JESSE'S JOURNEY
A Canadian Story

by John Davidson

Timberholme Books Ltd.
Suite 159, 19567 Fraser Hwy.
Surrey, B.C. V3S 6K7

Publisher's Foreword

I first met John and Jesse Davidson in January 1999 as John reached Victoria, British Columbia, after his 8,272-km marathon. There, among the many hundreds of supporters, I was lucky enough to observe first-hand, the impact of their journey. John embodied the spirit of giving to others, and Jesse humbly acknowledged his own role of spokesperson for genetic research.

A natural progression of events led to the involvement of Timberholme Publishing with *Jesse's Journey*. As an ambassador for Multiple Sclerosis, I have had experience in promoting the idea that those of us fortunate enough to be able to help others, should do so. We should do this even though at times we may feel as if we are such a small part of the mass of humanity that we couldn't possibly influence or change events – like being a grain of sand on an infinite beach. But I believe, passionately, that we can change things and that each individual can make a difference – and it all adds up!

Part of my personal challenge is to help illustrate examples of individuals who are shaping our future. John Davidson is one of those people who share a common factor – enthusiasm – the spark of life. John would want you to know that he is just a regular caring father, prompted by circumstances, trying to do his best. He would also want you to recognize the team that has helped him to achieve – his family, the core volunteers and organizers, and the thousands who have contributed time and money to help build the Jesse Davidson endowment.

John's dream is not yet fulfilled. We all have parts to play in spreading his story and following his example as our own circumstances allow. Ten million dollars is not easy to find. By the time you read this story, *Jesse's Journey* will have passed the halfway mark. Please do what you can to help make John and Jesse's goal a reality.

Tim Lawson
Langley, B.C.
July 2001

Foreword

This is a story of courage and an almost impossible endeavour – the chronicle of a determined man and his son.

Although he had been a longtime friend and colleague, and we had often met for lunch or just to sit down and talk, I was puzzled when John Davidson called me on a weekend in July of 1986 and suggested we meet as soon as possible. He seemed anxious and we agreed to meet for breakfast the next morning. Driving to our meeting that summer morning I was apprehensive, and when I sat down with John I knew something was very wrong. He's a pretty direct, no-nonsense guy and he got right to the point. I saw the beginning of tears as he told me his young son Jesse had been diagnosed with Duchenne Muscular Dystrophy. I could see that John was troubled by this devastating prognosis and what Jesse's future might be. John is not the type of person who backs away from a problem, and as devastated as he was, he was beginning to think about what could be done. No one could have predicted what road John would take in his quest to find an answer. It wasn't until some time later that we would learn why the word 'road' was the appropriate one. Most of his friends were amazed, as was the rest of Canada.

In 1972, newly married John and his wife Sherene left London for Vancouver where he went to work for the CBC in radio and television. As Program Manager at CFPL Radio, we stayed in touch and when John and Sherene decided they wanted to have a family, I urged John to come back home to London to work with me on my talk show. I think I may have put on a bit of pressure, but eventually John agreed and soon after we were working together again.

Life was full of promise when Tyler, the first of the Davidson's three boys was born in 1977. Jesse arrived in 1980, and when Tim came along in 1983, the family was complete. No one knew that Jesse was carrying a deadly gene until a summer weekend in 1986 when life took a drastic turn for the Davidsons.

Jesse grew and the disease progressed, while at home the rest of the family forged the beginning of a great support system. At my initial meeting with John he started to talk enthusiastically about the need for research so that some day families like his would not have to face the ravages of this disease. He went on to express his frustration about the lack of progress and about his need to do something to help. Even though I understood his passion and determination to further bio-medical research, I was shocked when he told me of his plan to push Jesse in his wheelchair, across Ontario. I tried to think of all the reasons I could to explain why this wasn't a good idea, but I knew it would be to no avail. My idea of a walk was from my car to the elevator and from the golf cart to the tee. But it wasn't long before people were buying into this father's dream of a province-wide journey to focus attention on the need for research. In May of 1995 the odyssey began as 49 year old John Davidson and his 15 year old son Jesse set out on what would become known as *Jesse's Journey*.

If Jesse was shy and reserved as he and his dad began their trek, he matured quickly as the days passed and the kilometres rolled by. This bright, determined young man was to become Canada's most committed and articulate spokesperson regarding the need for research. For 124 days this father and son persevered in a blistering hot summer through cities and towns, and when they rolled through their hometown enroute to Ottawa, Londoners welcomed them as they'd welcome royalty.

In this book, John Davidson tells the story of *Jesse's Journey* and the courageous son who brought a message of hope to people all across Ontario.

Day after day as they pushed on, their impact could be gauged by the selfless giving of strangers, as children who related to another youngster brought jars of nickels, dimes, quarters, loonies and toonies to the roadside in their no nonsense "let's help" approach. People passed bills of every denomination out the windows of cars, vans, transport trucks, buses, and motor homes all across the province.

In these pages, you'll also live part two of this father's dream, and the even more dramatic challenge, for now John had determined that Ontario just wasn't enough. The rest of Canada had to know the importance of research, and with the provincial walk still fresh in people's minds, plans were made to walk the entire length of Canada. Throughout the months of training John knew that this time he would be alone. It was a wrenching decision to leave his family and head out on what many considered an impossible adventure. The very thought of walking from "sea to sea" led many to express our doubts and concerns, as we urged him to reconsider. Of course he did not. In April of 1998, John Davidson undertook an almost unbelievable journey.

In his own words John tells his story – one of courage and fortitude and nearly overwhelming obstacles. This is the story of not just a Canadian hero but of a remarkable family and of a landmark labour of love.

Bill Brady,
London, 2001

Acknowledgements

After walking across Canada it did not surprise me that the team which helped in the creation of this book, reflects the size of Canada itself.

In western Canada, special thanks to Tim Lawson and the entire team at Timberholme Publishing in Langley, British Columbia for their vision in recognizing *Jesse's Journey* as a Canadian story waiting to be told. In Vancouver, editor Terry Teather showed immense patience and perseverance in overseeing and working through the many copies of the manuscript and pictures, which were transmitted back and forth across the country. Peter Whitelaw brought together the rest of the Timberholme team, working with Anya Wilson in Toronto. Brenda Lausanne and Alf Thomas from Marketing Communication in London provided the initial design concepts. In Vancouver, Laurel Swenson created the final design for both the book cover and compact disc.

On the east coast of Canada, my thanks to writer Kay Coxworthy from Bell Island, Newfoundland for transcribing my daily journal entries from 286 days on the road. Kay also provided research material from her own journals and interviews as well as completing the early edits of the manuscript along with editor Michael Nolan in London. Sincerest thanks to all those who made themselves available to be interviewed for the book.

In London, Ted Eadinger chaired the *Jesse's Journey* book committee. That team included Ron Calhoun, Willy Fry, Maureen Spencer-Golovchenko, Colleen Jones, Stephen Klein, Murray Morgan, Terry Roberts, Darrell Skidmore and Mike Woodward.

The London Free Press graciously gave us permission to use pictures taken by their staff photographers beginning at Quidi Vidi, Newfoundland where I dipped my shoes in the Atlantic Ocean. Bevin Palmateer provided additional 35-millimeter pictures and shot the vast majority of the video material contained in the compact disc.

Dean Chevalier, John McHale and the Ottawa Senators supplied additional photos. Alex Schmoll and his team, Shawn Lienweber-Miller, Mike Sebalj, Ben Playford and Evan Couch at Brick House Productions did the creative work on the compact disc. Additional footage was provided courtesy of CFPL Television. Thanks to video editors Serena Palmateer and Nancy Allen for their help in compiling the material. On the CD the voices of Glenn Bennett and Andi Hardy are heard in the song "A Hero in Everyone's Heart" written by Canadian singer/songwriter Glenn Bennett.

Ted Eadinger took the cover photo of the Rocky Mountains, and London Free Press photographer Sam McLeod took the photo of Jesse and I.

Daily and weekly newspapers across Canada provided copies of stories they published about *Jesse's Journey* through Ontario in 1995 and across Canada in 1998-99. Thanks to the hundreds of radio stations and television stations whose reporters and personalities provided both video and audiotape from interviews during both journeys.

To all of the sponsors, large and small, who helped in so many ways, thank you for coming to this project for the right reason.

And to all the people who came out to the road in every province across Canada, thank you for being there. You made the entire story possible.

Inspiration in a Pair of Running Shoes

Let me just say off the top, I'm not a very religious person. The Easter weekend, for me, meant having a very difficult time getting interviews with people. To make matters worse, many even took Thursday and/or Monday off. But there was one event that happened on Good Friday that gave the day's title new meaning.

No, I'm not talking about the anti-abortion (or is that pro-life?) protest at the Health Sciences Centre. The hundreds of people circling the hospital's parking lot didn't put the Easter spirit in me. After taking a few photos there, I raced to St. John's City Hall to record a little bit of history.

Ontario resident John Davidson was setting out for a journey across Canada to raise funds for genetic research. His son, Jesse, has a genetic disorder (Duchenne Muscular Dystrophy) that threatens his young life. Feeling a sense of helplessness no doubt, Davidson decided to walk across the nation in the hope of raising $10 million. With these funds, thanks to bank interest, the Foundation for Gene and Cell Therapy could give $1 million a year to research. Well, I guess there's at least one thing to thank the banks for.

From the steps of City Hall, Davidson, on a cellular phone spoke with Jesse. It was Jesse's 18th birthday, and what better gift could a father give than hope? As I jostled for position to get a good shot, I stopped to smile as the crowd began an impromptu chorus of *Happy Birthday*. I can only imagine that Jesse was smiling too as he listened to a crowd of Newfoundlanders sing to him over the phone.

Jesse's dad was soon off from where the Trans-Canada Highway begins. Passing the Delta Hotel, another father with two children at his side called to Davidson. One of the girls donated a couple of loonies and wished him luck.

Under a grey sky, the motorcade of RNC cruisers, fire trucks and Davidson's support vehicles followed him and those who decided to walk alongside for a while. Memories of Terry Fox, Rick Hansen and others filled conversations as the crowd dispersed.

As they went home to prepare big family meals or get out their Sunday best clothes for church, Davidson would soon be practically alone with the road. Hopefully, each community along Davidson's route will be just as supportive, or more so. I hope when he reaches the ferry at Port aux Basques, walks on board and rests his feet, that he has only good memories of this province. I hope his mind is filled with awe that Newfoundlanders came out in sunshine and in rain to donate a few dollars and to cheer him on. I hope he gets a good seat on the ferry and doesn't have to sleep on the floor, too.

Although we all have our little problems, few can claim to have loved ones in the grasp of a disease that could take their lives. Even fewer of us would have the dedication to do something about it, let alone travel on foot from St. John's, Newfoundland to Victoria, British Columbia. This man should serve as an inspiration to us all.

While the anti-abortionists circled and prayed, while churches filled with Easter songs, Davidson was doing something real. His faith, not necessarily involving a god, had him walking and looking out to the horizon, knowing he wouldn't catch up to it for some time.

What goes through a man's mind as he starts a walk that won't end for some 8,000 km? I guess I'll never really know. But I do know that I have a great deal of respect for Davidson, who would actually do something to help his son's situation, rather than simply wish it better.

We can all pray for world peace, an end to hunger and good health for all. The trick, the solution is to do something about it – or at least help those who are doing something.

Keep an eye open for Davidson over the coming weeks as he winds his way through the province. To help him is to help us all. And maybe, just maybe, he'll serve as an inspiration to help us change our world, instead of waiting for someone to do it for us.

Roger LeBlanc
The Express – St. John's, Newfoundland
April 15, 1998

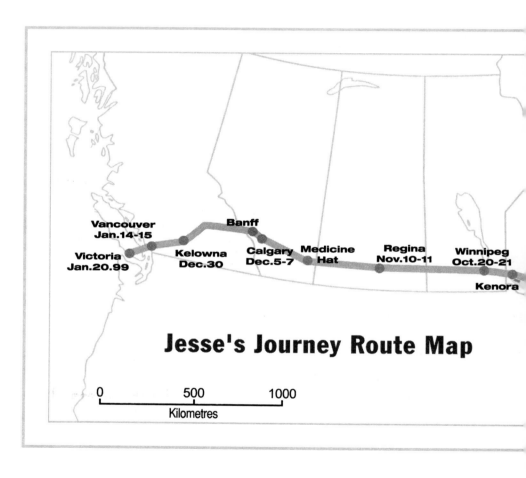

Victoria
Jan.20.99

Vancouver
Jan.14-15

Banff

Kelowna
Dec.30

Calgary
Dec.5-7

Medicine
Hat

Regina
Nov.10-11

Winnipeg
Oct.20-21

Kenora

Jesse's Journey Route Map

0   500   1000

Kilometres

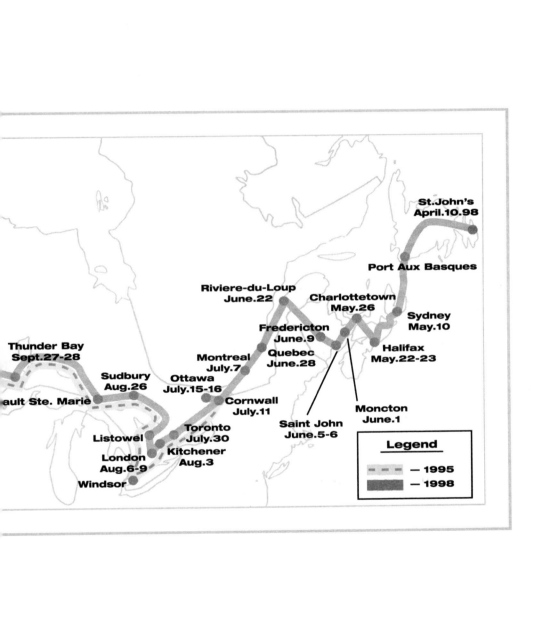

St.John's
April.10.98

Port Aux Basques

Riviere-du-Loup
June.22

Charlottetown
May.26

Sydney
May.10

Thunder Bay
Sept.27-28

Fredericton
June.9

Halifax
May.22-23

Montreal
July.7

Quebec
June.28

Sudbury
Aug.26

Ottawa
July.15-16

Cornwall
July.11

ault Ste. Marie

Moncton
June.1

Saint John
June.5-6

Toronto
July.30

Listowel

Kitchener
Aug.3

London
Aug.6-9

Windsor

Legend

— 1995

— 1998

Dedication

To every father.......
I did what I did because the life of every child is precious

Chapter One

THE DREAM IS BORN

"Out of difficulties grow miracles" –
Jean De La Bruyere

April 1998

Canada's youngest province was soon to celebrate its 50th anniversary in Confederation.

The jagged coast of Newfoundland has a narrow opening to the little harbour at Quidi Vidi, on the eastern edge of St. John's. The Atlantic Ocean rises as it pushes its way through the gap and the green and black waters climb the face of the rock cliff before sliding back in a white foam, pausing for just a moment before the cycle begins again. Nestled in the inner harbour, behind the breakwall that protects it, is a scene reminiscent of a Newfoundland postcard. Fishing boats in orange and blue are reflected in a saltwater mirror as they tug every now and then at the limp ropes that hold them to weathered wooden docks. Work sheds scattered around the inner harbour are draped in an assorted web of fishing nets that have been hung to dry.

Above the harbour, small houses cling to the cliff facing out to the sea. Some are red, some are white, and some are yellow. Most of them look worn by the weather. Smoke from the chimneys is quickly stolen away by the wind that's always there.

In the April cold, ice and snow cover the rocks and the roofs on the south side of the harbour, which is shaded by high cliffs. Some old snowdrifts are still tucked in between the houses. On the sunny north side, the wooden docks look warm and inviting. To the east lies Ireland, a shorter distance than Vancouver is to the west.

Here is where it will begin again. For a moment I close my eyes, bow my head, and pause to let my thoughts drift back to a summer that sometimes seems like yesterday, a summer day that has led to my being on this rocky shore on Canada's east coast.

It was June of 1986 and the summer that lay ahead held promises of barbecues and weekends at the beach. But the spirit of the season was soon to be broken.

In the darkness, the windshield wipers swept back and forth with a constant rhythm. Through the rain, the tail lights ahead were a blurred red line moving silently off into the distance. On the other side of the median the headlights made a similarly blurred white line moving in the opposite direction. Occasionally the sidelights of a transport truck would creep by the window and spray from the tires would blur the colours from the lights even further. Somewhere further down Highway 401 was London.

Driving home from the annual fishing trip to Lake Temagami in Northern Ontario usually takes about six hours. The final hour of the trip is always the quietest. It was no different this time as I stared out the window into the darkness and let my thoughts drift to home and my wife Sherene and our three young boys, Tyler, Jesse and Tim.

It was close to midnight when I pulled the car into the laneway. It seemed unusual to find that my wife Sherene, a very disciplined person who usually heads to bed early, was still up. In the minutes that followed came the shattering realization that something was dreadfully wrong with one of our children.

Jesse, our middle child, was born in 1980. A quiet, independent little boy with a shy smile, he had a normal early childhood, joining Beavers and then Cubs. He stuck pretty close to home with his younger brother Tim and always looked forward to going off to school with his older brother Tyler. Then just after he turned five, Jesse began to exhibit the first ominous signs that something wasn't right – and the medical consultations began. It was a parent's worst nightmare. Our fears were realized when the diagnosis of Duchenne Muscular Dystrophy was confirmed. It was a disease we knew little about but it would soon be as familiar as our heartbeats.

It couldn't happen to us, we reasoned. But in the dark of night, with our small sons sleeping soundly nearby, we had to come to grips with what was happening, how it would affect not only Jesse, but also all of us who loved him. DMD is the most severe of all the neuromuscular diseases; we had to prepare for what lay ahead.

The family faced a major crisis that could not help but tear emotionally at all of us. Every parent of a child with an illness goes through phases which torture the mind and soul long after the disease is a certainty. The initial denial gives way to guilt – is it something I did wrong? What could have prevented this happening to our baby? Eventually, the realization comes that analyzing the cause of the anguish is wasted effort. The day comes when you must put aside your own grief and begin the process of learning about the disease and the perceived barriers to a normal life. Life goes on, and your strength is better spent trying to keep the family strong.

The disease takes its inevitable toll on muscles and limbs. As parents you continue to explore every avenue that might prove to be the miracle. We quickly learned how little research had been done on Duchenne, and how time-consuming and expensive medical research really is. Looking back, we realized we hadn't given much thought at all to medical research on a conscious level, and now it was on our minds almost every waking moment. Jesse's diagnosis would forever change our way of thinking and would lead us to dream dreams and take on challenges we would never have thought possible.

As a broadcaster, I had been fortunate to develop a fairly extensive circle of friends and a network of media connections. I also had access to people who worked in medical research. Sherene and I were learning quickly that the biggest obstacle faced by researchers, including those involved in the study of gene-based illnesses, was the lack of adequate funding. Some of Canada's most prominent researchers were being enticed elsewhere with promises of better facilities and more funding. Governments didn't seem to be listening, and the public interest in, and knowledge of, genetic disease was limited. As parents we felt helpless and alone even though we were surrounded by caring family and friends who loved us and wanted the best for Jesse. Our concern for him had to be balanced with the needs of our two other children. The need to earn a living also had to be factored into the picture. We were a family of five and the road ahead was shaping up as a tough one.

We learned very quickly that parents of special children often find themselves walking a tightrope, trying to come to grips with medical problems while at the same time trying to take care of the needs of everyone else in the family. Those demands leave parents little time or energy to devote to each other. This is the turmoil that tears families apart, and we were determined from the beginning not to let this happen to us. In the early days after Jesse was diagnosed it was Sherene who shouldered most of the burden at home and we all drew strength from her. The extent of that strength in those first months seemed to surprise even Sherene herself. She's always been a strong, confident mother with a quiet forceful manner. Still, nothing in her life experience had prepared her for this.

As the 1980's moved along, so did Jesse. He grew into a determined youngster who was not about to let a thing like a disability keep him from doing what he wanted, and we treasured and supported that independence. His ability to keep smiling and to cope with the curves life had thrown him continued to amaze us while we continued to search for the answer that would make everything right for our little boy.

Part of the solution came in 1987 when Dr. Ron Worton and his team at Toronto's Hospital for Sick Children identified the gene that causes DMD. For the first time, Sherene and I saw something that looked like a small spark of hope. Science had never been my strongest subject in school and the genetics maze certainly looked like a very complex world that wasn't about to surrender its secrets easily.

I had read about how the blueprint for life is DNA (deoxyribonucleic acid). Like most people who have leafed through magazines in doctors' and dentists' offices, I recognized this as something that looks a lot like a spiral staircase. That was about it. What I needed was a picture I could draw in my mind that would make it easier to understand how it all fit together. Sitting on the bookshelf across the room, painted in red and green and gold, the answer was staring back at me in the form of a wooden doll.

Matriuschka dolls from Russia became very popular in the fall of 1972 when Canada and the Soviet Union met in hockey's historic Summit Series. The doll that was sitting on the bookshelf was one that Sherene and I had bought in Vancouver. It's about a foot tall and when you open it, there is another doll inside, and inside that doll is yet another one, and so on. The dolls keep getting smaller and smaller. Under the microscope, the genetics story did the same thing as the parts kept getting smaller and smaller.

We came to understand that the human body has as many as a hundred trillion cells and just like looking inside the first doll, there is a nucleus inside each cell. Much like opening the next doll, we found that each nucleus contains 46 chromosomes. The chromosomes are arranged in 23 pairs, plus an X and a Y chromosome. One chromosome of every pair comes from each parent. Working down toward an even smaller picture the chromosomes are filled with tightly coiled strands of DNA, making up the spiral staircase picture. Genes are segments of DNA and look like the steps of that spiral staircase connecting one side to the other. Those strips contain the instructions for making proteins – the building blocks of life itself. We now knew that the gene we wanted to see corrected lay on the X chromosome. But there were still more questions than answers.

Since the early fifties, scientists have known that DNA is the basic stuff of heredity. Its chemical structure was unlocked in 1953. DNA acts like a biological computer program that is some three billion bits long and spells out the instructions for those building blocks.

21

The picture was getting clearer to us. Our only hope was research and we had to face the reality that we were in a race with time.

Inspiration comes to us at the most unpredictable of times. It came to me on a Fall day in 1994. We had known for some time that the day would arrive when Jesse would have to face life in a wheelchair. It had been a heart-wrenching discovery to learn that Jesse suffered from a genetic illness for which there is no cure. As the years slipped by we felt helpless and the disability tore at us as Jesse's strength continued to be sapped by the disease and the need for a wheelchair was becoming more apparent. It didn't seem fair that this should be happening at one of the most vulnerable periods in a boy's life. Slowly we were becoming hardened to the reality that life makes no promises. No one could prepare Jesse for what lay ahead. Sherene and I were determined that as a family we would face this together and do something about it. But what?

On a beautiful October day in 1994 I was walking back home from the little town of Ilderton, about twenty kilometres north of London. I had taken up walking as a form of exercise to stay in shape. Looking back, it seems ironic that I was beginning to walk more than ever when Jesse was losing his ability to walk at all. It was about this time that I said goodbye to the game of golf. Jesse was at an age where it required both Sherene and I to do the lifting and moving. I couldn't leave Sherene to do it all alone and so I left the golf clubs in the garage and focused on more important things.

So there I was on that Fall day walking along on the gravel at the edge of the road. The sun was shining and the rolling countryside was well on its way to showing off that Southern Ontario tartan of copper, red and yellow as the leaves made ready for their grand finale. I loved walking because it gave me time to think. As I looked at the blue sky and saw the fields of grain waving in the wind, the thought came to me in the form of a question: I wonder if we could ever turn this walking into something meaningful? Almost as quickly as it came to me, the question faded away unanswered.

Although I am not a deeply religious person, as I continued to walk in the days that followed, I took time to think and to ask for strength if there wasn't to be a cure for Jesse.

As the days grew shorter and winter crept closer, the question kept coming back to me. Each time it did, it took longer for it to go away and I found myself starting to daydream. Was there something that one father could do to bring about an awareness of the need for more research funding?

I came to the realization that while one person probably couldn't do it alone, there is strength in numbers, and Sherene and I had been blessed with a wonderful extended family, lasting friendships and people who would stand by us in anything we decided to do. That was the source of our strength and slowly the die was cast in my mind. To dramatize the need for research funding, I would push Jesse, in his wheelchair, from the Manitoba border right through the heart of Ontario to Ottawa, and on to the Ontario border with Quebec. It was easy to say, yet it would prove to be a daunting challenge.

The idea for a wheelchair marathon, with me pushing Jesse across 3300 km of our home province, was initially met with the comment, "Are you out of your mind?" from just about everyone including Jesse, the central figure in the plan. I guess they had every reason to have doubts. I was 48 years old, and while all that walking around London meant I was in reasonably good shape, I was no athlete. I'd never tried serious competitive walking. Now I was planning to push a wheelchair eight hours a day every day for four months. But by now I was determined and, with Sherene at my side, the support began to build.

Jesse is a lot like his mom, who seldom acts on impulse. He likes to think things through before he makes a commitment. Eventually, as happens with situations that are maybe meant to be, Jesse championed the idea of this unique fundraiser for gene research.

23

It would be an opportunity for both of us to see our home province in a way that few people ever get to experience. We all knew it was an opportunity to reinforce the need for more funding. It was certainly going to be an educational experience and, as a dad, I was hoping it would be the thrill of a lifetime for my son.

It's one thing to have a dream; it's another to put the wheels in motion. Once the target was set and we were committed to making the trip across Ontario in the summer of 1995, the real work began. The first thing to be done was to find people with a positive outlook who would be willing to lend us both their knowledge and their energy.

This wasn't going to be easy because while we initially shared the dream as a very private family, we were now going to have to step into the public arena. As a broadcaster I didn't mind doing this, but I worried about what it would mean for my son and the rest of our family.

No matter what the project, you have to start somewhere and when it comes to recruiting volunteers, one of the best volunteers in Canada happened to live in the village of Thamesford just east of London. Ron Calhoun had been the national fundraising chairman for the Canadian Cancer Society in 1980 and had coined the phrase *Marathon of Hope* for Terry Fox. When the plans were laid out, Ron never hesitated in coming on board and *Jesse's Journey* was born.

Slowly we started to build the team – not by selecting people right away, but identifying tasks that needed to be done, and then finding the right people to do those jobs. There were times I thought the list of job categories was endless. We needed help with everything from transportation, communication and accommodations, to insurance, media and police, and just about everything else in-between. But always at the front of my mind was how we were going to take care of Jesse, because his health and safety came first. When we were in the planning stages, none of us really knew how gruelling the task ahead would be for a 15 year old boy in a wheelchair.

When the project was unveiled by the media, the volunteer floodgates opened, and I discovered I had moved the Davidson family into the public spotlight. It's a decision I still ask myself about. Was there any other way to accomplish the task? Was there something else I could have done as a father to showcase the need for genetic research? If there was, it had eluded me.

Things were starting to happen, often faster than I'd imagined they would. What was now called the home team was shifting gears and picking up speed. Former Toronto Maple Leaf captain Darryl Sittler, who had played in London as a junior, joined us as a spokesperson.

On a winter morning early in 1995, Darryl drove from his home outside Buffalo, New York to be at Jesse's high school in London when we announced what *Jesse's Journey* would be all about. When it was my turn to speak, I was gripped with nervous excitement. I knew that I was committed to seeing this project to its completion, but I also knew the reality that I was almost 50 years old and about to tackle the biggest physical challenge of my life. I remember looking at Jesse as he sat smiling. I couldn't remember when he had changed from a cute little boy to a handsome and confident young man. And then everything became clear again. This was what it was all about. It was for Jesse, and all the kids he represented, who battle just to get through the day. When I began to speak, I told everyone that "I could probably forgive myself if I couldn't complete the job ahead, but I couldn't forgive myself if I didn't go out and try."

Our launch date of May 16th was getting closer. The home team had been making the links that would be needed across the province. Jesse had been given the medical go-ahead and as part of the final preparation I kept pushing myself, walking longer stretches every day, getting myself ready. I still had some serious doubts about my ability to complete this trek, doubts that I'm sure were in the minds of most of our team, doubts they may have whispered to each other, but were kind enough not to share with me.

My parents and Sherene's parents, along with the rest of our families, probably had their misgivings as well, but all of them were there to do whatever they could to see this through. Gradually the idea began to take hold, first in London and then across the province. As the training continued, strangers passing me on the street would stop, shake my hand, and wish us well. It was the beginning of an outpouring of support that would strengthen my resolve and toughen my muscles throughout the months ahead.

Chapter Two

THE TEAM GATHERS AND HEADS OUT

"It is a fine thing to have ability, but the ability
to discover ability in others is the true test" –
Elbert Hubbard

The morning of May 16th, 1995 dawns clear and almost cold.
There is still so much to do, but we'll set out for our start point at
the Manitoba border and leave the rest to the home team. Media
interviews are critical to our getting the word out, so we make the
early morning rounds of the radio stations before our formal sendoff.
Jesse's shyness starts to fade away as he rises to the occasion, doing
his best to answer question after question about a road *Journey* that
has yet to begin.

There really is no template for a project of this sort. When the idea
of a wheelchair marathon first came to me several months ago, the
very early blueprints were mine alone. As those plans were shared
and the wheels put in motion, the team expanded. You have to be
prepared for the fact that you probably won't be aware of everything
that is going on around you. The truth is you hope that the project
will take on a life of its own and snowball as you make your way
toward your goal and at the same time, the need to delegate
becomes obvious. It's impossible for one person to micromanage
all the details.

On this particular morning I begin to see the results of the work done
by the volunteers who have joined our team. Some of them are
people I have known a long time, others I hardly know and some
I've never met. The events of the day are starting to unfold in a
lightning-like blur. There's Jesse on the radio, introducing a song
called *A Hero in Everyone's Heart,* by London singer and songwriter
Glenn Bennett. I would find out later that when Glenn was contacted
about writing a theme song for the *Journey*, his response was that he
had already written it!

Later in the morning Jesse and I are whisked through the crowd for the official sendoff at Victoria Park in the heart of London. From the stage we can look out at the familiar faces of friends and supporters, as the words and music of our theme song wash over the crowd, opening hearts to a cause our hometown clearly shows it's prepared to support.

There is a lot of emotion attached to the sendoff. The mayor chokes back tears as she reads a statement wishing us well on our *Journey*. As part of the ceremony Jesse is presented with a Montreal Canadiens sweater signed by his favourite player, goaltender Patrick Roy. I am glad when this happens because deep down I also want this to be a great summer adventure for a young boy. Too many kids like Jesse never get to have an adventure.

As we prepare to depart, the people of London leave us no doubt as to where they stand on the issue of genetic research – squarely on our side. Our task now, Jesse's and mine, is to bring the message of the vital need for gene research to the rest of the province. The campaign to show the need for research is now a central part of the fabric of our family.

On the grass at the park sits the motor home that will be our 'home away from home' for the next four months. It's another symbol to show that people support worthwhile initiatives. The motor home has come to us courtesy of a recreational vehicle dealer in St. Thomas, just south of London. Don Ferguson is another 'dad' whom I had never met before *Jesse's Journey* began. It's hard to imagine the feeling you get when someone hands you the keys to a fully outfitted 12-metre motor home and wishes you all the best with the casual yet confident words, "Bring it back when you're done." People begin to feel they want to take part in this project, not for personal gain through being sponsors, but because they realize how fortunate they are to have healthy families.

After leaving the park it's home for some lunch, and then we're saying goodbye to the rest of the family. For Jesse it's just part of another day. When you're 15 years old, saying goodbye to your 12 year old brother is pretty easy. You just say, "See you later, buddy," as if you'll be back by supper.

For me, saying goodbye to Jesse's brothers, Tyler and Tim, who would be staying behind wasn't that easy.

Hugging Tyler I was wrapping my arms around a very mature 17 year old who understood what was going on. Then I hugged Tim, our youngest son. Tim has always lived in the shadow of the light that's been focused on Jesse, a light that Jesse had never asked for. The hardest part for Jesse was saying goodbye to 'Charlie' our faithful little dog. Charlie knows something is happening and she knows she's not going. Then, climbing aboard the motor home with Sherene, it's time to go.

After months of training and preparation, the road team is finally on its way to our start point. The convoy consists of the motor home, two mini-vans and eleven people. There is a feeling of excitement as we cross the border at Sarnia heading up through Michigan to Sault Ste. Marie where we will cross back into Canada. From there it is around the top of Lake Superior and on to Thunder Bay before turning northwest to the Ontario-Manitoba border which lies just west of Kenora. That's where this adventure will begin.

The team members are settling in amidst a background of laughter as they try out the walkie-talkies that link the vehicles together. As the first few hours slide by they begin to stake out their own little areas on board the vehicles and to note each other's habits. It's something that becomes important when a group of people faces living in close quarters for a long period of time. The crew rotates assignments several times during the four days it takes us to reach our destination.

Glancing up from the road maps on the kitchen table of the motor home gives me a chance to watch the dynamics of the team and to speculate about how it will all turn out. Almost every expedition that has set out to conquer Mount Everest has known from the beginning that not everyone on the team will reach the top of the mountain. I find myself wondering which members of the road team will go the distance. And I ask the same question about myself.

There are only four of us in what will become known as the 'permanent' road team. The rest of the road crew is made up of volunteers who will come on board, generally for a one-week stint. I have no idea at this point how many times these people will end up telling me how much that one week changed their outlook on life.

The road manager is 23 year old Trish (Tricia) Federkow from St. Catharines, Ontario. A graduate of the kinesiology program at the University of Western Ontario, Trish is tall, athletic and has dark red hair that's never out of place. Like most of the crew she is feeling her way along in a job that seems to defy description. Until we have some history to attach to it, Trish's job is to keep the whole caravan moving day after day. In the months ahead it will prove to be the most thankless of jobs, with everyone second-guessing her decisions. Early on it's obvious Trish has a soft spot in her heart for the young boy at the center of this project and at times she seems more like Jesse's big sister. She quickly acquires the nickname Trish "The Dish."

Sean Bagshaw is also a kinesiology graduate from Western. He's also 23 years old and thinking seriously about a career in medicine. Sean will be Jesse's caregiver over the next four months, looking after all of Jesse's needs, especially the overnight ones. Sean bristles with the self-confidence that's often the trademark of youth. If he appears a little cocky, I'm betting some of the sharp edges will be worn away by the huge dose of maturing he'll get over the next four months. For now he and Jesse appear to be a great fit. If Trish looked like a big sister, Sean seems even more like a big brother. In the nickname department, Sean Bagshaw becomes "The Bagger."

Forty-seven year old John McHale was the last person to join the *Journey* road crew before we left London. John's bearded face makes it evident that he's the only member of the team who can truly say that he 'knows' Northern Ontario. Among his talents John has emergency medical training and he is experienced in the search and rescue field, a skill we are hoping we don't have to call upon. He knows his way around a video camera and can shoot still pictures as well. John can read maps and drive a motor home, but even more importantly, he knows how to cook.

Fifty-eight year old Michael Woodward has been a part of *Jesse's Journey* from the very beginning. Although he doesn't meet up with the crew until the end of week one on the highway, Mike knows the road well. He helped survey the Northern Ontario portion of the route earlier in the spring, noting where the Trans-Canada Highway has shoulder that will accommodate a wheelchair. The rest of the reconnaissance mission was used to chart distances between motels and to troubleshoot anything else that we should know in advance. One of his most valuable assets is that he knows how to deal with the media. With a 40-year career in television, most of it as a journalist, Mike is a stickler for detail and a jack-of-all-trades, which seems a perfect fit for the job at hand. Of all the members of the crew, I've known Mike the longest and his greatest strength is he's fiercely loyal and will give the project his all.

The rest of the road crew consists of the volunteers who will be with us for a week at a time. Although there will be many I have never met, I'm not worried about that group. Their enthusiasm will probably be enough to last the length of time they will be with us, even if the *Journey* doesn't meet up to their expectations. Our ability to make it across the province will be determined by the chemistry that exists within the group that's been chosen to go the distance.

Like a rock band on tour, it takes time for us to get used to moving in and out of motels night after night. Eventually it will become a routine we'll be accustomed to. But in the first few days sleep doesn't come easily. As I lie awake on this first night on the road, I find myself hoping that I haven't committed us to more than Jesse or I can handle. The marathon is something of a leap of faith for both of us. I'm certain in my mind that my son and I will be able to forge an unbreakable bond, but there is a risk involved. It's a risk we are willing to take, if what we accomplish allows us to create an awareness of the need for gene research, especially research into Duchenne.

I'm certain in my mind that awareness is what's needed in order to create a fund that will enable researchers to work toward a day when kids like Jesse can have a chance at a normal life.

The springtime scenery along the north shore of Lake Superior is spectacular as our little convoy continues to make its way along the Trans-Canada Highway, stopping in little towns to take on food and fuel. Just before we arrive in Thunder Bay we get a glimpse of the Terry Fox Memorial. For a few minutes, a silence settles over the motor home, as each of us is alone with our thoughts. What an inspiration this young man is to the world, but never more so than at this moment, when a 15 year old boy in a wheelchair, facing his own challenges, has his determination and courage reinforced by the spirit of the indomitable Terry Fox.

Saturday, May the 20th, 1995 begins cold and windy at the Manitoba border. I've been awake since 3:30 a.m. The adrenaline rush, in anticipation of the morning, has blocked any chance of sleep. Though I'm not hungry I force myself to eat some toast and honey before we drive the 50 kilometres west from Kenora to the point where Manitoba and Ontario meet. As the icy rain that's blowing sideways stings our faces I double check to make sure that Jesse is bundled up warm. His serious smile lets me know he's ready to go.

Ron Calhoun reminds the group that "Genetic illnesses don't wait for a perfect day to strike and we aren't waiting for a perfect day to strike back." Now the moment – we are on our way, emerging from

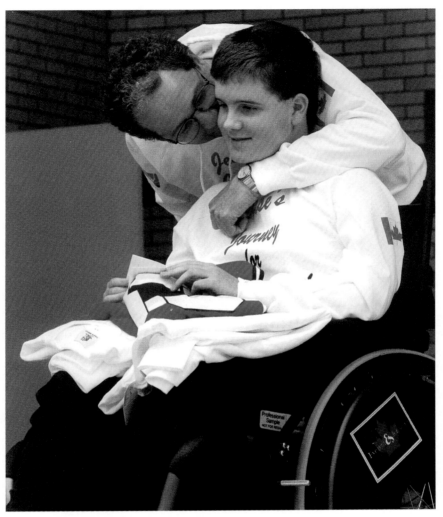

Before setting out to cross Ontario, Jesse smiles after being presented with a Montreal Canadiens sweater autographed by goaltender Patrick Roy.

Journey volunteers Mac Haig and Michael Woodward stand at the Ontario-Manitoba border.

the circle of family, friends and supporters who are huddled together in the cold at the front of our motor home. As I take the first few steps pushing Jesse in front of me, I know that those who are watching us from behind are probably asking themselves "Can they actually do it?" For a brief moment I wonder the same thing and even though the question will continue to come back to me more than once during the days ahead, I remind myself why we are here. I'm doing what I think fathers are supposed to do: Do everything you can to make sure your children enjoy the best possible quality of life. This is how all of us in the Davidson family can make a solid contribution to the hope that a cure will be found for DMD.

In the early days of the *Journey* we manage a full 30 km, even though it's been cold and raining. We wind our way along the Trans-Canada Highway through small towns that show signs of tough economic times, but still the generosity of the people continues to amaze and inspire us every day. Here in Northern Ontario, it's still winter. Slowly the kinks are ironed out and both Jesse and I are pleased with our progress. At the end of the week we say goodbye to Sherene who is going home along with Ron Calhoun and his wife Fran, who have been with us since we left London. We'll miss all of them, but my sister Dorothy and her husband Peter are still here and, in a few days, Mike Woodward will be arriving to complete our road team.

As the days blend together, it seems the hills never end. Some are bigger than others, but all of them are more than anything I ever faced in the months of training on the flat lands of Southwestern Ontario. It makes me wonder how we ever managed to build a railway across this country. The downhill stretches are a real strain, as the hand brakes on the wheelchair aren't gripping the way they should. We've been tinkering with the brakes almost every night, but we just don't seem to be able to get them right and that means I have to drag back on the wheelchair to control it on the downhill portions of the road. And when you're battling the logging trucks for space on the road it becomes a major challenge.

Every day there is another sign spring is coming. The bright green buds are starting to show that they will soon burst into bloom. The lakes and rivers we come to are welcome sights, as most days we are faced with hours and hours of evergreens and rock. Trish starts to work some social activities into the program for Jesse. Movies are his favourite. School groups come to meet Jesse and to hear all about what we are doing. There is no doubt as to the real star of the show. Service clubs are greeting us and providing meals and donations as we make our way further south heading toward the Lakehead and Thunder Bay.

It's time for another changing of the guard. My mom and dad arrive from Brantford, Ontario while my sister Dorothy and brother-in-law Peter leave from Long Sault to begin the train ride home to Brantford. As we continue to tackle the hills one at a time, we're joined on the road early one morning by a huge moose. We've been told that moose will come to the roadside early in the morning looking for road salt that has gathered in the cracks of the highway where the asphalt has eroded.

Slowly the weather is getting warmer; we're already into June and before long it will be unbearably hot. Jesse is doing fine and even with the protection used to cover him, he is starting to get a tan. We kid him about his raccoon sun tan as he now has a patch of white around his eyes from where his sunglasses sit.

Jesse and I are starting to get our rhythm in sync. My leg muscles feel good although I certainly appreciate a rubdown at the end of the day. We are spending long hours on the road, sharing our thoughts and seeing our home province from a whole new perspective. We roll through the pulp mill town of Dryden where a few years before a tragic plane crash brought national attention. No one here talks about it. Around the top of Lake Superior you can smell the pulp and paper mills long before you see the smokestacks. When you're from Southwestern Ontario, you never get used to the smell of a pulp mill town. All you can do is hope for a favourable wind. Every day as the wind keeps getting hotter, the radio is full of news about the spread of forest fires throughout the region.

As the kilometres of jagged rock and forests of fir slip behind us, Jesse and I fill the hours talking about everything from sports to music. We explore a lot of questions we'd probably never think about had we been at home. One day, after noticing how few homes are made of brick in Northern Ontario, we talk for a long time about housing and then about what makes people choose to live where they do. When things are really quiet, we pass the time counting pop cans in the ditch. We're amazed at how dominant Pepsi-Cola is over Coca-Cola in Northern Ontario. We count thirty Pepsi cans before we find one Coke can. Jesse thinks somebody is missing a good marketing opportunity. Sometimes we talk about home and what Jesse's brothers are probably doing. It reminds me of how much I miss them.

Despite what seems like a pretty steady routine, every day on the road something new happens. One morning it's a phone call from Darryl Sittler, who's just checking in to see how we're doing. Darryl says he hopes to meet us later somewhere along the road. It's a thought which causes a buzz of excitement for a father and a son who are hockey fans. The former star centre of the Toronto Maple Leafs gives us our boost for the day.

Leaving the town of Ignace and heading for English River in Northern Ontario, we make the switch from Central Time to Eastern Standard Time. By midday we reach the concrete watershed marker, where everything that flows north will go to Hudson's Bay and the Arctic Ocean, and everything that flows to the south will eventually reach the Mississippi River or the Atlantic Ocean.

Making our way across Northern Ontario donations keep coming in, so we know the word is getting out. Still, it's slow going. Some days are exceptional. On other days we do our 30 kilometres with little to show for it beyond sore muscles. But we never lose heart. We know that our best hope to raise funds lies in the more densely populated area of Southern Ontario. Even in these early days, Sherene reports that donations are coming in, which gives all of us a lift. Meanwhile Jesse continues to do interviews. It's amazing to see how much sharper his ability becomes to explain the precise reason we are on the road.

Most of our days are tedious and blisters make the job more difficult. Because of the punishment it takes, the wheelchair continues to give us problems. We can't seem to get all the bits and pieces and nuts and bolts to work together. Just when we get the brakes set properly, the shock absorbers start giving us problems. But each time it happens we get closer to finding the smooth glide we're looking for while always making sure that Jesse is comfortable. It's a test of both our patience and commitment. We manage to get a passing grade.

As a city boy, I had never thought about animals along the road. On a muggy June morning we have our first encounter with a bear, a reminder of the need to be constantly on the lookout. A young cub crosses our path, and I slow my pace to keep us closer to the escort vehicle. I remind the crew to be ready to get the back hatch open fast in case we have to get off the road in a hurry. Where there are cubs, there is usually a mother and we need time to get Jesse safely loaded on board the van.

The occasional sight of a moose or a bear causes a ripple of excitement. But it's what Jesse has labeled our 'dog of the day' that gives us an opportunity to judge which ones are friendly and those to be avoided. The small canister of pepper spray attached to my belt is to be used only as a last resort for protection. The dogs come in all shapes and sizes. Bounding down farm lanes, they sound a warning bark. During my months of training along rural roads, I learned how to handle a dog that appears aggressive. Generally, a dog is only interested in guarding its own territory. The trick is to figure out where the dog has drawn the 'magic' line that it doesn't want you to step across. In the country it's usually a line that's parallel with the road, about where the mail box is located. One thing you don't do with a barking dog is to look right at it and make eye contact. Dogs seem to interpret that as a direct challenge.

I guess the most important indicator is to check and see if the dog is wagging its tail. Jesse and his little pal Charlie, still back at home, are about as close as a boy and his dog can be. Maybe that's why Jesse has such rapport with the dogs we meet along the road. Whatever the case, they all seem to arrive wagging their tails.

As the days continue to get warmer, the highway stretches out before us in a long black line that rises and falls and twists around the rock cuts carved by dynamite when the Trans-Canada Highway was built.

Along the road and in the small towns that link Northern Ontario together, people continue to support and encourage us. I notice the number of people, children particularly, who want to meet Jesse and to shake his hand. In nearly every town, we're met by groups of school kids and teachers who come out to the road or who often invite us to visit their school. Jesse obviously enjoys spending time with these young people. Not surprisingly he is just as comfortable with kids his own age as he is with a group of adults. He has perfected his after-dinner speaking, and his ability to exchange greetings with people along the roadside continues to develop with each passing day.

It's hard not to feel a sense of pride as I listen to Jesse. I watch the faces of the people he speaks to, and I know they're as touched as I am by his honesty and his courage.

We're attracting lots of attention on the highway from what feels like the entire blackfly population of Northern Ontario. The blisters and bites appear to be some kind of rite of passage. As we soldier on, we are nearing 650 km on *Jesse's Journey* and the weather just keeps getting hotter. For the first time, it's taking its toll on my strength. I find myself looking forward to my short naps after our lunch breaks.

The crew teases me about how fast I can fall into a deep sleep after a morning in the heat and humidity. They love to tell the newcomers the story about the day I slept through a dozen bikers who roared up to the motor home to have their picture taken with Jesse and to present him with $500.

We roll on past Kakabeka Falls where the water echoes its way down into a steep rock canyon. From there it's mostly downhill into Thunder Bay. We have now been on the road for three weeks, and reaching Thunder Bay we receive word that we have passed the $100,000 mark in donations. That's the first real shot of adrenaline for the road team since leaving the Manitoba border.

On the eastern edge of Thunder Bay I push Jesse up the hill to the Terry Fox Monument which rises high above the road. It's along this stretch of the Courage Highway that the one-legged runner was forced to postpone his *Marathon of Hope* in September of 1980. The monument itself looks out over Lake Superior and, with a clear blue sky overhead and a breathtaking view, it's a day when anything you can dream seems possible.

From Thunder Bay the road winds north to Nipigon, one of the many tiny towns that boomed at one time, but whose prosperous days disappeared when the logging ended and the steam engine was replaced. But there is a golden moment in Nipigon. Jesse is invited aboard the "Morning Star" by Captain Jack Dampier, who everyone in Nipigon knows simply as Cap'n Jack.

The evening cruise gives Jesse a chance to look at 800 year old Indian pictographs carved in the rock cliffs that surround Nipigon Bay. It isn't something that every youngster will have a chance to do in the summer of 1995, and it's all part of the great adventure I want Jesse to enjoy.

When we reach Terrace Bay on the north shore of Lake Superior, a local doctor makes Jesse an offer he can't refuse – the chance to try salmon fishing. When Trish and Jesse get back with the news that Jesse caught a two-pound salmon, we all share in the excitement. Of course for Jesse the catch means a phone call home to his mom and his brothers to tell his first 'fish story'.

For some dads maybe it isn't a big event when their son catches a fish. But when your son has never been salmon fishing, that first fish is big news. The thrill of catching the salmon makes up for a bit of homesickness, missing Charlie and suffering through the blackflies. It's great to see Jesse so animated. It's another memory we will be able to share long after our days on the road come to an end.

We spend Father's Day 1995 in Marathon, Ontario. It's a sunny day, but the wind is very cold. Jesse and I shiver and my hands are numb as we arrive for the first of two church appearances that are on the schedule for today. The entire road crew joins us for the morning service at the United Church in Marathon. In the warmth of the church, away from the cold and wind, amidst the flowers, wooden pews and stained glass, one of the funniest moments on the *Journey* is about to unfold.

The church is packed. We can see entire families, dressed in their Sunday best, standing next to one another. You can tell these are people who work together, play together and look out for each others' children. The minister gathers the children at the front of the church where some of them sit on the steps and some of them sit cross-legged on the floor. After playing his guitar and singing a song, the minister asks Jesse to speak to the kids.

Genetics is not an easy subject to explain to adults, let alone children. But Jesse has a clever way of explaining to kids just how tiny genes really are, in a manner that kids understand. Jesse starts off by asking the kids to imagine taking a loonie and cutting it into a million pieces. His words bring some 'oohing' and 'aahing' from the smaller kids. Then Jesse asks them if the pieces would be very small. The kids all nod. Next, Jesse wants them to imagine taking just one of those million pieces and cutting that into a million more pieces. That brings even louder 'oohs' and 'aahs' from the smallest kids in the group. When Jesse asks them if they are able to see one of those tiny pieces, the kids all shake their heads to say no. When he asks them what they would need to see something that small, one of the kids answers with "a great big microscope".

It's at that moment that a little girl of six or seven puts up her hand. Up to this point Jesse's science lesson is going along fine. He looks at the little girl with the ribbon in her hair and then glances at me with a 'What should I do?' look. I shrug my shoulders as if to say 'Go ahead and see what she wants to say'. Now you have to remember that Jesse has just asked these kids to imagine cutting something into a million pieces not just once, but twice. The little girl with her hand up is stuck on the thought that she now has two million pieces of something, even if she's not sure what it is. When Jesse asks the little girl if she has a question to ask, she opens her mouth and says, "That's OK because we have a vacuum cleaner for that!" It's a classic 'out of the mouths of babes' moment and the entire church erupts in laughter, including the little girl. The kids are laughing, the moms and dads are laughing, and Jesse and the road crew are all laughing. Looking out at the flowers, the wooden pews and the stained glass windows, it is nice to hear laughter in a church on Father's Day.

In the evening we are invited to the Anglican Church in Marathon for a barbecue. The church is typical of the many churches in Northern Ontario. It's made of wood, painted white, has a huge spire on top, and at the front there's a steep set of stairs that lead to the double doors at the main entrance. We're right at home with the smell of hot dogs and hamburgers coming from the grill of the barbecue. Lots of people bring cameras and there are plenty of pictures snapped with the road crew posing with kids and moms and dads. We eat in the church basement and after dessert and tea, poured from the biggest metal teapot I've ever seen, it's time to say goodbye, which is always the hardest part.

Little do I know the evening will end on a down note. Three or four people are helping to carry Jesse in his wheelchair down the front stairs of the church. Suddenly one of the armrests comes loose and Sean, who is always extremely careful whenever it comes to lifting and moving Jesse, loses his grip. The wheelchair tumbles backwards and I can hear the thud as Jesse's head hits the wooden stairs. There is a moment of panic as everyone scrambles to stabilize the situation. And to complicate matters, Sean gets his foot caught in the outdoor carpet on the stairs. Through all this, Sean has the presence of mind to grab hold of the chair and he bears the weight of both Jesse and the wheelchair.

As I turn to see what's happening it's like I am seeing everything in slow motion. I can see hands coming from everywhere to prevent the wheelchair and Jesse from crashing further down the stairs. We quickly pack some ice on the back of Jesse's head and I heave a sigh of relief when Jesse looks up at me, grimacing and smiling at the same time. I know then that he's going to be all right. I feel sorry for Sean who is visibly upset over what's happened. The incident serves as a reminder again that life makes no promises. A couple of days after the incident Sean has the armrests bolted permanently to the chair. We never have another accident like that.

Leaving Marathon we are back on the Trans-Canada Highway and approaching the first of three monster hills that we have to climb. Jackfish Hill isn't the biggest hill on the north shore of Lake Superior, but it is one of the most intimidating. From the foot of the hill you can look straight up as if you're at the bottom of a ski jump. I check to make sure that the tether line connecting me to the wheelchair is clipped in place. The tether line is something that's been added for safety in the event that I fall, especially if we are going downhill. Today I am not leaving anything to chance. I check with Jesse to make sure he's ready for the climb. Then, there is nothing I can do except put my head down, grit my teeth and start up the hill.

If you can't have your best friends with you when you're chugging up a hill, then it's nice to know you can have your best friend's parents. Dave Meadows is a lawyer who lives in Halifax. We first met when we were both working in radio more than 25 years ago. His mom and dad, Don and Pat Meadows, have joined us as volunteers for a couple of weeks. I am glad to have Pat beside me as we make the long climb up Jackfish Hill. I don't bother looking up from my position behind the wheelchair, but every now and then I ask Pat to pour some cold water over me. As the sun beats down on us, like all good moms, Pat just keeps telling me, "It's not too much farther now."

After what feels like an hour, rubber-kneed and drenched in sweat, we reach the top of Jackfish Hill. There's a round of applause from everybody on the team and as I lean against the motor home for support, Sean pours water over me and congratulates me with the words, "That was a test of character." For just a moment I think to myself, 'I'm almost 50 years old, what am I doing out here?' As soon as I catch my breath, I am back behind the wheelchair with Jesse in front of me. The wheels are turning again and we're heading for Wawa.

Chapter Three

ON TO WAWA

"Do what you can, with what you have, where you are" –
Theodore Roosevelt

From Marathon heading south to Wawa, the Trans-Canada Highway swings inland away from Lake Superior. The heat coming off the pavement is over 40°C and everywhere around us things are tinder dry. It hasn't rained for days and the heat and humidity are intense. Mike Woodward has gone ahead of us to scout the road and make arrangements for us to stay in English River and then Wawa. His phone call back to the team is a double dose of bad news. The road ahead has a very broken shoulder and we will have to be extremely careful because we're going to have to move Jesse and the wheelchair further out onto the travelled portion of the highway. To make matters worse, there are forest fires ahead. Mike reports that the water bombers fighting the fires are making low passes right over the place where we'll be staying in Wawa. There is still no sign of rain.

On June 22nd, just past the longest day of the year, hot and tired, we roll into Wawa. It's here that fate has another twist in store for us.

Pirkko Gravelle lives in a little place called Hawk Junction, northeast of Wawa on the winding road to Chapleau. It's another of those northern towns that seem to have been abandoned after the heyday of the railroad. Pirkko has a Scandinavian background and with her blonde hair and beautiful smile you might mistake her for a fashion model if you saw her in downtown Toronto. But she prefers the northern life in Hawk Junction where she has a small farm with horses and a team of sled dogs. While Jesse and I are working our way through another hot and muggy day on the road, Pirkko Gravelle stops by the motor home while she is in Wawa. This wonderful mother is about to turn something tragic into something magic.

43

Pirkko's young daughter Leije lost her battle with Muscular Dystrophy not long before *Jesse's Journey* took to the road. Leije had been looking forward to naming a new foal they were expecting at their farm, but died before the foal was born. That's what brings Pirkko to the door of the motor home. She wants to know if Jesse will come up to Hawk Junction and give the new pony a name. And so on a warm summer night the road crew piles into the vans and sets out to find the farm at Hawk Junction.

We arrive to see the ten-day-old colt standing on somewhat shaky legs, with a wet black nose and huge brown eyes peering through the fence at us. I hold Jesse's hand out for the little pony to lick. He's a golden brown colour with four white socks and a patch of white down his face. After thinking about it for awhile, Jesse decides the little creature looks as though he has just walked through the snow, and names him 'Snowy.'

When it's time to leave I ask everyone if Pirkko and I can have just a few private minutes together. I thank Pirkko and as we hug one another we are both fighting back tears. We stand there for a moment, two parents united in grief. I think it helps both of us.

Back on the road the next morning we reach the 1000-kilometre mark and still there is no relief from the 40-degree heat. Ahead lies the highest and the longest of the hills at Montreal River Harbour. This one has become a personal challenge. As I tuck my head down behind the wheelchair, Jesse and I decide to put one more hill behind us.

The next big hill is just outside of Sault Ste. Marie. What the locals call 'one mile hill' awaits the unsuspecting. It's actually longer than a mile and like Jackfish Hill, it's almost straight up. Jesse and I don't mind the heat and humidity during this climb, because we know that just beyond the top of the hill we will be reunited with the rest of the family.

Sherene, Tyler and Tim meet us at a traffic light in the middle of four lanes of slow moving rush hour traffic. A lot of motorists are honking their support as they see the road crew, kids, a boy in a wheelchair and a man holding up traffic as he kisses his wife in the middle of the intersection.

Jesse is happy to have his brothers at his side and he begins planning activities for the three of them. It's easy to see how much he's missed both of them. All we're missing is Charlie. With her the picture would be complete. The hours that follow are spent filling the family in on our road adventure and catching up on family news from home.

Canada Day, July 1st, leaves us with little to celebrate. The weather takes another 180-degree twist as we take part in the International Bridge walk from Sault Ste. Marie, Michigan to Sault Ste. Marie, Ontario. Crossing the bridge the temperature dips to the minus numbers on the Celsius scale. The weather turns a bitter cold; it's raining and you can see your breath in the air as Jesse and I are among the fastest to cross the bridge. In the cold and wet we hurry back to the motel and settle in for the day since the events we are scheduled to attend are all cancelled because of the cold weather.

When we get ready to roll east to Sudbury there's a serious setback for the road team. John McHale has developed pneumonia. And to make things worse, Mike Woodward has strep throat. Some decisions have to be made and quickly. Despite protests that he's recovering, arrangements are made to fly John McHale home, as he's too sick to remain on the road. Mike Woodward, who is taking antibiotics, will stay. It's decided that I will sleep on board the motor home to keep a watch on Mike. Sean will lend a hand with the driving. It's a plan that leaves us spread thin, but at this point we don't have the luxury of adding to the permanent road team.

The road continues to rise up to meet us, and through all our troubles, Jesse does well. He doesn't seem to be bothered by the heat and humidity and he continues to amaze me with his personal growth, the rapport he's developed with the team and the way he relates to strangers who stop to meet him.

Rolling through Bruce Mines, Iron Bridge and Blind River, the dollar figures continue to climb. Hearing that kind of news is like putting fuel in the tank as we face the next set of hills. The weather slips back into a long string of hot and muggy days.

Heading east in the mornings Trish always makes sure both Jesse and I are slathered with sunscreen on our faces and arms. When the sun swings over to the west in the afternoon, it's time for another coating of sunscreen, this one on the back of my neck and the backs of my legs. Every day it seems as if the sun jumps into the sky early and then lingers there for hours before plunging rapidly late in the day. My skin has gone from a pinkish white to a richer looking copper colour. Jesse's 'raccoon eyes' are even more prominent.

There's a noticeable steadiness and routine that everyone on the road has settled into. Sometimes when things are quiet, I listen to the pitter-patter of my running shoes and the smooth hum coming from the tires of Jesse's wheelchair. Out here on the road, emotions sometimes run close to the surface when we meet disabled kids who have come to the roadside with their parents to cheer us on. It's especially tough meeting other boys with Duchenne. Jesse seems to be a source of inspiration and hope for them. More and more I'm feeling like we're doing the right thing and that our time together on the road will make a difference in people's lives.

Moving east along the Trans-Canada Highway, we turn north to Elliot Lake, the 'Jewel in the Wilderness.' Fur trading, the lumber industry and the lure of silver and gold have all played a part in the history of Elliot Lake. It was the discovery of uranium in the 1950's that had the town basking in the glow of prosperity. By the time *Jesse's Journey* arrived here in July of 1995, 11 of the 12 mines in the area had closed and the last mine still operating was scheduled to shut down in the following year.

But Elliot Lake is a town that has gambled and won. Perhaps sensing its most industrious days were behind it, the community literally set about the job of reconstructing itself. The little town, which is now heavily populated with seniors, focused on the Toronto market and soon the homes that had become vacant as the mines shut down were springing to life again. Senior couples, widows and widowers, tired of the traffic, concerned about safety and missing the company of friends in their own age group, sold their $450,000 homes in the south and headed north where a two-bedroom bungalow could be purchased for less than $20,000. The move meant not only fresh air, trees and water, but also plenty of friends to share the retirement years. For those who loved hunting or snowmobiling, Elliot Lake turned into a paradise. And for those who didn't care for the cold and the snow, they now had money in the bank for the winter months in Florida.

It's amazing to find a location this far north with such a vibrant downtown. Almost all of the stores are occupied, including such specialized shops as those offering merchandise for stamp collectors and coin collectors. Watching Sean line-dancing with a group of seniors in a community centre one morning, I think of Elliot Lake as the little town that picked itself up by the bootstraps and turned a negative into a positive.

On the afternoon that we roll into Elliot Lake, we have no idea it will be so difficult to say goodbye. Heading into town we suffer our first flat tire on the wheelchair. It's the only thing that goes wrong here. Our hosts Ron and Debbie Kruger do a great job of making sure that small town hospitality shines at its brightest. We are given an escort into town by the police department and an escort to City Hall by the fire department. We are presented with cheques and plaques and Jesse gets to meet 'Miss Elliot Lake.' And on a warm summer night we are able to take Jesse out on a pontoon boat with a group of new friends who we know will always welcome us back. Before we leave Elliot Lake, people along the streets start to applaud Jesse as he passes by, and still more people are coming out of their homes to shake his hand. Mike Woodward is right, the hardest part of this *Journey* is having to say goodbye.

Espanola is another northern Ontario town with a pulp mill. It's west of Sudbury and just a couple of kilometres south of the Trans-Canada Highway. There are puzzled looks on the faces of the team when we find out we are staying at some place called the Anishinabe Spiritual Centre just south of town. A small wooden sign that can easily be missed points the way to a gravel road that winds its way through the woods and opens up to a lake and a place that we know we are going to like as soon as we set eyes on it. Any television or movie images we had of priests and nuns are gone in an instant. Father Mike and the Sisters, Dorothy and Pat, are dressed as casually as we are and they greet our little band of strangers with hugs and a warm welcome. Jesse is given his own special welcome by 'Frisky' and 'Mooch', two senior citizens of the golden retriever world. I can tell this is going to be a golden opportunity to recharge our mental batteries before moving on to the next leg of *Jesse's Journey*.

The Spiritual Centre is run by the Jesuits, whose history in this part of Canada reaches back to the splash of the Voyageur paddle, before both the Hudson's Bay Company and the North West Company had established trading posts in the area. The Centre is designed to bring spiritual leadership to people of all faiths. The log cabins on the property are really very solid log buildings with stone fireplaces. One of the most incredibly beautiful structures in Northern Ontario is the chapel that stands among the tall trees overlooking Lake Anderson. The chapel is round and made entirely of wood that was cut and milled on the property. The amazing thing is there isn't a nail in the building. The chapel was built using mortise and tenon construction that dates back to twelfth-century England. The bright, colourful paintings done by native people add another dimension to the warmth of the wood. The sunlight that filters through the trees, the windows and the skylights, leaves you with a feeling there is no division between indoors and outdoors. It gives you a chance to experience nature and creates a feeling of quiet.

Sister Dorothy and Sister Pat have been working together for more than 25 years. Their past several years have been spent at Espanola. Sister Dorothy Regan is kind and caring. She's also the take charge person. Sister Pat Hassett is tiny, with boundless energy and a twinkle in her eye. And its clear to see they have both taken a liking to Jesse. They're up early to pick the blueberries that will be in the morning pancakes.

The evenings spent at the Anishinabe Spiritual Centre, after days on the road, are all too short. But I'm glad the team has a chance to rest. Trish tries her hand at kayaking while Jesse and Sean settle in with some of the local kids for what sounds like the world championship of Monopoly.

We reach Day 50 during our stay in Espanola, and it coincides with Mike Woodward's 28th wedding anniversary. We celebrate the occasion with a barbecue and Jesse acts as Master of Ceremonies at an impromptu party. He does a great job with his toast, "Here's to the past and to the future," which I think relates to each of us sharing this special place.

There are a few tears as we say goodbye to everyone at Anishinabe who, along with so many along the road, have become like family to us. Our police escort as we leave Espanola is Sgt. Bob Andrew. We are proud to learn that after thirty-nine years and seven months on the job, his final assignment before retiring is to escort *Jesse's Journey* as it moves on down the road heading for Sudbury.

Along the roadside people continue to stop to take pictures of Jesse and me and to make donations as we push on to Sudbury where Jesse is looking forward to visiting Science North. For people from Southern Ontario, Sudbury conjures up images of long winters, heavy snowfalls and freezing cold temperatures. But with the heat we've been through on the road, at Science North we are glad to be indoors where it's air conditioned and cool.

49

The time spent at Science North becomes one of those parts of the *Journey* where a father wants to step away from fundraising for a few minutes and just watch his son enjoy himself. And enjoying himself is exactly what Jesse does. First it's a chance to touch a real live milk snake. Jesse makes a bit of a face before I hold his hand out to touch the snake's smooth skin. Then in the glare of the TV cameras, he smiles as he is allowed to pet one of the half-dozen baby beavers born a few days before our arrival. After doing an interview with MCTV in Sudbury, Jesse and I are hamming it up for the cameraman as I hold a set of antlers on top of Jesse's head. I ask if they are deer or moose antlers because I can't tell one from the other. The staff seems to find that pretty funny. At the IMAX theatre we watched a show about sharks. Jesse thinks they look scary. I fall asleep.

Back on the road making our way through Sudbury, the heat and humidity are really sapping our strength. Trish and Sean, who are always pushing Jesse and me to drink more water, double their efforts to make sure that we are both taking on plenty of fluids. I know that Jesse is feeling the intense heat coming off the pavement, but he never complains and sticks gamely with me as we continue to generate donations along the road. Then, in the middle of afternoon traffic in Sudbury, with sweat pouring off me, my knees start to wobble. Sean and Trish jump in right away, taking control of the wheelchair and getting me off the road. Trish makes the decision that we are through for the day. I don't argue. Walking the highway in 40-degree heat is a test of both the human body and spirit. Some days nature wins. This is one of those days.

Friends along the road provide more than the usual support through the long days of what will become the hottest summer on record in Ontario. Since eating in restaurants day after day stopped being a treat many kilometres ago, the offer of a home-cooked meal becomes a treat we gratefully accept whenever we can. One of the hardest times of the day is right after suppertime when I look at the clock and see the few precious minutes between supper and bedtime slipping away like sand through an hourglass.

With the steady routine that we maintained, these were the only minutes of the day that I felt belonged to me. Trish and Sean would always do their best to see that Jesse enjoyed the evening, while I made my phone calls and wrote my journal entries before heading to bed as early as possible. Even though the heat made sleeping difficult, I rested better knowing there were a lot of people who wanted to make sure that for Jesse the end of each day was filled with as much fun as possible.

People might think that sitting in a wheelchair all day is easy and effortless. It's not. It's hard work and what Jesse is doing day in and day out is giving hope to a lot of people, particularly young people who never get to have an adventure. With every turn of the wheels on Jesse's chair, the hopes of a better future grow brighter for those young people.

Two months to the day after leaving London, I push Jesse through the rain on a quiet Sunday morning in Sudbury. Through the downpour, motorists continue to stop to make donations. There's another memorable moment when a police officer who is just coming off duty stops to wish us well. It's obvious that he is very moved by what we are doing and he is apologetic that he has left his wallet at the police station. I can see that he wants to do something and in an instant he reaches up to his collar and takes off his silver police department medallions. Handing them to Jesse he says, "Jesse, the public can't always get these and I want you to have them."

On Day 61 we break through a banner in the little town of Powassan, just south of North Bay, Ontario. We are halfway across the province.

Our *Journey* is giving Jesse and me a greater understanding of how Ontario is really a province of small towns. It's a tremendous feeling to know we have made it this far and a great relief for me to know that Jesse is doing fine. It's another hot, sunny day and I pour a bottle of water over my head after breaking through the banner.

For a little town like Powassan, our arrival is big news. From the side of the road, I smile as I watch Jesse surrounded by a sea of young children, all of them waving small Canadian flags. Jesse spends the next half-hour signing his name on the flags.

The halfway mark seems to give everyone on the team both a physical and mental lift. Knowing that we now have less distance left in front of us than behind us permits me to shift gears. If the human body can be compared to an engine, I'm well tanned and my legs are working like two pistons as the kilometres continue to click by. The honking and cheering has become constant, and as we head further south we begin to hear the echo of young voices yelling "Go Jesse Go" from the cars and vans that pass us.

We push deeper into Muskoka cottage country, passing through South River, Sundridge, Burk's Falls, Huntsville, Bracebridge and Gravenhurst. No two days on the road are alike. Every day is magical, as there are stories from every town we visit. There are receptions and dinners, funny times, sad times and times we wish we were a million miles away. The team is humming now like a well-oiled machine. As July draws to a close, media interest intensifies on the young man at the front of the parade who is capturing hearts wherever we go. In his own quiet manner, Jesse handles the pressure like a pro.

Rolling south on Highway 11, our police escort becomes concerned about the volume of traffic. Families with kids and cameras are crossing the road to see us. Transport truck drivers stop their huge rigs in the middle of the highway to make a donation.

When I look up from my position behind the wheelchair I see smiles and tears and I hear the spontaneous bursts of applause. Among the many who want to shake Jesse's hand on this particular day is a mechanic who comes out to the edge of the road from an automotive garage. He has on a pair of overalls and is wiping his hands with an oily rag. He leans over and kisses Jesse on the head and tells him,

"Be strong and keep up the good work." As quietly as he arrived on a hot afternoon, he slips away through the crowd and is gone. We never even learn his name, but he becomes a part of the magic.

Volunteer traffic becomes intense with people arriving and departing at a pace faster than anything we have experienced since leaving the Manitoba border. The increase in activity is visible everywhere we look. Trish is almost always on the phone, either in the motor home or in the escort vans, setting up interviews, coordinating police escorts and finalizing plans for the stops we are now making in almost every village and town we pass through. Sean is keeping an even more vigilant watch on Jesse to see that he doesn't become dehydrated in the heat or overtired from the accelerated pace. And both Trish and Sean become the 'foot doctors' for the volunteers who have pushed tender feet to the point where they are badly blistered and bleeding by the end of the day. They may limp to bed at night but none of them ever complains while they're on the road. And in the morning they're back again, ready to go.

Sherene and her brother, Glen, are welcome members of the team for a few days as volunteers are shuffled in and out. They take turns walking alongside us and sharing news from home – the latest dollar figures, new sponsors, new fundraisers being planned in various parts of the province, and the plans for our arrival in Southwestern Ontario. Jesse and I are content to take it one day at a time.

Ron Calhoun joins us for a day on the road and I'm glad he arrives on a busy day so he can get a first-hand look at how things work out here as traffic backs up along both sides of the highway. Meanwhile Jesse puts in another good day on the road – but then again he always does. Soon we're in more familiar territory and closer to home. We turn west, travelling through Owen Sound and Collingwood as we head for that section of the *Journey* that will take us down the eastern shore of Lake Huron and eventually on toward Windsor.

The crowds grow as we make our way toward Port Elgin, and the geography changes from the pine trees of cottage country to rolling farmland. At the ends of farm laneways, entire families are waiting with their children to take a picture of the boy who is travelling across Ontario to help battle genetic illnesses. The volunteers with us are quick to ask if they can hold the camera and click the shutter so that 'Dad' can be in the picture along with the rest of the family. Jesse and I smile, time and again, before shaking hands and moving on.

Day 73, moving south from Port Elgin, brings both fear and suspense. An alarm goes off inside me as the gruelling pace finally takes its toll on Jesse. The summer sun is beating down on us as we push on through a hot dry wind that licks at us like the flames of a fire. All of us are dripping with sweat when suddenly Jesse's head begins to sway back and forth as if his neck has turned to rubber. I can tell right away that he's in trouble. In a matter of seconds from the time I alert Sean to the problem, he's at Jesse's side. The back hatch of the van is opened, the hydraulic ramp comes down, I'm unclipped from the tether line, and Jesse is hustled from the heat and humidity into the air conditioning inside the van. Exhausted by the heat, his day on the road is over. It's a time of high anxiety.

The next morning, after checking with the crew and with Jesse to make certain that he is ready, we're back on the road. I'm glad we have our police escort, as people seem to be coming from everywhere as we roll through Southampton. We can see very plainly how understaffed we are, especially in the cities where the crowds almost overwhelm our volunteers.

We're now into August, and for the first time we can officially say this project ends next month. It's a comforting thought as we face another hectic day on the highway. Twin sisters, one of them in a wheelchair, join us for a few kilometres of road, just wanting to be a part of something they know is important to a lot of people. They're real charmers, and again the roller coaster of emotions starts its crazy ride.

Up and down the lakeshore people stop in cars and vans and climb down from trucks and farm tractors. Throughout the day we know we are falling behind schedule by taking pictures, but we are trying to accommodate as many people as we can because every person is important to us and to our cause.

Through the villages of Amberley, Kintail and Kingsbridge we keep moving. Despite being greeted by bagpipes or presented with town pins, we are always doing everything we can to keep the research dollars flowing. Sometimes in the chaos I have to force myself to remember why we're here. Alone at night, the faces of the hundreds of people we have met flash before me, many of them little children in wheelchairs who are counting on what we are doing to make a difference in their lives. Just before I fall asleep, I think about how my motivation is right in front of me every day. No matter how tired I feel, I know I'll be ready to go in the morning. I'll be there because I know Jesse will be there, and if he's ready every morning, what possible excuse can I have?

The pattern of shuffling in and out of motels along the shoreline of Lake Huron is broken every now and then when plans call for us to spend a night at a private home or at a cottage with family friends. The hospitality is always appreciated even though I am a poor house guest, with an agenda that calls for getting our laundry done, loading fresh water on board the motor home, and being in bed just after eight o'clock. Still, I always enjoy hearing the next day about how warm the water was for those who went swimming or how much the team enjoyed just sitting around telling our hosts stories about our travels and feeling for at least one night that they are part of our *Journey* family. Time always governs the things that I am able to enjoy in the few hours between the end of our day on the road and time to go to sleep. In that small window of opportunity, I like to linger over a home-cooked meal, with the first corn-on-the-cob of the season and a freshly baked pie. That always makes writing the nightly journal a little bit easier.

If the evenings are a time to unwind, the mornings are a different story. The pace increases drastically with everyone on the team in a hurry. I'm sure that must disappoint some of our hosts who want us to take our time at breakfast and then pose for some pictures. We always find ourselves looking at our watches, knowing we have a full day of roadwork ahead and schedule deadlines that have to be met in the towns and villages further down the highway. Breakfast is usually eaten quickly, the pictures are snapped in a hurry, and saying thanks is easier if it's kept short. We've been through this too many times. No one likes doing the goodbyes.

Chapter Four

THE PRETTIEST TOWN IN CANADA

"Your imagination is your preview of life's coming attractions" –
Albert Einstein

Goderich and its surroundings remind me of the hills we left behind in Northern Ontario. The road makes a long winding sweep up to the top of the hill that looks out over the harbour and Lake Huron, before turning in to the center of town. Traffic slows to a crawl in both directions and there is a lot of honking and cheering as I push Jesse up the hill, escorted by members of the Fire Department. One of the firefighters gives Jesse his helmet to hold in his lap as we make our way along the crowded streets and it isn't long before it is stuffed full of bills of every denomination. When we stop at the Tourist Bureau there are hundreds of people and a lot of media attention; for the first time I notice the television cameras are really right in Jesse's face. Although I know he is hot and tired, he just keeps smiling. Still, I keep a close eye on him to see if this kind of pressure is going to be a problem.

After a series of donations and presentations from various community groups, Jesse and I both make short speeches. It should be old hat to me by this time but I'm still amazed at how many people come out in the sweltering heat to support us. I know that it will be the people who will keep us going through both the good and the bad times, and it will be the people who ultimately make *Jesse's Journey* a success. While the crowds get larger, the days even hotter and the pace more hectic, our resolve to see the *Journey* through to its completion at the Quebec border hardens like steel.

On the outskirts of Goderich, as we leave "the prettiest town in Canada", Jesse and I come to a large group of seniors in wheelchairs parked along the sidewalk waiting to see us go by. They are all quite elderly and as we stop to say hello, I hold Jesse's hand out so he can shake hands with each of them. There's something special about elderly people and it seems we never have time to stop and hear their stories. Like most seniors, this group is well dressed.

The ladies have straw hats to protect them from the sun, while the men have shirts with ties, and wear nicely polished shoes. The values and manners of people of this age should be models for all of us to follow.

The frail hands, many with blue veins and well-worn wedding rings, reach out to squeeze the hand of the young man who has inspired them and made them think about grandchildren they haven't seen in a long time. There is a sparkle in the watery eyes we leave behind, many I know I will probably never see again. I can only hope we brightened their day.

The summer resort of Bayfield is a favourite spot for sailors. Weekends find the lake dotted with white sails snapping in the wind as the sailboats tack back and forth around the marker buoys on the lake. The village itself is lined with tall trees, as well as antique shops, art shops, tea rooms and restaurants which are a Mecca for tourists. Bayfield is on the list of places to visit for people from both Canada and the United States who are travelling the area, enjoying summer stock theatre and staying at the many bed-and-breakfast locations.

When we roll into town on what can only be described as a perfect summer day, this village is a showcase of Canadiana. In the shade of the tall trees that line the streets, it's like looking through a kaleidoscope at all the colours. Looking up from behind the wheelchair, I see glimpses of stained glass in the windows of many shops and the glint of silver from the sets of wind chimes dangling above storefronts along the main street. In one direction it's the white linen tablecloths and polished silverware at an outdoor café, and in the other direction, the red, white and blue sails of a model ship in still another window. And all along the main street there is the lustre of copper and brass in the antique shops.

As I hold up Jesse's arm to wave to the people who are applauding at the side of the road, I think that the entire team that is on the road on this particular morning must look a little worn. The T-shirts that always start the day fresh and clean, with the crisp red and black lettering that boasts *Jesse's Journey for Gene Research,* are now soaked with sweat.

The wheelchair is covered with a layer of dust from along the side of the road, and the running shoes I'm wearing are scuffed and dirty. The sweat and dirt have been hard-earned since I started pushing Jesse's wheelchair back at the Manitoba border.

People don't seem to mind as they line the street to make donations, and our volunteers find themselves lugging buckets that are overflowing with money. And we have no idea of what's in store for us further down the road.

Heading south along Highway 21 toward Grand Bend we meet a woman using a walker who is standing at the side of the road waiting to see the parade go by. As we pause to say hello, her son stands with her, his eyes moist. He tells me his mother, a diabetic, hasn't been out of the house in ten years but she wants to say she's seen the young boy who everyone is talking about. It's another of those moments that will stay with me for a lifetime.

Looking down the highway through the shimmering heat wave that obscures everything in the distance, we can barely make out the edge of Grand Bend. We are in familiar territory as this is where we have always vacationed as a family. Long before we reach the village, we can see through the haze that there is a huge crowd on both sides of the road. Traffic slows in both directions as the Ontario Provincial Police escorting us scramble to keep everything under control. Everyone on the road team takes a deep breath before we plunge into the sea of red balloons and cheering people wanting to shake hands and make a donation to support gene research. I know the team is looking forward to reaching Grand Bend because the schedule calls for a three-day break here, our first real rest in seventy-seven days.

Grand Bend is the hub of the lakeshore villages that make up what the tourist people call Ontario's West Coast. In the off season, it's a quiet village of fewer than a thousand people. In the summer months, Grand Bend is bursting at the seams with as many as fifty thousand people, most of them seeking the sun and the fun. It's an eclectic circus with everyone doing their own thing and it creates a lot of visual contrasts.

The streets are usually crowded with families in T-shirts, shorts, sandals and sunglasses, strolling or browsing through the shops, reading the sometimes funny and sometimes rude sayings on the brightly coloured tops and hats that fill the stores. Grand Bend's main street seems to be a constant carnival. In the air there's the smell of coconut-scented suntan lotion that has been slicked onto the hundreds of young bodies soaking up the sun on Grand Bend's main beach. On the long weekends, what's commonly known as 'The Bend' is a popular destination for young people looking for the nightlife.

Add to the mix the theatre crowd, in town for an evening of entertainment at the Huron Country Playhouse, one of the mainstays of Grand Bend's summer life. The theatre-goers fill the trendier restaurants in the area, while their vehicles make a statement of tradition parked next to the SUV's, mini-vans, pick-up trucks, motorcycles, several hundred bicycles and the odd dune-buggy that make up Grand Bend's transportation system. On long weekends, the village can even boast of gridlock as all these vehicles jostle for position at Grand Bend's only traffic light, at the main intersection that leads to the beach.

Then there is the sailing crowd. Some of them are yuppies who are relatively new to the game of sailing, and some are dyed-in-the-wool sailors who have experienced the lake's many moods. They seem to spend their time washing decks, polishing brass fittings and re-arranging rigging. Sometimes the air along the river that leads out into Lake Huron is filled with the smell of steaks being barbecued on hibachis attached to the sterns of the sailboats. Walking along the river, you can count on overhearing a conversation about the amount of money tied up to the slips. Alongside the fleet of local boats with Canadian flags dangling from their sterns are some of the big boats that have made the trip from Detroit or some other American harbour.

On the other end of the seafaring economic scale are the enthusiastic 'trailer sailors' slipping their boats into the water in the morning and hauling them out at the end of the day.

Just south of Grand Bend, still a central part of the community, is Pinery Provincial Park where campers pitch their tents for a more rustic back-to-nature holiday that includes swimming, soaking up the sun and toasting marshmallows over a campfire.

The smells, sights and sounds of Grand Bend include french fries with vinegar and jet-skiers flitting across the lake like water spiders with no set pattern. There are the cigar boats whose drone can be heard for miles and the parasailors dangling in the silence high above the water.

On the quiet side, you can see moms and dads snapping pictures of each other on the shore as they help their preschoolers build sandcastles. If you walk along the beach, you'll find people snoozing in the sun with copies of the latest paperback propped open beside them, often on about page three. And if you look along the pier that leads to the lighthouse, you'll find young boys and old men with fishing poles, both daydreaming about yachts, speedboats and bikinis, and sometimes catching a fish. Mostly, Grand Bend is a lot of people watching a lot of other people. And it's all fun.

The roadside leading into Grand Bend is jammed with kids with signs. Alongside the kids are their parents and grandparents, clapping their hands, waving and calling out words of encouragement as we enter town.

At a civic reception and barbecue Grand Bend shoots to the top of our record book, generating more than $20,000 for *Jesse's Journey*. It's an experience that makes me feel my highest hopes can become a reality if I just keep trying hard enough. And in saying "thank you," I have trouble finding the words to reflect what I am feeling. Everywhere I look, I see familiar faces. These are people who have worked long and hard to make this day a reality. The emotions that I normally hold in check are running dangerously close to the surface.

True to his word, Darryl Sittler catches up to us while we are in Grand Bend. Darryl gives Jesse a Toronto Maple Leafs hat and an autographed copy of his book, which he has inscribed with the words, "continued success in helping others and thanks for including me in *Jesse's Journey*." The hot dog lunch Darryl attends raises more than $1,000. Just as I expect, Darryl is as much a gentleman off the ice as on the ice, taking the time to fill each and every request for an autograph.

Just when things are looking up, our buoyant mood is shattered when the team suffers a real setback. Mike Woodward falls and breaks his collarbone. We are all relieved when we learn that Mike will be fine once he has time to mend. While we know he will be working for us from home, the bad news is that on the road we are going to have to get along without Mike for the rest of the *Journey*.

National Geographic Magazine once listed Grand Bend, Ontario as one of the three best places in the world to watch a sunset, and during our brief stopover we are treated to a spectacular show. The cloud deck takes on a fiery red colour before changing to orange and then to a rich copper hue as the sun slips below the horizon. We'll have to carry the picture of the sunset in our minds as we head back to the road in the morning.

The *Journey* continues with one small snag. I've developed a nagging cough that will not go away. This is a real concern because it's using up energy, but it will take a lot more than a cough to keep me off the road.

Rolling on through Thedford and Ravenswood, we are met at a farm gate by John McIntyre of the Vancouver Canucks. He and his dad come walking down their farm lane to say hello, and John gives Jesse a hat that has been autographed by the Canucks. His father's rugged-looking hands are evidence of a life of hard work on the farm.

They both wish us well and, waving goodbye, they head back up the laneway toward their farmhouse. Walking side by side with a little cloud of dust around their feet, I saw a father proud of his hockey-playing son, and a son proud of the sacrifices his father had made to help make his son's dream come true.

On toward Sarnia we stop at the Kettle and Stony Point First Nations Reserve, where about a hundred and fifty people are waiting to meet us, many of them in native costumes. Jesse is presented with a dream-catcher. I have seen dream-catchers hanging from the rear view mirrors of cars, but never really paid attention to them. Dream-catchers look like a stick that has been bent into a circle with a series of loose cobweb-like threads that criss-cross from side to side. In the middle of the cobweb pattern there is a hole, and the legend is that the dream-catcher will snag all the bad dreams in the cobweb but let the good dreams pass through the hole.

There are no bright costumes when I push Jesse past Ipperwash. The remains of partially burned logs block a portion of the road. Little do we know that a month later the situation will escalate to a full-blown crisis with gunfire and a death. At the time we pass by, I wonder what it will take to bring peace to the troubled area. We move on with the question unanswered.

The trip through Sarnia in the heart of the chemical valley is a blur of radio and newspaper interviews. And while we collect more than $6,000 on the road, things are not getting any better on the health front. My legs are aching, but the real problem is the cough that keeps getting worse. My throat has become ragged and by the afternoon of Day 84, as we head toward Chatham, we have to call it off. Jesse is too hot, and the heat and humidity overcome all the road crew and volunteers. The hottest summer on record is making us pay a price if we want to raise funds for research.

In the sticky moist air that makes breathing difficult, I begin to wonder if Chatham is going to be the end of the line. Trish doesn't hesitate in making the decision that I am going to the Emergency Department of Chatham's Public General Hospital. I'm told that I need antibiotics and plenty of rest. By the next day, my throat is getting worse and I know I'm in real trouble. I can't remember if I was being stubborn but I guess I must have been because the next thing I remember is Ron Calhoun arriving on the scene. Then I am heading back to the hospital where more tests are conducted and new drugs are ordered to combat the problem.

We lose 48 hours in Chatham and that forces a real scramble on the telephones to rearrange our schedule. While we are back on the road again, I am still suffering the effects of the infection and both Trish and Sean are working overtime at every break to keep cooling me off with wet towels. Packed in ice and resting in the back of the motor home after our lunch break, I must look pretty funny. But I don't care. I just want to sleep, and as I lie there I think about how valuable Trish and Sean are to this project, two young university students showing maturity beyond their years. Through this last stretch of heat and highway, I don't think I could keep going without them.

Entering Windsor, I'm still trying to get as much sleep as possible to get my strength back. Jesse picks up the slack and takes over making all the speeches. He is front-page news in the *Windsor Star* and there's a story on CBC television's evening news. When Sean takes Jesse to the observation deck of our hotel on the Detroit River to look at the skyline of Detroit, Jesse is very impressed. When he comes by to say goodnight, he tells me that some older women gave him a kiss. He's quick to add that he's decided he wants to start

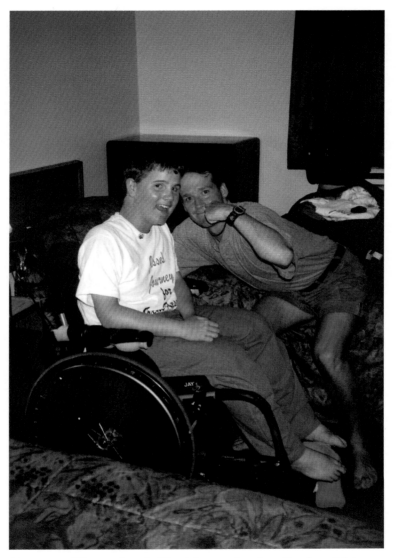

University of Western Ontario Kinesiology student Sean Bagshaw didn't meet Jesse until just three weeks before the road team left London. Shuffling constantly in and out of motel rooms, Jesse and "The Bagger" soon became like brothers.

One of the many special moments Jesse and I shared together in 1995 was the summer night Jesse was asked to travel to Hawk Junction to name a ten-day-old foal.

Of all the pictures of Jesse and I together as we crossed Ontario, my favourite was taken by Sam McLeod of the London Free Press when we reached home in August of 1995.

Jesse and I are welcomed "home" by a huge crowd in London in August of 1995.

In August of 1995, tired at the end of another long day, Jesse asked me in a whisper how long it would be before we could go home. It was a constant worry of mine that perhaps I had asked Jesse to take on too much.

meeting younger women! I laugh even though I am still feeling pretty rough. My thought is: What a wonderful kid!

By Day 89 I am starting to feel like I'm on the mend. We are back on the road and in the groove again. After the *Journey* makes the turnaround at Windsor, for the first time we are facing northeast toward Ottawa and the border with Quebec, our final destination.

At this point on our *Journey*, fate deals us three favourable cards. We reach mid-August and the humidity drops, the road becomes smooth and flat, and home is almost in sight. The farmland of Essex and Kent counties, which produce tons of tomatoes and corn, is ready for harvest as we travel through Tilbury and Kent Bridge en route to the little community of Wardsville.

The sun is shining and there are red-winged blackbirds sitting on the fence posts along the edge of the farm fields. The barns we pass are sometimes red and sometimes just boards that have been bleached in the sun. Most of the barns have surnames painted on them, followed by the proud words 'and sons'. There is a warm wind blowing and we are moving along nicely when Sean jogs up from behind our police escort to whisper a message. There is a lady up ahead waiting to see us.

The compassion and understanding of the people we meet is remarkable. Meeting the lady Sean had told me was waiting is another of those moments that no amount of advance notice can prepare you for. Smiling, she appears to be in her sixties with just a touch of grey in her hair. She is standing by the tall grass at the side of the road, waiting to make a donation. There are no speeches, no fanfare, and no politicians, as she quietly gives Jesse a little envelope that contains more than $1,000. It's a quiet meeting for a father and a son and another family's mother – a mother who has lost both her sons to Duchenne. Hugging this woman, I thank her as we share a moment only the parents of children who face a struggle every day can understand. Grappling with my own emotions, the reason we are here is again that much clearer.

As the kilometres continue to mount up, so do the donations. What takes place in the little town of Wardsville is typical of the many nights we share as a team – a team that has been living in each other's shadow for three months now. There is a meal of piping-hot scalloped potatoes and ham at the Masonic Hall. After dinner, Jesse and I both speak, and then there seems to be an endless line of people waiting to make donations. It's as if every service club, group and individual in Wardsville wants a chance to meet the young boy whose *Journey* across Ontario is carrying a message of hope. At the end of the day, Wardsville, with a population of four hundred people, has donated almost $3,000 to *Jesse's Journey*. It's another example of the kindness we find in small communities all across Ontario, generosity that's the backbone of our country.

We pick up the pace as I push Jesse through West Lorne and Dutton, villages that are jammed with people. There are little kids with signs and balloons, youngsters in baseball uniforms, farmers, seniors and politicians. Everywhere I look, there are families and moms and dads with cameras. I hold Jesse's arm up to wave so they can take a picture. Maybe someday they can look back at that photograph and remind their families of the day they met a very courageous young boy. I can see in their faces how thankful they are for their families' good health. I don't envy people very often, but passing through these little villages, that feeling is close to the surface.

Day 91 is special in a different kind of way. We know that for the first time since leaving in May, we are close enough to home that we can sleep in our own beds. The thought picks us up as we pass all the people and cars that are parked along both sides of the highway heading toward St. Thomas. I put my head down to push Jesse's wheelchair up a steep hill that leads to the giant statue of Jumbo, the circus elephant killed at a level crossing in St. Thomas in 1898. This statue is at the top of the hill at the Tourist Information Centre, and marks the western entrance to a city whose railway heritage is its signature.

With sweat dripping off my chin, I can see out of the corner of my eye that our volunteers are struggling to keep up with the donations that are pouring into the buckets they're carrying.

The crowd surges forward from the side of the road and Jesse and I are being swamped. This is a serious concern for me because I've noticed in the past couple of days that Jesse has been a little testy. I wonder, not for the first time, if maybe the length of the *Journey* is starting to wear on him, and all of us, more than we realize.

On the steps of City Hall there are speeches and the formal presentation of donations. As I do so often, I hold the microphone for Jesse as he speaks to the crowd. When it's my turn, I lean over to tell Jesse he spoke very well. It's then that he reminds me to keep it short with the whispered message, "Don't ramble dad!" That's when I know he is doing fine.

After planting a tree at City Hall before heading back out to the road, St. Thomas remains in my mind as a series of still pictures. There is an image of the mayor walking with us through the crowd on the main street of his city collecting money with one of our buckets, and it's hard to tell which one of us feels more pride. There is Jesse signing the city guest book and receiving the key to the city. There are more interviews, pictures to pose for and autographs to sign. And in every picture I can see the road team and volunteers in their *Jesse's Journey* T-shirts, making sure that everything runs smoothly. The weeks we have spent together have taught us how to keep to a schedule. We have reached the point where seldom when I'm speaking anymore do I see Trish subtly pointing at her wristwatch to remind me it's time to go.

Our days on the road end with somebody either spray-painting a mark on the road, hammering a stake into the ground or tying a ribbon to a fence post to mark where we have finished for the day.

As that was being done there were others who would open the back hatch of the van and get Jesse on board once the hydraulic ramp came down. Then they would latch Jesse's wheelchair to the floor and frame of the van, and the road convoy would head to our motel to get settled in for the night.

But on August 18th the road pattern is broken. For the first time in 91 days on the road, we are driving home. I can't help smiling as I glance at Jesse every now and then on the short drive home to London. His eagle eyes are taking in everything and I have to remind myself that he is only fifteen years old and he's been away from home for three months. This must be a little bit like Christmas.

When we pull into the driveway, I'm not sure whether Charlie is happier to see Jesse or the reverse. Charlie jumps on Jesse's lap and has the tail-wagging, face-licking and affectionate moaning in high gear, and Jesse has a smile that could light up a dark room. As brothers do, Jesse and his younger brother Tim try to pretend it's not a big deal to have been apart from each other for such a long time. Tim and Jesse have always been best buddies as well as brothers, and secretly I think they're glad to be back together, even if it's only going to be a short stay. As Sherene and I watch all the fussing that is going on, and without saying a word, we both know we have made the right decision in pouring our energy into *Jesse's Journey*.

For the next three nights we'll be at home, but I caution myself not to think of this as a rest break. The days and nights are going to be busy with events and appearances and I don't want to lull myself into a false sense of relaxation. Any thoughts I have about a mini-holiday of some kind are shattered right after supper. Jesse and I are on the move again; this time it is an appearance at the stock car races at the half-mile track just outside of London.

Parents of disabled children spend a lot of time searching for fun for their youngsters. They struggle doing everything they can to try to make life as normal as possible for their children. There can be a lot of tension when that struggle is sometimes waged at the expense of a couple's other children. And all too frequently, parents punish themselves for not being able to be in more than one place at a time. That might sound silly, but it's a reality for parents whose kids can't play hockey, soccer or baseball, ride a bicycle, roller blade or go swimming. Spectator sports are a great outlet, and for us stock car racing is one of the best. It's outdoors, it has lots of action, lots of colour and for a young teenager, lots of noise.

Our three boys were just little kids when I first started taking them to the races. Like most little kids they liked the crashes, but they didn't want to see anybody get hurt. So we went to a lot of 'endurance' races where they fill the entire track with pretty beat-up cars, usually with rookie drivers. They drop the green flag and then see who can last for 250 laps. We always picked our favourites (usually based on the most outrageous paint job) and followed their progress. It was a great way to spend part of the summer, sitting on top of a grassy hill, watching the chaos on the track and enjoying all the action, noise and laughter.

As they grew up, the kids still liked the french fries and hot dogs. They still enjoyed the sunshine and sitting on the grassy hill, but now they were developing a keener interest in what the drivers were doing. They started to follow the strategy involved in stock car racing at the levels above endurance racing. They weren't as interested in the crashes as they were in watching drivers jockey for position or keeping track of pit stops and noting who was on what lap. The good part was there was still a lot of colour, a lot of action, a lot of noise, and a lot of laughter.

It's another action-packed night at the races. Jesse gets to go around the track with his wheelchair mounted in the back of one of the track service vehicles. As I hold his arm up to wave to the crowd, the thousands of moms and dads and kids in the grandstand and on the grassy hill give Jesse a standing ovation. Tim is happy because he gets to follow right behind in the pace car.

What really makes this night so special is something that people seem to be doing wherever we go. Jesse's good friend, Erica Hill, whom he has known since grade two, is there with her mom and her dad and her brother. They are the ones wearing the *Jesse's Journey* T-shirts and manning the buckets collecting the dollars that are pouring in. That night, like so many volunteers before and the many that would come after, they are the real heroes.

And the driver who won the feature race donated his winnings to *Jesse's Journey.*

It's late when we arrive back home that night, and finally it is quiet. I take a few minutes to let the whole idea of 'home' come back to me after so many nights away. It feels good to be there, even though I know it will be a short night and that we'll be back on the road in the morning.

Chapter Five

THE VALUE OF FRIENDS AND TEAMWORK

"The best mirror is an old friend" –
(Proverb)

The village of Port Stanley, on the north shore of Lake Erie, is one of those lakeside resort villages that have seen lots of changes. In the era of the big bands, it was the music of Guy Lombardo and his Royal Canadians that filled The Stork Club on the shore of the lake. The Stork Club is gone, lost to a fire several years ago. Condominiums now line the fringe of the beach and the village's most visible link with history is now the Port Stanley Terminal Railroad. A restored diesel hauls carloads of passengers up and down a rail line that long ago was a major transportation route. Now it's almost a Disney-like experience for children – children whose grandparents smile as their minds wander back to a gentler time.

Port Stanley is also an ocean-going seaport, and there is still a lighthouse at the end of the pier. Artists and photographers have captured the lighthouse from every angle, but the pier itself has been fenced off for safety. Lake Erie, which is the shallowest of the Great Lakes, can change its mind in an instant, sending huge waves crashing over the top of the pier. Ocean freighters still slip in and out of Port Stanley, and in the spring, the mandatory picture of a ship's captain is taken, smiling and wearing the top hat that symbolizes that he is the master of the first ship into harbour in the new shipping season.

Like most lakeside villages, geography dictated where the streets would go. The village has a lift bridge and offers a retail mix that runs from traditional to trendy. It's another of the ideal spots to spend a lazy summer day, the kind of day that doesn't get started too early.

The day on the road starts under a clear blue sky at the point where the beach sand gives way to the pavement. It is Day 92 and our road team is about to be joined by a marvelous group of people.

They say that if you can count your real friends on one hand, you're a lucky person. On that Saturday morning in the little village of Port Stanley, I would have needed a lot of extra hands. The people I had worked with for the better part of two decades as a reporter at CFPL Television in London were about to show me all over again what being a family is really about.

It probably sounds corny to say we were a family, but it's true. Most of us had known each other throughout our careers with microphones and cameras in both radio and television. We had been there for each other. We had celebrated the marriages, seen each others' kids grow up and supplied the much-needed support when separation or sickness threatened to put a dent in that family.

We had survived the ugliness of downsizing when the unpredictable economy of the 80's and 90's had forced every sector of society to tighten its collective belt. We had played charity hockey games and pick-up baseball games together. We had partied together, laughed together and cried together. And on this day, we would all walk together. There is strength here and it shows on the faces of the people who are about to spend the day on the road with us.

One of those people is John Lees. With a 'salt-and-pepper' beard and a full head of straight hair, John is pushing 50 and still defying age in the same manner that he has defied a lot of things since his youth. I have known John since we were in high school. A lifelong swimmer, he is a rebel who loves the outdoors, and a deep thinker who has always looked after himself physically. He is also a *Journey* veteran and a good friend. John and his daughters had walked the highway with Jesse and me down through the Muskokas doing all the things that volunteers do to keep everything moving.

There was a day when I was slumped in the front passenger seat of the motor home, sweating with a towel over my head at the end of the day. John was driving me back to the motel for the night. He handed me a small book of photographs he had taken at the high school reunion I had missed because we'd been in Sault Ste. Marie at the time. The faces I had known in high school had changed. They weren't exactly strangers, but they were no longer the faces in the yearbooks. The guys I had known now had grey hair and some were baldheaded, which made the guessing game more difficult. Despite being tired, I think I stared even longer at the faces of the girls I once knew. The beauty of youth had slipped away gently, and been replaced by a different kind of radiance. Most had aged gracefully, yet from cover to cover I didn't get any of their names right. Perhaps a bigger clue would have come from the incredible messages of inspiration they had written in the back of the book. The words matched the people I remembered, when we were young and we'd thought those golden days would last forever.

I check my watch just before we set out to cross the lift bridge that leads to Port Stanley's downtown and the Town Hall where a huge crowd has already gathered. Time is always important. In the morning sun I watch the people I know so well stretch their muscles in preparation for the walk ahead. Trish makes sure that everyone has lots of sunscreen and plenty of water. The women from the television station are busy talking about what a great opportunity they will have to work on their suntans. The guys are lacing up running shoes and adjusting sunglasses for what they describe in a slightly macho manner as 'a great day for a little walk.' Slipping on the fingerless leather gloves that protect the palms of my hands as they grip the wheelchair, Jesse and I smile at each other. We know that by the end of the day, suntans and a little walk will be forgotten, replaced by the need for water, finding shade and fixing blistered and bleeding feet. We also know that every one of these people will last the entire day. That's what this family of co-workers is all about.

At the Town Hall there are cheque presentations, a teddy bear for Jesse, and a choir that urges us all to "live a little...laugh a little", something we have been trying to do since leaving the Manitoba border. Saturday traffic is heavy and John Lees quickly has the rest of the volunteers working like pros, collecting donations from the windows of cars and trucks and vans whose drivers are most generous. By midday the temperature reaches 34°C and the heat reflecting off the pavement is truly intense.

The sound of car horns honking their support is mixed with the sound of air horns from transport trucks below as we pass up and over Highway 401, the province's number-one corridor for commerce between Windsor and Montreal.

Sunburned and tired, our volunteers spend the day lugging buckets of cash, as well as gifts of cider, blueberries and apples from the fruit stands we pass. Finally we approach the sign that says 'London – population 316,000.' After 92 days on the road we have 'officially' reached home. One by one, the family of volunteers hug Jesse and me as they leave, and even though they are exhausted, they thank us for a great day and the opportunity to take part in *Jesse's Journey*.

For Jesse and me, and the rest of the permanent road crew, the day isn't over. There is still another appearance to make, this time an evening parade through downtown and a concert in London's Victoria Park. With a police escort, marching bands and hundreds of people walking with us, we stop to shake as many hands as possible making our way along the parade route. When we finally reach the park it seems ironic that Jesse and I are back where we started in May.

When we're introduced at the park, both Jesse and I are given a standing ovation. While the cameras are clicking, one of those photographers takes what will become known as the 'signature picture' of *Jesse's Journey*. Standing beside Jesse, holding his arm in the air with his small Canadian flag waving back and forth, I know the applause we are hearing belongs to every member of our team and every volunteer who has come out to the road to help make a dream come true.

I am very worried when we finally arrive back home because I can see that Jesse is really tired. We had stayed at the park longer than we had planned, posing for pictures, signing autographs and shaking hands. I'm relieved when Sherene and I have Jesse tucked into bed. He's done a remarkable job throughout what has been a long and grueling day. In the quiet, alone for what seems like the first time in months, Sherene and I talk for a few minutes, knowing that the next day we'll all be able to sleep in. In the morning it will be August 20th and we'll have exactly one month to go.

Since Sunday is meant to be a day of rest, that is exactly what I wanted to do. But when the sun comes up, Charlie greets me with one little bark right outside our bedroom door. I guess I had forgotten she did that. She jumps up on the bed and snuggles down to claim her bit of space. With her tail wagging, she looks up at us as if to say now that we're all home, everything is right with the world.

For one day it's sheer pleasure to do normal things like reading the newspaper and enjoying a second cup of tea. It's nice not to have to pack up in the morning and board the motor home to get to our start point. It's nice to walk around on the grass in my bare feet. And for just one day, it's satisfying to know I don't have to open the door to another empty motel room. For a day there's no unpacking and trying to make an empty room seem like home before moving on again.

Watching Sherene making breakfast for Jesse on Sunday morning, I start to realize just how much I have underestimated the amount of work this whole project has meant for her. While there was no shortage of enthusiasm in launching *Jesse's Journey,* we had no idea of the infrastructure that would be required. By the end of summer Sherene and her mother will have hand-written more than seven thousand thank you notes. And that was just the beginning. Through it all Sherene never complained, and I never knew how lucky I was.

Monday morning comes all too quickly, and as Jesse and I prepare to head back to the road, gene research is about to get a tremendous financial shot in the arm. By 7:30 in the morning, there are a half-dozen radio interviews stacked up before we can get underway. Trish and Sean and the rest of the road crew are scrambling to get everything organized for departure. Quickly they run through the checklist. Cell phones are tested for strength, vehicle drivers checked in on the walkie-talkies, police escorts are confirmed along with their positions and use of lights and sirens. Flags and signs are clipped into place. Cold water and nutrition bars are loaded on board the escort vehicles. Fuel levels and oil readings are noted. First aid kits are checked and both the drivers and walkers are given instructions. Trish cautions the walkers to drink lots of water and make sure they use sunscreen. The walkers are also cautioned not to cross the road through traffic to collect donations. Volunteers on the other side of the road will look after those people wanting to make donations.

With the safety concerns addressed, Trish looks down the list one last time before she gives me the go-ahead to clip on the tether leash that connects me to Jesse's wheelchair. We are set to go for another day. I double-check with Jesse to see if he's ready. And then we're underway.

There are hundreds waiting to see us off and with this many people we know there is a danger in getting bogged down and falling behind schedule. But this is what it's all about, bringing the issue of the need for research to the public, gathering support for our dream of broadening the base of genetic knowledge.

As the day grows hotter, the crowd becomes larger while we make our way steadily along the road. There are kids with colourful signs of encouragement and banners telling Jesse he's their hero. There are also people in wheelchairs, and it's here that we always try to stop to say hello and to shake hands. People are pressing cash and cards and cheques in our direction. Jesse is getting swamped, and the escort van is quickly filling up with flowers and balloons and teddy bears that people along the side of the road have handed to the volunteers.

By the time we reached City Hall, where London Mayor Dianne Haskett and her young daughter Annie join us, we are starting to feel as if the entire population of London is in the streets. In the square beside City Hall is another huge crowd of people, gathered to see the courageous young boy who is making a difference in the lives of the people he's met and touched.

The Master of Ceremonies for the event outside City Hall is an old friend of mine. Bill Brady isn't one of those people who live their life as if it's a rehearsal. A well-respected broadcaster who loves to travel, Bill is also a great cook, a writer and a stained glass worker who has given back to his community countless times, serving on numerous boards and being a champion of almost every cause imaginable. But most of all, he likes to have fun.

When Bill was a little younger he seemed, almost with reckless abandon, to live each day as if it were his last. In those days he poked barbs at what was seen as London's establishment. Now he's highly regarded by the establishment he used to take to task.

The formal ceremonies include a lot of cheque presentations along with the announcement that the city plans to name a park after Jesse. The park is a beautiful piece of land where children can play, not far from our home. It's a place that will forever remind our family of the generosity of the people of our hometown. Jesse Davidson Park will always remind me of the real hero in all of this, Jesse himself.

Before we leave City Hall to return to the road and the kilometres we still have to complete in the afternoon, everyone sings the national anthem. It catches me off guard. There are lots of Canadian flags in sight, and as we turn to leave, this is one of the most emotion-charged moments of the entire *Journey*. If the hills of northern Ontario had been a physical challenge through the first half of the *Journey*, the sheer volume of people and the outpouring of support we are now receiving has become the mental challenge of the second half.

Leaving London behind us, I push Jesse on toward Ron Calhoun's
hometown of Thamesford where there's a fire engine waiting to
escort us to a barbecue for the whole road team. Jesse and I talk for a
few minutes about how many fire engines we have seen since May.
We decide there have been dozens of them, some old, some new –
some with wailing sirens and some that were antiques spewing out
smoke when it was already muggy and difficult to breathe. But on
this summer night, everything is fine. We've had a great day on the
road. We are back in small-town Ontario, and August is winding
down. We're starting to feel like we're on the home stretch.

Rolling on through Ingersoll and Beachville, we are greeted with
cheers and applause. Next up is Woodstock where I made my start in
radio in 1966. As I push Jesse up the hill that leads into Woodstock,
we pass the radio station that holds so many memories for me, back
in a time when not everything we did on air went quite as planned.
I smile to myself when I think back to all the fun we had in those
early days of my radio career. In the mornings, there were only two
people in that little building; there was me and there was Howie
Hilyer. Howie had been in the military and was in his late fifties
when I started in radio. He had lots of stories to tell, like the day he
was on the air in Goose Bay, Labrador, just after the war. The station
signal barely reached beyond the edge of the base. It was a quiet
Sunday afternoon, and Howie was doing his regular music show that
helped pass the hours for those on the base. It was snowing pretty
heavily when there was a knock at the door. A man in a thick,
fur-trimmed parka appeared and introduced himself simply as 'Ed'.
He explained to Howie that he was on his way back to New York
from London, England and there was going to be a delay while the
ground crew fixed some mechanical problem with the plane. He
asked if he could 'sit in' for a while. Howie and 'Ed' chatted through
the afternoon and Howie read the news on the hour and played some
records and read the weather reports. Late in the afternoon a young
officer came by and knocked on the door. He took a look at Howie
and apologized for interrupting. Then, looking at 'Ed' he said, "Mr.
Murrow, your plane is ready sir!" Howie had just spent the afternoon

with broadcasting legend Edward R. Murrow, who just wanted to 'sit in' for a while.

They say you can never go home, but just for a moment as I push Jesse along the main street of Woodstock, I think that maybe they're wrong. If I close my eyes, I can still hear the high school marching band, the late night whispers on endless summer nights, the purr of car engines cruising the main street, and the sound of teenagers who really did hang around on street corners mimicking the latest 'doo-wop' songs. I think everyone growing up as a teenager in a small town in the 60's felt like they had lived the real life version of *American Graffiti*. On a hot summer day in 1995, it was like revisiting the set, only all the main characters had moved on.

The downtown streetscape in what's called the "Dairy Capital of Canada" had changed and yet it hadn't since I had gone to high school. A lot of the shops whose signs once heralded familiar family names now displayed the logos of chain stores. Some of the best pieces of architecture had been saved and given new life. Woodstock is like many of the small towns and cities we have been through, where the downtown is still the heartbeat of the community. We can feel the pulse of the city in the smiles on the faces of the people who line the streets, many of them clapping their hands or reaching out to pat Jesse on the head. Every now and then there is a familiar face in the crowd, a former teacher, an employer or an old friend, who reaches out to shake hands and say 'welcome home'.

At City Hall, I stand in the shade of one of the flower baskets that hangs from downtown street lamps, and like so many times before, Jesse and I deliver our message about the need for research dollars. This is an audience that understands when I tell them that all we want is for every youngster to have a chance to grow up and experience the type of youth I enjoyed in Woodstock. We don't need to say any more. It's time to move on again.

There are some volunteers who never make it out to the road. They labour long and hard, far from the limelight, making sure that the way is paved for *Jesse's Journey* to keep rolling. In Woodstock, Fay McFee is that key person. Like so many before her and so many to come after her, Fay is the sparkplug who does everything that has to be done. As we roll out of Woodstock, it isn't the first time I know that we have left behind another of the real heroes who are making *Jesse's Journey* a success.

Pushing on through Paris we reach Brantford, where I attended public school. Brantford is the home of Wayne Gretzky. In my sports career I had an opportunity to interview Wayne, but it was an interview with his father, Walter, that I will always remember the most. Walter Gretzky and I sat down to talk about families one day when he was making a promotional appearance at an event in London. I couldn't resist asking Walter if it had been difficult when Wayne was growing up, knowing full well that there was a superstar living in his home. Walter told me about an evening when the kids were practising on that legendary little rink behind the Gretzky home in Brantford. Wayne was having no difficulty with the drill they were working on, but for his brother Keith it wasn't quite as easy. Walter said he made a big mistake when he said, "Come on Keith, why don't you do it like Wayne?" Keith stopped skating, dropped his gloves, looked at his father and said, "I'm not Wayne!" Walter told me how at that moment it became so clear to him that our children are all different. I knew exactly what he meant.

I was aware that our children are all different, that they are like snowflakes with no two the same, and that we must remember to encourage them in whatever it is they choose to do. As I think back to that interview, I know exactly what Walter meant when he said that our children all have different abilities. I also know that some of our children have disabilities, and with my motivation sitting right in front of me I feel more than confident that Jesse's commitment to what we are doing is going to make a difference.

Not enough can be said about the teamwork and incredible chemistry our crew exhibits and the support they offer day after day. It's in Brantford that I notice how Sean and Jesse have become more like big brother and little brother rather than just Jesse and his helper. Sean is always making sure that when Jesse isn't on the road, there's something happening. At lunchtime they play gin, in the evenings it's sometimes a movie. Most nights when I stop by their room on the way to bed, I find Jesse and Sean with about four other people and a pile of pillows all curled up on one bed watching their favourite sitcom, *'Friends.'*

While Sean is busy with Jesse, Trish takes on the job of making sure that the volunteers find their days a rich and rewarding experience. This includes having some fun. Volunteers are very special people, and we have the very best. These are people who have given up a week of their lives to take part in *Jesse's Journey*. Their days on the road are hard work and making sure they have some fun is the least we can do.

Pushing Jesse through Brantford, we are escorted by local firefighters who conduct a boot drive for us. The volunteers for the week are two of the funniest ladies I ever worked with. Jo Ann Reed and Janet Ferguson both love to laugh. They described themselves as "middle-aged, married women, away from home and somewhat giddy at the appearance of the hunky firefighters." I think it has something to do with men in uniforms. All week these two are kidding Trish about how they are going to find her a man. And in Brantford, it looks like there's a pretty good chance to do that.

At night, during a barbecue in our honor, these two starry-eyed volunteers are raving to their dinner partners about how the Brantford Fire Department is the best-looking department in Ontario, and how they are looking for a handsome young firefighter for Trish. This is probably a big mistake, since one of the dinner guests works for the Fire Department. A quick phone call is made and shortly after that a fire truck arrives complete with sirens and lights, and plenty of

young firefighters decked out in boots, yellow coats and helmets.
Maybe they thought that there was too much smoke coming from
the barbecue!

It doesn't take long before the cameras are clicking and our
middle-aged volunteers and Trish are putting on the boots, coats and
helmets and posing with their favourite firefighter. They can't stop
laughing the entire time. The room is in an uproar and for these
volunteers it's like Fantasy Night on *Jesse's Journey*. It's also the
kind of night that makes being a volunteer more satisfying, not only
knowing that you're helping, but having fun while you're helping.

Chapter Six

NEARING THE FINISH LINE

"Life begins when you get out of the grandstand and into the game" –
P.L. Debevoise

At the end of Day 98 on the road, we reach the outskirts of Guelph where we pack up quickly and head to Toronto. The days in and around Toronto are going to mean a lot of dashing in and out of Canada's busiest city. It will be hectic, but we know there are media nuggets that can be mined that will help us carry the message. There is quite a buzz among the road crew as we drive on toward Toronto and I can tell Jesse is pretty excited about what's in store. On this particular night the Toronto Blue Jays and *Jesse's Journey* are both playing at the Skydome.

The events of that night unfold in a blur as Jesse and I are hustled from one location to another to meet people, shake hands and pose for pictures. Prior to the game Lou Gossett, Jr., who starred in *An Officer and a Gentleman,* comes over to meet Jesse in front of the Blue Jays dugout. He's very interested in what we are doing and he kneels down beside the wheelchair to ask Jesse about his travels across Ontario. With microphones being jammed in between the two of them, Mr. Gossett pauses and looks at the media people before quietly telling them in a big bass voice, "This is private conversation!" As he stands up and shakes hands with me, he tells me I should be very proud of my son.

Then with our video playing on the Jumbo-Tron, Jesse and I are introduced and we start making our way around the bases at Skydome. As I hold Jesse's arm in the air so he can wave his small Canadian flag to the crowd, thousands of baseball fans rise to their feet and applaud as they salute the young man who is leading *Jesse's Journey.* As we round third base, there is a cluster of television cameras and still photographers waiting for just the right moment. With my hand holding Jesse's forearm and his flag aloft, we pause for just an instant. And as we look up at the crowd and smile, all of the photographers' cameras click at the same time. I hope that is the picture the morning papers will use, because I want every disabled youngster and their parents to know that kids in wheelchairs do amazing things when they try. It's a special moment and a moment I know will never come again.

Jesse is given a Toronto Blue Jays shirt with his name on the back, and Devon White of the Blue Jays, who we are told doesn't like to be interrupted while he's getting his 'game face' on, signs a ball for Jesse. Jesse gives the ball to Jo Ann Reed for her 9 year old son Andrew, who really wants to be a baseball player.

After doing several radio and television interviews with the Toronto media down at field level, it's upstairs to be on the radio with Blue Jays announcers Tom Cheek and Jerry Howarth. They are both very generous with their time and after interviewing Jesse and me they talk at length to the entire radio network, telling listeners what *Jesse's Journey* is all about. Before we leave Jerry Howarth takes off his headset, comes over and says, "Good luck and God bless you, Jesse."

It has been a good day for *Jesse's Journey*, but as we leave Toronto Jesse is tired and we still face the long ride back to Guelph. Driving through the darkness there's an afterglow of excitement over being at Skydome. Jesse is very quiet. I wonder if he's going to be able to keep this up for almost another month. It will be a short night and we'll be back on the road in the morning.

The next morning dawns a beautiful summer Saturday and Jesse is ready to go. Pushing our way through Guelph, the traffic is bumper-to-bumper and slowed to a crawl in both directions. For the first time since leaving the Manitoba border back in May, our police escorts are seriously concerned about the number of volunteers and donors who are on the road. Trish calls everyone together to spell out the ground rules again, and eventually the chaos settles down. As the day wears on, the donations for genetic research continue to pour in and I continue to push on. By mid-afternoon the alarm of concern in my mind is going off again. My shoulders are aching, I want to sleep and, worst of all, the sore throat is back.

Sunday morning marks our 100th day on the road and I'm feeling tired even before we start. I do my best as I pick up the pace rolling through Acton, hoping I'll forget about my sore throat. But after 22 km, Trish orders a halt. We are looking for medical help again, this time at Peel Memorial Hospital. The specialist who examines me says my throat is extremely raw but the vocal cords are OK. After prescribing a strong antibiotic, he allows us to return to the road where our day ends up being a financial success, probably the best medicine I can get.

The days are now running into each other with what seems like no beginning and no end. There are fire engine escorts and receptions at city and town halls mixed with the hours spent pushing Jesse along the road and the constant shuffling in and out of motels night after night. In Etobicoke, I fall asleep right after we check into our motel. I miss supper and sleep through the fire alarms that keep going off throughout the night. By morning I'm more tired than I want to admit and I'm concerned that maybe I've taken on more than I can handle. I tell myself we have just three more weeks to go and then I can take Jesse home, knowing we've done our best. I decide to dig deeper than I have ever done before and to call on all the reserves available.

The Toronto mornings are busy. It's still dark as we drive through the early morning traffic to do yet another television interview. After appearing on CTV's *Canada AM* with host Valerie Pringle, Jesse is up the next day again just after five a.m., to do an interview with Ann Rohmer on CITY TV's *"Breakfast Television."* Heading east on the Gardiner Expressway, we notice how the rising sun puts the skyline of Toronto in silhouette and Jesse mentions that he has never seen a sunrise before. For a moment, there's silence as everyone in the van stops to think about how many children are totally dependent on someone else making sure they see the things that so many of us just take for granted day after day. I add that sunrise to the long list of special memories shared during our incredibly eventful days on the road.

Travelling through the tangle of traffic and intermittent gridlock of Toronto is complicated at the best of times. Pushing a wheelchair through the heart of the city makes it that much more difficult. Still there are some memorable moments, among them one that was either destined to happen or a remarkable case of defying the odds. It happens after another hurried breakfast and a dash across the city to reach our start point at a service station on a busy downtown corner. When we ask the service station owner if we can use his parking lot for a few minutes to assemble our road caravan for the day, he says certainly as he tells me about his 21 year old brother with DMD. He and his mechanics give us a donation, one of the very few we receive in Toronto where we are swallowed up in a city of three million people. We have to laugh as we make our way down Yonge Street, where people are actually asking us for money! We can't wait to get back to small-town Ontario. But before leaving Toronto, we have one more visit to make.

The Hockey Hall of Fame is our final media stop in Toronto and both Darryl Sittler and Don Cherry are there to greet us. Don shakes his head in amazement as he smiles at Jesse and says, "So, a hundred days down eh?"

I remember a chilly, raw night in Kenora back in May. It was only our second or third day on the road, and a couple of our crew had gone to do laundry, another of those thankless jobs that volunteers took on whenever it had to be done. People waiting for the washers and dryers to complete their cycle were watching the Stanley Cup playoffs on the television at the laundromat. As the clean *Journey* shirts were being folded and repacked in duffel bags, there was Don Cherry giving our cause a great plug on "Coach's Corner." People immediately recognized our group as the people Don was talking about and right away they wanted to buy the *Journey* shirts that had come hot out of the dryer!

Darryl and Don present Jesse with an autographed "Hockey Hall of Fame" sweater and hat. After lunch we are all given a guided tour of the Hall. Then, sitting among the National Hockey League's most prized trophies – the Hart, Norris, and Lady Byng – Jesse poses for the Toronto Star, the Toronto Sun and CBC television with the biggest prize of all, the Stanley Cup.

The skyline of Toronto is falling behind us as we push on to the east with Ottawa now less than three weeks away. It feels like we are back in our comfort zone as we're again in familiar territory, the little towns of Ontario. We are now officially into our fifth calendar month on the road as we push along the north shore of Lake Ontario, and again there are more nuggets for the memory mine. On the edge of Toronto, an elderly woman stumbles and falls as she tries to take Jesse's picture while making a donation. Jesse and I stop to make sure she's all right. There's a trickle of blood from a cut on the bridge of her nose, dirt smudges on her face, and plenty of grass stains on her clothes. As she sits up, she laughs and says, "Well Jesse, it looks like I have really fallen for you!" Sean is quick to administer first aid, and when he offers the woman some water, she smiles at Sean and says, "Haven't you got anything stronger than that?" Jesse cheers her up with a picture he autographs for her and seeing again that she is all right, we move on.

Further down the road, we find ourselves moving parallel to a major highway construction zone. Looking down on the construction work from where we are, backhoes are filling dump trucks. There are graders, bulldozers, and steamrollers stirring up a cloud of dust that hangs in the hot air. One of the construction workers looks up and when he sees us, climbs down from the backhoe that he's operating. He is a big man with well-tanned muscles beneath a very sweaty T-shirt. He leaves a line-up of dump trucks waiting as he climbs up the hill and over a fence to shake Jesse's hand and make a donation. His accent leaves little doubt about his Italian heritage. I could only guess that he's probably a dad who has worked with his hands all his life. It's moments like these which brighten our days on the road. Like so many others we meet, we don't know who this man is, but as I shake his hand and thank him, I'm proud to have met him.

Through Pickering, Ajax, and Whitby, the routine settles into a steady pattern with the road being extremely busy with donations and the volunteers tireless, although I know they must be hurting. Jesse is doing great and although I'm tired, I have seen the torn and bloodied feet of new friends and old friends, people who have spent hot days working the long lines of traffic and sharing our highs and lows. People are drawn to this project by the magic and the hope that a young boy is weaving into the hearts of people all across the province. Jesse and I agree that we never would have made it this far without these dedicated workers.

Jesse and Sean continue to build a friendship that will carry on when our days on the highway end. They've become very close and I feel a bit like we struck it rich when fate brought the two of them together.

By Day 110 we reach Port Hope, and for the first time there is a snap in the air to indicate that fall is coming. On a quiet day along the road, we get to watch a movie being made in Cobourg. As we look at what is supposed to be a high speed chase, I can't help thinking that after all we have seen in the months we have been on the road, this stuff looks pretty tame. It's amazing how different things look on the big screen when Hollywood has time to add all the sound effects and dramatic music. It also makes you think about how far Hollywood is from reality.

Back in our motel room at night, we watch as the Baltimore Orioles' Cal Ripken, Jr. plays in game number 2131 of his career, a chunk of history as he breaks Lou Gehrig's 'Iron Man' record set in 1936.

With records that have stretched that long and stood up for such a long time, our 110 days suddenly don't seem that long.

It's about this time in *Jesse's Journey* that the weather decides to test us again. We have run into an endless wall of rain that's crossing the lower Great Lakes and after just two kilometres, we are forced off the road. In a way I don't mind. Jesse's health is always our number one concern and I know that everybody on the road team welcomes a break, even if it is unscheduled. Trish, who is suffering from a sore throat, goes to a walk-in clinic while the rest of us catch up on sleep. By the time we reach Brighton that evening, we definitely know it's fall. It's raining and the wind is blowing. Jesse is very cold as we end our day with 28 km completed. It's the coldest day we've faced since Kenora and we are all chilled and tired. The good news is that donations for research are still pouring in and we have just ten more days to go.

Reaching the outskirts of Kingston, I notice for the first time that the leaves are starting to change colour. It's September 11th and we're about to receive two messages and send one very important one ourselves.

The day begins with a long uphill run that takes longer than usual because muscle fatigue is now a major problem for me. I'm trying hard to make sure that the little energy I have left is spent wisely over the final few days of the *Journey*.

The first of the two messages we receive comes on the cell phone from one of the radio stations in London that's been keeping track of our progress. The newsroom wants to let us know that the annual *Terry Fox Run* has attracted more entrants than usual and organizers are attributing that to what Jesse and I are doing. Despite the sore muscles, that message gives me a lift both physically and mentally.

The second message comes in the afternoon from Darryl Sittler. Jesse's eyes are smiling when I relay the message from Darryl.

The Ottawa Senators have asked if Jesse and I will drop the puck at centre ice when the Senators host the Toronto Maple Leafs in a pre-season exhibition game just two days before we finish the *Journey*. Even though this is our final week on the road and our schedule is brimming over, I know this is the kind of moment that every father wants his son to enjoy.

The next day we send a message without knowing it. The day starts out the way most have begun. The checklist has been run through and the volunteers have been given instructions. The police have arrived and, like a lot of mornings, a fire engine has pulled in behind Jesse's wheelchair, providing me with the protection that we have to have every time I step onto the highway. But this day will turn out a little different.

I always made sure I went back and introduced myself to our police escort and whoever was driving the firetruck, as well as anybody else that might be riding in the cab or on the truck. That morning, I have a feeling that the driver has never heard of *Jesse's Journey* because he doesn't seem very interested in his assignment to provide us with an escort. I wonder if he has something else on his mind or is maybe just having a bad day. When we start moving along the highway I think about what the driver behind me must be seeing. He'd be looking at a father wearing a hat, a white T-shirt with a map of Ontario on the back, a pair of khaki-coloured shorts and a pair of running shoes. He'd see that man pushing a young boy in a wheelchair. He would see them stop from time to time to shake hands with people, sometimes families, sometimes kids and sometimes people who have pulled their car to the side of the road to make a donation that the volunteers will collect. From time to time he would see the father hold up his son's arm up so the youngster's Canadian flag is held high as they pose for pictures being taken. Sometimes the father would wipe the sweat from his forehead and sometimes he'd pour cold water over his head even though the days were getting cooler. That's what he would see. That's the message we were sending.

But by the time we reach midday and the man driving the firetruck is leaving us, it's obvious he now sees things differently. As he says goodbye, the driver of the firetruck asks me where we are having supper. After we tell him our night time location, he makes a donation, wishes us luck and I can see his eyes are wet as he turns and walks away. At suppertime the same volunteer fireman shows up with his son. My journal entry notes his son's name is Andrew and he's a boy of about nine or ten. His father just wanted him to have a chance to meet Jesse and to shake his hand.

Before they leave, Andrew's father reaches into his back pocket, takes out his wallet and pulls from it a very worn silver badge with the words 'Ernestown Fire Department' and the number '14.' He tells Jesse he's had that badge in his back pocket for 17 years and he wants Jesse to have it. It is something that means a lot to that firefighter, and it means a lot to us too.

We had received two important messages the day before. Both of them made us happy. As Jesse accepted that firefighter's badge, a very special gift, we were aware that we had sent an even more important message – about the need for research dollars and what *Jesse's Journey* is all about. That made us feel even happier.

Chapter Seven

THE FINAL STRETCH

"He who influences the thought of his
times influences the times that follow" –
Elbert Hubbard

The days are dwindling as we roll on toward Ottawa, but they aren't
getting any easier. On Day 115, still battling muscle fatigue in my
legs, I put in just 22 km behind the wheelchair. I decide to be even
stingier with the small amount of strength I have left. I want to spend
it carefully and not get carried away just because we are so close to
the finish line.

Jesse is holding up fine, and I can see he is having fun on these final
few days. Still, I know that he's anxious to get home and back to
school. Coming home has been a dream that Jesse and I have shared,
but never talked about since we left the Manitoba border, and every
day as we get closer to Ottawa, the anticipation is growing. With just
eight days left, I finally feel that we will be able to complete our
Journey together. The team, including Jesse and I, has become like a
large family out on the road, and in just a few days, we will all be
going our separate ways after saying that final goodbye.

We are now rolling north up Highway 29, passing through the
villages of Forthton, Addison, Frankville and Toledo, en route to
Smiths Falls. In Frankville we stop at a public school where about
125 cheering youngsters are waiting to see the boy they've been
hearing about. Realizing it's the first time we have spoken to
students in the new school year, I'm aware of just how long we've
been on the road, carrying our message of hope.

The morning of September 18th, 1995 is clear and crisp, and we
wake up knowing that, like a lot of dads and their sons, we're going
to a hockey game tonight. And that when this day is over, there will
be just two more days to go. But before then we have work to do.

Pushing up the road toward Nepean, the recognition factor is high
and the donations are pouring in. But then, once again without any

warning, there's another of those moments you can never really plan for. Waiting up ahead at the side of the road is another couple who's lost a son or a brother to Duchenne. Sometimes I never hear the whole story; it's happened so many times, and it's about to happen again. These are people, whose feelings I understand. They've come to the side of the road to connect personally with me by pressing a small golden 'guardian angel' pin into my hand. Through the tears that have welled up in their eyes I can see their inner belief that the pin they have given me will be the only one of these I'll receive on this *Journey*. It's always a very emotional moment. Even though Jesse and I are both feeling the drain from almost four months on the road, I pause a moment and thank them and assure them that what we are doing is going to help us find the answers we're looking for. It's a brief meeting that only lasts a few seconds. Sometimes these people give me a quick hug or I pat them on the back. I'm not very good at wearing my feelings on my sleeve or my shirt. Hoping that I'm not hurting the feelings of these very caring people, I gently slip the pin they have given me into my pocket with the other 'guardian angel' pins already there, as once again Jesse and I move along down the road.

The game of hockey has been very fortunate that its superstars have always been real gentlemen. People like Gordie Howe, Jean Beliveau, Bobby Orr and Wayne Gretzky have brought not only great talent to the game, but also a real touch of class. In Ottawa we are in the company of two more of the game's best ambassadors, Darryl Sittler and Brad Marsh, both of whom captained the London Knights as juniors.

Going to a hockey game is relatively easy when you have a ticket. You just show up and find your seat. Going to a hockey game when you're part of the pre-game festivities is a little more complicated. You have to find a specific parking area before connecting with the person you are to meet at a predetermined entrance. And you have to arrive earlier than everyone else to be given instructions by people with walkie-talkies who run you through what will be happening before they park you somewhere while you wait your turn on the program. But in Ottawa that doesn't happen. The Ottawa Senators' Brad Marsh looks after us from start to finish.

One of the special moments we share happens as Jesse and I wait for the pre-game warm-up to end. Behind the Toronto Maple Leafs' net, where the players enter and exit to the dressing room, we watch the players. As they leave the ice, Jesse and I are talking about how big they are when they walk by on skates. One of the last players to leave the rink is the Maple Leafs' Mike Gartner, who nods as he walks by us and then turns and comes back. In a very polite manner, with the sweat dripping from under his helmet, he asks if I'm the gentleman who is pushing his son across Ontario. When I tell him I am, he pulls his hand out of his hockey glove to shake hands and to say it's an honour to meet me. Reaching down to take Jesse's hand, Mike Gartner, one of the classiest guys in hockey, tells Jesse he should be very proud of all he has accomplished.

As we are introduced and we make our way to centre ice for the pre-game ceremony, the crowd rises to its feet in a standing ovation that goes on for a long time. As I push Jesse across the ice, it's an emotional and proud moment for me as the father of a young boy who can't skate like other children can. Here is a young boy who is bringing a message of hope as his wheelchair glides toward the red carpet at centre ice. His message is a simple one: that through research we can find a way to make sure that more and more children will be able to skate.

Brad Marsh presents Jesse with an Ottawa Senator jersey with 'Davidson' emblazoned on the back, and Darryl Sittler gives Jesse a hockey stick that has been autographed by all of the Maple Leafs. Following the ceremonial face-off, the crowd is on its feet again as Jesse leaves the ice. The standing ovation continues as I lift Jesse's arm one last time and turn his wheelchair so he can wave his Canadian flag to acknowledge the crowd. It's sheer magic.

Just as we are leaving the ice, Brad Marsh leans over and whispers to me, "You have another younger son at home, don't you?" When I mention Jesse's younger brother Tim, Brad says, "We'd better step into the dressing room and get an extra stick." Brad Marsh and Darryl Sittler are a class act – two former players who see themselves as ordinary people giving back to a game that has given them so much. Hockey can use more people like these two former London juniors who have helped keep the game of hockey dear to people's hearts in Canada.

On the morning of Day 123, we complete a short 90-minute walk, picking up where we left off the day before, and positioning ourselves for the final day. Then, with our *Journey* set to finish in just over twenty-four hours, we are off to Rideau Hall to tour the Governor-General's residence. Jesse is presented with a newly-minted coin. Canada mints a new coin every time we have a new Governor General, and this coin bears the likeness of Governor General Romeo LeBlanc and his wife. It's a striking gold piece and certainly shiny and new. But it lacks a story, and can't rival the volunteer firefighter badge Jesse received a few nights before. That smooth and well-worn badge has a special warmth this one lacks.

In the afternoon we attend Question Period in the House of Commons. Prime Minister Jean Chretien's Office provides us with special seats so we can look down from the gallery directly at the Prime Minister. Across the green carpet from the Prime Minister, and directly below us, sit Lucien Bouchard, leader of the Bloc Quebecois, and Preston Manning, leader of the Reform Party. It's important to remember that our *Journey* is coming to an end just six weeks before the Quebec referendum, and our country's future is once again on the line. I am pleased to have Jesse here to see history unfolding. And it is extremely gratifying that, despite the fiery rhetoric that echoes across the floor in the House of Commons, the members of all three parties stand and applaud as we are recognized by the Parliament of Canada.

Canada's Parliament Buildings were never designed with the disabled in mind. After taking an elevator to the second floor to get

Hockey fans applaud as Jesse shares the spotlight at centre ice with Doug Gilmour and former London Knight Captains Darryl Sittler and Brad Marsh along with Martin Straka of the Ottawa Senators.

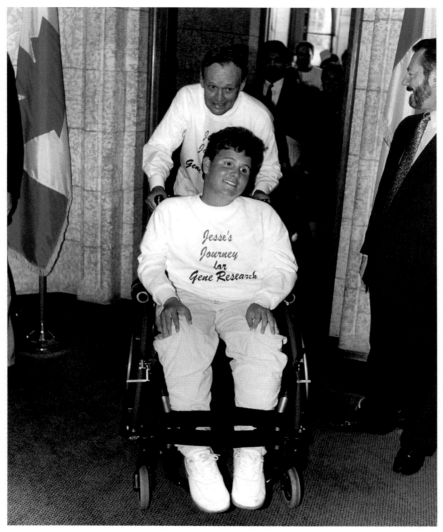

After posing for "official" pictures, Prime Minister Jean Chretien grits his teeth as he and Jesse go for a "run" down the corridor outside the PM's office. Jesse's "raccoon eyes" are visible where his sunglasses shielded his face throughout the summer.

The Lieutenant Governor of Ontario, the Honourable Henry N.R. Jackman shakes hands with Jesse as he presents him with the Order of Ontario, September 26th, 1996 at Queens Park in Toronto.

Jesse changed from T-shirt to tuxedo as he and I pose with Canadian astronaut Lieutenant Colonel Chris Hadfield at the Order of Ontario investiture.

After shaking hands with Her Majesty Queen Elizabeth II, it was a proud moment for me as I introduced Jesse to the Queen while Deputy Prime Minister Herb Grey and Ontario Premier Mike Harris looked on.

Jesse and I assisted Her Majesty the Queen with a little "gardening" as we planted a Sugar Maple in London's Victoria Park on June 26, 1997. Jesse wore a tie given to him by Don Cherry, whose wife Rose had passed away earlier. Jesse thought it might cheer up the hockey analyst to know he wore Don's tie to meet the Queen.

Jesse into his seat at Question Period, it's necessary for Sean and me to lift Jesse and his wheelchair down a small flight of stairs leading to the narrow hallway that runs along the back of the side gallery in the House of Commons. Then we have to lift Jesse out of his wheelchair and carry him through a narrow doorway and down a couple of steps to his seat.

There is an embarrassing moment as we are leaving the gallery. We have to complete the whole procedure in reverse to get Jesse back into his wheelchair. Holding Jesse under his arms, while Sean takes his legs, I'm walking backward into the narrow corridor where we have left Jesse's wheelchair. Backing through the doorway, I accidentally step on the foot of a woman in a brown dress suit who has come to meet Jesse. I'm very apologetic and this lovely woman in the brown outfit smiles and doesn't seem to mind at all. She just wants to reach down to take Jesse's hand for a moment and to tell him she thinks he is a very brave young boy. Apologizing once again, we begin to move Jesse backward down the hall, as there isn't enough room to turn his wheelchair around in the narrow corridor.

With the huge oil paintings of previous prime ministers staring down at us from under the little lights that illuminate their pictures, we are escorted down a series of corridors that lead to the Prime Minister's private office. As Sherene and Jesse's brothers, Tyler and Tim, together with our road team, make their way into the office, you can't imagine the embarrassment I feel as I look up at the smiling face of the woman in the brown dress suit. Just minutes before I had stepped on the foot of the Prime Minister's wife as she waited to meet Jesse. We smile a knowing smile at each other and I feel I've been forgiven.

Political stripes didn't mean anything when it came to *Jesse's Journey*. And on this occasion, the Prime Minister seemed more like every youngster wants his grandfather to be. He had no hesitation in taking off his jacket and pulling on a *Jesse's Journey* T-shirt, grabbing the back of Jesse's wheelchair, and in that unmistakable voice of his, saying to Jesse, "Come on, my friend, we go for a run down the corridor!" They shot out the door and down the corridor with security people smiling, along with a battery of television cameras and still photographers in pursuit. After Mr. Chretien wheeled Jesse back into his office, Jesse looked up at me and said, "Dad, I think I have whiplash. He goes faster than you do!"

As a father, the Prime Minister was very interested in hearing all about what we were trying to accomplish. I indicated to the Prime Minister our feeling about the need to invest in all of our children because they are the future of Canada. I hoped that my words would find their way to those who control the purse strings.

Jesse would later receive a picture of himself taken in Mr. Chretien's office with the Prime Minister standing behind Jesse's wheelchair wearing a *Jesse's Journey* T-shirt and beaming like a proud father. At the bottom of the picture the Prime Minister had written, "Jesse, you are a very courageous young man." I think we made our point.

A tour of the Parliament Buildings and the Senate capped what had been another busy day, and back at the hotel there's a tremendous sense of anticipation. The next day will be our last day on the road. I can only contemplate how much we have to be grateful for, including the hundreds of volunteers and an incredible road team, who, through all the ups and downs, have allowed Jesse and I to achieve our goal.

Chapter Eight

A DREAM REALIZED

"I am a slow walker, but I never walk back" –
Abraham Lincoln

Finally it's here, September 20th, our 124th day on the road. This is the day we've been dreaming of, the end of the road and the realization of a dream. There is the usual morning confusion getting vehicles and equipment organized. Murphy's Law has decided to toy with us one last time. A wrong turn makes us fifteen minutes late in reaching our start point. Normally when this happens, it really tests my patience. But today, four months to the day since we started at the Manitoba border, fifteen minutes doesn't seem to mean much in the grand scheme of things.

When we reach our start point, a police motorcycle escort meets us along with the usual fire trucks and media vehicles. The biggest surprise of the morning comes just as we push off on what will be the final stretch of *Jesse's Journey*. Thirty-three of the people I have spent so many years working with at the television station in London spring up from behind parked cars along the side of the road. They chartered a bus on their own time and left London at three o'clock in the morning to be with us for the final steps of our marathon *Journey* across Ontario. I'm speechless as the shock wave rolls over me. These are the people I have shared a large part of my life with, and having them with us makes it an even more incredible day. I'm grateful for this moment in a *Journey* that's been filled with special moments.

The roadway becomes a sea of colour as people cheer from the porches of their homes, from offices and stores, and from the balconies of high-rise apartment buildings. All through the crowd there are the familiar faces of those who have been with us as volunteers, some of them from as far back as the Manitoba border. I've been the only person to push Jesse's wheelchair while we've been on the road crossing Ontario, but now it's time to share that magic feeling with those who have helped. One by one, they come forward to take a turn pushing Jesse in the slightly-battered wheelchair that has gone through six sets of tires, as we've logged more than 3300 km across Ontario. Still wearing the leather gloves I have worn for the past four months, I keep one hand on the wheelchair just to keep things 'honest' as we roll toward the finish line. I listen carefully as everyone who comes forward to take a turn behind the wheelchair has something special to say about *Jesse's Journey*. Mostly, they tell Jesse and me about how they have been forced to rethink the direction life is taking them. It's humbling to hear this thought from so many people.

With a light rain falling, we start up a small incline. From my familiar stance behind the wheelchair, hunched over to push on the uphill grades, I lean forward to tell Jesse, "I think this might be the very last hill."

In the heart of Ottawa, the entire road team is joined by a Shriners' Band and a fleet of funny little cars doing circles around Jesse and me and around the police at the intersections we pass through. The police officers, with their whistles in their mouths, keep working the traffic with their hand signals as they smile at the antics of the Shriners. It's obviously a great day and everyone's in the mood for laughter and celebrating the joy of being alive and able to make a difference.

Pushing Jesse up Wellington Street toward the Parliament Buildings, there's a familiar face in the crowd. John Gerrard is Canada's Secretary of State for Science, Research and Technology. On the morning we began our *Journey*, 124 days earlier, he had driven out to the Manitoba-Ontario border from his home in Winnipeg to see us on our way. On that bitterly cold and snowy morning west of Kenora, he had walked along with us as I took those first steps pushing Jesse in his wheelchair. When he left us that morning he had said, "Jesse, I walked the first kilometre with you, and when you get to Ottawa, I'll be there to walk the last kilometre with you."

And now there he is, standing on the corner in his trench coat with a huge contingent of his party colleagues, ready to keep his promise. Stepping off the curb, John Gerrard takes his turn among the politicians who have spent a busy autumn lunch hour pushing Jesse's wheelchair closer and closer to the finish line on the far side of Ottawa's Alexandra Bridge.

What started out as a team, most of whom hardly knew one another, has grown to be a family that has crossed a lot of bridges in more ways than one. In Sault Ste. Marie, we crossed over the huge steel expanse that links Canada and the United States, and we have walked both the big and the little bridges that span the hundreds of creeks and rivers that wind their way across the province. On a personal level we have built and crossed the bridges of trust in one another and in our volunteers. We have pulled together to bridge the gaps in difficult times. With every bridge we crossed, we matured, learning more about the art of listening and the value of compromise. There were times we may have felt like lashing out, but we have realized the futility of burning bridges. And so bridges have come to represent more than just structures of wood, concrete or steel. They're symbols that represent life's challenges. Along the route we have crossed them all, and now there is just one bridge remaining.

The Alexandra Bridge, which can be seen from the back of the Parliament Buildings, crosses the Ottawa River and connects Ottawa, Ontario to Hull, Quebec. It isn't on the list of tourist attractions like the Peace Tower and the Parliament Buildings, The National Art Gallery or The Canadian War Museum. But on the morning of September 20th, 1995, the Alexandra Bridge is the only thing on our list of things to see in Ottawa.

Now that we are on the bridge, with Jesse's wheelchair rumbling across the wooden planks of the walkway, a wave of bittersweet emotion engulfs me. In a minute, the walk will be over. Everything will change. The routine we have followed for the past months will be gone. There's no time to think about what comes next. There's just the reality that ahead of us two RCMP officers in their red serge outfits are holding the banner that Jesse and I will break through in just a few seconds.

The crowd of people following us across the bridge pauses to let Jesse and me go on ahead – just a father and a son, the way we had started so many days before. I stop and turn Jesse's wheelchair to face the crowd, all of whom are now chanting his name. I hold Jesse's arm in the air one last time, and he waves his Canadian flag as a way of saying thank you to all those who have made our dream come true. With the television cameras focused on Jesse, it's his way of thanking those people all across Ontario who have worked so hard to make this event a success.

With that final wave, I turn and push Jesse on to the finish line and break through the banner. For just a split second, I'm completely drained. I hug Jesse and tell him I love him. Then, looking up, I see we have been swallowed up in a sea of friends, volunteers, and family who are smiling and laughing, some of them through tears.

I have to take off my glasses and wipe my own eyes after embracing Sherene, and Tyler and Tim. Looking back at Jesse, he grins from under his hat that now holds so many pins from cities and towns in the 3300 km we've travelled.

There are more special moments that unfold very quickly in the time between our crossing the finish line and finally heading home. They begin right at the finish line with one of the two RCMP officers holding the ends of the banner that Jesse and I broke through. Throughout our *Journey*, I never knew when I would meet people who had lost a child. As he smiles and a father's pride sparkles in his quiet eyes, the officer presents Jesse and me with RCMP pins. Shaking my hand, he leans over to whisper to me alone that it was just two years ago, he had lost his son to Duchenne. I wasn't expecting to hear that news and it really rocks me. I guess I must have let my guard down a little after we crossed the finish line. Maybe with all we've been through I'm a little more fragile than I realized. I can only hope that we've opened the eyes of Canadians and their governments to the reality of the desperate need for genetic research.

After a short walk to Ottawa City Hall, our own Member of Parliament, Sue Barnes, presents Jesse with a Canadian flag that has flown over the House of Commons from the top of the Peace Tower. The day before, it was her voice that rang out with pride and admiration as she introduced us in the House of Commons.
As I listen to the speeches, it is sad in a way to realize that the faces I am looking out at will soon go their separate ways, back to their hometowns, back to their families and back to their lives. This wonderful group of volunteers will probably never be together like this again. They have mothered us, nursed us and gotten us lost several times since we left the Manitoba border four months ago. They have shared an incredible period in our lives, and together they have helped make our impossible dream become a reality. They are the 'family' that helped us to beat the odds to make genetic research a winning cause.

It has been quite a *Journey* – one we wouldn't have missed for the world. It has had its ups and downs, but with the help of family and friends, Jesse and I have managed to stay with it. And although we didn't know it right away, when the final numbers came in, we discovered we had raised $1,500,00 for genetic research. And along the way, we'd given hope to a lot of people.

I know I'm sharing this final day with every family, especially those who have a loved one suffering from a genetic disease. I can only wish that every father in Canada will take the time to make a contribution and help us fund the research which is so vital. I hope that no father will ever have to look into a child's eyes, as I once did, to try to explain the cost of research to a youngster who wants nothing more than to ride a bike.

By the end of the day we are exhausted and emotionally spent. When it is my turn to speak, I remember thanking everyone, particularly

Sherene, Tyler and Tim for their love and support during the time Jesse and I have been on the road.

Earlier in the day someone stuck a little red heart on Jesse's cheek and when he looked up at me, he smiled that great smile of his and winked. It was then that I knew we had made it.

As I looked down at Jesse, I was almost unable to speak. *Jesse's Journey for Gene Research* was to have a lasting impact. I thanked Jesse with all my heart, and then just like that it was over. At last, the time had come. We were going home.

Chapter Nine

MAPLE LEAFS AND MAJESTY

*"In spite of everything, I still believe
that people are really good at heart"* –
Anne Frank

When the idea of pushing Jesse across Ontario in his wheelchair had
first come to me nearly a year earlier in October of 1994, I had
imagined us shaking hands with people and doing our best to explain
to them the need for and the benefits of research. We had thought we
would try to raise $100,000. But by the time we had reached Ottawa,
our 'little project' as we'd called it, had snowballed to something
much bigger than we'd ever imagined and it wasn't about to stop.
Suddenly there were speaking engagements and appearances, as
everybody wanted Jesse to be at their event. The calls began as soon
as we arrived home. And one of the first was a most pleasant surprise.

We were just starting to organize the appointment calendar when
Darryl Sittler called to say the Toronto Maple Leafs would like us to
drop the ceremonial puck at Maple Leaf Gardens when Toronto
opened the hockey season against the New York Islanders.

It seemed like just yesterday that the Stanley Cup playoffs were
getting underway as Jesse and I were starting out on our *Journey.*
And, here we were already at the beginning of another hockey
season. We were both very excited about the night as we headed off
to Toronto. When we arrived at Maple Leaf Gardens we were
whisked through security and into a world of VIP's, not something
either of us was used to.

Tuxedos with bow ties and evening gowns made it difficult to
remember we were at a hockey game. There were chefs in tall white
hats with razor-sharp silver knives carving roast beef. There were
varieties of seafood and fresh fruit, and decorative garnishes cut to
look like flowers. The entire arrangement was a feast for the eyes as

well as the taste buds. Pushing Jesse's wheelchair across the room, I couldn't help but notice the depth of the carpet and the one huge navy blue Toronto Maple Leaf logo that left no doubt we were in one of hockey's most famous buildings.

Jesse met Steve Stavro, the owner of the Maple Leafs, and people like Toronto businessman, 'Honest Ed' Mervish. I met the Leafs' general manager, Cliff Fletcher, and learned something about the 'behind the scenes' business of hockey. Cliff explained how the Maple Leafs had sought out defenceman Dimitri Yushkevic from the Philadelphia Flyers. I had always wondered how the mechanics of player acquisition worked. Mr. Fletcher outlined how Toronto had run a computer search of the player rosters of all the NHL teams. The computer search looked for defencemen with a minimum of four years NHL experience, whose statistics met Toronto's demand, and who were in the salary range that fit the Maple Leafs' budget. When the shortlist of names surfaced, the Maple Leafs did their homework to see which of the half dozen players the computer came up with could actually be acquired and would fit the mould Toronto was trying to shape. Listening was a fascinating experience and Cliff Fletcher went into such detail that even his own people had to remind him it was almost game time and that he had to leave.

At ice level there was a laser show shooting pencil-thin green streaks of light through the darkness. One by one, as the players were introduced, they skated through a pyrotechnics show that fired a burst of flames and smoke across the ice as the crowd welcomed back each of their hockey heroes.

Dressed in our tuxedos, and with the sound of the drums and bagpipes of the 48th Highlanders filling the building, it was showtime. As I made my way to centre ice from the player's bench, Toronto Maple Leaf captain Doug Gilmour pushed Jesse in his wheelchair to centre ice. As we all gathered in the spotlight there was a thunderous ovation from the fans. Over the noise of the crowd, Doug Gilmour took the time to lean over and to say to me, "You guys are doing a terrific job." That type of encouragement confirmed in my mind what I was already thinking. *Jesse's Journey* wasn't over. Driving home from Ottawa at the end of the *Journey* across Ontario, I had thought to myself that perhaps I could have done better. That was when I first knew that I would try again. As 1995 was coming to a close, it was a thought that for the short term would remain mine alone.

In the spring of 1996 I received a letter from Toronto. Jesse and I were asked to be at the Provincial Legislature at Queens Park on the 26th of September. *Jesse's Journey for Gene Research* must have had some impact. The letter advised us that we were to be presented with the Order of Ontario. Looking at the names of those who were to be honoured, I could see that we were going to be among some very distinguished people. Among the other recipients to receive the award were Canadian country singing legend Tommy Hunter, actor Al Waxman, artist Trisha Romance and Canadian astronaut Lt.-Col. Chris Hadfield. The presentation would be made by the Lieutenant-Governor of Ontario, the Honourable Henry N. R. Jackman. This was pretty exciting news and certainly not something anyone in our family had ever dreamed would happen.

The main foyer of the Legislature was packed with family and friends who had gathered for the evening of presentations. There was a great deal of pomp and ceremony including a musical program with the Royal Regiment of Canada. The Premier of Ontario, the Honourable Michael D. Harris, and the Lieutenant-Governor presided over the parade of award recipients who walked across the red carpet to be presented with the Order of Ontario.

A ramp covered with red carpet had been built to permit Jesse access to the stage. It's difficult to find words to describe the feelings I had as I watched Jesse, dressed in his tuxedo, glide up the ramp to be honoured by his province. He no longer looked like the young boy who had started out on a great adventure with me more than a year before. He was now a young man, and anxious to carve out a life of his own, equipped with confidence that he could tackle any challenge. I hoped we had shown disabled people all across Canada that they can do anything that they want to do, if they just try. And in the wake of our *Journey*, I wanted the people of Ontario and Canada to have a better understanding of the huge dividend that is paid when we invest in the future of our children through research. I remember watching as if I was frozen in time. In that moment, I took great pride in what Jesse had accomplished. My son, who had never been able to play on a baseball or hockey team, was about to receive his very own championship medal. The boy who couldn't ride a bicycle had touched people's hearts as he championed the cause of genetic research. That would far exceed any baseball or hockey championship I could imagine.

After the formal ceremonies, there was a reception in a portion of the Legislature which houses a private residence and office used by the Lieutenant Governor. Jesse had his picture taken with an astronaut, and then with his brothers and his mom. In one of the pictures Jesse and his Grampa Davidson smiled at the camera. It was the first time in his life my father had worn a tuxedo. Jesse would never know how many magical moments he had made happen.

Like most teenagers, Jesse wasn't all that impressed with the fine china, tea that was poured from silver teapots or the desserts that were balanced on small paper serviettes with the embossed gold emblem of the Lieutenant Governor. At the end of the ceremonies, we 'borrowed' a small handful of gold-embossed serviettes. They ended up in one of the drawers of our kitchen table. Every once in a while we would have a little fun at home when we would ask our dinner guests if we could pass them a serviette. Even if Jesse wasn't impressed with the serviettes, our guests usually were.

I didn't think there would be a moment that would surpass the Order of Ontario ceremony when it came to a father's pride in a son. But as I began to think more and more about what was next for *Jesse's Journey*, there was another surprise waiting for us.

Early in the spring of 1997 I received a phone call from London's City Clerk, Jeff Malpass. He told me he had been talking to CSIS (Canadian Security Intelligence Service) as well as the RCMP, and he wondered if he could come and have a talk with me! Needless to say, my first thought was, 'Now what have I done!' I didn't think I was in any kind of trouble, but I was certainly wondering what this was all about. On the afternoon that the City Clerk stopped by for our little chat, whatever fears I'd imagined vanished when he asked if Jesse and I might be available in June to plant a tree with Her Majesty the Queen during her visit to London. I was so shocked that after a long pause all I could think to say was, "Can we keep the shovel?" Then, Jeff paused a moment before saying, "Sure you can."

A royal visit may look like a very casual and relaxed affair on television, but there are a lot of details to be checked and double-checked. Security is probably at the top of the list. The route that the royal motorcade would take from the airport to downtown London could not be revealed until a day before the visit. Manhole covers have to be welded shut and hospital operating theatres are put on standby and must have an ample supply of the Queens blood type. And that is just the beginning. There are the hundreds of little things that need to be done and of course, there is the protocol that has to be followed. And all of this had to be put in place for something that would last only a few minutes.

The sun was shining and the 26th of June 1997 was a gorgeous summer day. There was a lot of excitement around the house as everyone was fussing with last-minute details. It's not every day that you get to meet the Queen. In the midst of all the attention to detail, Jesse casually did another of those thoughtful things that he does so well. He decided to wear a tie that hockey broadcaster Don Cherry had given him when we were in Toronto. Don had lost his wife just days before and Jesse told me he thought it might cheer Don up if he knew that Jesse had worn his tie to meet the Queen of England.

In advance of the official party, Jesse and I arrived at Victoria Park, the emerald green and heavily-treed gem in the heart of London. The city had built a walkway, about 15 metres wide, with white picket fence along both sides. Long before Her Majesty was scheduled to arrive crowds began to assemble, some of them staking out lawn chair locations behind the picket fence. There were older people whose roots tied them to the monarchy; the women were finely dressed as if they were going to church on a Sunday. Most of them were wearing summer hats. The men's shoes had been polished to a fine lustre, and even though it was warm, jackets and ties were the order of the day. And so were cameras. This would be an occasion to remember.

There were young families everywhere. There were little girls, whose hair had been neatly arranged and tied with ribbons, carrying bunches of flowers. Their mothers, in bright summer dresses and wearing generous smiles, wondered where best to stand, hopeful that Her Majesty would stop and speak to them. There were teenage girls with braces on their teeth, wearing fashionable blouses and elegant long skirts, doing everything they could to look grown up. There were fathers in expensive business suits and fathers in casual clothes, some with teenage sons whose hair looked as if they had just showered. There were small boys wearing little tweed jackets and bright tartan ties. And everyone seemed to be holding a flag. There were Canadian flags and multi-coloured Union Jacks being given practice waves by excited children. Film was being loaded into cameras and families were posing beside flowerbeds, in the sunlight that filtered through the tall trees. There were television people checking cables and making sure everything was ready. And in advance of the Queen's arrival, there were security people with walkie-talkies trying their best to look inconspicuous with curly little wires that emerged from the backs of their collars and led to plastic earpieces. The veterans of both World Wars took their places, some seated in chairs, some standing proudly as they leaned on canes. Though a number of the men and women wore military uniforms, most of the veterans were dressed in navy blue blazers with insignias and medals pinned to their jackets.

Then a strange thing happened. As Jesse began to roll along the fenced-off walkway with me beside him, people on both sides began to applaud. It was the most unexpected thing. It was the kind of recognition that confirmed in my mind that *Jesse's Journey* was not over. We took our place beside the young sugar maple tree that had been planted in the park.

Our instructions were that the Premier would introduce me to Her Majesty, and I would introduce Jesse to the Queen. I would then give Her Majesty the silver shovel and ask her to place a scoop of earth at the base of the tree to signify the official planting. After that, I would help Jesse shovel a small scoop of earth onto the base of the tree, and then the whole thing would be over. At least that was the plan.

Surprisingly, the Queen was much shorter than I had imagined. She was wearing a finely-fashioned pale blue dress and a wide-brimmed straw hat. She had a friendly smile, and I couldn't help but note she had a very smooth complexion. I also noticed the Queen does indeed have very Wedgwood-blue eyes.

The Queen chatted briefly with Jesse and me about our travels and what we had been able to accomplish. Her Majesty said she understood we had managed to raise quite a bit of money. She then told me, "Keep up the good work." Now, sometimes when people ask me why I am doing what I am doing, I tell them that I am doing it because the Queen of England told me to!

When I passed the shovel to Her Majesty, I expected her to lift a polite shovelful of earth and place it at the base of the tree. She surprised us both when she pushed her purse further up her arm and dug in as if she was gardening! After three pretty good shovels full, Jesse and I responded in kind and did the same thing.

If there's one thing I'll always remember about our brief meeting with Her Majesty, it's her incredible ability to focus on the conversation. Throughout the time Jesse and I chatted with the

Queen, her eyes never left those of the person she was speaking with, despite all the noise that surrounded us. There were people waving flags and yelling, "over here!" and there were cameras clicking all around us. With a lifetime of discipline, the Queen never once looked away. As she left us and moved toward the barricade for a royal 'walkabout', I invited the little kids in the crowd to come and use the silver shovel to help us finish planting the maple tree.

Chapter Ten

JESSE'S JOURNEY: A FATHER'S TRIBUTE

"Perseverance is not a long race; it is
many short races one after the other" –
Walter Elliott

On Labour Day weekend of 1997 I put on my familiar walking gear, laced up my running shoes, set my pedometer at zero and began training again. This time the vision was clearer and the target was bigger. I kept in mind the old Chinese proverb about how a secret is best kept between two people if one of them is dead. For awhile, I was the only one who knew what I had in mind. I wanted to create a lasting legacy to pay tribute to Jesse for what he had accomplished in his historic crossing of Ontario. The goal was simple – create an endowment fund that would eventually generate a million dollars a year, every year, forever, to fund genetic research. It was the method by which we would do this that caused me to examine every possible aspect of what I was planning to do. I intended to walk every step of the distance from the Atlantic Ocean to the Pacific Ocean and the start date I had in mind was just eight months away. I would have to do this alone, but I would be doing it as a tribute to Jesse. That's what the project would be known as: *Jesse's Journey – A Father's Tribute.*

In 1995 Jesse and I had set out to cross Ontario with little more than determination fueling our dream. The infrastructure was limited and mostly consisted of meeting minimum requirements. In the beginning we had just a small group of volunteers who helped put the building blocks in place. Once we had secured our transportation and communication needs, we worked on things like insurance, accommodation, and police and media help. Beyond that it was pretty much a 'wing and a prayer' kind of project. While Jesse and I were battling the hills in the heat, Sherene and her mother had tackled the job of writing hundreds of thank you notes to people who had made donations to *Jesse's Journey for Gene Research.* I knew we would have to do things differently this time.

We were going to need a much bigger and more organized team. As the training continued, mostly alone in the dark, through wet and windy nights in the fall of 1997, the task of assembling a team began again.

Not all of the key players from our *Journey* across Ontario were still available. Jesse's companion, Sean Bagshaw, had moved on to medical school at the University of Calgary. I knew that the new team was going to be a combination of old and new faces. This time the task was bigger than any of us could imagine and I was faced with the same questions I'd had to focus on in 1995. Who would make it to the finish line in Victoria? And the more haunting question: Would I make it to the finish line in Victoria? I didn't spend a lot of time thinking about that but rather kept busy with the training routine, identifying the jobs, and filling the positions.

Ron Calhoun agreed to come back, this time as National Co-ordinator of the event. Mike Woodward, the wordsmith jack-of-all trades who had handled reconnaissance, and driven the motor home and worked with the police and media, was quick to commit to another stint on the road. I think I felt Mike had been shortchanged when he fell and broke his collarbone in 1995. When I stopped by his home to share the news that I planned to walk across Canada, he smiled and started to sing Willie Nelson's song, "On the Road Again."

Trish Federkow, who had been our road manager in 1995, was shocked when I called to ask if she would be available to take on the job again. She asked if I was certain I wanted to do this. She reminded me that I was now 52 years old and that Canada is a very big country. She wanted some time to think about the offer, but when I called her back, she agreed to take on the job. When I asked her what had made her decide to take on the challenge of getting us across Canada, she said she just couldn't stand the thought of somebody else doing the job!

There was only one new face in what would be the permanent road team. It was a name I had never thought would be involved at all, but in the end it turned out to be one of the most satisfying additions to the team.

Bevin Palmateer was that newcomer. He was a high school student when he first came to work at CFPL television as an 18 year old part time sports reporter. In the newsroom he was incredibly creative, and not yet ready to be reigned in by the parameters that television still presented in the early eighties. Bevin's youthful ways often landed him in hot water with management. A hopeless romantic as a youngster, Bevin would go to great lengths to impress the ladies he was dating. On the birthday of one of the ladies in his life, Bevin didn't think there was anything wrong with hiring a male exotic dancer to perform on her desk where she worked in another part of the television station. Everyone found it hilarious – everyone except the senior managers who had to stifle a smile as they made a half-hearted attempt at some form of discipline.

Bevin stuck with television, suffering through all the zany things that were done to try to make a high school student look a little more 'mature' in front of the camera. One of the plots that was hatched had Bevin wearing glasses with no lenses in them, just to try to capture that 'mature' look that seemed so all-important at the time.

Maturity came to Bevin as his life experience increased, and as the years went by, his work became more polished. Viewers saw one of his best pieces of work in the late eighties. Bevin had clipped an article from *Island Magazine* about a man in California who had built a yacht that looked like an island. The man had literally defied the old Mark Twain adage to 'buy land, they've stopped making it.' Bevin passed the article along to the news director with the thought that he should be sent out to interview the guy in California. Much to Bevin's surprise, the next day he was asked by the news director if there were 'any other weird things out there' that Bevin could find. Bevin's idea was about to become a reality. The show was to be called *"The Perfect Gift."*

In five days, Bevin and a cameraman visited five cities – San Francisco, Los Angeles, Dallas, Toronto and London. They looked at gifts of all kinds, including the floating island. There was a quarter-million-dollar gold bracelet, a Rolls Royce, gold-plated bathtubs, mink coats and a hot air balloon designed for one, called the *Cloud Hopper.*

The show ended with Bevin back home where he found a young boy of about seven who could not speak. He had never been able to communicate with his mother. Bevin showed them working with something new called a 'Light Switch Talker.' For the first time in his life, the little boy was able to 'talk' with his mother. The Light Switch Talker brought them together. It was a great ending that captured the true Christmas spirit and it really did exemplify "The Perfect Gift."

One day as Christmas 1997 was approaching, Bevin, now in his mid 30's, called me at home to say he wanted to go across Canada with me! I was taken by surprise. As Bevin's career continued to unfold, his adventures had continued. He had flown to Paris, France to have dinner with a girlfriend. He had been in the passenger seat of a Porsche on the track at Mosport with racecar driver Scott Goodyear, and experienced the thrill of driving 225 kilometres per hour while Goodyear fiddled with the car's stereo system! Bevin had owned his own art shop, and had even flown with Canada's precision flying team, the Snowbirds. So I was at a loss to figure out why he would want to make this trip across Canada with me!

When we met, I was aware that Bevin had at one time wanted to go to film school in London, England. He had also flirted with the idea of going to work in television in the United States, and like most young broadcasters he had mailed his fair share of audition tapes. But somehow he had always stayed in London, Ontario. When I asked Bevin why he wanted to go on the *Journey* across Canada, his answer could not help but touch me. Bevin's mom had died of cancer in 1995 and he told me about his stepmother, who three years before had been a very vibrant woman and who, by the time we met, was no longer able to feed herself, a victim of the ravages of ALS (Amyotrophic Lateral Sclerosis, also known as Lou Gehrig's Disease). It was the first time I had ever seen Bevin choked with emotion. It was then that I knew we had found our fourth person for the permanent crew.

Hundreds of volunteers would take part in *Jesse's Journey – A Father's Tribute* in the months ahead. But fewer than a hundred would be volunteers who would serve as the day-to-day road crew, experiencing everything that the *Journey* had to offer.

The names and faces of the permanent road crew had been identified. Their jobs would dovetail to clear the path for me, to allow me to walk every step of the way from the Atlantic Ocean to the Pacific with the single purpose of raising dollars to fund research.

That left just one position still to be filled. I had learned from my experience with Jesse when we crossed Ontario that we would need greater infrastructure for the walk across Canada. There had to be a home office to co-ordinate the new project.

I first met Maureen Golovchenko, an energetic five-foot-two woman with jet-black hair and green eyes, at London's Fanshawe College, where I had been asked to teach a course on media ethics in the mid-eighties. She had made a brave decision. Maureen was a 29 year old single mom with a degree in psychology who had gone back to school to become an electronic journalist. Her co-workers in the insurance industry wondered why Maureen, with an 8 year old son in daycare, would want to leave the security of a full time job to go back to school to pursue a career path that can be a minefield. Maureen, who has a stubborn streak, had no trouble looking them in the eye and saying, "I just don't want to be 60 years old and saying to myself 'what if?'"

My friends usually snicker when they hear about the course on media ethics. Invariably they end up asking the tongue-in-cheek question, "What would anybody in the media know about ethics?" The aim of the course was to get these new young faces that were about to pick up a microphone and become reporters, to do some serious thinking about ethical considerations in journalism. I worked out a series of hypothetical situations, such as: There is a fire in a major city at a gay nightclub. Nine people are killed. Among them are the deputy mayor, a prominent religious figure in the city and two highly-respected and well-known business people. Whose names do you use in this story and why? The situations I outlined for the students may have been a bit bizarre, but they certainly sparked dialogue among all those young people and very quickly my job was to act as referee while the sparks flew. There was no problem getting people to take part. The difficulty was getting them to be quiet while others had the floor. Maureen was always a participant and she wasn't shy about expressing her opinion.

We seldom saw each other in the years that followed Maureen's time at college. After four years of working as a broadcast journalist, Maureen moved into the charitable sector. With the skill set she had compiled, Maureen Golovchenko was about to step into the most taxing job she had ever faced, quarterbacking the 'home team' that would co-ordinate getting the 'road team' across Canada.

With the key players in place, it was time to build the volunteer army, muster all the supplies we would need, and get underway.

The training continued through the fall and on into the winter of 1997-98. The number of kilometres being logged each day continued to climb, and by Christmas of 1997 I was walking more than 25 km per day in preparation for what lay ahead. My plan was to reach 33 km a day by the middle of March. Thirty-three kilometres per day was the target figure for every day I would be on the road. Making that objective would get us home by Christmas of 1998. I didn't want to reach the 33-km-per-day objective any earlier than March, for fear that I would be burning myself out before I even started the walk across Canada.

Right from the moment I started training, I could feel the rust peeling away as I searched for the rhythm that had worked in pushing Jesse's wheelchair 3300 km in the summer of 1995. Even though I was making steady progress in getting back into shape for the road, I had to remind myself that I was now three years older. Taking on a challenge of this size at age 52 was going to require some discipline.

I had measured and mapped a series of routes that would get me the training distance I had to complete daily. Leading up to the day of departure for Newfoundland, there were plenty of times when I found the training sessions too repetitious, and when that happened, I would head out onto the country roads to test my legs.

One of my favourite routes took me 33 km north of London to 'Heart's Content Farm,' the home of my friend Peter Garland and his wife, Ann Hutchison. Peter hosts a morning radio program in London, and he was always kind enough to have some lunch ready when I would walk out to the farm from the city. The first time I completed that trek, I felt it gave me the right to ask myself if I could repeat that distance every day for almost 300 days. I think I might actually have looked up and asked, 'What do you think?' seeking an answer from the highest source.

Peter and I first met in 1973 at the London City Press Club. I was working for CFPL Radio, which at that time was a cornerstone of the Blackburn family empire that included CFPL television and the flagship asset, *The London Free Press.*

When we met, Peter was working at another radio station in London, and eventually over the years we developed an enduring friendship. Peter reminds me that I was practically a newlywed at the time. Sherene and I were married in January of 1972, just a few months before we moved to Vancouver where I had accepted a job with CBC radio and television. But I guess I was meant to be a Londoner. Sherene and I were young, and we didn't know anybody in Vancouver where I sometimes thought we were seen as 'Easterners.' We knew we wanted to have a family, and we knew that the educational facilities in London were excellent. And so we packed our bags and headed east to Ontario – back to London, and back to our families.

Peter and Ann saw Sherene and I go from newlyweds to parents with the birth of Tyler in 1977. Jesse was born in 1980 and Tim arrived in 1983. As the boys grew, they saw the pride that Sherene and I shared in our young family.

It was at the Garland's home in London in the late 1980's that Peter saw something that still stands out in his mind to this day. They were hosting a party for Gary Alan Price, another media colleague who was changing jobs. I arrived late and Peter, always a thoughtful host, was circulating among the guests. When he looked for me as the party was winding down, he noticed that Gary Alan Price and I were standing at the back of the garden, engaged in what appeared to be a serious conversation.

Peter remembers feeling certain he had seen tears on my face, although at that moment he put it down to being an illusion caused by the gathering dusk. It was only later he would discover that for the first time, I had shared the news with someone other than a family member that Jesse had been diagnosed with Duchenne Muscular Dystrophy. Like many others, they would watch as the years slipped by and Jesse slowly lost his ability to walk.

When Jesse and I decided to undertake the wheelchair marathon across Ontario to raise funds for genetic research, Peter Garland was there for us. He became involved, both as a friend and a member of the media corps that would follow our father-and-son odyssey as it wound its way over challenging hills and scorching pavement. As a friend he watched the bond between Jesse and me grow as we spent our days together on the highways, and shared experiences during a summer like none other in our lives. We were on Peter's show every week, and he remembers thinking, "Here they were out on the road, father and son, making this awesome commitment to a cause so close to their hearts and their lives. And I had the privilege and pleasure of walking with John when he and Jesse got close to London."

Walking the highway with us had the same effect on Peter as it did for so many people who came out to the road to join us. It was magical. And walking with us set Peter up for my announcement in December of 1997. He was at a news conference when our friend Gary Alan Price (whose initials led to the nickname Gapper) came up to Peter and whispered, "He's going to do it again."

With a puzzled look, Peter asked, "Do what?"

That's when Gary told him: "He's going to walk across the country."

Peter's immediate reaction was, "Good grief, the man is 51 years old!"

But Peter also knew that I was determined to walk across Canada to raise funds for genetic research. The target date had now been set. I would begin the walk in St. John's Newfoundland on April 10th, 1998 – Jesse's 18th birthday.

Meanwhile, the training continued as I prepared mentally and physically for the almost year-long separation from my family and the more than 8000 km and four seasons I would face before the end of the *Journey*. I started to push myself to the limit in the months prior to the walk, and by March, with the April 10th launch date rapidly closing in, I began to concentrate on more 'highway experience.'

Peter and Ann's 'Heart's Content' farm is just outside of Lucan, Ontario, which is north of London. There is an apple orchard south of Lucan, which Peter passes every day on his drive home. I asked him to mark the distance from the apple orchard to his home. If I walked the distance from the orchard to Peter's home and back, I would log 26 km, exactly the distance I wanted to do at that point in the training schedule.

I would make the walk, have lunch and chat for a while, and then walk back. Although Peter was devoted to what I was going to attempt in the months ahead, he could certainly be forgiven for entertaining doubts. He remembered me leaving his house in the rain and heading down that gravel road all by myself. That's when he thought to himself, "Buddy, you have got the world's courage in your heart to do this, and to look to a cross-country walk ahead of you." It was then that he said to himself, "OK buddy, you've got me. I'll do whatever I can for you." From that point, Peter made a commitment and he never looked back. It was a commitment that would lead to two of the most memorable moments in his long and storied broadcast career.

The logistics of a cross-Canada walk started to become a reality in the week before I left for Newfoundland. One of our first challenges was to get a 12-metre motor home and two escort vans from London, Ontario and have them in place and ready to go from St. John's, Newfoundland.

We had made arrangements with the Canadian military to haul the motor home on a Canadian Forces flatbed truck from London to the ferry terminal in North Sydney, Nova Scotia. From there, the first five volunteers who were driving the two vans to St. John's would pick up the motor home.

The generosity of St. Thomas recreational vehicle dealer Don Ferguson, who provided us with a motor home for our first *Journey* in 1995, made sure that the road team would have a 'home away from home' for the trip across Canada.

London car dealer Pat Kennedy, an Irishman with a kind heart and a sparkle in his eye, had donated the vans. The two vehicles were emblazoned with a larger-than-life picture of Jesse waving a Canadian flag and the map showing our route across Canada. Pat had been a solid supporter of *Jesse's Journey* from the beginning, providing a van for our *Journey* across Ontario. The first time I went to meet Pat in 1995, he wasn't in his office. A devout Catholic, Pat was out making his weekly pick-up of bread to be delivered to the Men's Mission, a longtime London mainstay providing emergency shelter. Don Ferguson and Pat Kennedy are models who represent the kind of people who are out there in every community across Canada if you just look for them.

In North Sydney the three vehicles would be loaded on board the ferry for Port Aux Basques, Newfoundland. From that point, the Trans-Canada Highway, which is really the only road that crosses Newfoundland, makes a big horseshoe-type loop across the top of the island. It's almost a thousand kilometres to St. John's on the southeast coast.

Making the crossing from North Sydney to Port Aux Basques, the volunteer crew found themselves travelling on 'dangerous cargo day' when only fifty-eight vehicles are allowed to board. When Trish Federkow, asked why the magic number was just fifty-eight vehicles, some of the ship's crew joked with her, "That's all the insurance we can afford!" Trish was told she should be thankful she wasn't crossing on 'double-dangerous cargo day' when they allow only 12 vehicles on board. That's when they carry things like nitroglycerin, dynamite, propane and butane. When Trish suggested the ship would probably go straight up if there was ever an explosion, one of the crew members was quick to tell her, "Oh no, Honey. If that ever went, she'd blow straight down!"

After reaching Port Aux Basques, the team bunked in for the night, as there was a gale blowing. In these conditions, driving anything at all was a white-knuckle experience, even for the islanders who knew the roads. Tackling the winding roads in the dark and in the treacherous high winds that sweep the west coast, was out of the question. With the snow blowing in all directions, the weather had served notice that Newfoundland was not going to be an easy crossing, either heading east on wheels or heading west on foot.

Chapter Eleven

ON TO THE EAST COAST

"God does not ask about our ability but rather our availability" –
Unknown

On Monday April 6th, 1998, just four days before I was to start my
walk across Canada, I left home knowing I wouldn't be back until I
passed through London on foot sometime in August. It was dark and
the boys were still asleep when the headlights of Gary Alan Price's
van pulled into the laneway. I hugged Sherene and as I kissed her
goodbye, I told her I would try to do my best, something we both
knew I would do no matter what. Jesse was going to be 18 on the
Friday of that week. It had been almost 12 years since he had been
diagnosed and our world had flipped upside down. I held Sherene for
a moment in the darkness and hoped I was doing the right thing. And
then quickly the luggage was loaded and we were on our way.

At the airport I connected with Bevin Palmateer, who would fly to
Newfoundland with me. With several bleary-eyed friends who were
there to see us off with good wishes, warm hugs and a few tears, we
watched the sun rise over the hometown I was leaving for almost a
year. It struck me just how many people cared about this project.
Once again, it was time to go.

The flights were uneventful, and my first image of Newfoundland
from the air brought me to the reality that this was it. My feelings
were a mixture of anticipation and dread. Was I up to the challenge?

The water that beaded on the window of the plane, revealed only
empty miles of dark green under a grey sky with a thick blanket of
white mist that drifted in the wind. As the jet bounced onto the
runway after the flight from Toronto, I thought of Jesse and all the
people who would benefit from the research dollars this *Journey*
would generate, and despite the sheets of rain hitting the tarmac
outside, I felt the adrenaline kick in. I was now close to the start

point, both in geography and time. In a few days I would leave St. John's City Hall and "Kilometre 0" and attempt to walk the more than 8000 kms of highway which link Canada's coasts.

Leaving the airport in St. John's, I was carrying everything I would need for the next nine months in one big red duffel bag with the words *Jesse's Journey – A Father's Tribute* stitched onto the side. Stepping out into the rain that was steadily falling, I thought back to the time Jesse and I had spent together on the road. I remembered how easy it became for us to pack our bags onto the motor home, which would head down the road to wait for us in another town at another motel. The hours I spent pushing Jesse along the highway in his wheelchair, as we caught up with the motor home, had been so rewarding. If this *Journey* came anywhere near that, it would all be worth it.

We could smell the salt in the air and I felt a sigh of relief when Trish, along with volunteer Bob Seaton, met us at the airport. The early hours of the first day in Newfoundland were spent figuring out where everybody was staying and making sure there were no problems. Bob Seaton, a 43 year old parts clerk at the car dealership that had supplied the escort vans, was one of the five-person crew assigned the job of moving the convoy of vehicles from London, Ontario to St. John's, Newfoundland. Since I had been worrying about them, seeing Trish and Bob in Newfoundland confirmed in my mind that the road team had arrived safely. But it hadn't been easy. Dashing across Quebec in the aftermath of the ice storm of the century, Bob Seaton and Mike Woodward were hard-pressed to stay ahead of the floodwaters as the ice melted. Hurrying through the Eastern Townships, roads were constantly being closed behind them as the water levels kept rising. The floodwaters and damage from the ice storm were scenes that haunted the entire team as they pushed on toward the Maritimes. Leaving the flood waters of Quebec behind them, the advance team ran into winter conditions in both New Brunswick and Nova Scotia.

Reaching the Gulf ferry terminal, the convoy grew in size as the advance team picked up the motor home that had been left waiting for them by the military people who had also battled some tough weather to get to their destination.

Then, after a windy and cold ferry crossing from the tip of Cape Breton, more of the same awaited them in Newfoundland. Leaving Port Aux Basques, Bob and Mike had to battle the high winds and snow that pounded the motor home and vans throughout the three-hour drive to Corner Brook, a distance of more than 200 km.

By the time they reached Grand Falls-Windsor, ice and heavy snow brought highway traffic to a halt. With the Trans-Canada Highway officially closed, Mike and Bob were forced to spend the next two days waiting out the storm.

It was late March and almost springtime when the motor home and escort vans left London. Like the rest of the advance team, Don and Jane Black probably didn't expect to witness the flooding, the devastation from the ice storm or a Maritime blast of winter before crossing the Gulf of St. Lawrence – nor the delay by the wind and snow in Newfoundland. Like Mike and Bob, the Blacks were also in Grand Falls-Windsor when the RCMP closed the highway. Don and Jane found a place to stay and they too settled in to wait out the storm. Finally, a week after leaving London, five very exhausted volunteer members of the advance team, one motor home and two escort vans rolled into St. John's, Newfoundland.

The permanent road team and the first wave of volunteer drivers were being housed in bed-and-breakfast accommodations scattered close to downtown St. John's. I was relieved to hear the Blacks were safely tucked away in nearby McCoubrey Manor on Ordinance Street. For Jane, arriving in Newfoundland was like coming home. Although she had never lived here, she felt this was her place and these were her people. Jane's parents had been born in Newfoundland, her father in Lewisporte, and her mother in Lower Island Cove.

The owners of McCoubrey Manor had beautifully restored the home and Don and Jane immediately felt a sense of warmth that would linger through their stay in Newfoundland. An intriguing piece of information about the home came to Jane through a cousin who passed along some family history. Of the five houses on that short, quiet street in the east end of St. John's, three had been built by one house builder – Jane's grandfather! They'll likely never know for sure, but they may indeed have been sharing superb Newfoundland hospitality in a home built so many years ago by a man who never dreamed that one day his granddaughter would sleep under its sloping eaves.

Driving through the narrow, rain-slicked streets of the oldest part of St. John's, I caught a glimpse of the harbour and the city's most visible landmark, Signal Hill. At the top of the hill stands Cabot Tower and it was near this spot that the Italian inventor, Guglielmo Marconi, received the first Trans-Atlantic wireless signal in 1901. In the days just before flying to Newfoundland, I had been busy with a lot of last-minute details, and I hadn't been able to get out on the road to train. I made a mental note that in the morning I would hike to the top of Signal Hill and give my legs a good workout.

Thanks to the wind blowing at the top of Signal Hill, I was rewarded with a sweeping panoramic view of the old port city of St. John's emerging through the fog. The harbour, the ocean and the coastline were all alive. With the sun shining and the wind blowing hard at my back, I looked out over the Atlantic Ocean, and in a moment of solitude, wondered what I was doing on this windswept hill, thousands of miles from home and family and friends. I could almost feel the pre-game nervousness of the athletes I had spent so many years reporting on for both radio and television.

Suddenly, the anxiety and self-doubt about my own ability to complete this job was gone. Mentally sharpening my focus, the anxiety was replaced by a sense of euphoria that I was being given a chance to do something extraordinary and for a noble cause.

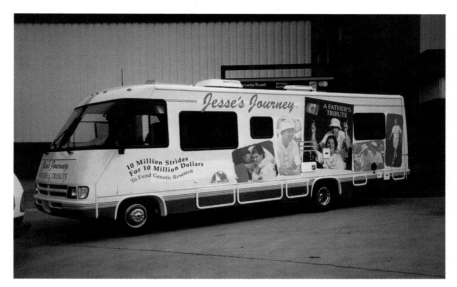

Waiting to leave London, to be transported by the Canadian Military, was the 10 metre Triple-E motorhome that would become the office, meeting room, lunch room, radio room, rest room and first aid station. In the rain and snow, the "Mothership" was always a welcome sight.

At the top of Signal Hill in St. John's, Newfoundland, with the Atlantic Ocean in the background, the shoes, road uniform and one of the escort vans all looked shiny and new. From where I am standing it's a shorter distance to Ireland than to Victoria.

From the top of Signal Hill, you can see why people call the island province "The Rock."
On the top right is downtown St. John's.

Beside City Hall in St. John's, I posed at Kilometre "0".

PEACE IN QUIDI VIDI   ST. JOHN'S, NEWFOUNDLAND

Bryce Bursey

Fishing boats tied to the wooden dock in the harbour of Quidi Vidi, Newfoundland, tug gently at their ropes. To the right is the channel leading to the Atlantic.

Looking out through the harbour entrance at Quidi Vidi I was just moments away from dipping my running shoes in the Atlantic Ocean. The journey of a lifetime was about to begin.

For me it was really like the second opportunity of a lifetime after the great adventure of crossing Ontario with Jesse three years earlier. It was as if the wind had blown the cobwebs of doubt out to sea, and the stage was set for a new cast of characters to step into the spotlight. A lot of the new players in my life were to be people I had never met before and they would be people I would call friends for the rest of my life.

In the days that followed, as we started to make final preparations for the launch of our *Journey*, there was a noticeable excitement in the air. This was the rally point and the clock was ticking.

Everyone working on *Jesse's Journey* knew that it was going to take an army of people connecting with one another to make the project a success. One of those magical links brought together two women from Newfoundland – mothers who had never met, and who for months would only know each other through e-mail, telephone calls and fax messages.

A push of the 'on' button of a VCR in Ontario and a glance at the 'Letters' section of a magazine in Newfoundland were about to spark a synergy that would open a floodgate of support.

It was Christmas 1997 when Joanne Dawson and her family from Summerford, Newfoundland arrived in Ontario to spend the holidays at 'Heart's Content' farm with her brother Peter Garland and his wife Ann. Just before Joanne and her family were to head back home, she and Peter were having a quiet brother-sister chat, when Peter leaned over and pushed the 'on' button. As the images of Jesse and me from the 1995 wheelchair tour of Ontario filled the television screen, Peter told his sister about my plans to walk across Canada. Her immediate reaction was, "I'll do anything I can to help."

Back home in Newfoundland, Joanne is a schoolteacher in Summerford, a relatively isolated community located on the south shore of Bonavista Bay. At first she wondered how she could help, but like so many *Journey* volunteers, she quickly came to realize that the power of one is awesome. When Joanne arrived home, she immediately began planning for the Newfoundland portion of my walk across Canada. Using her considerable energies and contacts, she began to enlist service clubs and church groups to provide meals, drivers, accommodations and all those things that would be required for a cause she now held dear.

Peter Garland had been born in the little Newfoundland outport community of Lower Island Cove, and his ties to his home province were as strong as the day he had set out as a youngster to seek fame and fortune on the mainland.

As he watched me pushing my 52 year old muscles to the limit in preparation for the walk, Peter made a commitment. He would do all he could to help get me safely across Canada, starting with the 960 km of highway from St. John's to Port Aux Basques, Newfoundland, a trek that would be compounded by some of the worst weather conditions imaginable.

His first thought was to contact his friend Ron Young, a long-time resident of Ontario and publisher of the magazine, *Downhomer*. Ron, a native Newfoundlander, had recently returned home, bringing his publishing empire to Water Street near the harbour in St. John's. The idea of a newspaper for expatriates had come to fruition in 1988. Now in magazine format and in its new quarters, the Downhomer has achieved phenomenal success among residents and expatriates alike.

Peter could not have known how the letter he wrote would affect one reader when it appeared in the January 1998 issue of the magazine. Nor could he have imagined how far-reaching its affects would be on the *Journey*.

Kay Coxworthy, from Bell Island, Newfoundland, had just been hired as marketing manager for the *Downhomer* when she took the latest issue of the magazine home on a cold January day to get 'up to scratch' on what exactly she had gotten herself into. On the ferry, "Flanders", making the five-kilometre crossing of what the locals call 'the tickle' heading home to Bell Island, she began to read the 'Letters' section of the Downhomer. There on page 57 her eyes settled on "Walking for a Good Cause", Peter's letter asking Newfoundlanders everywhere to help a father who planned to walk across Canada – not just to help his own son, but to further research to help all those who suffer from genetic illnesses.

As Ron Young tells the story, bright and early the next morning, Kay, who'd been touched by the heartfelt eloquence of Peter's letter, walked into Young's office and said, "Ron boy, we've got to do something for this fellow." Ron will also tell you that, like every publisher, he gets hundreds of letters from readers every month, twelve months of the year. So, after having another look at this one to see what his new marketing manager was so worked up about, he looked up at her and said, "We'll do whatever we can girl. You handle it!" And handle it she did, working in tandem with Joanne Dawson, hundreds of kilometres away in Summerford, Newfoundland. Together they became a formidable team, tapping computer keys on into the night, making calls and leaving phone and fax messages across the province, all the time without having laid eyes on one another. It wasn't until the night before the *Journey* began that Joanne and Kay finally met in St. John's at a birthday party for an 18 year old neither of them had ever met.

The birthday party for Jesse was held in Mount Pearl, just outside St. John's, and it marked the end of a whirlwind week of trying to get used to the culture, sights and sounds of Newfoundland. I had spoken to St. John's City Council, been interviewed by the St. John's Evening Telegram and the *London Free Press*. I had been interviewed on radio and television in both cities. I was feeling the way Jesse must have felt on the morning that we left London to cross Ontario, answering question after question about a *Journey* that had yet to officially start.

Earlier in the week, Trish and I had been to Government House to have tea with Maxwell House, a neurologist, and Lieutenant-Governor of Newfoundland and Labrador. The house is impressive, with its high ceilings, red carpet, and polished wooden floors that creak just the right amount to indicate their age. The glass greenhouse beside Government House was the source of the fresh-cut flowers that brighten the bleak portions of days that can turn from grey to gorgeous and back to grey again in just a few hours. The Lieutenant-Governor seemed most interested in what we were planning to do, and said he would like to do something more for us but is bound by the protocol of his office from much involvement. He invited me to come back to see him when it's all over.

I had spoken to the St. John's Rotary Club and dropped the official puck at a St. John's Maple Leafs playoff game. I had re-climbed Signal Hill to look out over the Atlantic at the white caps that indicate the strength of the wind blowing outside the "Narrows," the entrance to the harbour that has played a part of naval history for over 500 years. It had been sunny and warm at the top of the hill, but by late afternoon when the *London Free Press* wanted a picture for the next morning's paper, things had changed dramatically. We only ventured halfway up the hill, as the wind and rain were lashing the harbour entrance and it had turned bitter cold. It was a sneak preview of what lay ahead, crossing Newfoundland when winter had yet to let go.

I had shared an evening with Jeff Gilhooley, a radio colleague from the seventies, whose career had taken him from London to Lahr, Germany with Canadian Forces Radio before he'd found his way to Newfoundland with the CBC. Jeff was a little wider, and had a little less hair, but the sparkle in his eye told me he was just as curious as ever, always the sign of a good newsman. He plunged right in with plenty of questions about the project we were about to tackle. It was great to have a night off and relax with Jeff, Mildred and their black Scottish terrier, Angus, who wears a dog-sized Montreal Canadiens sweater.

We had a wonderful meal of salt cod and spent an evening reminiscing by the fireplace. Jeff's 106 year old home is, like everything else in St. John's, dated as either before or after the Great Fire of 1892 that pretty well destroyed the city.

It had been a busy week, and the birthday party for Jesse was a great success. The Royal Newfoundland Constabulary (RNC) in their dress blues and the Royal Canadian Mounted Police in their red serge mingled with representatives of city service organizations, and kids of all ages. As the sounds of "Justice Combined", a band made up of RNC and RCMP members filled the room, I was joined by a group of kids who helped me cut the huge birthday cake as everyone joined in singing, "Happy Birthday, Jesse." As the party began to wind down, Kay Coxworthy gathered the London contingent for the traditional Newfoundland Screech-In. Having kissed a cod and tried the famous local rum and the tongue-twisting dialect, we were declared Honourary Newfoundlanders, a designation we were all delighted to accept. The party was our first experience with Newfoundland hospitality. It certainly would not be our last. I just wished that Jesse and the rest of the family could have been there to share all of it with us.

Then, the moment of truth arrived. If I had been a tourist visiting historic St. John's, and taking in the sites and sounds of Newfoundland, then Friday April 10th, 1998 would probably have been just a routine morning. The smell of fresh coffee would have drawn me down to the kitchen of the Prescott Inn, our bed-and-breakfast on Military Road. But this wasn't just another day. After seven months of training, today the distance would start to count for real.

Looking out the window of my third floor room, I could see the day had started out overcast, and St. John's looked cold and quiet. Although it was just before seven in the morning, people were starting to arrive at St. Thomas' Anglican Church, across the street. Like most buildings in St. John's, the church, built in 1836, is made of wood. It used to be called the Old Garrison Church and it's the oldest wooden church in Newfoundland. The church was painted dark brown with white trim, and from the centre of my room, the window framed the wooden cross on the top of the church. Below my window, on the narrow street, a thick layer of frost covered the motor home and the escort vehicles, which would soon be warming up.

Across the street, people bundled up in coats and scarves were arriving at the church, carrying dishes of food. I had almost forgotten it was Good Friday. With people scurrying to get out of the early morning cold, I decided to start this *Journey* in a wind suit. That outfit consisted of navy blue pants and a bright red jacket with the words *Jesse's Journey – A Father's Tribute* in white stitched across the front. Lacing up my shoes and picking up my hat, I took a deep breath and headed downstairs to get the day started.

Motor home driver Mike Woodward, and van driver Bob Seaton were already in the kitchen, where the smell of coffee and toast filled the room. Mike was a veteran, having been on the road with Jesse and me in 1995. For Bob Seaton, the quiet guy with the brush cut, this was his first trip 'down East.' He'd been sitting at home reading the newspaper a few months ago, when the announcement of the walk across Canada and the need for volunteers caught his eye. Bob, who was scheduled to stay on with us as far as Goobies, Newfoundland, had been up since before dawn. He and I sat down to bowls of cereal and toast with a choice of a couple of Newfoundland treats, bakeapple or partridgeberry jams.

Looking past the potted geraniums on the windowsill, the sun started to stream in through the window. It was going to be a typical early spring day in Newfoundland, with the weather constantly changing. After breakfast, the motor home and vans were warmed up and running as everyone gathered in the parking lot of the Hotel Newfoundland to convoy out to the start point at Quidi Vidi. Cameraman Richard Johnstone from CFPL-TV in London had a rental car, and since he had no one riding with him I decided to jump in for the short trip to Quidi Vidi, just northeast of the old downtown area of St. John's.

Richard is extremely creative with a television camera. He has been assigned to shoot video of me dipping my shoes into the saltwater off Newfoundland, and filling a jug with cold Atlantic water. That water is to be carried across the country to be mixed with the waters of the Pacific at the end of the road ahead.

Richard Johnstone is also the father of three young girls, and more than most dads he understood the value of medical research. Richard and his wife Sherry's oldest daughter, Andrea, was born in 1988 with a very rare brain disorder that has left her profoundly disabled.

Like a lot of parents of disabled children, Richard has a tremendous sense of humour. He has been involved in his share of pranks, and he loves to laugh. I have sometimes wondered if God gives special children to people who can handle the task – people who don't pray for a lighter load, but pray for a stronger back.

On the way out to Quidi Vidi, Richard was very quiet. When we reached the harbour and the car rolled across the gravel to a halt, Richard paused for a moment as he put the car in 'park.' Then turning to me he said quietly, "John, when you get really tired, take a few more steps for Andrea." It was something that shook me, and I knew I wouldn't forget those words when I felt too exhausted to take another step. Like so many times before, and like so many to come, it was time to get going.

At Quidi Vidi, I wander out as far as I can on the tip of land that faces the entrance to the harbour. For a few minutes I am alone. With more than 8000 km of highway ahead of me, I take that quiet moment to make sure that my focus is crystal clear.

The little group of volunteers and media people spread out across the rocks, snapping pictures to record the event. I dip my running shoes in the frigid saltwater of the Atlantic Ocean, and fill a glass jug with water as some of the locals look out from behind curtained windows, snug indoors, probably wondering what this lot is up to on such a bitterly cold morning. I wonder how often they see someone do exactly as I am doing before heading off down the road or out to sea. And how often had those people disappeared down the road, never to be heard from again?

Heading down the road toward St. John's and the formal sendoff at "Kilometre 0", *Jesse's Journey* receives its first donation. Seventy-five year old Peg Magnone owns an antique shop housed in 'Mallard Cottage', the oldest cottage in St. John's, built in the 1750's by Irish immigrants. Early on that Good Friday morning she leans over her picket fence to donate $10. Peg Magnone had her own travel story to tell. Ten years earlier, widowed at age 65, she had packed everything she owned into a van and driven across Canada from her home near Vancouver to her daughter's home in St. John's. She told a reporter she remembered seeing me on television, and added how thankful she was she had four healthy grandsons.

The sun breaks through the clouds that have settled over the city just as I crest the hill and reach City Hall and "Kilometre 0." Because it is Good Friday and a holiday, most of the people of St. John's are probably just getting out of bed at the time we are holding the 'official' sendoff. As I walk on toward City Hall, I can hear again the music of "Justice Combined." After playing for us the night before, this great bunch of guys are back again filling the downtown area with traditional Newfoundland music. I will quickly come to learn about this kind of willing spirit shown by Newfoundlanders.

For London radio morning show host Peter Garland, it is a special morning. He is doing his show 'live' from his beloved Newfoundland. St. John's radio station VOCM, which people in Newfoundland say stands for "Voice of the Common Man," has provided their special events trailer, which serves as the mobile studio. The station's engineers have completed all the technical hookups required to make the broadcast back to CFPL Radio in London a reality.

Peter, who has been conducting interviews since dawn, has a surprise for me as he hosts the formal portion of the kickoff from the steps of City Hall. He has Jesse on the phone from London, and while I'm wishing him a happy 18th birthday and explaining how I kissed a cod the night before, something special happens again. The crowd, which had gathered around the fire trucks, police cars and even a city bus that had stopped to join in the excitement, spontaneously breaks into a chorus of "Happy Birthday" to a young man they have never met. A young man who is the inspiration for the *Journey* that is just beginning.

There is one other piece of business that has to be attended to before I set out on the road. On behalf of *Jesse's Journey*, I present a cheque for $250,000 to Dr. Ron Worton of the Ottawa General Hospital Research Institute, the discoverer of the gene that causes Duchenne Muscular Dystrophy. I make that presentation on behalf of The Foundation for Gene and Cell Therapy, the charity we had founded in the winter of 1993-1994.

A few more 'photo ops' in front of the "Kilometre 0" sign, a final wave to the crowd, and after eight months of training, I take the first of the ten million strides it will take to reach Victoria, British Columbia.

Chapter Twelve

Rugged Newfoundland

"You win some, you lose some and some get
rained out, but you gotta suit up for them all" –
J. Askenburg

Our travels in 1995 taught me that the crowd that joins you as you set off down the road soon dwindles to one or two people who will stay with you for a while. Leaving the city of St. John's and entering nearby Mount Pearl, the rain is falling steadily as the escort van drivers and motor home crew begin the process of settling into the routine of life on the road. By midday it's raining steadily as we take our first lunch break and heat some soup on the stove in the motor home. We're a pretty wet-looking troupe with a lot of high hopes.

Back on the road in the afternoon, the rain keeps falling and the temperature begins to drop. Before long, the surface of the Trans-Canada Highway disappears under a blanket of greasy white snow. The revolving amber caution light on the roof of the escort van is barely visible behind me. Slipping and sliding along the shoulder of the highway, I'm passing cars that have slid off the road and into the ditch. By the middle of the afternoon, the wind has come up and the snow is stinging my face. The RCMP advises us it's too dangerous to stay on the road. Our first day on the Trans-Canada Highway ends after 22 km.

Driving back into St. John's, the snow again turns to rain. To make up the shortfall in distance on the highway, I climb down from the motor home, set my pedometer, and walk from downtown St. John's back out to Quidi Vidi, and then back to our bed-and-breakfast. By the time I get back, it's dark, and everything I'm wearing is soaking wet. After a hot shower and some supper, I write in my journal and go to bed. It's the end of our first day on the road in Newfoundland.

I knew before leaving London that April weather in Newfoundland could be very hostile. Resting my head on the pillow, I consider the fact that it will be twenty-eight days before we reach Port Aux Basques on the other side of the province. All I can hope is that those twenty-eight days won't be anything like the one we just had.

On Easter Sunday we're up early. It's our first official 'moving day.' Over the next nine-and-a-half months, it will become a common sight to see the road team's red *Jesse's Journey* bags being loaded into the vans or onto the motor home as we 'move up.' I've now been in St. John's for six days, the road team even longer. We say goodbye to those who have hosted us at four different B & B's in the heart of old St. John's. It's funny how Canadians can establish a friendship in such a short period of time. Saying goodbye is still something we never really get used to doing.

It's a long drive out to our start point and the marker where we finished the day before. The morning is quiet, with very little traffic and just a few donations, but things are about to change. After lunch, the four-lane highway becomes a two-lane road and traffic quickly backs up for about one kilometre. For the first time, donations begin to pour in as Easter holiday traffic from 'around the bay' starts to make its way back toward St. John's.

As I concentrate on the road, Trish runs up and asks me to slow down. Behind me, the yellow-vested men and women of the Whitbourne Lions Club are darting in and out of traffic, taking donations being handed out the windows of vehicles backed up in both directions. There's one minor fender-bender and I feel a little guilty about being responsible for people being delayed. I apologize to a few drivers in the lineup heading home to St. John's. It's a relief to hear a lot of them say with their broad Newfoundland accent, "Don'cha worry boy, you just take your time and good luck to ya." By the end of the day, we've made lots of new friends and collected more than $2,300.

After a long day on the road, it's time for another slice of Newfoundland hospitality when the Lions Club of Whitbourne plays host at a 'Fish and Brewis' dinner – another first for all of us on the road team. 'Fish and Brewis' is made of hard bread which is soaked overnight. Before it's soaked, the bread is really as hard as a rock.

The hard bread is then cooked and mixed with salt cod, onions and scrunchions, which are small pieces of pork fat fried to a golden brown. 'Fish and Brewis' is an age-old Newfoundland dish, and after a busy day on the road it proves very popular with our crew of 'Mainlanders.'

In 1995, when we crossed Ontario, Jesse and I had always said that it was the people that made it so remarkable. And just as if we were still on the road together, I strike up a conversation with one of the Lions we are about to have dinner with, a muscular-looking man named Wayne. I was trying to guess whether he worked in the lumber industry or the oil industry. When I asked him where he worked, he just sort of smiled and said, "about 200 miles east of St. John's." He kidded with me that it took him two days to get to work and two days to get home. I learned he worked as a 'crabber' on board a fifty-five foot boat. The crew consisted of seven men, and they would stay out on the water for two weeks before heading home with fifteen hundred kilograms of crab. When I asked Wayne if it ever got very rough on the ocean, he was quick to reply, "Oh yes, boy. And the rougher she gets, the better I likes her." When he mentioned the ocean rising and falling, I asked him to tell me what you actually see when you're out at sea in those conditions. He paused a moment before he said, "Well, let me put her this way, when you're up top you see everything. When you're down below you don't see nothing!"

It's been a good day and we've made a lot of new friends. As I head to bed at the motel where we're staying in Whitbourne, Mike Woodward and Bob Seaton are off to discover one of the many outports that dot Trinity Bay. They're hoping to snap some pictures of whales breaching. I'm happy to hear they're doing that because I want everyone who is part of the *Journey* to be able to take home their own special memories. After Bob and Mike drive off, I head to bed, walking down the long, dark hallway to my room, three doors down from where Terry Fox stayed when he passed through Whitbourne almost 20 years before me.

In a way, Newfoundland is almost two islands. The Avalon Peninsula, bounded by Trinity Bay on the north side and Placentia Bay on the south, is the narrow land passage leading to St. John's and the easternmost pocket of Canada. It's across this strip of land that the cold air from the waters of Trinity Bay collides with the warmer air from the Gulf Stream in Placentia Bay and creates some dramatic weather effects for the Avalon Peninsula.

Crossing the Peninsula, we experience mostly rain, fog and a lot of very wet clothing. I spend my time on the road completing the assigned distance for each day. I like to get as close to 20 km as possible in the first half of the day, so the afternoon portion of the walk will seem a little shorter. My lunchtime routine is to close the bedroom door at the back of the motor home and sleep for about 45 minutes before heading back to the road for the afternoon. It's never much fun waking up to the sound of rain and looking at more grey sky. While I nap, the rest of the crew continue to fine-tune the daily routine. The list of little things that have to be done is almost endless, and in tight quarters, with everyone having their own way of doing things, there's bound to be friction, although everyone tries hard to make sure that doesn't happen. But when it does happen, at least nobody tells me about it. That's another reason I'm happy to hear about people going off to look for whales or moose – or just to see some of the colourful little Newfoundland villages. It gives everybody some breathing space.

One of the earliest overnight stops during the crossing of the Peninsula is at the 'Five Bays Lodge' at Goobies, Newfoundland. The lodge, which is right on the Trans-Canada Highway, consists of a motel, restaurant and bar.

When the owner, Len Manning, heard about *Jesse's Journey* and the walk across Canada, he organized a fundraiser and even brought in a band called "Medicinal Purposes." Most of the people who stay at the lodge on a permanent basis work on the Hibernia oil project. The lights of the motel are always a welcome sight to travellers along the Trans-Canada Highway. But on this particularly rainy, dark night in typical Newfoundland fashion, music and fun are the focus. The result is more than $1,000 raised for research.

Walking along the Trans-Canada Highway in Newfoundland is unlike walking anywhere else in Canada. There are waterfalls everywhere, and sometimes they're so close, I can feel the spray and listen to the wild rivers that rush under the bridges I'm crossing. At other times, I can see waterfalls in the distance, but they're so far off, there's only silence. These are the times when all I can hear is my own breathing and the sound of my running shoes on the paved shoulder of the road. Alone with my thoughts, this is when I store up the 'mental energy' I know I'll eventually need. And all the while, the kilometres keep slipping behind me at the rate of 33 per day.

Newfoundlanders have their own special sense of geography when it comes to tracking places on the map. And it doesn't take me long to understand that everything in Newfoundland seems to be marked by its distance from the closest Irving Service Station. K.C. Irving probably never knew his service stations would become such well-known landmarks throughout eastern Canada. Whenever we ask how to get to someplace, the answer always seems to start off with someone stretching their arm out, pointing and saying "Well, you go down to the Irving." And from that reliable marker point, directions can begin.

Besides serving as landmarks, the Irving Stations are drop-off and pick-up points for people using the airport, with mini-buses stopping regularly according to Newfoundland time. Both time and distance operate a little differently on the Island, and our dealings with this fact led to a funny moment on more than one occasion.

One Sunday morning, Ron Calhoun was preparing to return to St. John's for his flight back to Toronto. Just before I headed out to the road, Ron was making his way over to the Irving Station looking for information on bus schedules. When he asked a young man who was busily pumping gas, what time the bus would arrive, the fellow just looked at Ron and said in a very matter-of-fact way, "She gets here when she gets here!"

Not one to be deterred, Ron thought he would try a different tack, asking the attendant what time he should be there in order to catch the bus. Again, without missing a beat, the young man told Ron, "You should be here when she gets here!" Eventually they settled on a time and Ron made his flight back to Toronto.

There are hundreds of little fishing villages or outports that dot the rugged coastline of Newfoundland. At night time, the lights of these coastal villages stretch out like a diamond necklace against the black of the ocean. It's the people of these little towns and villages across the province who make us feel at home, hosting the *Journey* road crew night after night as we make our way across Newfoundland.

One night, after a wet day on the road, we came face to face with Canadian politics. We were sitting at a window table in an outport restaurant alongside the docks of a small fishing village where most of the people worked at the canning factory. We were talking about the hardships faced by Newfoundland fishermen, when Mike Woodward recalled a story from on board the ferry Caribou as the advance team had made the crossing to Newfoundland.

It was lunchtime on board the Caribou, and the road crew was among those lined up in the cafeteria. Mike was eyeing the cod that was listed on the menu. When he asked if the cod was fresh, the server replied in a strong Newfoundland accent, "She should be fresh bye, she came off a Russian dragger last night!"

I suppose, like a lot of Mainlanders, I had never given much thought to the economics of Newfoundland and to the hardships these incredible people endure. It was like a cold slap in the face to realize how dependent the province is on the fishing industry. To be subject to a moratorium on cod fishing, while the rest of the world seems to be able to fish the waters off Newfoundland and then sell those fish on world markets, just didn't seem fair.

I found myself wondering who really knows which countries' boats are fishing in international waters, and which ones are fishing in the territorial waters of Canada.

I knew that from that moment on, I would read newspaper accounts of the plight of Newfoundland fishermen from a completely different perspective. I also realized that this trip across Canada was going to include a big chunk of education for all of us. In training for the *Journey* I hadn't given much thought to that aspect of the project. It was going to be just one more thing to deal with while never losing my focus on the research dollars I had set out to generate.

The Trans-Canada Highway is shaped something like a horseshoe as it arches across Newfoundland from St. John's on the southeast coast, up and over to Port Aux Basques on the southwest. The highway, which opened in 1956, is really the only road across Newfoundland. The way the highway is laid out gave our road crew lots of material for *Wizard of Oz* jokes – to 'just follow the yellow brick road.' A week into the *Journey*, I was really starting to find my pace in the rugged terrain that rises and falls as it twists and turns its way across Newfoundland.

A couple of things happened as we continued north toward Gander. When we reached Clarenville, the road widened out to four lanes, with a nice wide shoulder for walking. The town of Clarenville, like so many settlements in Newfoundland, lies below where the Trans-Canada Highway sweeps across the province. Like many Newfoundland towns, it hugs the shoreline, where the water and the woods powered commerce in Clarenville's earliest days.

My first minor injury of the *Journey* occurs as I twist my ankle making my way up and down slopes on the main street of Clarenville. I feel a lot better when I reach the Town Hall and see the large number of young Sea Cadets, Brownies and kids with flags who are waiting to greet us. It hasn't taken me long to notice that the young people of Newfoundland are extremely polite and answer every question with 'yes sir' or 'no sir.' Hearing this also makes me feel a little older.

Clarenville is where Ed Coxworthy from Bell Island, Newfoundland, joined us as a volunteer. Ed was driving to the birthday party his wife Kay had organized for Jesse before we left St. John's, when she casually mentioned that we were still looking for a driver for two weeks in Newfoundland. Ed said, "Don't look at me, I've done my part for the world." He had no intention of leaving home for any reason, and certainly not to spend two weeks with a bunch of 'Mainlanders.' But after he heard me speak that night, he told his wife on the way home, "Maybe I'll go for a week." The truth of the matter is that Ed had another motivation. His daughter, Kari, is a cancer survivor.

When he joined us in Clarenville, we had no idea of what lay ahead for the two of us. If there is one thing that Ed brought to our team, it was a solid dose of Newfoundland humour. I began to think that if there was a Mr. Newfoundland who represented the fun, the dedication, the hard work and the love of his province – Ed was probably it. He liked to remind us he was a Newfoundlander and one who'd been born before Newfoundland had decided to let the rest of Canada join them in 1949. We were to learn that was a sentiment shared by people across the province who'd been born prior to Newfoundland joining Confederation.

If Ed was proud of his home province, Newfoundland could be proud of Clarenville. The people of that area donated $7,500 to *Jesse's Journey.*

The Trans-Canada Highway is the lifeline of Newfoundland. The ferry from North Sydney, Nova Scotia to Argentia, in eastern Newfoundland is only a seasonal run. So when winter holds the province in its icy grip, everything that's bound for St. John's arrives in Port Aux Basques, and then has to be trucked almost the entire thousand kilometres across the province. The fleet of transport trucks hauling everything from pencils and pantyhose to milk and motor oil, is constantly on the move along the Trans-Canada Highway.

The transport trucks making the cross-province run soon become a familiar sight. And as word of *Jesse's Journey* continues to spread across the province, truckers begin responding with a friendly blast of the air horn as they pass by.

Along a stretch of the Trans-Canada Highway that has a section of wide shoulder, a trucker pulls his rig to the side of the road and climbs down from the cab to shake hands and to make a donation. He has heard on the radio about a father who is walking across Canada to help raise money for research and he wants to contribute. He too is a father, and he understands why I'm on the road.

As he shakes my hand, my eye is drawn to the silver cross around his neck. It's bigger than any cross I have ever seen anyone wearing and I just have to ask about it. It's about three inches from top to bottom, and has a small diamond in its centre. There are four small coloured stones, two on each side of the diamond. When I ask about the significance of the stones he tells me the diamond is from his mother's wedding ring and that the four coloured stones are his children's birthstones.

It's just a brief meeting at the side of the road, and in a couple of minutes, he begins shifting through the gears and his tractor-trailer starts moving. Soon his truck becomes just another of the hundreds of rigs moving back and forth across the province. It has been another of those moments when two parents have reached out to each other.

Ten days into the *Journey* and moving farther away from the Atlantic Ocean, the rain and snow disappear, replaced by a brilliant blue sky. As I head north along the Trans-Canada Highway toward Terra Nova Provincial Park, I estimate the visibility to be about 50 km, and in the distance I can see snow-capped mountains. Newfoundland has decided to put on a show.

Despite the stiff breeze, there are smiles on the faces of the people in the escort van that follows along behind me like a shadow at five kilometres per hour. For the first time since arriving in Newfoundland, the road crew can roll down the windows and soak up the sunshine. The atmosphere in the motor home seems to change as nature teases us with a serious hint of spring.

But it's still early April and, despite the smiles and upbeat feeling among the road crew, I'm certain we will still face some hostile weather before we move on to the mainland. I set my sights on Glovertown, next up on the map of Newfoundland. I don't mind leaving Terra Nova National Park behind. Some of its monster hills have taken me more than an hour to climb. It's now just over a week since we left St. John's and my body has been giving me less-than-subtle reminders that I really am 52. But even with that knowledge and nursing the aches and pains, I feel confident that the months of training will get me through the *Journey*. I know there is no other way I can do something that will have such a lasting impact and help kids like Jesse.

Glovertown is really the first chance I get to take stock of how we are doing. By now, we have just enough history on the road that I can actually gauge how we are functioning. Considering that the road crew is still getting comfortable with everything that has to be done to keep us moving, things are running pretty smoothly. Many nights the only things to record in my journal are the routine events of another day on the road. On the day we reach Glovertown, the highlights include Trish finally spotting a moose, the laundry getting folded, the groceries being purchased and, for the first time, hearing

148

songbirds in the silence along the Trans-Canada Highway. Spring is finally coming to Newfoundland.

In Glovertown the road team is scattered in different locations – or at least as scattered as you can get in a small town in Newfoundland. I'm at the Lilac Inn bed-and-breakfast, operated by Doug and Linda Churchill. We actually met the Churchills earlier on the road when we were having lunch at one of the many Irving Stations across the province.

For the first time since we had left 'Kilometre 0' in St. John's, Glovertown makes me think of suppertime back home. Instead of a restaurant, we are sharing conversation and the story of *Jesse's Journey* with the Churchills, the Mayor of Glovertown and representatives of the Lions Club and the Women's Institute. I will soon learn how important the Women's Institute is in Newfoundland.

There are bowls of steaming-hot mashed potatoes, lima beans baked in molasses and all the goodies we can imagine being passed up and down the big dining room table. Wondering what they are having for supper tonight in London reminds me that it's time to make a phone call back home.

Bits of news, which confirm we are heading in the right direction, reach us each day. In Glovertown, the big news comes from Mike who reports that Irving Oil has agreed to provide us with free gas and propane across Newfoundland. It will be the only province where that kind of sponsorship will happen.

Joey Smallwood, Newfoundland's first premier, who liked to refer to himself in the 1960's as Canada's "only living Father of Confederation", was born in the little town of Gambo. The town which lies at the edge of the water that leads northeast out into Bonavista Bay, looks like it was probably a busy little place on the old roadway before the Trans-Canada Highway let travellers whisk on by without stopping.

149

At the end of the day we double back to Gambo where we are guests at a church supper. There are times when it is very quiet along the highway, with the exception of noise from passing transport trucks. That's when I find it difficult to figure out how, especially at night, more than a hundred people have heard about us and show up to squeeze into a church basement, share a pot luck supper, and hear the story of *Jesse's Journey*.

There are plenty of times walking along the road when I wonder if anyone knows I'm out here. And there are times in the evening when I bow my head and listen to someone saying grace in yet another church basement or another community hall, and I give thanks that these generous people do know I'm here and why I'm here.

At the end of another day on the road as we drive on through the darkness towards Gander, wet snowflakes are falling and with the windshield wipers keeping time, I close my eyes to try and catch a nap. I hear on the radio in the van that Paul McCartney's wife, Linda, has died of cancer. She was only 56 years old. It just isn't right.

In the morning, as we will do every day, all across the country, we drive back out to where we've left our marker the day before. The *Journey's* integrity rests on our always picking up where we left off. Every day we have to budget time depending on the distance we have to drive, either forward or backward, to reach the correct start point on the highway. It's another of the little things you might never really think about, but it's something we have to do every day. Mornings become a routine pattern once everybody has checked in onboard the motor home. Mike Woodward checks the batteries on the portable radios assigned to each van. Batteries don't do well in cold weather and keeping them charged is a constant problem. Trish gives out the road assignments, designating who will be out on the road with me for the first part of the day. Bevin gives me a rundown on what radio interviews we'll be doing and when. Most of the interviews are done by portable phone as I continue to log distance along the highway. The van drivers check to see that their vehicles are fueled up, the flashing lights are all working and that we have plenty of water on board. It's surprising how dehydrated you can become even when the weather is cold and wet.

Following breakfast there's a quick cleanup. We are very careful about our use of water, which is a precious commodity on the road. There is still the risk of freezing temperatures, and that has put an end to any hope of having running water on board the motor home during the Newfoundland leg of the *Journey*. This means we have to make do with the two red plastic five-gallon containers we are carrying. Running water will have to wait until we reach the mainland. And we know that when the cold weather sets in later in the year in British Columbia, we will have to shut the water down again, and get the plastic containers out once more.

Reaching the start point for the day, we sometimes have to get the motor home and the escort vehicles turned around to start heading west. After completing some stretching exercises and coordinating positions with our RCMP escort, it's time to get to work.

By the end of the day we are officially in Gander, 'The Crossroads of the World.' I have been making good time throughout the day, unlike on the previous day. I ask Ed Coxworthy to check my stride from the escort van behind me, and I am right in the groove I want – 125 steps to the minute. The day before I had covered 33 km on the highway, although my pedometer read only 31, an indication how short my steps had been walking into the very strong headwinds.

In Gander, we receive a $500 donation from the VOCM Cares Foundation. The St. John's-based radio station, with repeaters across the province, continues to be our main radio link with the people of Newfoundland.

In the gathering dark of the late afternoon, I finish my distance for the day. Gary Alan Price, who has flown out from London to join us,

151

rides with Ed and me back along the highway to a gravel road. The rough-cut road, directly across from the raised lights at the end of the runway at Gander Airport, marks the entrance to the 'Silent Witness Memorial.' The memorial marks where 256 members of the 101st U.S. Airborne Division, heading home from overseas for Christmas, were killed when their aircraft took off December 12th, 1985 after a refueling stop in Gander.

There is a light snow falling in the eerie silence that surrounds us. Directly in line with the north-south runway at Gander Airport is a huge clearing stripped of trees, exposing three levels of rock descending toward Lake Gander. The ill-fated plane, heavily loaded with fuel, came down in what was then a heavily-wooded area, hitting the top of the first hill and then the two levels of rock below.

The bald area of the crash site is dotted with little stone cairns, some with small wooden crosses tipped over by the wind. Draped from some are bits of ribbon or the remains of flowers, under a light dusting of snow. Faded and weathered pictures of wives, girlfriends, parents and children are at the base of many of the crosses.

The U.S. Airborne Division's Memorial to those who died in the crash is a larger-than-life bronze statue which depicts a member of the U.S. Airborne in full battle uniform, holding the hands of a little girl and a little boy, who are standing on either side of him. The children are holding olive branches in their hands. It's a very moving piece with an incredible amount of detail in the sculpture, and the faces of the soldier and the two little children are haunting.

It's starting to snow a little harder and it's getting dark as we turn to leave. I can't help but wonder what might have happened if that plane had cleared that first hill. Would it have made it as far as the lake, which was only a short distance away? We'll never know. It's time to move on.

In the morning I wake up in the dark to the sound of a snowplough clearing the parking lot. Opening the curtains and wiping the moisture from the window, I'm looking out at 10 centimetres of fresh snow. For the first time since leaving St. John's, I'm not certain we will be able to get started. And even if we do, I'm not sure we'll be able to put in a full day on the road if the snow keeps falling.

The snow is heavy and wet, and the spray from passing vehicles makes for a miserable and sloppy morning. When the snowplough goes by, it scoops up a carpet of white and curls it into a wall of watery slush at the side of the road. The driver gives us a friendly honk of the horn and the snowplough grows smaller and smaller as it moves off into the distance. With the shoulder scraped clean, the footing immediately becomes more solid.

By midday the sun has replaced the cloud cover of morning. Every now and then the silence along the road is broken as tree branches, sagging under the weight of the overnight snowfall, spring free when the heat of the sun loosens huge clumps of snow, which in turn fall onto the snow below with dull thuds.

A young woman and her husband stop to make a donation, on their way to St. John's from Cambridge, Ontario. I'm impressed that they stop because they are heading to St. John's for the funeral of the woman's father. I give her a hug and remind her that there will be happier days ahead. I didn't know what else to say, but I think about their long drive across the island, and the time she will probably spend thinking about her dad as they drive on to a destination that is bound to bring sadness. Such thoughts only make their donation mean that much more.

Late in the day, Newfoundland's weather turns nasty, so quickly it is as if someone has pushed the switch from 'off' to 'on.' The wind is blowing hard when a man in a truck stops to make a donation. He asks me to sign his autograph book and I feel as if the book is going to blow away before I can sign my name and thank him.

Events unfold constantly along the roadway. At one moment you're at the high point on the roller coaster, while the next moment you're plunging to a low point. And always there is something to learn from both the highs and the lows. It gives me a great boost when people who've heard me speak in a church basement, community hall or service club the night before come out to the road the next day. Through my experience on the road when I pushed Jesse across Ontario, I can tell by looking at them that they've come to see for themselves. They're curious to see this 52 year old father who is so determined to make a difference, that he is willing to walk the entire distance across Canada. In turn, that 52 year old father is just as thrilled to get the chance to meet those youngsters who are like his own son, for it is them and their families who fuel his fire of commitment to complete the thousands of kilometres that lie ahead.

On our final night in Gander we are the guests of a group of firefighters who give us a tour of their firehall before presenting us with a cheque. When we hear about the capabilities of the new trucks, and the history of their one almost-antique truck, our conversation swings around to who had been where on the night of the Airborne crash. When I meet the firefighter who had been the first to reach the site, I don't mention the crash. Although it's been 13 years since it happened, I can tell by the way he looks down and shuffles his feet that he doesn't want to talk about it.

A newspaper photographer from Gander arrives and we all smile for a formal cheque-presentation picture. I shake hands with the firefighters and thank them for their support before climbing back into the van. Gazing out into the black night as we drive back to the motel, I thought about that one firefighter and the terrible mental burden he must carry. Somehow my load seemed a little lighter.

Heading west, I have seldom seen the sunrise behind me as I walk along the Trans-Canada. On the morning we leave Gander and head toward our next stop at Lewisporte, it's like watching the curtain go up on a spectacular set. It is still very cold as daylight pushes aside the night to reveal the highway that sweeps downhill and disappears into the snow-capped mountains that sparkle in the early morning sun.

It's midday when I meet Michael Roberts from Bishop's Falls. He's everything an 8 year old is supposed to be with one exception. Like Jesse, Michael has DMD. Michael and his mom and dad, Mary and Dave, are the first Duchenne family I have met along the road. At lunch we are guests of the manager at the Irving Restaurant outside Bishop's Falls. I have to smile to myself as I watch Michael's eyes light up when he finds out he can have anything he wants for lunch. A couple of minutes later this little kid almost disappears behind a huge hamburger, a giant plate of french fries, and a milk shake. As Michael's mom helps him with the ketchup, I chat with his father. Like so many Newfoundlanders, Dave is unemployed and the family faces a four-hour drive into St. John's to get treatment for Michael. The hardships of life in rural Newfoundland are apparent almost every day, and it's difficult to imagine the struggle of dealing with a life-threatening disease in such a remote place.

Dave and Mary aren't the kind of people who complain about their lot in life. Instead, they have organized donations for *Jesse's Journey,* and as we walk through Bishop's Falls with a police escort, Michael is sitting up high in the front seat of a big red fire truck, which is making plenty of noise with its siren. As we make our way through town, the people who have very little to give, give everything they can.

Sometimes when we think of philanthropy, the picture that comes to mind is corporate giving, and we flash to the picture of a huge cardboard cheque being presented. It happens all the time, and thank goodness it does, because without those donations charities would suffer. But corporations have budgets. People along the road don't often have well laid-out budgets. They just see a need and they respond. Like the grassroots people of Bishop's Falls, they reach into their pockets and give. That's real philanthropy in action.

155

When our parade completes its loop through Bishop's Falls, it's time to get back onto the Trans-Canada Highway. As I lean over to say goodbye to my new friend Michael, he shakes my hand as he gives me an envelope with a cheque inside. Then he reaches up and puts his arms around my neck and gives me a big squeeze. He's only eight years old and yet it was as if he knows what the future holds and this is his way of saying, "Keep going John. Help us find an answer. All we want is a chance to grow up like other kids." I hold him for just a moment before his dad lifts him up to head back home. Dave thanks me for what I'm doing and as I turn away, I wonder if I'll ever see them again. Maybe it doesn't matter. What really counts is raising the dollars to fund research to find the answers for kids like Michael.

Later, what had started out as a majestic day turns ugly. The wind comes up and a stinging combination of rain and sleet is biting at my face for the final hour on the road, and yet people are still stopping to make donations. It's almost dark up ahead, when a car pulls to the side of the road. The driver, who leaves his emergency lights flashing, gets out of his car and comes back to meet me in the rain and the spray from passing vehicles. The wind blows his trench coat stiffly against his body, and sends the collar whipping up and down and striking his face. He had heard me speak at a reception in Gander. And here, in the middle of what is probably one of the most miserable hours I have spent on the road, he hands me a cheque for $500. He too has a son who suffers from Duchenne. If he has tears in his eyes I can't tell because the storm is lashing us where we stand in the headlights of the escort van. As we shake hands in the rain, it's the second time today that a father who understands exactly what I am doing has reached out to me. Without saying anything more he turns, walks back to his car and drives off. I know I will likely never see him again.

By suppertime we are in Lewisporte, north of the Trans-Canada Highway and tucked into the south end of the Bay of Exploits. Lewisporte is the Newfoundland departure point for the ferry that makes the 35-hour journey to Labrador.

Arriving in Lewisporte, I must have been quite a sight. Soaked to the skin and dripping water on the carpet, I shake hands with the dignitaries who are on hand at the town hall. We're all welcomed to Lewisporte by the sea cadet marching band and even though it's cold, wet and miserable outside, the town hall is packed. Everywhere I look, I see the smiling faces of parents and kids. Tired and wet, I speak for ten minutes about how kids everywhere will benefit from research.

Several groups present cheques and knowing we are still in the early days of the walk across Canada, I think to myself that if this is what I have to do every day to reach our goal, I'll gladly do it.

Our schedule has us at the Women's Institute in Lewisporte for supper. It isn't the first time we have been hosted by this fascinating group. After spending hours on the road each day, sometimes with very little response, at suppertime we often find ourselves guests of a Women's Institute. It amazes me how well organized and powerful they are. I have the feeling that if the Women's Institute in Newfoundland ever fields candidates, they will probably win enough seats to become the government.

Arriving in Lewisporte, I am still soaking wet so Trish brings me some dry clothes from the motor home. Trish is aware of the need to make sure that I don't get bogged down with a cold. That would really throw a wrench into things. It's a logistical nightmare trying to keep a project of this size moving day after day, meeting deadlines at towns and villages along the route. The last thing we would want to report to the home team in London is that we have lost a day.

Supper is served upstairs by the Women's Institute, which shares the second floor of the building with the town's Heritage Museum. I end up shedding all the wet clothing (everything I was wearing) in the empty silence of the museum under the watchful eye of a couple of mannequins dressed in period costumes. I have to laugh at the thought that there probably aren't too many Canadians being afforded the opportunity to stand naked in a museum in Newfoundland on this particular day! It's not exactly what I had planned when I got up in the morning, but it's rapidly becoming apparent that no two days on the road are likely to be the same.

About 150 Newfoundlanders provide us with another marvelous meal, and top it off with a dessert of bakeapple, the Newfoundland tradition. They then open their hearts and wallets to help *Jesse's Journey* take another giant step forward. These are people I have never met before. These are the people of Lewisporte.

The red duffel bags, that make us look like a hockey team, are loaded onto the motor home and into the vans, which are warming up in the pre-dawn stillness. To reach the marker at yesterday's finish point and our start point for today, we face a 55 km drive. The marker routine is to tie some fluorescent tape to a guardrail or a signpost at the edge of the road, and then reset the motor home's odometer to zero for the trip either backward or forward to wherever we are spending the night. Then in the morning we note the distance and set the odometer at zero before driving the same distance until we find our marker reflected in the headlights. This is our longest trip so far to reach our start point. From the front passenger's seat of the motor home, the headlights reveal nothing other than snow-covered trees and a long stretch of black highway. By nightfall we will be in Grand Falls-Windsor and halfway across Newfoundland. Walking the highway toward Grand Falls-Windsor, my friend Gary Alan Price joins me on the road. He had flown out from London to be part of the road team for a few days, and this is his final day with us before heading home. I'm looking forward to hearing what he has to say about his time in Newfoundland.

It's funny how we sometimes go through the course of our days spending so much time looking at computer screens, reading reports and memos, and answering telephone calls. Our conversations throughout the day are usually focused on work. Then television often dominates our evenings at home, and real conversation, where we exchange thoughts and ideas with others, seems well down on our list of priorities.

When you're on the road for seven or eight hours a day, you have a lot of time to listen to the people who are taking turns walking with you. You get to know them in a way you probably wouldn't have under different circumstances. The surface conversation is gone in a hurry, and it's then that you get the chance to learn about what really motivates people. That's a very rich experience.

Gary and I were deep in conversation as we walked along one of the loneliest sections of the Trans-Canada Highway. Hour after hour, there was nothing but trees on either side of us. Then in the distance we saw a small bridge and a sign, presumably with the name of the river that passed beneath the bridge. We still had more than a kilometre to walk before we would reach the bridge and that sign, the first printed word we had seen in about two hours. We resumed our conversation and the next thing we knew, we were a couple of hundred yards beyond the bridge and the sign when I turned to Gary and said, "What was the name of that river?" Gary laughed and said, "I don't know, I didn't read its sign!" We were so engrossed in what we'd been talking about that neither one of us had looked at the sign, even though it was the only thing for us to read since we'd started walking. That's conversation!

At noon hour I speak to a joint meeting of the Rotary and Kiwanis Clubs in Grand Falls-Windsor. What makes me happy about this stop is the fact that two service clubs have come together for the greater good, reflecting what I have been saying for a long time about the research community collaborating.

I'm a big believer in not re-inventing the wheel, and I feel that rule should be applied to research. I can't see the value of two laboratories doing exactly the same work, and for that reason I have always urged the partnership of scientific efforts in order to benefit those whose only hope lies in research.

The CBC tapes my after-lunch speech in Grand Falls-Windsor and I receive a standing ovation from the audience. It gives me a good feeling as we make the trip by van back to where I left the road. The meeting means I have to skip my after-lunch nap, which is an important part of my daily routine. I guess that's OK, because at least a lot more people now know what *Jesse's Journey* is all about.

The road team is scattered in a number of different locations for the overnight stop in Grand Falls-Windsor. I am at a bed-and-breakfast with a real country feel about it. The lady who runs the business has eleven horses and also operates a riding school. As we pull up to the gate there's a stop sign, which says, "Whoa Partner!" The sign on the fence where the horses are enclosed proclaims, "Please do not feed fingers to the horses!" Just up the road, I am about to see a real life sign of the times. Badger, Newfoundland is our next stop.

On a sunny day in St. John's, the double-decker bus ride takes visitors to the top of Signal Hill to look out over the rugged coast of Newfoundland. Then southeast from the mouth of the harbour is Cape Spear, the easternmost point of Canada. Standing in the shadow of Cabot Tower at the top of Signal Hill you can gaze out over the Atlantic toward Ireland.

As the tour winds through the oldest parts of St. John's, you can see the brightly painted 'jelly bean' houses that stand side by side, lining the streets that surround the harbour. These colourful houses, with their hanging baskets of flowers, have come to represent St. John's in the pictures that fill the art shops along Duckworth and Water Streets. On that kind of sunny day, Newfoundland is all about whale watching, boat excursions to see the icebergs or the puffins and visits to the outdoor cafés and restaurants. No one talks about the people of little towns like Badger, and their ordinary day-to-day struggles.

Badger doesn't reflect the usual tourist's view of Newfoundland. It's about as close to the centre of the province as you can get by road.

In the snow outside Deer Lake, Newfoundland, on the 28th of April 1998, I faced another 268 days on the road.

On rainy days in Newfoundland, I was always thankful for the flashing lights of the continuous escort provided by the RCMP.

It's also about as far from saltwater as you can get in this province. Before the railway tracks were torn up at the end of the 1980's, the town was a bustling logging community. Now Badger struggles economically with as much as 70 percent of the town's 1000 people on social assistance of some kind. Most of Badger's residents work for Abitibi-Price, either in the forest or at the mill in Grand Falls-Windsor. While spruce trees in the area are earmarked for the mill at Grand Falls-Windsor, the people of Badger are allowed to cut the birch, aspen and tamarack for firewood. Some of the tired-looking buildings in town date back to more prosperous times, and yet inside the town's proud little houses are some of the warmest hearts you could ever hope to meet.

When *Jesse's Journey* reaches the edge of Badger, men from the local volunteer fire department are waiting with not just one, but two fire trucks to provide an escort. Fire engines are a major part of celebrations in small communities all across Canada. Thousands of hockey players probably have memories of a ride on the fire engine in their hometown after winning a championship.

It's a cold spring morning, the kind of day where you can see your breath in the air. Smoke is rising from the chimneys of the little wooden houses. From behind curtained front windows and the warmth inside their homes, people smile and wave at the passing parade.

Even with the sirens of the Badger Fire Department splitting the morning silence, few people venture outdoors. Donations will be hard to come by here.

While I'm making my way to the public school, a 93 year old man stops by the motor home to make a donation because he wants to help. He has only a dollar to give and that's what he donates. I'm just sorry I don't get to meet him. If every Canadian will donate a dollar to research, then we will be able to leave a legacy of more than a million dollars a year, every year. Perhaps the old man's visit to the motor home is a preview of the kind of people I am about to meet.

There are just over 80 students at Avoca Public School in Badger, which enrolls grades one to nine. Avoca is an Indian word that means 'the meeting of three rivers.' The kids at the school are just like school kids everywhere, full of life and wanting to help. When the teachers heard that Badger would be one of the stops I would be making, they wrote a song. The result is very special as the kids in the junior grades sing "hello" to welcome me to Badger. It seems true all across Newfoundland, that the people might not have a lot of money but they all have the gift of song, and for that I think they are richer than most Canadians.

Officially welcoming us to the town, a young girl presents me with a cheque on behalf of all of the students at the school. It is 127 of the hardest-earned dollars we've received as I've made my way across the province.

I feel like the Pied Piper as I leave the school. All of the students join me in a walk through town as I make the loop back out to the Trans-Canada Highway. Walking along together, there is one little girl who never leaves my side. She is being quiet and every time I look down, her big blue eyes are looking up at me. Waving goodbye to the kids as they turn to head back to school, my new little friend looks up at me and in a very shy voice she says, "I'm going to be an astronomer when I grow up." Crouching down beside her in the snow and pointing to the sky I say to her, "Every night, you look up at the stars, because that's where your dreams are, and I hope they all come true."

Back on the highway in the afternoon, before turning and heading back into Badger for the night, I have a lot of time to think about the people of this little Newfoundland town and the lives they live. The surroundings don't reflect the spirit of the people of Badger, where the number one priority is taking care of each other. I feel this is about as far as I can possibly be from a life of four-lane traffic, cell phones, fast food, and too much noise.

At night, the 'Firettes,' a group that consists mostly of firefighters' wives, have a roast beef dinner waiting for us at the firehall. Just after the fire department was formed in 1961, the 'Firettes' hoisted the fund-raising banner and they've been hard at work ever since. The firehall is a beehive of activity when we arrive. It's nice to come in from the cold to savour the wonderful aromas coming from the kitchen.

We spend the night on World War II-vintage cots that have been set up in the firehall. There are times when I roll over that I'm almost certain my rear end is hitting the floor. But I know this is the best these people have and they are proud to share it with us. And I'm just as proud to have met them.

With my head on the pillow, thousands of kilometres from home, I'm grateful to these kind Newfoundlanders, but tonight I'm missing Sherene and the boys. The impact of having met the people of Badger is weighing heavily on my mind, and before trying to sleep I write in my journal that in Badger, Newfoundland, 'We have stared poverty in the face, and it has smiled back.' In the morning we will be moving into the most remote part of this province, and another test of my stamina and commitment to the *Journey* is just ahead.

After breakfast, we pose for pictures as the motor home and escort vehicles are warming up. We sign autographs, receive pins and say goodbye to the good people of Badger. Then it's back onto the Trans-Canada Highway where the road is now a little more dangerous. The wide shoulder is gone, and now the truck traffic seems that much closer.

From Badger, the Trans-Canada Highway turns north toward Springdale, which is tucked into one of the many inlets that lead to Notre Dame Bay. There is no view of the ocean in this part of the

163

province, and in the rain it's depressing. Along the narrow road is a large area destroyed by a forest fire about three years ago. When you live in the city and the closest you come to seeing a forest fire consists of television pictures, you can't imagine the destruction. The scars from this fire are still visible and no new trees have been planted. The day is a bit confusing as police cars shuffle back and forth so that officers can attend court. The officers tell me that most of the cases involve domestic disputes. By the end of the day we've had five different RCMP officers providing an escort. The good news is that whenever I look back, there's an RCMP vehicle behind me with its roof lights flashing. And in the big picture, that's going to help to keep researchers working in their labs.

There are few donations along this remote stretch of highway in central Newfoundland. There's a man loading a logging truck, who waves from off in the distance. He stops what he's doing and drives up to the road to make a donation. There is a group of little boys, who look cute, dressed in their Beaver uniforms as they wait to meet us at the turnoff to Springdale and to present me with the toonies they have collected. They're smiling, excited and proud to be helping other kids. And there's a man in a pick-up truck who drives by before turning around and coming back to make a donation. He shakes my hand and says he wants to help. There are tears in his eyes as he tells Trish and me that he lost his daughter just a month ago. When I grip his hand, I know I don't have to say anything. I just say "thank you."

I never get used to these moments when strangers find a way to release their feelings. As the pick-up truck eases back onto the highway and slowly pulls away, Trish and I walk on for several minutes without saying anything. If I had forgotten why I am here, I have just been reminded.

Long before I reach Springdale, a town I had never heard of a month ago, people have literally been stopping traffic to raise money. The Kinette ladies have organized a 'boot toll' and raised almost $1,000 for *Jesse's Journey*. Springdale is a town of just 2500 people, and less than a month ago, they had never heard of John or Jesse Davidson.

Dinner in Springdale, moose meat and scalloped potatoes, is followed by the Kinettes' presentation of a donation. Then a lady who has left her home on a rainy Sunday afternoon makes a donation on behalf of Springdale's Royal Canadian Legion membership. Newfoundlanders have a special place in their hearts for people who make sacrifices. Legion members have never forgotten those young people from across Canada whose last steps on Canadian soil were in Newfoundland before they crossed the Atlantic to fight for freedom. So many never returned.

There are times that if you don't laugh, you'll probably cry. Just beyond Springdale, Murphy's Law hits with a vengeance. We have entered one of those geographic pockets we've nicknamed 'Never-Never Land' or 'Cell Phone Hell' depending on how many problems we are up against. Without cell phones, we can't contact the rest of the world, and we have to get to a 'land' line in order to do radio interviews or talk to the home team in London. This makes for a lot of jockeying along the road to keep our time and distance accurate. To complete this major day for minor problems, Bevin's computer isn't working and Mike Woodward is having a tough time getting the walkie-talkie batteries to hold a charge in the cold weather. We've been promised that the scenery ahead is spectacular and that the road is flat. At least it isn't snowing as we make the turn toward Port Aux Basques and the ferry to mainland Canada.

On the last day of April, after what feels like three days in the wilderness, we finally reach Deer Lake. The weather alternates between rain and snow, both of which swirl in every direction. For three solid days we are constantly soaking wet and we consider ourselves lucky if half a dozen vehicles a day stop along the highway to make a donation. I remembered Darryl Sittler of the Toronto Maple Leafs telling me in 1995, "It's real easy when the television cameras are there and everybody wants to talk to you. It's when you're all alone in the middle of nowhere and it's pouring rain that measures your courage."

In a perfect world, Mike Woodward would drive the motor home seven or eight kilometres down the road where he'd stop and get fruit and tea ready for the first break of the day. In Newfoundland, the Trans-Canada Highway doesn't always lend itself to finding someplace where you can get a ten metre motor home completely off the road. Mike has developed a sharp eye for spotting places which are both convenient and safe. After the break Mike packs up and moves the motor home ahead, and the cycle begins again as we head toward the lunch break.

One of the thankless tasks is trying to figure out how many people will be on board for lunch. Sometimes our RCMP escort has to leave to go to court and sometimes there are unexpected visitors like reporters and camera people, who are always welcomed aboard. Although things are sometimes a little hectic at noon hour, no one ever leaves the motor home hungry.

Since I have to rest after lunch each day, I don't want to be lying down worrying that several tons of transport truck might be about to come through the motor home bedroom. Mike always does everything he can to make sure that I have a comfort zone in that regard. Sometimes it becomes a game of cat-and-mouse, as Mike will have the motor home tucked into the end of an abandoned laneway, partially hidden in the trees. With very little noise, these are great spots for getting a good rest.

Heading southwest toward Port Aux Basques, our next stop is Pasadena. Things are looking up as the sun is shining and Newfoundland's gorgeous scenery is again on display. The weather is now warmer and our clothing has finally dried out. The legs that have been struggling through snow are again starting to pump like pistons as the kilometres fall behind us. We are in the home stretch across Newfoundland.

Jesse has used a wheelchair since he was 12 years old. The cherished pictures from the years when he could still walk are locked away safely in my mind. I see Jesse walking home from grade school carrying the artwork he would show us at suppertime. I see him walking on the beach in the summer, standing at attention in his Cub uniform, trying his best to kick a soccer ball and leaning on my shoulder for a family picture. And every time I look at the faces of school children, like the kids in Pasadena, I replay those pictures over and over again in slow motion, because I want to be able to hang on to them forever. I saved every image I could with as much detail as possible, because I knew the clock was running out, and I guess I knew that a day would come when Jesse could no longer walk. It's something most parents never think about. Some of them chew their kids out for not doing better at baseball or hockey when there are parents like me who would give anything just to be able to see their son walk up the laneway.

In Pasadena, the public school is high on a hill overlooking the road below. The kids have been let out of class and they've formed a long line in front of the school. They are cheering and making lots of noise as *Jesse's Journey* makes its way through town. I get an extra workout as I climb the hill and shake hands with every one of the students. Looking into the eyes of these children, the smiling faces so full of life, the replay camera in my mind is flashing pictures from another time and another place.

Just outside Pasadena there is a young boy of about 11 waiting at the side of the road with his dad. He wants to give us $5 of his own money. When I was eleven, $5 would have seemed like a huge amount of money to me. The youngster asks me if I will autograph his hat. I don't know who has the bigger smile, the son or the father whose pride is written in every line of his face. Seeing the young boy standing with his dad takes me back again to when Jesse was his age. It's time to move on.

There's no time for a midday rest as we make a signpost our road marker before driving into Corner Brook for a noon hour luncheon with the Rotary Club. We'll return to the marker in the afternoon.

Sometimes I wonder what members of service clubs are thinking as they head off to their weekly meetings. Do they ask each other, 'What the heck is *Jesse's Journey?* Who is John Davidson? What's this all about?' I never assume that they know anything about *Jesse's Journey*. And whether there are 20 or 200 people in the group, I do my best to tell our story.

There are days when our road team must look like a ragged lot when we arrive at these functions. Quite often our hosts seat us at a table for special guests and there we will be, sometimes wet, sometimes sweaty or windblown with our *Jesse's Journey* outfits making us stand out in a room full of men in shirts and ties, and women in business suits. Each time that I stand up to speak, I find myself looking at an audience largely made up of business leaders who are used to making tough decisions. Telling them the story of *Jesse's Journey* always seems to hit a nerve, and I have watched businessmen who've been laughing over dessert and coffee suddenly become silent, sometimes even removing their glasses, exposing red-rimmed eyes. There are women in the audiences who reach into their purses for a handkerchief. All I'm doing is telling them about the courage of youngsters like Jesse. I never want their tears. I want them to take action and to help the Foundation we have created.

Back on the highway, having missed my noon hour rest, I'm very tired when I finish my daily regime. It's been a long day and there is still another appearance to make. Riding in the van as we head back to our motel, I try to sleep for a few minutes though I have asked Ed to stop when we reach the house of the young boy who had given us the $5. The boy and his father are busy working in the yard and when I give him the hat I have been wearing since leaving St. John's, his eyes light up like it's Christmas morning. Then I sleep in the van until we reach our motel.

The lights of the outports scattered along the coast sparkle in the dark, linking the little villages together. Night time in the small towns and villages in Newfoundland isn't like night time in any other part of the country. In the cities, night time for a lot of people is television time. In Newfoundland, it's 'each-other' time. Tonight's each-other time is at the firehall in Pasadena.

The sound of guitars, a stand-up bass and a mandolin mix with the clear, powerful voices of The Sharecroppers. The three singing schoolteachers from Pasadena have performed all over the island and around the world. Neighbours chat over coffee and sandwiches as Bevin captures the magic on videotape for one of his weekly reports that will be aired back home in London. There are young girls in kilts doing an impromptu Highland fling, and everywhere you look there are smiling faces, fingers drumming on table tops and toes tapping on the floor as people sing the lyrics to "Fogo, Twillingate, Morton's Habour, All around the circle." After speaking to the people of Pasadena about the *Journey* across Canada, there's another Newfoundland memory to be stored away as The Sharecroppers talk me into doing a solo. And, as a mainlander struggles his way through "I'se the boy that builds the boats" there's a lot of laughter. This is night time in Newfoundland.

On the first day of May we are just outside Corner Brook and looking up at Marble Mountain. Its pink marble, shipped all over the world, can be seen from the Trans-Canada Highway, which makes a dramatic sweep upward as it swings high above Newfoundland's second largest city. Besides its distinctive marble, Corner Brook boasts one of the largest pulp and paper mills in the world.

There are always frustrations along the road, and as I work up a sweat struggling to climb to the top of the hill at Corner Brook, I run into one of them. Using a cell phone to do an interview with CBC Radio in Corner Brook, it doesn't take me long to realize Bevin's hand-delivered media kit has been lost in the shuffle. I know the interview isn't going very well when the announcer first thinks the project is called 'Jesse's Dream.' From that point, things just get worse. Not only does he think I'm running across Canada, he thinks

169

I'm going in the other direction and finishing in St. John's. I try to be patient and do my best to straighten things out, since there is nothing to be gained by being upset. The announcer already looks foolish. There's no point in both of us looking that way. Turning off the phone and giving it back to Bevin, I just shake my head and remind myself it's just one interview.

The highest point on the Trans-Canada Highway at Corner Brook provides a panoramic view looking toward Frenchman's Cove and the Bay of Islands. There's a plume of smoke from the pulp and paper mill in the distance, rising straight up in the morning air. On the water, Canadian Forces HMCS Nipigon is just making her way into the harbour. From this height, the frigate looks like a toy floating in a bathtub. When I reach the very top of the hill, a team of people from the Dominion Store in Corner Brook catches up with us to make a donation of $1,500. That makes the climb worthwhile.

As Corner Brook fades into the distance, life on the edge of the road once again settles into a quiet time of logging distance as we move southwest. Although we won't be there for a couple of days, our next major stop is Stephenville, Newfoundland.

At the end of the day, the RCMP escort us back to Steady Brook, at the foot of Marble Mountain. A bagpiper leads us in to a dinner hosted by the Lions Club of Steady Brook. Although I'm starting to get anxious about finishing the Newfoundland portion of the *Journey*, there is another audience that wants to hear what *Jesse's Journey* is all about, and that's where I focus my attention. After dinner I speak about the hope that research holds for kids like Jesse. When I finish, the Lions are on their feet, and there are more donations.

Every night I am asked to speak, I do my best to make sure the audience knows I am not a doctor and that I have no medical training. I always make sure they understand that I am just one dad

170

sharing what I have learned in the years since Jesse was diagnosed with Duchenne Muscular Dystrophy. In Steady Brook, a doctor in the crowd thanks me for the information I have provided, some of which he says he was not aware of. The Lions of Steady Brook make a $500 donation.

Then, the weatherman gives us a break! Back on the Trans-Canada Highway heading toward Stephenville, the sun is shining and for the first time since the *Journey* began, it is definitely warm enough to put on a T-shirt. It's great to feel the warmth of the sun on my face.

A truck driver who stops to make a donation tells me he has passed me about 50 times. That is very important because if he has passed me that often, I'm pretty certain that a lot of other truck drivers also know exactly where we are on the road, and that makes life seem just a little safer. That thought is confirmed when Bevin spends some time riding in the police cruiser with our RCMP escort.

Bevin had noticed that the RCMP cruiser was outfitted with a monitor for CB radio. When he asked the officer if the truck drivers paid much attention to *Jesse's Journey*, he was told, "Oh yeah, you guys are a hot item out here."

The RCMP officer had no sooner made that comment than the voice of a trucker crackled through the speaker in the cruiser asking, "Who the heck is that guy walking down the road?" Another trucker answered back, "That's John Davidson from London. He's walking across Canada." When the first driver responded with surprise saying, "You're shit'n me," the RCMP officer smiled a sheepish grin at Bevin as he picked up his microphone, pushed the button and said, "OK boys, let's keep it down a bit." It was all a part of life along the Trans-Canada Highway.

One of the RCMP escorts with us as we move closer to Stephenville is a young man in his mid-twenties. 'Chris' has blond hair, a brush cut and a square jaw that makes him look just that much tougher.

He tells us he is being transferred to Hopedale, Labrador, north of the 55th parallel. I'm getting a geography lesson out here on the road, because I hadn't known that Labrador is three times the size of Newfoundland. The territory he's talking about means that Chris will be one of those responsible for policing Davis Inlet, where there are about 600 residents, mostly native people. The Labrador community has a very high rate of teenage suicide and has been in the news in the past few months with the tragic stories of people dying after drinking anti-freeze and sniffing gasoline. I can't imagine how you police a place like Davis Inlet where the only way in or out is by boat or plane. There are some tax incentives and isolation pay that go with the two-year posting. It certainly sounds like it will have its share of hardship, but Chris says that taking such a posting means moving to the top of the 'preferred transfer' list at the end of the two-year period, which means you can choose where you want to be posted. It still seems like it will be a long two years. The sunshine suddenly feels a lot warmer.

The giant Abitibi-Price pulp and paper mill is the backbone of Stephenville. On the day I reach the town, the wind has been blowing hard and it's been raining all day. For the first time since leaving St. John's, as I look west, I can see the saltwater of the Atlantic Ocean, which leads into the Gulf of St. Lawrence.
To reach the town from the Trans-Canada Highway, you have to drive across the Port au Port Peninsula east of town and past the hamlets of Lourdes, Grand Jardin and De Grau that were settled originally by French seafarers.

Stephenville was once the largest U.S. air base outside of the United States. On this rainy Sunday night, driving there is like stepping back into history. If you let your mind wander, you can almost hear the ghosts of yesterday. To reach the centre of town, you have to drive across miles of tarmac and past abandoned hangars that have been aged by weather and neglect. In the headlights of the van, sheets of rain are lashing the tarmac and the windshield wipers are whipping back and forth as I squint to look out at the empty buildings with their broken windows. Letting my mind wander, I can almost hear what it must have been like when thousands of young airmen were here during World War II. There would be the sound of Jeeps being driven, amidst the constant drone of military flights taking off and landing, and showing up on radar screens in darkened rooms. The runways are now fenced off and deserted. A fighter plane mounted on a pedestal in the centre of town is one of the last reminders of a time when Stephenville, Newfoundland was of strategic military importance. But that was long ago.

Brick buildings are a rarity in Newfoundland. In Stephenville, there are two of them, both built by the United States military. They have each been sold to the town for a dollar. The brick building we are staying in also houses the College of the North Atlantic, while the second brick building has been converted to a retirement home.

Every time we see the yellow vests of Lions Club members, we begin to feel like we're home again. After unpacking our bags and driving through the rain to a pre-arranged destination, a hot meal is a welcome sight for everyone on the road crew. With chicken and salad on our plates, and bowls of steaming hot vegetables being passed back and forth, we thank the Lions for their hospitality and generosity.

And I give unspoken thanks to the behind-the-scenes team back in London, who are working in military precision with our Newfoundland volunteers, to make sure that meals and beds are always there.

Stephenville is dark, wet and dreary as we head back to our dormitory for the night. The floor we are staying on is empty except for us. I decide to work on the blisters on my feet, which are in pretty bad shape after a day of pounding the pavement in the rain. Bevin and Trish decide they will join me so we fill the sinks in the washroom with sea salt and water. Bevin shoots some videotape for his next report, which he decides he will call 'Memories of

Newfoundland.' A blister-popping party consists of soaking your feet in very hot saltwater and then pricking the bubble portion of the blister with one of the small disposable needles from the first aid kit. We sit there in silence, with steam rising from the hot water in the sinks making the tile walls even clammier than they already were. We are listening to the rain that runs down the outside of the washroom window, a black rectangle of glass with a wire grid that separates us from the night. I think all three of us might be a little homesick. It isn't exactly our finest hour on the road.

As we snap out of whatever mood we were in, I head off to bed while Bevin and Trish join a couple of the volunteers at a concert to see 'Buddy What's His Name and the Other Fellers.' When this popular and very funny Newfoundland group introduces the road crew from *Jesse's Journey*, the audience gives them a great round of applause.

When I finally put my head to the pillow, I think back to the highlight of our day, when a group of volunteer firefighters had stopped by the motor home to make a donation. They were from Burgeo, an outport on the south coast of Newfoundland, and they had made a five-hour drive in the rain to meet us. It was another of those occasions where friendship was both instant and fleeting. Climbing on board the motor home, our guests had a chance to dry out and share a hot chocolate. It was plain to see they were really enjoying themselves.

We laughed and joked and smiled for the cameras as the volunteer firefighters took still pictures and videotape to mark the day they took part in *Jesse's Journey*. They are a proud group of guys who typify the spirit of Newfoundlanders. Learning about the little outport of Burgeo, I realized this is a once in a lifetime moment. A village I have never heard of, consisting of 2500 people, has just contributed $500 to help make life better for a lot of kids they've never met. It was another act of incredible kindness. We shook hands and wished each other well and as quickly as they had arrived, they disappeared in the rain, heading home. And tonight as I drift off to sleep, their names and faces begin to fade into the blurred stream of unbelievable generosity that has followed *Jesse's Journey*.

In the morning after climbing Gallant's Hill, the largest in Newfoundland, the scenery is incredible as the Trans-Canada Highway begins its plunge down into the Codroy Valley making its way toward Port Aux Basques.

The Gulf of St. Lawrence lies off to the right, bright blue and sparkling in the afternoon sun for as far as the eye can see. In the distance to my left, there are dark green mountains separated by what look like giant inland fjords. Fog sweeps down in long wisps from the almost flat tops of the mountains, like steam from a witch's cauldron. Wildlife seems to be everywhere, transforming this part of Newfoundland into the stuff of fantasy. Across a ridge are two moose, a cow and her calf standing absolutely still, staring as we log some of our final kilometres on the island.

On the other side of the highway, there are caribou and a red fox. For the first time since leaving St. John's, I'm wearing a T-shirt and shorts as I prepare to shift gears into warmer weather. Trish brings me some water and says she wishes she had brought her camera. I tell her that I don't think a camera can really capture the beauty or the immense size of the scenery we are enjoying.

After a final night back in Stephenville, the red *Jesse's Journey* duffel bags are loaded on board the vans and the motor home. This is our last moving day on the island. By nightfall we will be staying in Port Aux Basques, our final stop in Newfoundland.

After reaching our start point for the day, we head toward Port Aux Basques. Ahead lies a 16 km stretch of the Trans-Canada Highway known as Wreck House. Entering the high wind zone, the landscape in this area is dominated by Table Mountain, which rises more than 500 metres above sea level. The winds here come rushing down the flanks of the mountain and blow across the highway. There are huge yellow signs along the road cautioning you about the danger of 200 km/h winds. The wind's effect here is the stuff of legend – trains that had to be chained to the tracks and tractor-trailers that were tossed about like match sticks. Usually, in bad conditions, drivers are cautioned to wait out the wind before venturing through the area.

It's another day that starts out wet and cold, but by the time I am 10 km down the road the temperature is 10 degrees warmer. I shed three layers of clothing in less than 30 minutes, but I have to put it all back on again as the high winds sweep down from the mountainside late in the afternoon. Despite changing shoes several times during the day, the wet weather is again causing problems for my feet, which are becoming a serious concern.

There are only a few donations along the road, the most memorable from a lady with a disabled son. She apologizes that she can only afford to donate $3.50 because she's on Social Assistance. It's always moving when I see people who have so little to give doing everything they can to help. If those with good health and the ability to help would realize how vital research is, it would make all the difference. I have to tell myself there will be lots of days when there are no donations, and not to be discouraged. A day will come when we'll reach our goal and we will be able to give a million dollars a year, every year, to research. That's the goal I never lose sight of.

On the eve of our final day on the road in Newfoundland, we are invited to supper at St. James Anglican Church. Standing on the highest piece of land in Port Aux Basques, the white wooden church with its tall spire is like a beacon welcoming those who arrive by sea. Like so many churches in Newfoundland, St. James is a rallying point with a congregation that represents 900 families in Port Aux Basques and the surrounding area. The majority of those who have joined us for supper are older, and they all want to know about Jesse and the story behind *Jesse's Journey*. After I explain our reason for being on the road they decide to take up a collection. There is a funny moment when the collection plate reaches the minister. He looks at it, smiles and says, "I gave at the office!" Then, like so many Newfoundlanders, he reaches into his pocket to help.

When I set out to cross Newfoundland almost a month ago, I knew there was a strong possibility that at times the weather would be hostile. On my final day on the road in Newfoundland, Mother Nature decides to test my endurance just one more time. A driving rain and very high winds make the final 16 km of the Trans-Canada Highway a miserable experience. Dressed in fluorescent orange rain gear, I'm in a real tug-of-war with the weather as I lean into the wind, which sometimes blows me backward a step.

Early in the afternoon, with the caution lights of the escort vehicle behind me blinking through the rain, I officially reach Port Aux Basques, Newfoundland. After almost 1000 km, the first province is behind us.

There is a huge welcome waiting at the new train station in Port Aux Basques where the legendary 'Newfie Bullet' sits parked on the last 70 metres of train track in the province. The 'Bullet' has been fully restored. The engine, which once belched steam into the clear Newfoundland air, now stands silent at the head of the rail. The red letters CNR stand out on a background of dark green and black. Behind the engine are the baggage car, complete with a gleaming hardwood floor, and the passenger cars, where thousands of travellers have sat over the years. The leather seats have been redone and the car's pot-bellied stove looks brand new.

To say the 'Newfie Bullet' is legendary is an understatement. Speed was the farthest thing from anyone's mind when they boarded the train that was to become part of Canada's history. There are tales of how the train would stop for those who wanted to pick berries or flowers before climbing back on board to continue their trip. Newfoundlanders like to tell the story about the woman who gave birth on the train. When the conductor told the woman she shouldn't

177

have been travelling in her condition, she looked him in the eye and said, "I wasn't pregnant when I got on this train!"

The day we arrive, the new station hasn't officially opened as a tourist attraction. But, with the RCMP organizing events for us in Port Aux Basques, town officials decide the arrival of *Jesse's Journey* is a good time to open the building to the public. I am really happy to see so many people turn out to welcome us. The building is jammed with school kids, Sea Cadets, and people from service clubs, including a huge contingent of men and women from the Royal Canadian Legion. The Royal Canadian Mounted Police are also on hand to say goodbye as we prepare to leave for North Sydney, Nova Scotia.

I had been told back in St. John's that "the Force would be with us," and for a month, through the wind, the snow and the rain, the RCMP has been right behind me. In making my final speech in Newfoundland, I thank the RCMP for their help while I find myself struggling to realize that I have made it all the way across the first province.

There are still some things to finish up before making the ferry trip to Nova Scotia. I call Joanne Dawson back in Summerford to thank her for all the work she and Kay Coxworthy have done to pave the way for our crossing of Newfoundland. It has been a humbling experience for me to realize that people I had never met before have gone to such lengths to make sure that night after night we were fed and had a roof over our heads.

I call talk show host Bill Rowe at VOCM back in St. John's. The station has shown a keen interest right from the time I arrived in Newfoundland. Not only has the station made a financial contribution, but also it has followed us almost daily and provided listeners with progress reports.

Saturday May 9th, and I'm up at 5:30 in the morning. While most of Port Aux Basques is still sleeping, the motor home and vans are being driven onto the ferry for the 96 nautical-mile journey to the mainland. The warm waters of the Gulf of St. Lawrence will soon separate us from the people of "The Rock". But the friends we have made in the past month will keep us tied to Newfoundland forever.

Chapter Thirteen

ON TO NEW SCOTLAND

"The soil of their native land is dear to the hearts of mankind" –
Cicero

Standing on the top deck of the *Joseph and Clara Smallwood* as we slip out of the harbour at Port Aux Basques, I watch Newfoundland disappear into the fog. While I look forward to reaching Cape Breton, I replay in my mind the pictures I have collected and stored away in my memory bank over the past month.

There was the day in Corner Brook when the lobster season opened. It was a day that was marked by one of the most memorable conversations on the island. Bevin and Ed had gone down to the docks to do some shopping because they wanted to surprise me with a lobster supper at the end of another day on the highway.

When they asked, "How much are the lobsters by the pound?" they were told, "We don't sells them by the pound, we only sells them by the each!" When they inquired, "How much are they by the each?" they were told they were "$4.50 a pound." It was a round about way of discovering both the price per pound and the fact that you had to buy the whole lobster. And so it went day after day, all across the island.

There are pictures of history, pictures of poverty and pictures of hope set in the magical charm of Canada's newest province, a province that boasts such places as Blow-me-down, Bumble Bee Bight, Hearts Content, Ireland's Eye and Little Cat Arm, along with Butter Cove, Bread Island and Empty Basket. There was the wit and wisdom of the good people of Newfoundland. There were the smiles and handshakes of encouragement from moms and dads and grandparents all across the province. These are salt-of-the earth people who listened and gave thanks that their children have the ability to row a dory, climb the rugged mountains of Newfoundland and walk the province's saltwater shores. They are parents who want all children to be able to share in that experience.

Threaded through the pictures of the day-to-day life in Newfoundland is the ever-present humour that helps dominate its harsh climate. But most of all, there is the love of life, and the singing and laughter that keeps things simple. These are the things that create a buffer between Newfoundland and the fast-paced world it seems so far removed from. As the bow of the *Smallwood* cuts its way through the water, leaving a churning wake of turquoise bubbles, I flip through all of my mental snapshots from across the island.

Our trip to the mainland comes courtesy of Marine Atlantic. Shortly after boarding, Captain Ian Delgarno invites our crew to tour the bridge to watch the activity as the *Smallwood* puts out to sea. There are five captains who man the two ferries, the *Smallwood* and the *Caribou*. There are two captains for each ship. A fifth captain is available for sick days and holidays. The *Smallwood* and the *Caribou* make the six-hour crossing of the Gulf of St. Lawrence twice a day.

Captain Ian Delgarno, who came to Canada from Aberdeen, Scotland, lives in North Sydney, Nova Scotia. He's been a ferry captain for 26 years and says he plans to 'put his feet up' in about four years. But for the moment he is in charge of a ship that can carry 1200 passengers, 370 cars and 77 tractor-trailers. In the summer months the *Smallwood* has a crew of 106. In the winter that number shrinks to 68.

Computer screens dominate the bridge of the *Smallwood*. Amidst all the technology, the one thing that seems to be missing is a steering wheel. I suppose Hollywood's influence through movies like *Titanic* has conditioned us to expect a large wooden wheel to be the centrepiece of the bridge.

The computer screens are the type you touch and they provide even more information. The captain shows us a small fishing boat on one of the screens. As he touches the screen again, more information

182

pops up, telling us the size of the vessel we can't see in the fog that surrounds the *Smallwood*, the course the fishing vessel is on, and at our current speed, the time we will pass each other. Any area of the radar screen can be isolated and enlarged to provide even more details. A similar tour of the engine room reveals more computer screens. One of the many screens is monitoring fuel consumption. The information flashing on the screen indicates that the *Smallwood* is drawing diesel fuel evenly from tanks on both sides of the ship to maintain perfect balance, and that the fuel is being eaten up at the rate of 94 litres for each nautical mile.

Lunch on board the *Smallwood* is again courtesy of Marine Atlantic as we continue to plow through the fog and the calm waters of the Gulf of St. Lawrence. I give Captain Delgarno a copy of the video story of Jesse and I crossing Ontario in 1995. While we are having lunch, I look up at the television monitor and there we are, Jesse and I slugging our way up a hill in Northern Ontario. Captain Delgarno has ordered the video played throughout the *Smallwoods'* in-house video system. In the main lounge, which is almost like a theatre with dozens of comfortable seats facing the video monitors, passengers sit quietly watching our story.

The motor home and escort vans provide major clues that the *Jesse's Journey* team is on board. Some of the passengers have seen Jesse's picture on the sides of the vehicles, smiling and waving a Canadian flag. After watching the video story, there are passengers who come over to shake hands and to make a donation.

The fog finally lifts as we arrive in North Sydney. Captain Delgarno invites all of us back up to the bridge to see the ship coming into port. The docking is a piece of precision work with a lot of tinkering at the controls to guide the ship gently into its slip. Once the lines have been secured, the bow of the *Smallwood* opens like the mouth of some giant sea monster to disembark its cargo of vehicles and people.

Under a blue sky and to the strains of bagpipes, I step onto the Nova Scotia soil of Cape Breton Island. My longtime friend from Halifax, David Meadows, and his wife, Susan, are there to greet us, along with a Mountie in his bright-red dress uniform. But most importantly there is a 10 year old boy named Trevor who suffers from Duchenne. Trevor is there to welcome us, along with his dad and his grandfather. It's for kids like Trevor that I have come to Nova Scotia. *Jesse's Journey* is for him and all the incredible young boys like Trevor who show us every day what real courage is all about.

I give Trevor my hat, and he and his dad and grandfather come on board the motor home for a little tour. Like most 10 year olds, Trevor thinks the motor home makes a pretty neat clubhouse. He is another link in the chain of youngsters I will meet along the road. And Trevor is the next link in what will become for me, a chain of inspiration.

The day after we arrive in Cape Breton is Mother's Day. It's Sunday May 10th, and early in the morning I'm back on the highway, this time walking the road from North Sydney to Sydney, Nova Scotia. Sydney had been the capital of Cape Breton Island from 1784 until 1820 when the Island became a part of Nova Scotia. It's a rugged part of the country where coalfields and iron ore deposits led to industrial development in the mid-19th century and made Sydney 'The Steel City.' In an area that conjures up pictures of smokestacks and slagheaps, along the highway there are tulips that are just about ready to bloom. Early in the morning the grass is a rich green as it soaks up the moisture from the morning dew. The sun is finally beginning to feel warm on my back, and the road ahead seems to hold a promise of spring.

The first donation of the day comes from a young lady driving a pick-up truck. She has her three young children with her and she tells me she drove out to the highway to shake my hand for what I'm doing. Like every person I have met along the road, she too has a story, and is visibly struggling with her emotions as she tells me about her children. This conversation lasts less than a minute, but has real impact, and again reminds me of the importance of what we are doing.

I can't believe how fast the traffic is moving in comparison to the slower pace in Newfoundland. One driver, after looking to see what we are doing, almost runs into the car in front of him, hits the brakes, and sends his car fishtailing back and forth across the highway. He's lucky there was nothing coming the other way on this narrow section of two-lane road. Shortly after that incident there's another close call. A transport truck screeches to a halt just short of the car in front of it. Blue smoke fills the air and there's the smell of burning rubber as the truck shudders to a halt leaving two long back skid marks on the pavement. We haven't been in an accident and I'm hoping today isn't going to be our first. I do a couple of radio interviews along the road and we end the day with 33 km completed before driving back to North Sydney for one more night. I pack the red duffel bag in preparation for morning and then phone my mom in Brantford, Ontario. It's moving day tomorrow, but tonight it's still Mother's Day.

Highway 4, which runs along the south shore of Bras d'Or Lake, is a difficult stretch. The road is narrow, with no shoulder to walk on, and there are lots of twists and turns. There are plenty of hills and although they're short hills, they are very steep, not like the long gradual grades of the Trans-Canada Highway. With no police escort available in the afternoon, for the first time I feel we are in some danger. While there are few donations along the road, I'm not discouraged. There really isn't any place to stop a vehicle without becoming a real hazard.

The good news is that donations are picking up steam back home, as more and more people are watching Bevin's weekly updates on television.

185

Here in Cape Breton, *Jesse's Journey* is attracting more media attention. After an early morning interview with CBC Radio, a Global Television news crew joins us on the road for our first TV interview in Nova Scotia.

Reaching the top of one of the short steep hills, my friend Dave Meadows and I are surprised to see Bevin part way down the next hill. Bevin is busy shooting videotape of David and me as we walk toward him. I can't understand why Bevin is shooting in our direction, because behind him there is a fabulous view across Bras d'Or Lake that looks like a travel brochure for Scotland.

When we reach where Bevin is standing, he just keeps shooting videotape as he asks me if I notice anything special about this spot. Other than some little yellow buttercups that are blooming at the side of road, I see nothing outstanding about this piece of the highway. With the camera still rolling, Bevin breaks into a smile and says, "Congratulations my friend, you just finished the first thousand kilometres!" With some back-slapping hugs and handshakes, we pause for a couple of pictures and a little roadside celebration. When we get going again, the hills seem easier and my pace just that much quicker.

The air here is warm, and with a huge blue sky overhead, the scenery has again reached the spectacular level. Bras d'Or Lake is a bit deceptive. It's actually a part of the Atlantic Ocean, and was formed when the sea flooded a glacier-depressed valley. St. Peter's Canal to the south, and the Great Bras d'Or Channel to the north, link the lake and the ocean. Bras d'Or Lake is known as the "Great Inland Sea" and has 70 km of coastline, barely perceptible tides, and a salt level that is half that of the ocean.

The few days along Highway 4 on the shore of Bras d'Or Lake are very quiet. After the rain and cold weather in Newfoundland, I take advantage of the time to let the sun warm me during the day. I settle into a routine of soaking my feet in sea salt and cold water three times a day. They seem to be starting to get tougher.

Mornings at bed-and-breakfast locations are always difficult. You can count on a breakfast of orange juice, bacon and eggs, toast and jam and hot tea. The sad part is you know in a few minutes' time you will have to say goodbye again to people who have been more than just hosts. They have become friends, and above all else, they want to help.

South from Big Pond, Nova Scotia toward the Straits of Canso, we say goodbye to Pat and Keith Nelder and their two young daughters, Allison and Dayna. Pat has a wonderful English accent, a great smile, and she loves to laugh. She went to school in Montreal before she and Keith, who is a boat builder, opened a business in the Caribbean. From there, they moved to Cape Breton where Keith now runs his own charter company on Bras d'Or Lake. On the road we get a chance, for just a few hours each day, to peek into people's lives, and I find myself wondering what it would be like to live in a place like Cape Breton. Could I live where they live and not miss the life I've grown used to?

The few communities in this area are spread out along the highway. White clapboard churches surrounded by green lawns mark the villages of Ben Eion, Big Pond, Irish Cove and Johnstown on the shore of Bras d'Or Lake. The stones in the graveyard tell the history of the area.

Walking the narrow roads of rural Cape Breton, I see old wooden houses that have been abandoned. These are the kind of deserted houses you find in the pages of black and white photography books. The story in this part of the country is that people who came from Scotland once occupied these farmhouses. Many of them arrived in Cape Breton late in life and didn't have children. When they died, the farms fell into ruin. The way the law is structured in Nova Scotia, squatters who might want to occupy a house are reluctant to do so in case 'long lost' relatives suddenly surface after money has been spent to restore the property. And so these houses sit empty, a hollow reminder of earlier times in a harsh land.

The moments that stay with us in life often come without warning. One of those unscheduled moments began with a knock at the door of the motor home one day in Cape Breton. It was lunchtime and we were just north of the Mikmaq Reserve at Chapel Island. A young woman named Donna Laneman, who teaches on the reserve, asked if I could please stop and say hello to the children at the school which is right along the roadside. I told her I would be happy to do that, not knowing it would turn into another of those special moments. Before leaving to return to the school, this energetic teacher told us that when she began teaching at Chapel Island Reserve there were just 13 children taking classes. There were now 75 kids attending school.

When I reached the school early in the afternoon, I was immediately surrounded by dozens of happy, smiling children. One of the young students was a little girl in a wheelchair. Six year old Mary Isaac has Cerebral Palsy. She looked up at me with the biggest brown eyes I have ever seen.

With all these Mikmaq children happy that I stopped to say hello, Mary Isaac reached up and handed me an envelope that contained a cheque for $100 from the children of Chapel Island School. That is what children do when they want to help other children.

Chapel Island Reserve is home to a lot of caring people. They are proud of who they are and what they have achieved. The homes on the reserve have window boxes with flowers and there's orderliness about the place. The reserve is the complete opposite of the stereotypical images I've been carrying in my mind. The years in the media have left me with an erroneous view of native people as living in unfinished homes with tarpaper siding and a collection of derelict cars scattered across the property. It isn't a pretty mental image but now I realize a lot of that stereotype is false.

Before saying goodbye and moving south with our native police escort, the chief of the reserve presents me with a book of poetry.

As I head down the highway, three ladies from the Chapel Island Women's Club come to the roadside to make a donation. The people of Chapel Island have opened my eyes.

Pushing south past Soldiers Cove, Bras d'Or Lake slips from view as we reach St. Peter's. At the end of the day, for the first time in a month and a half, I find myself sitting behind a steering wheel. Bevin wants to sit back and enjoy an ice cream cone, so I ask him if I can drive us back up the road to where we are staying at a bed-and-breakfast. The roller coaster road is a bit of a challenge, but it also gives me a chance to hear about how Bevin is feeling about being a member of the road team. Bevin's job includes the advance work to establish media contacts and to set up events. I don't know how we'd manage without him in these areas. I'm sure there are times it must seem like lonely work. Bevin is a great addition to the road team and I see him growing and gaining life experience daily as we keep moving across Canada with our message of hope.

The final day on Cape Breton Island is warm and sunny. This is the first time I feel content to be here rather than in Ontario where it's a sweltering and sticky 31°C. Heading toward Port Hastings and the causeway that crosses the Straits of Canso, it's 28°C in a light breeze under a clear blue sky.

We cross the Canso Causeway just before lunch on May 14th, 1998. Built in 1952-55 and almost two kilometres long, it's the world's deepest causeway, reaching a depth of 75 metres. To move 10 million tonnes of landfill in the 1950's, it cost $20 million, a pretty meagre amount by today's standards when it comes to a major construction project. In hindsight it seems a small price tag for such a big job.

Sometimes friends and relatives come out to the road to take part in *Jesse's Journey*. Reaching the mainland of Nova Scotia is one of those days. South of the Straits of Canso, Jim Mustard, my wife's cousin, brings his entire family to meet us. The Mustards live an

189

interesting life working with foster children in a remote part of Cape Breton Island. They live in the village of Upper Margaree, close to the West Coast of Cape Breton in what must be a nightmare for the post office. Along with Upper Margaree, there's Margaree Harbour, Margaree Forks, Northeast Margaree, Southwest Margaree and Margaree Valley!

The day starts with radio interviews in Ontario and Nova Scotia. There are also interviews with Atlantic Television and the *Halifax Herald*. We're getting lots of media coverage but on a busy highway it's difficult to convert that into donations. In the afternoon, I finish my 33 km listening to Jim Mustard as he tells me about life on Cape Breton Island, with three young children, 14 horses, no television and lots of books. The questions that went through my mind as we left our bed-and-breakfast this morning are in my head again. What would life be like living on Cape Breton Island?

Checking in and out of motels we push deeper into Nova Scotia. Kilometre after kilometre and hour after hour I press on, sometimes struggling to stay focused, as I tend to tire mentally. On the days when there is very little activity in the way of donations, my thoughts drift back home to Jesse.

The tires of the escort van behind me make a soft crunching sound as they roll over the gravel at five kilometres per hour. Walking alone, I want some time to check my focus. The key is research. I keep reminding myself if research is the only hope for a brighter future, then I have to do everything I can to find a way to fund that research. I have to sharpen my focus and always keep the dream in front of me that someday we will be able to provide research with a million dollars a year, every year, forever.

There is no room for doubt even though I know there are those who don't think I'll make it. With more than 7000 km still ahead of me, I'm going to have to be patient and stay the course. Building an endowment of $10,000,000 is no easy task, and I'm in for the long haul.

Since we began in the winter of 1993-94, a brand new charity has been built in The Foundation for Gene and Cell Therapy. Thousands of people have given their time, energy and hearts to *Jesse's Journey,* the fundraising wing of that new charity, whose mission is "to strive to improve the lives of people, especially children, by funding the expansion of genetic knowledge. Through investment in research the Foundation seeks to inspire the scientific community to find treatment and cure for neuromuscular genetic disease."

The parents of disabled children who face life-threatening diseases for which there is no cure find it difficult to use words like patience. They find it difficult when they live each day in a race with time, and the clock keeps steadily ticking. Alone on the road, there is no choice except to be patient. It's not easy to tell myself that maybe young people like Jesse have only a slim chance. But I also know that if I stop walking, maybe they won't have any chance at all. This is all I can do. The reality check is over. Regardless of how much or how little is raised each day, the big picture is clear. It's time to move on.

Fields of blue and purple, and pink and white lupines are starting to bloom along the highways of Nova Scotia. I'm on the road with Dave Meadows who has decided his Halifax law office can survive without him for a week. He has something more important to do that he'll remember the rest of his life. Dave and his wife, Susan, together with their friends, have been working tirelessly to smooth the way for the Nova Scotia section of this cross-Canada walk.

David and I are two fathers who met in the summer of 1969 when we were in our early twenties, still single and living at the same fraternity house in London. We were both working on radio in what the music world would label "the summer of love." In upstate New York, Woodstock was about to go from being a small rural community to a generational landmark. The musical "Hair" was riding the crest of a pop wave, and "Aquarius" was one of the most popular songs of summer. Zegar and Evans were on the charts with

'In The Year 2525' along with Sly and the Family Stone and 'Hot Fun in the Summertime.' Beauty, horror and triumph were all performing on a psychedelic stage. It was the year that saw Ted Kennedy's hopes for the White House dashed at Chappaquiddick, and the horrific Manson murders take place in California. It was also the summer the world stood still as Neil Armstrong stepped onto the moon.

After law school, Halifax became home for Dave and Susan while Sherene and I moved west to Vancouver where I started working for the CBC, broadcasting sports on radio and television. None of us were parents. None of us knew what lay ahead.

When Jesse was diagnosed in 1986, Sherene and I took some time away together to adjust to a circumstance that was going to change our lives. In Halifax we stayed with Dave and Susan, who made us feel at home. Sherene and I didn't talk with our friends about the news we were still struggling to come to terms with. For me it was a comfort to know that through the years that followed our meeting in the summer of 1969, Dave and I had never lost touch.

Scottish roots run deep in the university town of Antigonish, Nova Scotia, where a civic reception marks our arrival. Heading into Antigonish, I walk through a portion of the campus of St. Francis Xavier University, which has been here since 1861. Another of the architectural highlights of Antigonish is St. Ninian's Cathedral. Built from locally quarried blue limestone between 1867 and 1874, the cathedral honours the fifth-century saint who brought Christianity to Scotland.

Walking the Trans-Canada Highway from Antigonish to New Glasgow I'm joined on the road by two politicians. At thirty-two-years old, Peter McKay is a rookie Member of Parliament for the Nova Scotia riding of Pictou, Antigonish and Guysborough. Peter's father, Elmer McKay, was the veteran Member of Parliament who gave up his seat to provide an opening for former Prime Minister

Brian Mulroney. Peter is young, enthusiastic and a possible future party leader. Listening to him talk, I can appreciate even more how sons so often follow in the footsteps of their fathers.

John Hamm is the leader of the provincial Conservative Party in Nova Scotia, who will go on to become Premier of the province. A tall man with a long easy stride, the 62 year old Hamm has no trouble walking the highway and helping collect donations. For me, on the other hand, the warning light in my mind is starting to flash as a lot of little physical problems are starting to pile up. Along with the constant blister problem, I now have to ice both knees as well as the ankle I twisted back in Newfoundland. It's a nuisance fussing with these things, but I have a long way to go and a lot of people are counting on me. I have to be careful and deal with each problem as it comes up.

The days along the road to Halifax have become what I call "paying your dues" days. Donations are few, despite the media coverage we're receiving. Some days there's a nice surprise like the Sunday afternoon our volunteers collect more than $750 at a stock car racing track outside New Glasgow. But on Victoria Day, along the road to Truro, we raise only $40. In my mind I have already dealt with the issue of 'good days-bad days.' Not everything is about money. I keep on walking.

The first 18 km of our route from Truro to Halifax has me walking southwest along Highway 102, a multi-lane divided highway, before I have to shift over to Highway 2, which runs parallel to 102. It's pouring rain as traffic speeds by, rushing back into Halifax at the end of a long weekend. The past couple of days in the rain have been a series of blurred pictures and conversations. There was the mayor of Truro presenting town pins, a car dealer dropping by the motor home with a cheque for $100, and a picture of steam rising from the Irish stew and hot chocolate that Ed served us at lunch. There's the mental snapshot of members of an old car club donating $200. There's me

193

soaking my feet while doing a radio interview, and an image of cars and trucks honking and spraying us with water as they whip by in the rain. There is a picture in my mind of a mother and father from New Glasgow, along with their son who suffers from the same disease as Jesse, coming out to the highway to make a donation and offer their support. I hold on to that picture longer than the others.

Steve Casey, who was born in Nova Scotia, has come from London and joins me on the road as we walk through villages and towns like Stewiacke and Shubenacadie in central Nova Scotia. The sun has finally broken through to shine on the farming communities. Steve had been with us on the road when I pushed Jesse across Ontario in 1995. A welcome addition, Steve is one of those guys who likes to work in the background and who will do whatever has to be done to keep the whole project moving. I guess Steve can tell the past few days have been tough when it comes to donations. After making it up one of the longest and steepest hills in Nova Scotia, Steve asks me if I ever think of giving up. I tell him that quitting isn't an option.

Six kilometres into the day, we mark the highway and head into Halifax for a news conference and an unexpected moment.

The room is packed with supporters ranging from business groups to school kids, including a young boy in a wheelchair with Duchenne. Having been in their place before, I know the television and radio reporters are looking for the right 'sound bite' for the six o'clock news or the right 'audio clip' for the day's newscasts on radio. The news conference begins with a short video of Jesse and me on the road together in 1995, after which the Mayor of Halifax, Wayne Fitzgerald, is scheduled to welcome us to his city. I'll speak to the crowd after the mayors' remarks.

The lights are dimmed and the video runs before a hushed crowd. When the lights come up and the mayor steps to the microphone to welcome *Jesse's Journey* to Halifax, there is a long pause, and a very unexpected moment. The mayor is suddenly so choked with emotion he can't continue. With tears running down his cheeks, Wayne Fitzgerald takes a handkerchief from his pocket and wipes his eyes as he struggles to gain control of his emotions. After what seems like a long period of time, he faces the microphone and begins his remarks. It isn't necessary, but he apologizes to the gathering as he dabs his eyes with his handkerchief. Then, with a little smile between the sniffles, he says, "You know I've been in politics a long time and people who know me will tell you I'm never short of something to say, but today you got me!" That comment breaks the ice and brings a warm round of laughter, after which the mayor gives us a heartfelt welcome to Halifax.

There are interviews to do after I speak to the audience and try my best to explain what we are all about. There are donations made as part of the news conference, among them a cheque from the employees of Manulife Financial who make the first of a series of corporate donations that will continue across the country.

Before returning to the road, it's my turn to be a little choked up as I say goodbye to Ed Coxworthy, who is heading back home to Newfoundland. We have been very lucky to have a volunteer like Ed, who in tough times and tough weather has kept us laughing. Ed's stories have quickly become legend. There was the day Ed stepped off the motor home after lunch and spotted two rabbits doing what rabbits do. We were reduced to tears when Ed described the scene, "By the Jesus Johnny, he was just a stitchin' her coat something fierce! A sewing machine didn't have anything on that boy!"

Ed has been on the road with us for 37 days, and after saying goodbye to the crew, he thanks me for showing him parts of his own province that he has never seen. We know we are going to miss this Newfoundlander who dropped what he was doing and gave us a chunk of his life, not just by entertaining us but by helping to look after us along the road. Steve Casey probably put it best when he said, "I know that if you ask any of the volunteers, they'll all have similar stories about the things Ed said and did on the *Journey*. He's one heck of a guy, and I know he was totally devoted to John and what he was doing. I guess when you have a sick child of your own, the desire to help goes right to the core of who you are and what you believe in."

The events in Halifax mean I am now behind schedule. Back on the road, I walk until almost six o'clock. We collect $20 in donations. As I edge closer to Halifax it's another case of the highs and lows. Charting a course through Halifax and staying on course both in terms of road distance and promotional appearances, leaves no margin for error and it means sticking to a very tight schedule.

Our first full day in Halifax starts before sunrise with an interview on *Breakfast Television*. Bevin and I will eventually get used to making these early morning trips to television studios. I kid Bevin that by the time we get to Victoria he will know his way around just about every major city in Canada. I had no idea how accurate that statement would turn out to be.

The *Breakfast Television* host, Liz Rigney, is genuinely interested in helping, and she has the mayor live on the telephone with me as he champions our cause and challenges other mayors across the country to raise more money.

Riding in the van to a Rotary Club breakfast meeting in Halifax, I do two radio interviews back in London. Talking with Peter Garland on CFPL Radio, I can hear in his voice how much, after his trip to Newfoundland to broadcast our launch, he would like to be back on the road with us. On London radio station Q97.5 the morning hosts, Rich Grevin and Elaine Sawyer, have Sherene on the phone to talk with me live from a *Jesse's Journey* fundraising breakfast being hosted by the Royal Canadian Mounted Police.

Driving through the morning's rush hour traffic in Halifax, Bevin hears me finish the interview by saying goodbye to Sherene with the words, "I love you, honey." There was a time when those words would have seen Bevin rolling his eyes with that 'oh brother' look. But Bevin is maturing. He has even told me about a late night phone call he'd received from his girlfriend in London when we were still in Newfoundland. They were talking about how far apart they were and how much they missed each other. Over the phone line from Newfoundland, Bevin asked his girlfriend to step outside the door of her home in London and look up at the moon, the same moon that Bevin told her he was looking up at in Newfoundland. He was maturing, but he was still an incurable romantic!

Province House, built in 1819, is the oldest and smallest provincial legislative building in Canada. When Charles Dickens visited Province House in downtown Halifax in 1842 he labelled it "a gem of Georgian architecture." Seated in the gallery, the road team receives a standing ovation when Premier Russell McLellan introduces us to the House.

Province House is one of those Canadian landmarks steeped in history. Touring the building I sit in the chairs used by U.S. President Bill Clinton and Russian President Boris Yeltsin when the G7 leaders met in Halifax in June of 1995.

Following question period, the Premier invites us to his office where there is a cheque presentation and a photo opportunity as the Province of Nova Scotia donates $500. Shaking hands with the Premier while cameras flash, I have no way of knowing that Nova Scotia will be the only province in Canada to make a donation to our cause.

Leaving Province House we stop by Gorsebrook Junior High School to visit a young boy in a wheelchair who has been collecting money for *Jesse's Journey*. He wasn't well enough to come to the news conference that had been held the day before. I sign my hat and trade it for a million-dollar smile from the boy in a wheelchair who is really happy we've come to visit him at his school.

The weekend is spent winding our way from the Halifax suburb of Bedford along city streets that are full of traffic which has slowed to a crawl as people roll down their windows to donate. Our volunteers are sweating as they scramble from vehicle to vehicle, and road manager Trish asks me and our RCMP escort to slow down a bit to give the volunteers, who are still stuck in traffic, a chance to catch up.

It isn't often that I am asked to slow down because of the volume of work the volunteers have to contend with, so in a way this is a nice problem. I ease off my pace as the police officer behind me honks and points out the cemetery where many of those who drowned in the sinking of the *Titanic* are buried. Since the release of the movie *Titanic*, the city of Halifax has been working hard to make the cemetery a tourist attraction. The hero of the Hollywood movie is a young Irishman named Jack Dawson. The RCMP officer tells me there actually is a gravestone marked 'J. Dawson.' History records his name as a stoker in the engine room of the doomed ship. That hasn't deterred those who are caught up in the romance of the film, and the cemetery is having problems with people wanting to chip pieces off 'J. Dawson's' gravestone to take home as souvenirs.

Trish catches up with me again to make sure I'm drinking lots of water and then gives the RCMP officer and me the green light to pick up the pace. We are quickly approaching the harbour as we pass under the Angus L. MacDonald Bridge, linking Halifax and Dartmouth.

Founded in 1749, Halifax has one of the world's largest harbours, and it has played key naval and military roles. Commercial shipping has long been a source of wealth for Halifax, which acts as Canada's gateway to commerce, particularly when the St. Lawrence River is frozen in ice.

Throughout the afternoon of our fourteenth and final day on the road in Nova Scotia, traffic is tied up several times. People are in a buoyant mood as they honk horns and call out words of encouragement. At one point, traffic is moving slowly as it comes down a ramp that merges with where we are on the Bedford Road. As cars crawl along, there are two women who are waving and smiling, when all of sudden one vehicle runs into the back of the other. It looks like there's very little damage and I look back at the RCMP officer right behind me to see if he wants to stop. He just smiles as he wipes his hand across his mouth and looks off in the opposite direction. I think he's saying, 'I didn't see that.' We keep going and at the end of the day, a tired but happy group of volunteers finish in the heart of Halifax with 32 km completed and hundreds of dollars in donations.

At night time there is an almost eerie silence in my hotel room in downtown Halifax. The noises of the day are gone, and as I write my journal notes, I can see the flickering lights of Dartmouth across the harbour from my eighth floor window. Every now and then there is an opening in the clouds and the moon shines on the water.

Below me, through the darkness, I can make out a harbour shed alongside the dock. The building gives no hint to the role that it played in Canada's history. There are no signs that during the war years, 368 thousand troops left from here. Too many would never return. There is nothing to indicate that two million people coming to Canada passed through its halls in the 43 years before the building was closed in 1971. When I was two years old, I passed through that building, the last standing immigration shed in the country. This was the arrival point, the gateway to Canada. This was Pier 21.

In 1995 my mother, Sarah, and my father, Jack, watched as I pushed Jesse across Ontario before taking on the challenge of walking across Canada to help research find the answers parents and grandparents pray for. Reading newspaper stories and watching television reports from along the road, my mom and dad always had

199

a smile when they heard the skirl of the bagpipes in the background of those news reports where they saw Jesse and I being welcomed in cities and towns across Ontario.

It was at those moments that they both thought back to their younger years in Scotland, where I had been born in January of 1946, two years after my sister Dorothy was born. My mom and dad were young, with their whole lives ahead of them when they made the decision to come to a new country and a new life. When my parents were planning their wedding, a grandmother I never knew told them, "If you two are smart, you'll get yourselves away to Canada as soon as the war is over." That was a piece of advice they followed and never regretted.

My dad was the first in our family to come to Canada, arriving in Toronto on board the first all-Scottish emigration flight in 1947. Then in April of 1948, with two small children in tow, my mother boarded the Cunard liner *Ascania II* to make the long crossing of the Atlantic, leaving Scotland behind and opening a new chapter in our lives.

During the trip my sister came down with the measles, so we were isolated and spent most of our days and nights crossing the ocean in sick bay, away from the rest of the passengers. I never did get sick, and my mom remembers me as a little boy with red curls, wearing my Davidson tartan kilt and spending eight wonderful days entertaining the crew. Remembering how seasick she was at the time, my mother laughs now about how hard it was then, and still is, for parents to keep a 2 year old confined, "especially when you're so seasick that you would be happy to die!"

For me it was wonderful. I spent all my time having fun either in the doctor's office, or else in the ship's engine room with the engineer, who just happened to be from our hometown, and who seemed to have an unending supply of candy!

Following the train ride from Halifax to Toronto, our family was reunited at Union Station. In 1948 my mother and father didn't really know a lot about the new land that would be our home. They knew Canada was a huge country and, like thousands of other families emigrating after the war, it was the country they had chosen in which to carve out a new life and a better future for their children. We settled in Brantford, Ontario where my mom and dad both went to work for Cockshutt Farm Equipment at a time when factory whistles told us the time of day. Our family was completed when my younger brother Alastair was born in 1957.

The subjects I enjoyed most in public school were current events and history. I liked clipping newspaper stories, and at night I'd put on a very bulky set of earphones to listen to short-wave radio signals from all over the world. The orange glow from the glass vacuum tubes of the radio was the telltale sign that I wasn't asleep and I think my parents knew that. I'd listen to everything I could, events in some far-off corner of the world or maybe the voice of Foster Hewitt from the gondola at Maple Leaf Gardens.

In 1960, we moved to Woodstock, Ontario, where my dad was working for Massey-Ferguson. My mother was a reporter at the local newspaper, *The Daily Sentinel Review,* so I guess it wasn't much of a surprise when I started working at CKOX radio in Woodstock as a news reporter.

In 1986 we shared the heartbreak with our families that our middle child, little blonde-haired Jesse, had been diagnosed with Duchenne. This was a word none of us had ever heard before. Too soon it would become all too familiar to us.

At Christmas of 1994, I shared with the family my plan to push Jesse across Ontario from the Manitoba border to the Quebec border at Ottawa. The route would take us to Thunder Bay and then across the top of Lake Superior to Sault Ste. Marie and Sudbury, before heading south through the Muskokas and down the eastern shore of

Lake Huron to Sarnia and Windsor. From there I would push Jesse home to London and then finally on to Toronto and Ottawa. There was a kind of stunned silence when I outlined the four-month *Journey*. My sister broke the quiet when she asked, "How can we help?" From then on they never looked back. They did whatever had to be done from fundraising to cooking and laundry. They did whatever it took to keep *Jesse's Journey for Gene Research* moving forward. Now that seemed like such a long time ago.

For a while I stood and just looked at Pier 21 in Halifax, where new lives in Canada had begun for so many people. It had been exactly 50 years to the day from the time I'd passed through Pier 21 to the day I dipped my running shoes in the saltwater of the Atlantic Ocean at Quidi Vidi, Newfoundland, setting out to try to help build a brighter future. It was time to get some sleep. Tomorrow it was on to Prince Edward Island.

Chapter Fourteen

PICTURESQUE PRINCE EDWARD ISLAND

*"With ordinary talents and extraordinary
perseverance all things are attainable" –*
T.F. Buxton

It's windy and raining in Caribou, Nova Scotia when I walk onboard
the ferry to make the 22 km crossing to the picturesque island
province made famous by Canada's best-known fictional character,
the green-eyed redhead *Anne of Green Gables*. Signs along the road
sometimes make me think of Canada itself as a fictional place. There
is the sign at Port Aux Basques telling you it's illegal to take
potatoes off Newfoundland. Boarding the ferry leaving Nova Scotia,
there's a sign stating it's illegal to transport honeybees to Prince
Edward Island. I suppose they both make sense. Those signs remind
me of a farm gate in Cape Breton, which instead of the word 'old,'
proudly boasted 'Young' MacDonald's farm. In a fun way, it all
seemed to make Canada seem like a rather comical place.

I do two interviews while crossing to Wood Islands, the Prince
Edward Island terminus for the ferries that still run daily despite the
1997 opening of the Confederation Bridge. The wind is howling on
the aft deck of the ferry as a young woman from Island Cable
interviews me. Then a couple from CARP Magazine (Canadian
Association for Retired Persons) decides they'd like to sit down
indoors with me at a window seat with a cup of hot chocolate. I was
happy to cooperate with the Island Cable reporter who was looking
for a wild and windy location. But with memories of the rain and
sleet in Newfoundland still fresh in mind, I am just as happy to be
indoors telling the story of *Jesse's Journey* to the writers from CARP.

Nova Scotia gets smaller in the wake of the ferry, and my thoughts
take me back to Chapel Island Reserve on Cape Breton Island. The
big brown eyes of 6 year old Mary Isaac, the little girl in the
wheelchair, and the donation from the kids at her school are among
the things that are driving me on.

The ferry docks at Wood Islands on the southernmost tip of Prince Edward Island after its 75-minute journey from the Nova Scotia mainland. In a matter of minutes the ship disgorges its cargo of cars, vans and cyclists who head off to explore the island. For these people, there's very little emotion attached to arriving on Canada's smallest province. The dock at Wood Islands isn't like an airport, train station or bus depot. In those locations you can see business people with briefcases and laptop computers meeting and shaking hands before scurrying off to waiting cabs. In airports, if you watch long enough, you'll see tears of joy as families are reunited. There will be husbands and wives kissing each other, grandparents hugging children and grandchildren, and lovers embracing. For a brief moment on a Sunday in May, the Wood Islands ferry dock was like an airport scene with friends greeting each other. Here it was not just a greeting, but a reunion.

Rich and Cindy Beharrell are waiting on the dock as the *Jesse's Journey* motor home and vans roll down the ramp and onto Prince Edward Island. Rich is a videographer I worked with for several years in London. He and his wife and their young sons Benjamin and Jonathon moved to Prince Edward Island in 1996.

Rich was a part of the incredible television 'family' that worked together in London. We were a tightly knit group of reporters, camera people, editors, on-air anchors and managers who worked together through good times and bad. We danced at weddings, played baseball and partied together. We watched each other's kids grow up and lent each other a hand when times were tough. Seeing Rich and Cindy, I remember a day came when Rich talked to me about a decision that he and his wife were facing.

Cindy's parents were living on Prince Edward Island with Cindy's brother Paul, who has Down Syndrome. Cindy was just like the rest of the television family. Her parents were getting older. It was time to think about family and time to think about going home to PEI. With two young boys in school, there were reasons to want to stay in Ontario. With Cindy's brother almost thirty, there were reasons to want to be in Prince Edward Island.

Rich had been weighing everything from the charm of the island to uprooting the kids when he asked my opinion. I remember telling him, "there are probably lots of reasons to make the move, just make sure when you think about family, that you go for the right reason." When I walked off the ferry and saw their faces, I knew that Rich and Cindy had made the right decision.

We form a caravan and the Beharrells lead the way as they guide us to their home at Stratford, just outside Charlottetown where Rich, Cindy, Benjamin, Jonathon and Paul treat us to a lobster supper.

It's Sunday the 24th of May, and after writing my journal I call home. I'm happy to hear Sherene's voice and she tells me how the boys are doing. From the time I stepped off the ferry, it has been a good day to think about families. Now it's time to get some sleep. The morning will bring the first of six days of walking across Prince Edward Island.

It is sunny and cool in the morning when we reach our start point for the day. With its red soil, Prince Edward Island lies waiting under a huge blue sky. The Trans-Canada Highway from Wood Islands winds through Belle River, Pinette, Flat Creek and Orwell, as it makes its way toward Charlottetown. Passing through the historic village of Orwell I'm just a kilometre east of St. Andrews Presbyterian Church, where they still hold services in English and Gaelic. This part of the Trans-Canada is a real treat because there is a very wide apron at the edge of the road. Rich and Cindy are walking with me when we pass an elementary school at noon. I am swamped by about 300 kids who are clapping and cheering and chanting, "Go John Go!" After signing as many autographs as I can, it's time to move on again. After the lunch break, a CBC television crew from Charlottetown comes out to the road to shoot a story about *Jesse's Journey*.

205

It's late in the afternoon of our first full day on the island when we mark the road and head into Charlottetown to take part in some special events. Charlottetown is often referred to as "The Cradle of Canadian Confederation." Our first stop is Province House, built in 1847, which now serves as the meeting place of the provincial legislature. The Speaker of the House greets us and we are given a tour of the building. We learn it was here in 1864 that a meeting of the Fathers of Confederation led to the British North America Act that created the Dominion of Canada. The room where that meeting took place, the Confederation Chamber, has been restored to how it looked when that historic meeting took place three years before Confederation. We are shown the long table where the idea of a Dominion of Canada was conceived. Our tour guide is bubbling with enthusiasm and very proud that she had also shown Terry Fox and Rick Hansen through Province House when they had passed through Charlottetown.

From Province House we hurry over to the CBC where the local weatherman, "Boomer" Gallant, a very funny guy who obviously loves life and loves what he does, has me read a part of the weather forecast. Then it's back out to the Trans-Canada Highway to finish my distance for the day.

The sun is sitting low in the sky when Bevin puts his creative genius to work along the highway. With his video camera he captures shots of my shadow moving across the red soil of Prince Edward Island and the fields of potatoes that are just beginning to sprout.

Walking along the highway, I sometimes have to hold my breath as Bevin scrambles back and forth across the road to get the shot he's looking for. At times he is on roller blades shooting videotape while skating backwards. Sometimes that video camera is right in my face and at other times Bevin is way off in the distance with the camera mounted on a tripod while he waits for me to appear. Regardless of where he is, he's out there every day, and I marvel at his dedication.

When the walk across Canada was being put together, Bevin's boss back in London, CFPL television News Director George Clark said he was floored when Bevin approached him for a leave of absence. George recalls thinking, "Here was this young man, whose mother had died of breast cancer, whose stepmother has ALS, and he obviously felt so helpless. He felt there was nothing he could do, but then along came *Jesse's Journey*." Bevin knew this was a project he wanted to be part of and one morning he told his boss, "George, this is something I can do, and I really feel I should give it all I've got, so can you give me the rest of the year off?" If George Clark was floored by the request, Bevin was probably just as floored when George said "Yes!"

It takes dedication to ask yourself, "Can I afford to live without a regular salary for a year?" I think Bevin's heart helped him answer that question with another question, "Can I afford not to do this?" Bevin has made a great personal sacrifice to be part of our team, and now here we are in the late afternoon sunshine with the shadows growing longer, trying our best to make a difference as we make our way across PEI.

Early the next morning, on our way out to the start point on the road, there are wisps of fog. At times the air is cold until the sun makes it over the horizon. The first glitch of the day finds us outside of cell phone range for a radio interview with "The Fan" in Toronto. We finally find a phone booth and make the connection with Toronto. The Fan is a sports talk radio station and they are interested not only in the fund raising aspect of the *Journey* but also the athletic story of a father who intends to walk more than 8000 km across Canada. The program coordinator, who takes our call, puts me on hold, and then puts me on the air with the announcer. At the end of the interview he comes back on the line to say goodbye. I'm surprised when he says, "Thanks a lot John. We love you for what you're doing." It's an interesting comment from someone I've never met.

There is no shortage of people stopping to make donations as I move closer to Charlottetown. Entering the city we have lots of flashing lights and sirens as both the police and fire departments escort us to a civic reception. An honour guard of police officers in their blue dress uniforms salute as we enter the building where Charlottetown Mayor George McDonald welcomes us. When it's my turn to speak I take full advantage of the opportunity to tell the audience our story. Bevin tells me after the reception that it was the best speech he has heard me make since we left St. John's.

Each day on the road there are more and more people who want to shake my hand, and donations are definitely picking up as we continue to move across the Island. The rolling hills are offering some of the prettiest scenery imaginable. In the sunshine, parked on the lawn of an Anglican church at the top of a hill in Bonshaw, the view looking out over the West River is absolutely storybook. The Island reminds me of a model train set-up without the train. Everything seems so well laid out. It's as if God himself decided, "This little white church will look right if we put it here, and this little green tractor with the yellow wheel rims will look just right parked over there." Wherever you look, the green fields and English-looking hedgerows along with the red soil and the ocean make the Island picturesque. People, young and old, are stopping their cars or walking down farm lanes to make a donation to *Jesse's Journey – A Father's Tribute*. Prince Edward Island has heard our story and Islanders are responding.

Looking into the sun and squinting through a late afternoon haze, I catch my first glimpse of the Confederation Bridge, the $840,000,000 engineering marvel that we will be crossing in a couple of days. The 13 km of reinforced concrete that links Prince Edward Island to mainland Canada is the world's longest multispan bridge over ice-covered water. The bridge arcs over the Northumberland Strait, and from a distance, it looks like some kind of giant centipede standing in the water.

With one more day left on the island, we head back to 'Molly's Bed and Breakfast' and our host Velma Owens, whose sister Olive Bryanton is coordinator for the Prince Edward Island portion of our *Journey*. Olive is another of the hundreds of volunteers who have been working in the background. Their names are seldom heard but it's their dedication that has paved the way to keep *Jesse's Journey* moving day after day.

There isn't an actual person named Molly at 'Molly's Bed and Breakfast' in New Annan, Prince Edward Island. Molly is one of the two little dogs who make Velma Owens' establishment seem just like home. Molly is a 12 year old Lhasa Apso while Charlie is a nine-month-old Shih Tzu. At the end of the day, while I soak my feet in saltwater, the two little dogs make me laugh as they tumble after each other bumping into furniture while slip-sliding across the floor. While Charlie wants to play all the time, it's pretty obvious that Molly is a senior citizen of the dog world.

Velma is the owner of Molly's Bed and Breakfast, which backs onto Malpeque Bay, famous for its oysters which are shipped all over the world. A shy and yet determined woman, Velma lives a quiet life on Prince Edward Island. She was a hospital administrator in Ontario for 16 years before moving to the Island. In 1989 Velma was seriously injured in a head-on car crash in Nova Scotia while on her way to a food show in Halifax. She's had a rough ten years. On the morning of our last day on the Island, over a breakfast of pancakes and bacon, Velma sums it up when she says, "I just keep going." Her greatest strength is her positive attitude, which seems to be fed by the easy pace of island life. After all the years she spent in central Canada, Velma admits her heart is in both Ontario and Prince Edward Island. Given a choice, Velma would have had things turn out differently, but add Molly and Charlie to the mix and you come up with a contentment that few people enjoy.

In the early morning sunlight, the emerald-coloured fields of Prince Edward Island resemble a travel poster for Ireland. At Victoria-by-

the-Sea, the fields of green grass sweep down to the red sand that
curls around the harbour to the pier. At the end of the pier, awash in
sunshine, there's a white wooden lighthouse, flying a Union Jack.
The perfectly still backdrop of blue water beyond the harbour makes
this place a living postcard.

Admiring Victoria-by-the-Sea, I'm walking the road with 52 year old
Paul Naylor, from Bonshaw. Paul is what the islanders call a 'CFA',
which means "comes from away." He had been an employee of Air
Canada for twenty-six-and-a-half years before he and his wife
Wendy moved to the Island in 1986. Paul told me the story of how
he scouted the Island for a property that could be made into a
bed-and-breakfast. Finding the spot he was looking for was the first
step. Then he tackled the thorny problem of purchasing the land.
Prince Edward Island has some rules about residency that make it
difficult for CFA's to be landowners. Once he understood that part of
the equation, Paul crunched the numbers and crafted his plan. He
would return to Ontario and live on $20,000 per year for two years
in order to save enough money to make his island dream come true.
Two years later, Paul and Wendy purchased more than 33 acres of
land on Prince Edward Island. The three-bedroom bed-and-breakfast
called "Sickles" sits on 6 acres of land that includes a barn, which up
until 1989 had been used as a wood mill. Paul spent the first six
months clearing the land by hand of the scrap slabs of wood that
littered most of the acreage. Paul said in hindsight, that the scrap
wood all over the place was probably the reason nobody wanted to
buy the place. Today, Paul and Wendy Naylor are the proud owners
of a bed-and-breakfast on Prince Edward Island, with their own
private 27-acre woodlot.

I listen with interest as Paul Naylor continues to tell me more and
more about Prince Edward Island while I log my final kilometres on
the island. It doesn't surprise me to learn there are no soft drinks in
plastic bottles or cans on this pristine little island. Crossing the
province on foot, it's easy to see that soft drinks in glass bottles have
kept roadside litter to a bare minimum. When Paul and I reach
Englewood School just outside Summerside, the school kids make a

$100 donation. The school won the National Science Award, and it's easy talking with kids who have an understanding about genetic illnesses and the need for research.

By the end of the day we reach the Confederation Bridge. I've finished the Prince Edward Island portion of the walk across Canada. In the morning we will move on to New Brunswick, the only province I have never visited. It will be our 50th day on the road. Three provinces down and seven to go.

Chapter Fifteen

DOWN HOME NEW BRUNSWICK

"Money is the most envied, but the least enjoyed.
Health is the least enjoyed, but the most envied" –
Charles Caleb Colton

From Newfoundland to Cape Breton, Marine Atlantic gave us a warm welcome and free passage. Getting from Prince Edward Island to New Brunswick is the exact opposite. Our letter outlining what *Jesse's Journey* is all about and our request for a "freebie" in crossing the Confederation Bridge, has brought a negative response, making it clear that nobody gets a free pass. We make one last appeal as the motor home and escort vans, which have been on television and in the newspaper all week, roll up to the ticket booth on the bridge. This appeal brings the cold response, "That'll be $112." When we clear the approach ramps on the New Brunswick side of the bridge, the drivers of the 'Bridge Authority' trucks seem to be keeping an eye on us. I think they're making sure I'm not walking on any part of the roadway that is considered part of the bridge. As the mammoth structure slips further and further behind me, I have to admit it is an engineering marvel. It's too bad our experience with the people behind that same marvel turned out to be as cold as the bridge concrete itself.

It's almost June when I take my first steps in New Brunswick. The winter weather is supposed to be behind me, from now until late fall in Saskatchewan. But on the first day in province number four, a combination of high wind, rain and sleet is tearing at my face.

This is the day the Acadians, Hector Maillet and Evariste Cormier, walk into my life. The two Rotarians are waiting in a parked car about 2 km from the Confederation Bridge. Waiting for someone they've never met, they are the next links in the chain, ready to play their part in making *Jesse's Journey* a success.

The wind and rain are buffeting the motor home as it comes to a stop beside the parked car. Like the pilot of a World War II bomber sitting on the runway, Mike Woodward slides the side window of the motor home open and yells into the wind, "Are you Hector?" With confirmation that these are indeed our next two volunteers, Hector and Evariste climb aboard the motor home and join the team.

My hands are cold, red and raw as I shake hands with the newcomers. Mike Woodward pours everyone a hot chocolate as the introductions are made and we quickly run through the daily routine. As they listen to all the instructions, I feel a little sorry for Hector and Evariste, who look like they're wondering what they have got themselves into. I have seen this look before and yet I know that by the end of their time with us, they will be veterans and friends who will be wanting to stay longer.

Then it's back onto the Trans-Canada Highway to log the first 33 km and receive the first donations to be made in province number four. The route through New Brunswick calls for a zigzag pattern that will take us through the major centres of Moncton, Saint John and Fredericton.

The following day, the wind is still blowing hard as I walk southwest along the Trans-Canada Highway toward Sackville. The lupines are in bloom and fiddleheads are growing along the roadside. I manage two stretches of 11 km each before lunchtime. Only a handful of people stop, as traffic moves fast along this stretch of the Trans-Canada, which is now a four-lane divided highway. One woman who stops to make a donation is very moved by the whole project. She makes sure she takes a picture of 'Jesse's dad' and donates $50 before driving away.

There's a long gentle slope to the Trans-Canada Highway as it sweeps down into the wide expanse of the Tantramar Marshes east of Sackville. Acadian dikes reclaimed the wetlands three centuries ago and the meadowlands that resulted have been labelled "The world's largest hayfield."

Off in the distance, Mike has the motor home parked almost a kilometre back from the highway, tucked in at the base of the 12 signal towers of Radio Canada International. The wires connecting the towers seem to be laid out in a criss-cross pattern, strung out over the marshes. The saltwater of the Tantramar Marshes acts as a giant reflector for the short-wave radio signals. There's a small museum exhibit about short-wave radio in one of the few buildings, but mostly this communications giant seems strangely devoid of people. Computers in Ottawa allow Radio-Canada International to change the configuration of broadcast patterns that are beamed around the world.

In the motor home, Hector Maillet supplies us with large tins of frozen lobster for lunch. Hector and his family own a lobster packing company in Shediac, New Brunswick. The company processes two million kilograms of lobster each year. Their customers are along the eastern seaboard and the west coast of the United States. Hector smiles as he says, "There you can sell lobster. But not in Texas. There you sell steak."

The day ends in Sackville, home to the campus of Mount Allison University. The university has the distinction of being the first in the British Empire to grant a degree to a woman – a Bachelor of Science to Grace Annie Lockhart in 1875.

On a quiet Sunday morning, I make my way along the tree-lined streets of Sackville. The tall oak trees, the Georgian architecture, the fine older homes, and the pond full of swans in the centre of town enhance Sackville's image as a university town.

The schedule calls for a 'site visit' at the end of the day. After logging kilometres for seven and a half hours, the *Journey* caravan heads to Shediac. Hector and Evariste, our volunteers for the week, are taking us to their hometown for a parade and barbecue.

There are hundreds of people, as well as sirens and flashing lights as we make our way through Shediac. A huge steel lobster bolsters the town's claim to being "The Lobster Capital of the World." When you look at a 14 metre high steel lobster that weighs 80 tonnes, you have to think there's little doubt about the community's claim to that title.

Smoke is rising from the barbecues where the Rotary Club of Shediac is hard at work, raising money for *Jesse's Journey – A Father's Tribute.* I am impressed with the hospitality and generosity of the people of Shediac who celebrate our arrival in both English and French. It's windy and cold as I speak to the crowd gathered in the park, and I thank them for their help. My French is terrible but nobody seems to mind. When I finally get to bed, I think about how genetic diseases don't recognize language, and how today people who speak both English and French, people I've never met before, have come together for the common good. That, I decide, is how it's supposed to work. The people of Shediac have been very generous. It's been a good day.

On the first day of June, fresh from a great turnout in Shediac, I feel really pumped about how we are doing as I pound the pavement of the Trans-Canada Highway leading into Moncton. Little do I know *Jesse's Journey* is about to make front-page headlines, but not with the story we are looking for.

When we reach the heart of the city they call "The Gateway to Acadia," there is a formal welcome to Moncton in the foyer at City Hall. True to their word, our friends from Manulife are on hand to make a $1,000 donation as I pass yet another Manulife branch on the sweep west. Officials from the West Moncton Rotary Club present our team with $250. And, as we shake hands and pose for the cameras, the newly elected Mayor of Moncton, Brian Murphy, makes a donation on behalf of the city. Immediately after the ceremony, as the mayor is heading to the elevator, a newspaper reporter from the *Moncton Times and Transcript* hurries after him to ask about the donation from the city.

The next morning there's a newspaper story about the arrival of *Jesse's Journey* in Moncton and the city donating $10. I have no idea how the city decided on that amount, but from there things only get worse. I feel sorry for the mayor when later in the week there's a front-page story saying, "Red Faced Mayor Admits $10 Donation a Rookie Mistake." The mayor promises that the city will establish standards for making donations. I just look at it as $10 we didn't have before we came to Moncton. The following day I'm asked to be the guest speaker at Hector and Evariste's Rotary Club. The club donates $4,000. And so the roller coaster ride continues and once again, it's time to move on.

From Moncton the Trans-Canada Highway continues its zigzag pattern as it swings southwest, passing through Petitcodiac and Sussex before reaching Saint John. The daytime temperatures are now in the high teens and sometimes beyond 20 degrees. There's a steady flow of people stopping to make donations, and the air horns of transport trucks are becoming a familiar sound as we are getting a lot of recognition in this part of the province. Maybe peoples' interest has been sparked by the media coverage in Moncton!

As the days flow into each other, there are mornings I have to look at the schedule to know where I am. Day 55 on the road would probably have been noted in my journal as a 'routine' windy and wet day along the Trans-Canada. But it turned out to be anything but routine, as I spent the day listening to the story of New Brunswicker Armand Belliveau.

Out on the highway, the motor home stops on the gravel as we reach our marker. As the escort van moves into position behind me with its lights flashing, I finish stretching my legs and getting ready for another 33 km chunk of highway. And like most other days, there is someone ready to walk with me. Today that someone is Armand Belliveau.

217

Armand and his family own a kitchen cabinet business in Shediac. He tells me they import oak and maple from the United States because there are very few hardwoods in New Brunswick. The bulk of the finished product is shipped back to the United States, for sale in Massachusetts and Maine.

Armand has had an interesting life. For a number of years he lived in the United States, and his children have dual citizenship. He served a year in Korea with the United States Army, and as a younger man he was a boxer. He had fought two fighters Muhammad Ali defeated on his rise to glory. I can see that Armand is in great shape and isn't going to be a walker who will start off great and then fade as the day lengthens.

He is like a lot of people I have met along the road. Listening to his story, I can tell he has mellowed with the passing years. He has set aside the games of his youth, and Armand and his wife are now ballroom dancers. The man who stepped into the ring in his younger days is now convinced that boxing will be banned within his lifetime. I'm not quite so sure about that, but Armand's strong view is underscored further when he says, "We don't let animals fight in a ring, why should we let humans do that?"

As the day grows longer, and people continue to stop, or honk and wave as they pass by, Armand shows no sign of tiring as we continue to count the kilometres. Holding his arms out as if he's exaggerating the size of a fish he caught, he tells me his philosophy of physical life and his story of the two clocks.

To start with, Armand says, "The human body should last for 120 years." Waving his left hand he says, "On this side there's the clock that is at zero and starts ticking when you're born." Simulating life unfolding, Armand's left hand goes up and down in a series of little ticking motions as his arm moves slowly to a spot out in front of him. Reaching his other hand as far to the right as possible, he described it as a person's 'body clock' at the 120-year mark.

As Armand talks about how a person may smoke too much, drink too much, not eat properly, lack in exercise, his right hand goes up and down in the same little ticking motion as it comes closer and closer to meeting his left hand. When he eventually clapped his hands in front of himself, Armand summed up life by saying, "When those two meet, you're out of here!" It was an interesting philosophy.

Late in the afternoon we finally hear the honk I wait for each day from the escort van which has come to a stop. We are at the end of the day with the distance completed. It's another of those special moments as I shake hands with Armand and congratulate him on becoming the oldest person to date, to walk an entire 33 km with me. Armand Belliveau is 58 years old.

Leaving the Trans-Canada Highway, the switchover to Highway 1 is a little scary as a steady stream of vehicles pours south into Saint John. The placenames along Highway 1 reflect the history of the area. There are the French names like Quispamsis, English names like Bloomfield and Native names like Nauwigewauk.

The little town of Hampton, New Brunswick donates $100, which is matched by the Rotary Club of Hampton as I walk on, ending the day at Rothesay, on the outskirts of Saint John. It's cold on the day I walk into Saint John, the oldest incorporated city in Canada (1785). When Samuel de Champlain arrived on June 24, 1604, it was the feast day of St. John the Baptist, and he christened the river The Saint John.

Like Newfoundland, New Brunswick's weather is unpredictable. Winds from the Bay of Fundy can bring quick changes. The wind, rain and the spray from the tires of trucks and cars that whiz by on the stretch of four-lane highway leading into Saint John make for a poor day financially. But, by the time I reach City Hall in the centre of downtown Saint John, the sun is shining. I sign the city's guest book and the mayor presents pins to everyone on the road team.

219

The heart of Saint John is a model for any city seeking to preserve its heritage while stepping into the future. A $250,000,000 facelift has revitalized the core of the city. Brunswick Square, together with the waterfront Market Square and the Saint John Trade and Convention Centre, are all linked by "pedways." There's visible evidence of rejuvenation in a downtown core that's full of people.

The shops, restaurants and outdoor cafés in this historic seafaring city are all busy. More and more, as I reflect on the places I've seen, it's becoming obvious how cities and towns focus on their heritage to build their future. Regardless of whether it's a geographic feature like a waterfall or a historic claim to fame, they build on what they have. It reminds me of the number of times I have heard hockey coaches talking about their playoff strategy with the words, "We're going to go with what got us here." When it comes to redevelopment, Saint John, New Brunswick has done it right.

At night time, we walk through the enclosed pedway system to the downtown arena complex, where the crowd stands and applauds as I am introduced at ice level. Hearing the cheers from the crowd that's here for a Saint John Flames, American Hockey League playoff game gives me a lift since we have been through some pretty lean days on the road. It's nice to know our message about research and the hope for a brighter future is getting through to people.

Leaving Saint John, I walk north for the next three days toward Fredericton where we will rejoin the Trans-Canada. There are no towns or villages along the road and the days are quiet. Bevin and Trish joke with me that my 'office' is four feet wide and 33 km long, and all I have to do is walk across my office once a day. My first day out of Saint John, I walk across my office in my fastest time yet since wetting my running shoes in the Atlantic Ocean. I finish by 4:15 in the afternoon.

We look a little different leaving Saint John. The roof of one of our two mini vans is now equipped with a pair of powerful strobe lights that face back toward traffic coming up to pass us. The lights are a gift from a policeman in Saint John who thought we should be a little more visible. The lights make the van look as if it has ears like the world's most famous mouse. From that point on the escort vehicle is nicknamed "The Mickey Van." By default the second mini-van quickly becomes known as "The Other Van."

We are now in the rolling countryside of New Brunswick, where I see deer standing in a field not far from the side of the road. They turn their heads, and their doleful brown eyes watch with a passive curiosity as I walk along the edge of the road, the escort van behind me with its flashing lights. Then in an instant, they disappear into the woods.

It's early in the morning on our way to Fredericton, when the tall grass along the roadside is still wet with dew, and a huge black bear crosses the road about a hundred feet in front of me. I decide quickly that he probably has the right of way. Coming out of the woods and through the wet grass, the bear leaves big moist paw marks on the pavement before vanishing into the grass and trees on the other side.

When I reach the spot where I can see the bear's paw marks on the pavement, I put my hand on the road to compare sizes. When my hand is spread out I can span an entire octave of eight white keys on a piano. The paw mark on the road is about two inches bigger than my reach. My guess is that if the bear were to stand on its hind legs, it would probably be about seven feet tall and weigh about 300 kilograms.

The narrow road to Fredericton eventually widens to become four lanes, with a huge paved shoulder to walk on. Dozens of Canadian Forces vehicles are moving back and forth along the highway from the military base at Gagetown, New Brunswick.

Jeeps with long communications aerials that whip back and forth, purr as they pass us. Big green army trucks with canvas tops growl their way along the highway in mini-convoys. Most of the vehicles look like kids are driving them. Some of them honk. Some of them don't. None of them stop. It's probably military regulations.

As Bevin and I walk along the highway, we listen to the sound of gunfire from a shooting range. It's a little unnerving, because while we can't see it, we can certainly hear it. We don't know if the small arms fire we are hearing is live ammunition or not, but we make what we think is a safe assumption that, regardless of whether it's live or not, the ammunition isn't being fired in the direction of the highway. It's also nice to think that, in terms of the rest of the world, when you hear military weapons fired in Canada, it's either a practice session or something ceremonial.

In the afternoon, a single green army truck passes us with one end of a canoe sticking out from under the canvas tarpaulin. As the truck drones on down the highway Bevin and I look at each other and I joke with him saying, "Bevin, there goes Canada's Army – and Navy!"

A day away from Fredericton, I'm putting in a routine day on the highway, looking forward to the afternoon break to get some juice and fruit. I can see the motor home parked a couple of kilometres up ahead, and I can make out someone walking toward me. It only takes a few minutes to close the gap between us and then I'm holding Sherene in my arms. We must look funny to passing motorists as we kiss each other in front of a small audience at the side of the highway. I don't care. It's been more than two months since we've seen each other and in the 27 years we have been married, it's the longest time we have ever been apart.

Sherene is a welcome addition to our little band of road warriors. For the next few days she becomes part of the team, helping Trish, Bevin and Mike with whatever has to be done. She quickly fits into the rhythm of life on the motor home, and adjusts to the breakfast routine, which is a well-orchestrated dance in tight quarters.

Sherene has brought mail and messages from the home team in London. She knows when to help, and probably even more importantly, she knows when to stay out of the way.

Pitching in with whatever needs to be done, Sherene ends up driving a news van for the CBC television crew who are shooting a story on *Jesse's Journey.* It's a familiar routine – the cameraman sits, facing out from the open hatch in the back of the news van. I watch his legs dangling almost on the road, while he shoots videotape of me walking into Fredericton. The daily goal of 33 km has started to take its toll, but getting through that, together with the backlog of media interviews, becomes a little easier with Sherene by my side.

Fredericton is where Sherene gets to see one of the many civic receptions I've described in my phone calls home. It's also where she decides I should get a haircut. The last time I'd been to a barber shop was in Port Aux Basque, Newfoundland and Trish has been kidding me about auditioning for the job of 'Crusty the Clown' on *The Simpsons.* I don't think it looks quite that bad.

Usually when you go for a haircut they just ask you how much you want off the top or the sides or the back. They don't often ask if you want a beer with your haircut! I didn't know it at the time, but I had wandered into what is believed to be the only barbershop in the country with a liquor licence. It's not something I can just let pass, so while I'm getting my haircut I ask the barber why the shop is licensed. The story is that when a group of four or five young guys from Camp Gagetown come into Fredericton for a night on the town, they want to be able to enjoy a cold beer while they wait for their buddies to get a haircut.

It took a zoning change, and because the city wanted to make sure that haircutting would still be the shop's main business, there's no bar in the shop. The beer is merely a convenience kept in a fridge that's out of sight. Still, it's pretty novel and when it is time to leave, *Jesse's Journey* adds one free haircut to its list of 'gifts in kind.'

Sherene leaves for home the morning we leave Fredericton and begin the walk to Woodstock. Walking along the Saint John River, the weather is starting to feel like a preview of what we can expect in Ontario. The river is smooth and for the first time, the day is hot and tiring. It's one of those days filled with a range of mental snapshots I am collecting in my journal. There's a man and his two young daughters who come to our table during dinner to make a donation. It's one of the few donations we receive that day. There's Bob and Donna Gallagher from Ilderton, Ontario, our volunteers for the week, returning from a visit with some New Brunswick friends. Their friends donate $409. The $9 came from their friends' two grandchildren who donated money they had been saving for toys. They said they wanted to give it to Jesse. Kids always amaze me.

The concerns about my well-being have surfaced again. Trish spends time each day working on my legs before icing my ankle. Ron Calhoun calls from London. He wants me to get a medical, which I'll do when we get to Edmunston.

In Woodstock, the Rotary Club organizes a parade through town. There are pins and another guest book to sign as the mayor welcomes us. As donations are being made at a presentation ceremony, two little kids donate $10. They are busy looking at the map of Canada on the side of the escort van, so I point out London and tell them, "That's where Jesse and I live." I guess they aren't very impressed because the next question is, "Where's Disneyland?" Everyone has a good laugh before we head back out to the highway.

A lot of people from Ontario stop to make donations on my way to Hartland, the home of the world's longest covered bridge. Covered bridges are sometimes called "kissing bridges" because back in the days of the horse-and-buggy the darkness of a covered bridge was the ideal place for lovers to steal a kiss.

The legend of the covered bridge at Hartland is that if you can hold your breath while you cross the bridge, your wish will come true. Walking across that bridge, I know exactly what I would wish for, but 391 metres is a long way to try to hold your breath while you're walking as fast as you can. Maybe I can't hold my breath for that distance, but it doesn't matter. It's foolhardy to hold your breath and wait for wishes to come true. I've decided that to generate a million dollars a year for research, I'll take a lot of breaths, go the distance and stick with what I'm doing.

Eighteen kilometres further up the Trans-Canada, we reach the quiet little town of Florenceville. The Saint John River flows right through the town, which was renamed in 1855 to honour Florence Nightingale, the Crimean War heroine. Before the change to Florenceville, the two little villages along the side of the river had the storybook names of *Corn Silk Flats* and *Buttermilk Creek*. No disrespect to Florence Nightingale, but I like the old names better.

Dave Morgan is the Mayor of Florenceville. He's also the town crier and a good-hearted man, whose daughter Michelle suffers from Cerebral Palsy. Florenceville is a milestone for *Jesse's Journey*. We are greeted at the Town Hall by an honour guard of Beavers, Cubs and Scouts, with flags and banners waving. Dressed in his full town crier uniform, ringing his bell and in his best 'Oh Yeah, Oh Yeah' voice, Mayor Dave reads the official proclamation of welcome to Florenceville.

During a reception at the Town Hall, the people of Florenceville present us with over $2,000. That's more than $2 per person in this little New Brunswick town.

There's another reason that Florenceville is a milestone. When we arrived, we'd been met not only by the honour guard but by a big part of the population. Breaking through their welcome banner felt especially good because I knew it meant I was a quarter of the way across Canada.

The highway is quiet on Sunday morning and we're moving further north when the Morgan family joins us on the road. The Mayor and his wife Ethel have brought their daughter Michelle out to the road in her wheelchair to be part of the *Journey* experience. We transfer Michelle from her chair to the front seat of the escort van, because we don't have a police escort and it is too dangerous to have Michelle's wheelchair on the highway. Michelle is now officially part of the road team. She and her mom and Trish are spending their time in the escort vehicle, deep in girl talk, while keeping an eye on Michelle's dad, as he and I walk the road.

Dave Morgan works for McCain Foods, whose corporate headquarters is in Florenceville. As we walk past kilometre after kilometre of potato fields, Dave tells me about his job and his travels to Japan and Korea for McCain. He goes to the Orient once a year, and when the Japanese come to the McCain plant in Canada, they love to bring their golf clubs. Dave says that in Japan, a round of golf can cost $300 U.S. and you can expect a five-hour trip to get to the course. When I ask him why the Japanese come to New Brunswick each year, Dave grins as he looks at me and says, "Just to make sure those potatoes are really there!"

A short while later, Dave points across the Saint John River to a house that had been the home of Wallace McCain. The family feud that rocked the McCain empire has left the $1,500,000 mansion sitting empty, except for a housekeeper and a gardener. Knowing it's empty makes the house which had once been a home look sad – another example where wealth hadn't brought happiness.

On this stretch of the Trans-Canada through New Brunswick, the magic of *Jesse's Journey* brings a couple of terrific volunteers back out to the road. Susan Meadows and Jane Morrison, nicknamed "The Halifax Robo Babes" have driven from Nova Scotia to be with us for the quarter-way mark. They're finally over the exhaustion from their last stint with us. I remember the weekend in Halifax, looking back and seeing Susan and Jane with their T-shirts soaked in sweat, running from car window to car window, collecting donations. It was times like that when I felt I had the easier job.

Out here on the highway, I feel comfortable with an RCMP escort rolling along behind me, the flashing red and white lights of the cruiser providing an extra margin of safety. Through this countryside, which has become more rugged with fir trees and green fields giving way to steeper hills, it has to be difficult for Sgt. Ron Lature to keep his cruiser right behind me in the 'guard' position. Here is an RCMP officer whose son was killed in a motorcycle accident just a week ago, and he's out here helping another father do all he can for his son and children just like him. Maybe it's his way of coping. Maybe it's because he's a father.

It's getting warmer with the first day of summer fast approaching as I walk through Perth-Andover and Grand Falls on the way to Edmunston. This will be the last stop in New Brunswick, before we cross into Quebec. I don't know at this point, but the end of New Brunswick and the beginning of Quebec will be the start of two remarkable stories for two remarkable people.

There's to be a changing of the guard at Edmunston. Ted Eadinger from London will become part of the permanent road team. Ted will take over for Road Manager Trish Federdow, who is heading home to St. Catharines, Ontario to take a break. And a young schoolteacher named Mario Chioini, born in Montreal and fluent in both French and English, will also arrive from London to help us for the 21 days we will be in Quebec. For Ted and Mario, *Jesse's Journey* will be a life-changing experience.

Sometimes things come along at just the right time for people, and I think that's true for my friend Ted. It's raining when we shake hands outside the McDonald's Restaurant in Edmunston.

227

Ted grew up in Saskatchewan where he'd been involved in all kinds of community work and volunteer projects. Our paths first crossed when he became general manager of the television station in London. It was Ted who had OK'd my leave of absence in 1995 to push Jesse across Ontario. In January of 1998, three months before I left for Newfoundland to begin the walk across Canada, Ted's wife Chris died of cancer. At 58, Ted Eadinger was on his own.

Making my way through traffic with a police escort in downtown Edmunston, I'm hoping our next volunteer will arrive soon. Behind me I see a studious looking young man in his thirties. He has steel-rimmed glasses, slightly long hair, and is wearing a T-shirt, khaki shorts and hiking boots. When I ask, "Are you Mario?" he nods and smiles, and again I see a smile that asks, 'What am I getting myself into?' Handing Mario a collection bucket and a handful of brochures I say, "Just try to do what everybody else is doing." For the next three weeks that is exactly what he does, and a whole lot more. Before the year is over, our meeting along the road will lead to an international adventure for Jesse and Mario. But neither of us is aware of that as Mario begins handing out brochures, collecting donations, and speaking French with the people on the streets.

There's been increasing pressure over the past few days for me to see a doctor. Bevin Palmateer is standing by to make sure I keep an appointment with a local doctor in Edmunston. But first I meet the mayor and speak to the audience at a jazz festival in the centre of town. The people are very attentive as I tell them what *Jesse's Journey* is all about. When I finish there's applause, and people reach into their pockets to help. After making my final speech in New Brunswick, Bevin whisks me away to the doctor's office where, despite having rather chewed up feet, I'm given the green light to keep on going.

Chapter Sixteen

LA BELLE PROVINCE

"Do not let what you cannot do interfere with what you can do" –
John Wooden

By now it feels like we've all been together for a lifetime. Nearing
Quebec there is great chemistry as people begin stopping along the
road. Mario walks the first 20 km of the day with me and I see how
proud he is as we take his picture in front of the fleur-de-lis on the
big royal blue sign that says, "Bonjour, welcome to Quebec." Mario
Chioini is in his home province and ready to shine.

On the motor home, Mike Woodward celebrates our arrival in
Quebec with a lunch of hot pastrami sandwiches. Regardless of
whether Mike is making hot chocolate, cutting up fresh fruit,
preparing peanut butter and jam sandwiches, writing and faxing
news releases, charging batteries or changing the oil, he's a key
member of the team who does what has to be done to keep
everything moving. I think Mike sees the motor home as his ship.
He once told me that he always wanted to be a tugboat captain.
And even though this ship is on land, he's the "skipper".

This is the first time since we began in Newfoundland that *Jesse's
Journey* has an 'all-guy' crew. Dave Meadows rejoins us from
Halifax and Doug Goodman, a nursing home administrator, and a
Rotary Club president, arrives from London. It's going to be an
interesting few days as the road crew now consists of seven men.

We have now moved well into province number five. Mario's
enthusiasm during his first day on the road has come at a price.
As I struggle up and down the steep hills leading into Degalis,
Quebec, Mario walks 20 km with me before being confined to
driving the escort van and nursing a badly blistered foot. But a bad
foot doesn't stop him. As the escort van crawls along behind me, I
can hear Mario speaking in French as he does interviews with radio

stations along the route – a route which will take us through
Notre-Dame-de-Lac, Cabano, and the village with the unforgettable
name of St-Louis-de-Ha!-Ha!

Mario plunges himself into his work. He translates everything from
media interviews to menus. He keeps the trip smooth and free of any
problems in the areas of accommodation, transportation and
communication. Mario is pouring his heart into making the
Quebec portion of *Jesse's Journey* a success, and along the road
we see the results.

The sweat is pouring from both Doug Goodman and Dave Meadows
who have been 'working the road' collecting donations and handing
out brochures as we head toward Rivière-du-Loup. Their T-shirts are
soaking wet, partially because Mario is working overtime with the
media, getting us into parades and events wherever he can. More and
more we see people waiting at their laneways with cameras in hand,
waiting to shake hands with a father from English Canada.

Doug notes how hot and sticky it is between noon and two o'clock
in the afternoon. But still, in the distance, in all that heat, you can
see young children waiting with their mothers and fathers to make a
donation and to offer, in French, their words of encouragement. At
first we just thought people saw a flashing light and were curious to
see what was going on. But as Doug jogs from house to house, he
finds a tiny hand offering a "loonie," and at the next house it's the
same. It's as though the message has been passed from house to
house and children are waiting to give.

Help arrives for Mario in the form of the doctor I had seen in
Edmunston. The doctor stops at the roadside with his wife and
children. He brings along some ointment for my feet, but I decide
that Mario needs the attention more than I do. The doctor's wife,
who met us the day before when Bevin took me for a checkup, is
very moved as she watches our road team in action. With her arms
around her daughter's shoulders, she smiles and pretends she doesn't
have wet eyes as people stop to make donations.

At nightfall on our third day in Quebec, we reach Rivière-du-Loup. It's the longest day of the year and as the sun sinks low in the sky, I look out at the St. Lawrence River, reflecting on the day's 33 km completed. It is just one more hot day in what has now become a long series of hot days. The all-guy team is in a buoyant mood. I feel tired and tonight I'm missing Sherene and the boys. In my room, I eat by myself and rest awhile before telephoning my dad in Brantford, Ontario. I'm sure it's just because I'm tired, but I don't tell my dad my concern that I still face thousands of kilometres of highway and another winter. Instead, I try out the French that Mario has taught me earlier in the day. "Bonne fete des péres" – Happy Father's Day!

It's eighteen years since Terry Fox passed through Quebec, and the response at that time was less than spectacular. I was cautioned back in April, before leaving London for Newfoundland, not to expect to do well in Quebec. Leaving the Trans-Canada Highway, we head into Rivière-du-Loup. I know I won't be back on the highway until we reach Sudbury in late August. For the next three weeks, we'll be meeting Quebecers face-to-face in the villages and towns on the smaller roads along the south shore of the St. Lawrence.

The *Journey* vans and motor home are right behind me along with police cars and fire trucks, as I make my way into downtown Rivière-du-Loup, holding up traffic all the way. There is a carnival feeling as people come out of houses, retail shops and businesses to make donations. Behind me I can hear the growling engine of a tractor-trailer that's stuck behind the motor home. Doug says he can just imagine how many gears that truck has, and how hard it must be to keep it inching up the hill we are on. I tell Doug that when we're finally out of his way, this truck driver just might have something nasty to say to us for holding him up. But when he finally gets a chance to pass us, the driver just gives us a wave as he works his way through the gears. Leaving Rivière-du-Loup after another city hall reception, another guest book signed and another pin added to the collection, I'm feeling good about the reception we are receiving in Quebec.

231

Summer arrives, with a breeze which is nothing more than a hot sticky wind blowing off the St. Lawrence River. The road we're on, Highway 132, cuts through miles and miles of low-lying land that has been reclaimed from the St. Lawrence River. On both sides of the road the hayfields swish back and forth in the wind. The economy here is built on the eel fishery. In the tidal waters there are weir traps, which look like rows and rows of wooden posts in the water. This is where the eels, which are shipped around the world, are caught.

Through the heat and haze, I can see the twin silver spires of the Catholic Church in the village of Kamouraska. The further I walk into Quebec, the more I can feel the influence of the Catholic Church. As farmers in this part of the province plough their fields, the church is always there. Every time they finish ploughing a row and turn their tractors back toward home, there in front of them gleaming in the sun are the ever-present silver spires of the church.

Few people stop here, where the air hangs heavy. But sometimes, despite the heat, people get out of their cars to shake hands, take a picture and make a donation. Although there is a constant breeze from the St. Lawrence, it doesn't move the haze or bring any relief. It's almost difficult to breathe with the temperature beyond 30°C and the heat radiating over 40°C from the pavement. There is nothing to do except to keep moving.

With another stretch of 33 kilometres behind us, at the end of what feels like a day in an oven, Murphy's Law strikes again. Exhausted and drenched in sweat, we get back to our motel to discover we have no luggage. With the heat and humidity, probably no one was thinking clearly in the morning when the plans for the day were being worked out. Bevin and Mario have gone to Quebec City to begin their media blitz, without realizing the van they are driving contains the road team's luggage. By the time they return later that night, we are not only tired, we're sweaty and dirty. And yet we still have to laugh as we tell Bevin and Mario that we're not sure whether we want to slug them or kiss them.

On June 24th, St. Jean Baptiste Day in Quebec, we reach the town of La-Pocatière and we are now less than 100 km from Quebec City. Trying to beat the heat, we start our day earlier. It doesn't work. In La-Pocatière, where Bombardier manufactures subway cars for New York and Montreal, Dave and Doug work feverishly in the heat as they hand out brochures and receive donations.

Watching them work, I know I'm seeing volunteerism in its purest form. Dave and Doug are two guys who don't have to be here, but they are giving everything they have to help make this project a success. I keep moving forward in the heat, extending the unbroken line that began in Newfoundland. Maybe it's the heat, but I struggle with my emotions as I watch two guys who never stop working and who never complain.

The day is another scorcher as it drags on into the afternoon. There are moments when I feel dizzy even thought we are all drinking plenty of bottled water to avoid becoming dehydrated. The heat vapours rising from the road ahead are playing games with Doug's mind.

Doug recalled that years ago, when he was a child, his parents had taken him and his brother on a holiday to Quebec. He thought it might have been the heat from the pavement, but he said there were times he could swear that he saw in the distance, his parents and their '38 Dodge parked by the side of the road with two young boys waiting for a picnic lunch. When Doug saw the church spires in the small towns we passed through in Quebec, they brought back memories of those childhood excursions.

Doug described walking through Quebec with me as a powerful experience for two reasons. It gave him an opportunity to see firsthand the extraordinary power of the human spirit, and it took him back to the days of his childhood, the days we only learn to appreciate with the benefit of time.

For about 40 km of road between La Pocatière and Montmagny, Quebec, the wood carving shops become a feast for the eyes. The heat has finally broken as I walk past dozens of artisan's shops jammed with carvings and the aroma of fresh cut wood. Outside some of the shops there are full size carvings, sometimes of a man holding an axe or of a woman with a broom. In front of another shop there's an entire family, including the children and a dog, all carved in typical Quebecois style.

Further west we stop in L'Islet-sur-Mer and the mayor welcomes us. We all sign our names in the town's Guest Book, where an entire page of beautifully scripted calligraphy refers to *Jesse's Journey – A Father's Tribute* and our walk across Canada.

Across the square from City Hall, where the motor home is parked, there's a very old and historic church. I don't usually go to see these kinds of things, opting instead to sleep before getting back on the road. But this time, the church is so close that I walk across the street with the rest of the road crew to have a look. There is an elderly couple on duty, serving as volunteers showing tourists through the building. The church is a masterpiece of stained glass. There's a beautifully carved raised pulpit. The wooden pews, ornate statues and bronze plaques tell the story of the town's history through the families that have belonged to the church. The old people showing us the church are proud Quebecers who speak in a matter-of-fact way about how the church was built in 1605. The main portion of the church is no longer used for Sunday services as the congregation has dwindled. Services, we're told, are now held in the smaller and newer part of the church. The 'new' section is only a hundred years old!

L'Islet-sur-Mer is where the hydrofoil Bras d'Or 400, perhaps the finest seagoing combat vehicle ever built in Canada, now sits on shore as an exhibit at Canada's largest maritime museum. The Bras d'Or, the one and only hydrofoil of its type built in the 1960s, suffered a fate similar to the Avro Arrow, the state of the art warplane scrapped by the Diefenbaker government. The Bras d'Or 400, which was so fast on the water that it had difficulty training its guns on a target, now sits on land with a huge hole cut in its side to let tourists on board to see what might have been.

The days leading up to Quebec City are a blur, and at times I feel dizzy and disoriented. The hours seem longer than ever before. To add to my confusion, there's a big increase in people traffic, with volunteers and permanent road crew members shuttling in and out as some of them head home to take a break. Sometimes at breakfast I'm not sure who is here for the day and who is heading home.

It's almost the end of June when we reach Montmagny, 50 km east of Quebec City. Along this part of the river, the saltwater comes to an end and the St. Lawrence becomes fresh water. The mayor of Montmagny tells us all about the town's fall festival, which coincides with the arrival of 600,000 snow geese heading south. The geese feed on plants that thrive in the waters of the St. Lawrence, which at this point contains about five per-cent saltwater. The mayor says that in just one week, the geese will eat all the plants and then, much like our road caravan, it will be time for them to move on.

At Montmagny I say goodbye to Dave Meadows, who is heading home to Halifax. Back in Nova Scotia Dave became a member of what was loosely called 'The 33 Club,' walking a full 33 km with me in one day. But long before that Dave had been in Ottawa with his son Jason when I'd finished pushing Jesse across Ontario. Dave had shown Jason how it's more important to give than to receive. And now three years later, the Meadows family, Dave and Susan and Jason along with their friends in Nova Scotia, have done all they can to help make this *Journey* a success. As we hug one another and slap each other on the back, I thank Dave and I take a moment to tell him that if the situation were reversed, I would be there for him and his son. That's what friends do for each other.

The traffic jam of volunteers sorts itself out at Montmagny. Dave and Doug leave for Montreal to catch flights home.

Two new recruits arrive from Drummondville, André Trenqua and Marc-Olivier Roy. Trish has returned from her furlough to St. Catharines. Ted Eadinger and Bevin Palmateer also head for the airport in Montreal where they park the 'Mickey' van before catching their flights home. The final piece of the logistical bottleneck is getting the van that's parked at the airport back to the road team. Bringing 'Mickey' back from the airport in Montreal is Ann Hutchison's job.

In 1988, two years after Jesse had been diagnosed with DMD, Ann had a bittersweet year. In July she got married, and in October she was diagnosed with cancer. There is no doubt that Ann knows, perhaps more than anyone who has been on the road with us, the value of research. Ann also brings with her an infectious enthusiasm that affects the entire team. Surveying the new recruits, it continues to amaze me how people who have never heard of us before willingly join us for a week, and sometimes longer, leaving behind their families and the comfort of their homes.

We nickname André Trenqua, 'The Gentle Giant.' He is from Drummondville, Quebec, and lost his left leg in a farm accident when he was four years old. Marc-Olivier Roy, also from Drummondville, is a handsome young man who should probably be at home spending his summer nights with a girlfriend. Instead, 'The French Connection,' André and Marc-Olivier are on the road.

The first thing we discover about André and Marc-Olivier is that neither of them speaks English. It's incredible how much you can communicate with hand signals, the odd word here and there in French, a lot of smiles and a good dose of laughter. When those who speak only English and those who speak only French work at this, there are few problems left unsolved. And when there is a difficult hurdle to get over, bilingual Mario is there to help us out. Secretly, I think Mario enjoys watching us struggle for a bit before he jumps in with the translation.

Leading to Levis, across the river from Quebec City, the new road crew is complete when Scott Shakir arrives from St. Thomas, Ontario. Scott teaches a grade five class in the village of Sparta, and has a couple of things working in his favour. He can speak a little French and, to prepare for his time on the road, he's been walking the 14 km from the public school in Sparta to his home in St. Thomas at the end of each school day.

On the Sunday of the July 1st weekend I complete 15 km of highway before we mark the road and everyone piles into 'Mickey' for the short ferry ride from Levis, across the St. Lawrence to the Lower Town of Old Quebec City. From there, motorcycle police escort us up the steep hill to the Chateau Frontenac, the jewel in the crown of Quebec City. On a holiday weekend, Quebec City is alive with tourists taking in the city's atmosphere and history.

Samuel D. Champlain founded Quebec City in 1608. Looking east down the St. Lawrence River toward Ile D'Orleans you can quickly understand why Quebec City is sometimes called "The Gibraltar of North America" and why hundreds of years ago it was clear that whoever controlled Quebec City controlled access to North America. It was here in 1759 that British and French forces fought for control of North America on the Plains of Abraham. The battle lasted less than 20 minutes and claimed the lives of both the British Commander, Sir James Wolfe and the French Commander, the Marquis de Montcalm. With great pride on a Sunday afternoon 240 years later, English and French speaking peoples sing, dance and make music together as they host tourists from around the world. It's here in Quebec City that those same tourists marvel at Canada's cultural success.

On the south shore once again, the morning after our visit to Quebec City, people begin making donations as soon as I'm on the road. Donations to *Jesse's Journey* sometimes seem to come from everywhere. At night time after supper in yet another restaurant, a man and his wife come to our table to meet us and shake my hand. They leave a donation of $500 before quietly slipping away.

237

When Scott Shakir joined us, he brought with him a $1,200 donation from the kids at the public school back home in the village of Sparta, Ontario. Newfoundlander John Hodder, who had been with us for a week in our earliest days on the road, stopped on the highway on his way to Ontario. He dropped off $2,000 he had collected in his hometown of Baie Verte, a large part of it from school kids who'd held a 'cool day' where they'd each paid a dollar to dress 'really cool.' In the snow of Newfoundland almost three months earlier, John Hodder, the absent-minded schoolteacher, had kept us laughing through some difficult times. He was upset that his hometown hadn't made a contribution, so when he returned home he became the driving force in making sure that Baie Verte, Newfoundland would be counted as a part of *Jesse's Journey.*

André 'The Gentle Giant' leaves us at Quebec City. I wonder if I'll ever see him again. He's another of those volunteers who knows when to work and when to laugh. We've shared a couple of funny moments together. There was the day the knee on his artificial leg was squeaking and we had to get out the wrenches and a can of WD-40 to fix the joint. And I'll never forget the rainy day when three or four of us were lined up in the aisle of the motor home stretching calves and thighs, and doing knee bends before getting out on the road. André was sitting watching us with his artificial leg crossed over his other leg. Out of the blue he picked up his metal leg and, mimicking our exercise routine, he threw it over his shoulder! Needless to say we all collapsed in a heap. That's when I knew that laughter sounds the same in English as it does in French. When it was time to go, André hugged each of us and then, as quietly as he had arrived, slipped into the wake of the *Journey* as we moved further westward.

Before leaving the motor home for the last time, young Marc-Olivier Roy made a little speech in his best attempt at English. He thanked us for a great week and apologized that he didn't have much money.

With the kind of smile you have when you've made new friends, he reached into his pocket and pulled out a ten-dollar bill for *Jesse's Journey*. Marc-Olivier Roy was 18 years old.

One of the most memorable moments in Quebec happened off the road. It was about eight o'clock in the evening on the day we'd arrived in Quebec City, when I heard a knock on the sliding glass door of my motel room. I opened the door and, standing there in the summer twilight with her mother was a little girl in her pyjamas. Michelle Gagnon is from Oshawa, Ontario, and her mother said that after they read our brochure, Michelle told her she wanted to donate something "to Jesse." The little girl in her pyjamas handed me a ten-dollar bill. Michelle Gagnon was eight years old. In the morning as we prepared to get underway again, I signed my name on my *Jesse's Journey* hat and left it at the front desk for the little girl in her pyjamas. It was time to move on.

On Canada Day, July 1st, people begin making donations as soon as I am on the road walking west toward Montreal. In the roller coaster world we've become used to, I hear the sound of a woman applauding from her veranda as *Jesse's Journey* passes her home in the early morning sunshine. By mid-morning it starts raining heavily. And then, just as quickly as the skies open up, donations dry up, and we spend the rest of the day being washed by the spray of passing vehicles.

From Quebec City, Highway 132 hugs the shore of the St. Lawrence as it winds through quiet villages where the scent of wild roses fills the air and painted window boxes sag as they overflow with flowers. The villages of Berniere-St-Nicolas, St-Antoine-de-Tilly, St-Pierre-les-Becquets and Ste-Angele-de-Laval on the way to Nicolet are made up of small houses, painted all the colours of the rainbow. These homes appear to be dozing in the sun, and wedged shoulder to shoulder as they crowd right up to the roadway.

239

Alongside the St. Lawrence River, in these European-looking villages, there's a tremendous sense of history, almost as if time has stopped. For days on end we can look out on the St. Lawrence River, where Samuel de Champlain and Jacque Cartier sailed all those years ago.

It's a summer morning and the grass is still wet with dew, when I see stone ovens just off the side of the road. Smoke is drifting up from the ovens and the air is filled with the smell of fresh-baked bread. The ovens, which are round and about five feet high at the centre, are smooth and shaped like the igloos you see in children's books. In each oven there's a main shelf for baking. At ground level there's an orange glow from the coals, giving each of the ovens a toasty look like the hearths you see on Christmas cards. Through the open doors of one oven, sitting on the shelf, there are loaves of bread turning a golden brown as they slowly bake.

With a picture of hot buttered bread in my mind as I walk on, I come to a spot where there's an older woman who is removing the bread from her oven. She has a kerchief on her head and holds a huge wooden paddle, which she's using to lift the finished loaves from the oven. The woman is so busy that when she finally looks up she seems a little startled. She says, "Bonjour monsieur" almost as if she is asking a question. This isn't a commercial bread-making operation. This is one woman making bread for her family. Handing her one of our brochures, her eyes light up and a smile comes across her face as she sees that the brochure is printed in French! We printed our brochures in both English and French because *Jesse's Journey* is a national project and we want all Canadians to feel welcome in taking part.

Between Sorel and Longueuil, Quebec, the early summer sky churns in shades of grey and black. Driving sheets of rain cut visibility to a minimum and jagged bolts of lightning are ripping through the dark sky, lighting up the road for an instant and frequently forcing us to stop and take cover in the safety of the escort van. The rain finally eases up, and a soggy troupe with running shoes that make squishy noises, steps back onto the road to complete the day's 33 km.

In the dismal weather, donations are few and far between as I trudge on toward Montreal. I have to call on the reserve of discipline I built up in the seven months of training before setting out to walk across Canada.

I don't want to burden anyone on the road team, but the weather has left me with a feeling of loneliness, being away from home for so long. It isn't self-doubt about my physical abilities that I'm fighting, although I have asked myself a couple of times if maybe I'm needed at home more than out here on the road. There's a danger that this can become an emotional tug-of-war. It's time to remember that I made the commitment to the walk back on those dark, windy, wet and cold nights when I was training in London. It was then I decided that if I could stay with it when there was no one there, then maybe when the sun was shining and there was someone to say "keep going," I just might be able to make it.

The physical challenge of that set distance of road each day is mandatory. The only thing that's optional is how that job gets done. It's back to the basics of focusing on an almost mindless routine, through constant repetition at the exclusion of everything else. Again, I tell myself to stay the course. Quitting is not an option.

The road team must think I have an obsessive need for routine, but timing is how I cope in the stressful times. It isn't always exciting, but it works for me. I use the same template day after day, and that's what gets me by. Through good days and bad days on the road, timing is the one thing that remains a constant. I go out to the road every morning at the same time and repeat the same pattern. It's a routine that works for me, and I know I have to maintain that pattern if I'm going to survive 8000-plus kilometres of highway and more than nine months on the road. When almost no one stops, it's important to remain a creature of habit to ride out the stormy days.

Out here on the road, the little things mean a lot. With the skyline of Montreal now visible in the distance, there are two moments to remember. The first occurs when a truck driver pulls his tractor-trailer to the shoulder of the highway. Climbing from the cab of his rig, he makes a donation, grips my hand and says, "You're a good man." He probably never knew how much encouragement he gave me at a time when I really needed it.

The second is a visual moment. It had been raining heavily all day, and it seemed like an eternity before we heard the honk from the escort van to let us know we had made our distance for the day. When I looked to my side I saw one of those pictures that no camera can do justice to. There was Ann Hutchison, soaked to the skin with water dripping from her chin, her hair wet and tangled. She was beaming with a smile that said 'I did it!' Ann Hutchison, a cancer survivor, had just become the first woman to spend an entire day on the road with me, walking a full 33 km!

The Olympic Stadium and Place Ville Marie in downtown Montreal are the most recognizable landmarks across the river on the north side of the St. Lawrence where the Jacques Cartier Bridge links Montreal and Longueuil. It's now three months to the day since I left home. Trish spends a lot of time talking to me about the mechanics of the next few days and getting through the biggest city in the country. I think Trish also wants to caution me not to expect a lot of donations while we make our way through Montreal. Trish was with Jesse and me in 1995 when we crossed Ontario and I'm sure she's recalling our Toronto experience where I pushed Jesse down Yonge Street in his wheelchair, and people asked us for money!

The journey through Montreal is surprisingly smooth, with very few delays. There's one moment of chaos in the parking garage underneath Place Ville Marie, the day we marked the road and headed off to the mayor's office. The parking garage had minimum clearance for vans. We never thought about the height that had been added when the two strobe lights were mounted on the roof of the 'Mickey' van.

The strobe lights scrape a couple of overhead pipes and that starts alarms ringing. Suddenly, security people are running everywhere and before long they surround us. We still have no idea what all the excitement is about. When Mario Chioini translates for us, we apologize while trying hard not to snicker because the security guards aren't very happy with us.

The whirlwind visit to downtown Montreal includes signing the Golden Book at City Hall, and happily accepting another donation from our friends at Manulife Financial as they continue to keep their promise to donate $1,000 every time I pass one of their branches. In downtown Montreal we also learn that Royal Bank has come on board as a sponsor. On the streets there's a lot of media attention. Making my way along a Montreal street where there are plenty of outdoor cafés, people are applauding and I find myself surrounded by television cameras from CBC, CTV and Global Television, along with still photographers from both the *Montreal Gazette* and *La Presse*. Still, the most memorable contact made in Montreal didn't happen on a quiet street with outdoor cafés, but rather in the middle of a freeway in rush hour traffic.

The freeway system in Montreal can be a little scary at the best of times. At rush hour it's frightening, especially when you're walking in the middle of that traffic. Even with police cars and lots of flashing lights both in front of me and behind me, I'm not very comfortable. Transport trucks are just a few feet away as they rush past me in the lanes on my right and my left. Over my shoulder I see a man of about 40, with disheveled hair and a scruffy-looking salt-and-pepper beard, running to catch up with me through the traffic which has slowed to a crawl. He has a leather satchel slung over his shoulder, and I think that he's a journalist wanting to do an interview. It turns out the man is from Paris, France and he doesn't want to do an interview. He has something bigger in mind.

Jean-Luc Robert is in Canada to ask if Jesse will come to Paris, France in December. This is not what I'm expecting to hear as I drink some tea and eat some fruit at my mid-morning break. In Canada, *Jesse's Journey* is not associated with the Muscular Dystrophy Association of Canada, which turned us down when we asked them to take part in the 1995 crossing of Ontario. But it seems The French *Association le Dystrophe Musculaire* is impressed with what Jesse has accomplished and they want him to take part in their annual telethon. The plan is to have a television crew from France visit Jesse in London and then join us on the road in northern Ontario. The crew will shoot video, which will be used to tell the story of *Jesse's Journey* in conjunction with Jesse's visit to France. Jean-Luc Robert asks me to think about it, and slinging his leather bag over his shoulder, he disappears through the dense traffic.

There's a long drive to Valleyfield, Quebec, that night to attend a Rotary Club function where $2,300 is donated. Riding back in the van, my mind drifts back to the events of the morning and Jean-Luc Robert. I have lots to think about. If Jesse decides he wants to go, and if we maintain our schedule on the road, I'll be entering British Columbia about the time Jesse will be on his way to Paris. On the road the next day, after talking with Sherene about the proposed trip to France, it's time to take the next step.

I don't usually rush to judgement, but for almost three weeks I've been watching Mario Chioini's dedication to *Jesse's Journey* and the ease with which he switches from English to French. Born in Montreal, Mario's pride in his French heritage rings clear in his voice with every interview on radio and television. The camera lens captured that same pride three weeks ago when a photographer took Mario's picture as he stepped into his home province of Quebec. I've enjoyed his sense of humour and his always-positive attitude. Now it's time to talk.

Life-changing experiences sometimes come to us unexpectedly. I'm not surprised to see Mario with a somewhat shocked look on his face. After all, it's not often that someone asks you right out of the blue, "Mario, do you think you could take my wife and son to Paris, France, in December?"

It takes Mario a second to realize that I'm serious. Then his eyes begin to sparkle, as the question I asked leads to a lot more questions. Walking the road toward Ontario with Mario, we discuss some of those questions. As a teacher, can Mario leave school for a week in early December? What role will he play in Jesse's travelling to France? Is Jesse up to making the trip?

Obviously there are a lot of things to be worked out before December, but the bottom line is that Mario agrees to escort Jesse and Sherene if it can be worked out. The trip to Paris, France is looking like it's now a 'go.'

On his final day on the road, as we cross the border from Quebec into Ontario, Mario walks 33 km with me. Later in the year he will travel several thousand more kilometres for the *Journey,* only this time it will be with Jesse.

Chapter Seventeen

ONTARIO, MY HOME PROVINCE

"Be yourself, who else is better qualified?" –
Frank J. Giblin

It's mid-July when I take my first steps in Ontario. The towns and villages with distinctively French names like Les Coteaux and Rivière Beaudette soon become towns and villages with decidedly English-sounding names like Lancaster and Summerstown. In a way, I am home.

In the distance I can hear the sound of bagpipes pumping some life into the humid summer air. By the time I reach the Ontario information kiosk, the young men and women in kilts have worked their bagpipes to a fever pitch. There is the military snick of the snare drums, and the soft thump of a bass drum that rattles in my chest as I break through the banner held by my mom and dad. I'm officially in Ontario, province number six.

In front of the motor home, escort vans and police cars, Ron Calhoun, the National Coordinator of *Jesse's Journey – A Father's Tribute,* welcomes us to our home province. The last time I had seen Ron was in Whitbourne, Newfoundland, on the Easter weekend. In the crowd is Dr. Ron Worton from Ottawa. On the steps of City Hall in St. John's, Newfoundland, the morning I began my walk across Canada, I had presented Dr. Worton with a cheque for $250,000 for research. Sherene and I will be seeing Dr. Worton in Ottawa, where a laboratory is being named in Jesse's honour.

Bevin is busy shooting videotape of the arrival of the *Journey* road crew in Ontario as several American tourists at the information kiosk are wondering what's happening. There's one family from Boston, Massachusetts standing in the sunshine patiently listening and learning about us. When the formal welcome ceremonies are over the father comes over to meet me. Reaching into his pocket he donates $60 as he shakes my hand and says, "You're doing a good thing." At night I write his words in my journal, a journal that for the first time has a dateline at the top of the page that says, 'Ontario.'

Corn on the cob is one of the lunchtime treats Mike Woodward prepares in the microwave to celebrate our arrival in Ontario. Corn on the cob is one of nature's sinful delights where you lace the yellow rows of kernels with butter and salt and you don't tell your doctor about it. It's also one of those taste sensations that serve as a calendar in Ontario, the same as strawberries in June. Enjoying the taste of summer, there's a thought about the calendar in the back of my mind. August is not that far away and we have just entered Ontario. While the heat is tolerable, my mind wanders ahead to Manitoba, which we won't reach until well into October. That is going to mean a dash across Saskatchewan and Alberta before winter closes in on us in the Rockies.

We are now on the north shore of the St. Lawrence River. On the road to Cornwall donations are very good. Aurèle Houle along with his wife Judy and son Corey seem to know how to read our every need from the moment we first meet. Aurèle is the owner of a Petro-Canada station in Cornwall, and his first order of business is to see that the motor home and escort vans are washed and the gas tanks filled. That is just the start of the Houle family's generosity. We are a group of strangers being shown the kind of caring for one another that Eastern Ontario exhibited in one of the toughest times in its history – the late winter ice storm that crippled a huge portion of eastern Canada early in the year.

Stories like the ice storm seem far away and not quite real until we're shown a front-page picture from an old newspaper. The magnitude of the storm becomes very real when looking at collapsed hydro towers with wires dangling in the snow, and cars with collapsed roofs pinned under toppled trees, and everything coated in a thick layer of ice. When you're at home and you can flip to the

Crossing over from New Brunswick to Quebec with the first "all guy" crew. Pictured from the left are: Michael Woodward, Dave Meadows, Bevin Palmateer, myself, Mario Chioini, Ted Eadinger and Doug Goodman.

Peter Garland of CFPL Radio in London was one of many radio announcers who conducted regular weekly interviews with me as I made my way across the country.

sports pages or the comics over a hot cup of tea or coffee, there is no ice storm. When you're in another part of the country and you're alerted to the need for food, blankets and generators, the need to help begins to register. When you're living through it, you get busy.

The Houles, Aurèle and Judy, share some of the incredible stories of courage and selflessness that resulted from the ice storm. Aurèle tells us about how he broke about half a dozen windows on cars and trucks, just trying to get the ice off. He had pictures of vehicles covered in ice that was twelve inches thick. It took days to melt, even when the vehicles were indoors at Aurèle's service station. In this part of Ontario you don't have to look too hard to find telltale traces of storm damage.

On the road through Cornwall, I can see the work ethic that the Houle family values has been passed on to their son, Corey. Here is a teenager who spends his day on the run, handing out brochures and collecting donations for *Jesse's Journey*. Back at Aurèle and Judy's home at the end of the day, I watch Corey limp into the house on a badly blistered foot, and there's his mom with supper organized, and our laundry cleaned and folded.

On a Sunday night as we prepare to leave Cornwall and head for Morrisburg the Houle family has a special sendoff planned. At the motel where we are staying the Houle family arrives with a giant picnic supper. Aurèle, whose family has fed us and serviced and fueled our vehicles, even lent us a van to shuttle volunteers back and forth at the next changing of the guard in Ottawa. With the ice storm, the people of Eastern Ontario had been through a lot in the past few months. And like the Houle family, they knew where to find their strength. They know what it means to work hard. They know what it means to do something for others.

From Cornwall along the north shore of the St. Lawrence I pass through the eastern Ontario towns of Long Sault, Ingleside and Iroquois before we mark the road and make a detour that takes us to Ottawa.

249

Since the time I crossed the Quebec-Ontario border, two more members of the Price family, Jeff and his father Al, have been our road crew volunteers. For Jeff Price, his time on the road as a volunteer with us has had a tremendous impact on him. I'm not sure Jeff knew just what to expect when he joined us, although I'm sure his brother Gary, who had been with us in Newfoundland, probably told him it would be a very worthwhile experience.

Jeff learned the ropes quickly. On days when the sweat was dripping from his chin and his T-shirt was stuck to his body, it was Jeff who was making sure that I was drinking enough water. His energy seemed boundless, yet as the days rolled by and he saw people's response to *Jesse's Journey*, Jeff was beginning to ask himself questions about his own life and his future. While Jeff began exploring new possibilities in his life, his father's name surfaced in my daily journal. Al Price quietly slipped into the record book as our oldest volunteer to walk and work 33 km in one day. Al accomplished this at the age of 71!

As well as being the nation's capital and home of the Tulip Festival, when people think of Ottawa, they think about skating on the Rideau Canal and how snowy it can be in the capital of Canada. But in the middle of July, Ottawa is sweltering. It is humid and the thermometer seems stuck at 35 degrees.

Motorcycle police escort *Jesse's Journey* to Parliament Hill. At the top of Wellington Street I pause to look at the statue of Terry Fox. When reporters ask me what I think about Terry, I tell them, "Terry was in a league all by himself and as Canadians, we were lucky to have had him for the time we did."

At the eternal flame in front of the Parliament Buildings, I give a little boy a loonie to toss into the water and make a wish. Watching him flip the coin into the water surrounding the flame, I think about how this is where Jesse and I ended our *Journey* together in 1995. The rest of the way across Ontario I'll be retracing virtually the same route Jesse and I shared three years earlier.

250

The extremely humid weather is making everything difficult, including breathing, so I really appreciate Deputy Prime Minister Herb Grey leaving his centre block office on Parliament Hill to meet me. Photographers' cameras click as the Deputy Prime Minister and I talk about the need to increase funding for medical research in Canada. I mention to Mr. Grey that among the G7 nations, Canada has a poor track record in funding medical research. Since waging his own battle with cancer, I think the Deputy Prime Minister has developed a greater understanding of the need for research dollars. We shake hands and as Mr. Grey walks back up the steps to his parliamentary office, I'm left with the feeling that he genuinely cares about what I'm doing.

The highlight in Ottawa is seeing Jesse on videotape and hearing him speak to researchers at the Ottawa General Hospital Research Institute. This is the institute headed by Dr. Ron Worton, the discoverer of the gene that causes DMD. As Sherene and I watch Jesse's image on the video monitor, I feel very proud of my son who has given hope to so many people who suffer from genetic illnesses. After the video, Sherene and I, along with Dr. Worton, unveil a plaque officially dedicating the Jesse Davidson Laboratory in Genetic Research.

Touring the laboratory, it's interesting to watch the youngest members of our road crew, Trish and Bevin. Bevin and his video camera are face-to-face with science, and he is busy videotaping digital readouts that are blinking on several pieces of research equipment, printing the results of experiments.

We have plenty of questions for the technicians and researchers who seem glad to take the time to explain their work. Scanning a lab that's full of equipment, and seeing researchers working at the bench, reminds me of why I am making this trek across Canada. Maybe I don't know a lot about research, but I know one thing; without money, it doesn't happen. It's time to get back to the road.

251

In Ottawa there is a heavy media workload and everywhere we go, there are cameras and microphones and, in addition, there is the relentless heat. Leaving Ottawa, it's time to say goodbye to Mike Woodward, who is finally going to get a well-deserved rest. He has been on the road, driving the motor home for more than three and a half months, since leaving London in March. It is the 17th of July, and after 113 days away from his wife Irene, Mike doesn't have to drive today. Instead he's boarding the train for home. The job of motor home captain is turned over to Ed Coxworthy, who is back from Bell Island, Newfoundland.

Back on Highway 2 at Iroquois, *Jesse's Journey* begins moving west again, through Cardinal and on toward Brockville. There are people waiting along the road, and at almost every stop now there are town pins, hats, T-shirts, guest books to sign and pictures to be taken. And most of all, there are donations.

Saturday July 18th, is my 100th day on the road. Ed Coxworthy says he can see that my legs are no longer the same size. Ed, who went home to Newfoundland when we reached Halifax, says the difference in size is easy to see. He measures my calves and finds that my right leg is now a full three centimetres bigger than my left leg. I assume that the difference comes from the right leg having to work harder because of the angle of the road. But the size of my legs doesn't seem to matter. What's important is the need to increase the frequency and intensity of stretch and massage routine. My muscles are feeling the distance.

The heat and humidity are still a strain for all of us as I make my way through Rockport and Gananoque on the road to Kingston. There are times when the road ahead shimmers in the heat. At least Ed keeps us laughing with his Newfoundland interpretation of the situation. Ed describes our circumstance as, "Like walking on a hot stove and breathing soup!"

There's another changing of the guard as I approach Kingston, which at different times has been an Indian settlement, a French fort, a

British citadel and for a brief period, Canada's capital (1841-1843). My sister Dorothy and my brother-in-law Peter join us as road crew, along with Grace Roca, one of our most petite, quiet and yet energetic volunteers. Grace came to Canada from Portugal when she was 12 years old.

She left school when she was very young and was married when she was 17. She was only 19 when she and her husband John celebrated the arrival of their son, Rob. The heat didn't seem to bother Grace, who Ed nicknamed "Gracie." She grew up working in the fields, picking tomatoes. She already knows what hard work is all about. Quietly and efficiently, Gracie tackles every job she is assigned. With her *Jesse's Journey* T-shirt stuck to her in the heat, Gracie jogs from house to house putting hundreds of brochures in mailboxes along the route.

Kingston is where one of the most unusual stories occurred when Jesse and I were together crossing Ontario. What made it so unusual was that the story didn't unfold for us until Jesse and I were making an appearance at a convention in London in 1996, a year after we had been through Kingston together.

A mother from Kingston, whose name I never knew, rushed over to meet Jesse and me in the lobby of the downtown hotel where we were appearing. She told us a story that had happened when she and her sister had met us a year earlier on a hot afternoon along the road to Kingston.

She was obviously excited to meet us again, and asked if Jesse and I could wait for just a few minutes while she went upstairs and brought her daughter, who has Cystic Fibrosis, downstairs to meet Jesse. We said that of course we would wait. It was while Jesse and the young girl chatted that I learned what had happened on the road in 1995.

This lady and her sister had been driving west when they passed Jesse and me heading east toward Ottawa. She said to her sister, "That's John and Jesse. We have to turn around and make a donation." As they got in line in the slow-moving traffic, the woman asked her sister to push the button and make the window go down. Her sister reminded her that the window hadn't worked for years. The lady was insistent and while she played with the master switch for the window, her sister continued flicking her switch for the power window. Nothing was happening. Then all of a sudden, just as they pulled up beside Jesse and me, the power motor hummed and the window glided down. They made a donation and drove straight on to the service station where the woman's husband worked as a mechanic. When they told him the story he said, "Honey, the window didn't go down. It hasn't worked for years. I'll show you." With that he took off the door panel and the wires that powered the window were several inches short of each other! It was a remarkable story told by a woman who I knew had no capacity to lie.

I have never been a very religious person, but there have been nights when I've put my head on the pillow and asked myself, 'What did make that window go down?' Alone on the road on a hot afternoon in Kingston, it was nice to recall one of the special moments Jesse and I had shared along the road.

At this point, on the road to Belleville, it seems as if there is some kind of divine referee keeping the forces of good and bad in balance. Today, the scale tips toward the bad guys as Perry Zavitz, one of our volunteers, who has driven all the way from London to take part in *Jesse's Journey,* has his car stolen. Police find the car later in the day with the driver's side window smashed and the steering column damaged where the car was hot-wired.

On the other hand, a woman stops at the motor home at lunchtime and donates $100. She is followed by a young couple from Quebec, who are teaching their children what it means to give to others. These two little kids timidly make a donation to help some other kids.

Passing through the Tyendinaga First Nations Reserve east of
Belleville, I do an interview at the little 80-watt radio station. The
interviewer, who is also the on-air announcer, is a young blind man
named Ky. He looks to be about 20, and has a genuinely warm smile
and long black hair kept neatly in a ponytail. "Shake my hand," he
says. "I'm not weird, I'm just blind." This is Ky's first live interview.
He uses an unusual-looking Braille typewriter to write out some
questions before we go on the air. I can't believe how fast he is with
the typewriter. During the interview, I do everything I can to make
things go smoothly. I leave, thinking that Ky is another of the
amazing people spread over six times zones who make this
country work.

The daily routine of describing, in morning radio interviews, where
we are and what things look like from the roadside, now has a new
piece of information. When we reach Trenton, I can now say the
water we are looking at is Lake Ontario.

A large group of cadets marching inside the fence at the Canadian
Forces Base in Trenton cheers and applauds as I walk by with a
police escort right behind me. The Base is Canada's largest military
air base, and there's an almost constant roar of what sounds like
thunder, as giant military planes rumble down the runway before
lifting into the sky. At a commercial airport you see the brightly
painted planes of airlines from around the world. In Trenton,
the aircraft taking off and landing are all the same shade of
military green.

Along the road there are stories of courage and stories of hope
almost every day. There are also sad times, and I hear one of the
most heart-wrenching stories in Trenton, while walking with a
member of the Lions Club who has both a son and a grandson with
Duchenne. Here is a man whose troubles I cannot imagine, and as
we walk along, the tragic story that continues to unfold is almost
beyond comprehension. This man is a paramedic whose twin
grandchildren died of crib death 21 days apart, one at four months

255

old and the other at five months. In both instances, the man beside me was the paramedic who answered the call. Some days the stories are more than I can handle.

Sharing a cup of tea on board the motor home before bed, the emotional strain of the day makes it difficult for me to share the story with Ed. After listening, Ed pauses before saying to me, "Johnny, if we could all throw our troubles into a hat, you'd want to draw your own back out."

Back on the road next morning, I pass the 'Big Apple', set back from the highway in one of the many orchards in Colborne. The world's largest apple is just one of the dozens of roadside attractions I will pass in the weeks and months ahead. More than 650,000 people a year visit the bright red, four-story apple shaped structure, inside which there are audiovisual displays of the local apple industry. Along the road there are lots of people who want to shake hands, and there are motorists who give me the thumbs up sign and shout, "Keep it going!" One motorist claps with both hands as he drives by. I have no idea who might be steering the car.

Through Cobourg and Port Hope, media attention from Toronto increases. There are radio interviews to be done, and television cameras are now with us almost every day as I make my way through two of the prettiest lakeshore communities in Ontario.

For years, towns and cities across Ontario have been wrestling with the question of how to save their downtown core from decline in the battle with suburban malls and 'big box' retailers. Cobourg and Port Hope both look like they have found the winning formula. The two communities have managed to preserve the Victorian architecture of their stately homes, churches and public buildings. Gas lamps and hanging flower baskets complete the Victorian streetscapes that have captured the attention of film and television production companies in both Canada and the United States. The retail mix on the main streets of these two towns seems to have capitalized on the theme of 'the butcher, the baker and the candlestick maker.' There are bookstores, flower shops, barbershops and antique stores. All of these shops give the appearance of a long-term commitment to the downtown core. There are no empty stores. Local residents tell me that there's a waiting list to acquire a shop on the main street.

People are making donations, and traffic slows to a crawl as I climb the hill leading out of Port Hope on a hot Sunday afternoon. Back on the road, pushing on toward Oshawa, in a time when so many downtowns seem to be struggling in a world of franchise and big box competition, I'm leaving behind two confident little towns, each with a solid and vibrant core.

In the days leading up to Toronto, I speak to city councils and at other times with provincial or federal politicians. Through Whitby, Ajax, Pickering and Markham, I tell the story of *Jesse's Journey* and our goal of providing the research community with a million dollars a year, every year, forever. Day after day I deliver that message. People might think it's easy to repeat the story over and over, but it isn't. Maybe it's the heat, or maybe I'm just tired, but every time I speak, it's a struggle to keep my emotions in check. I'm aware that I'm talking about a disease that marches on relentlessly. More than that, this is my son I'm talking about. We are a family like so many others, in a race with time.

The kilometres click by, one by one, as people along the road open their hearts and their wallets to proudly take part in *Jesse's Journey*. Nearing Toronto, a woman who operates a chip wagon at the side of the road donates $11. It's all she can afford. Giving her a copy of our video story, she breaks down in tears. She has lost three nephews to Duchenne.

The challenge of getting through Toronto begins in the pre-dawn darkness as Bevin drives us into the heart of the city to appear on City-TV's *Breakfast Television*. The show's host, Ann Rohmer, who remembers Jesse and me from 1995, interviews me on the street

257

outside the studio. She is gracious, and while the interview on the fast paced morning show lasts only a couple of minutes, we do very well. Climbing back into the van, I shut my eyes and try to sleep. Bevin tells me later that when the interview wrapped up, Ann Rohmer went back inside, leaned her head on her producer's shoulder and said, "God, I love that man." I feel embarrassed, but not nearly as embarrassed as when Bevin and I discover that neither one of us has the price of a cup of coffee in our pockets. Murphy's Law has struck again and suddenly the cup of tea and the doughnut I had back at *Breakfast Television* is starting to feel like a Christmas dinner.

The next stop is Metro Hall where Toronto Mayor Mel Lastman introduces me to City Council. All the major television networks – CBC, CTV, Global, CITY and CHCH-TV are there, together with the *Toronto Star* and the *Toronto Sun*.

After speaking to City Council and taking part in a media scrum outside, we head off to meet the people at Manulife who send us on our way with an armful of cheques and cash. I think to myself that, if the rest of corporate Canada follows the lead of Manulife, we will be able to meet our goal of $10,000,000 for genetic research.

On the fortieth floor of the Royal Bank Building in downtown Toronto I speak to executives of the bank. These are people of power and influence. Here in the heart of Canada's financial district, bankers who are often portrayed as cold and aloof, are moved by the story of *Jesse's Journey* and my reason for being on the road.

At night, inside Toronto's Skydome, the public address announcer introduces me. Then, at field level, with video footage on the giant Jumbo-Tron showing Newfoundland and the early days of the cross-Canada *Journey*, I circle the bases Jesse and I had circled together three years earlier. Upstairs in the broadcast booth, I'm on the air with Blue Jay announcers Tom Cheek and Jerry Howarth, and the announcers from TSN (The Sports Network). We talk about

Jesse's Journey as they show the video of my rounding the bases. But the most memorable moment at Skydome isn't seen by any of the fans. It's one of the highlights of my marathon walk – one of those moments that truly touches people.

In a private area deep inside Skydome, a group of parents and kids gather as three ladies from Oshawa and Whitby, the mothers of children with DMD, make a very special presentation. With their young sons in wheelchairs beside them, Marian Stafford and Heather Peters join their friend Kerry Lyon to present a cheque for $60,000 in memory of Kerry's son Bradley, who passed away in the spring of 1997 at the age of 20. Tears of joy and sadness mix together in a very emotional moment. These three moms, part of a Toronto-based group of parents of children with Duchenne, have worked hundreds of hours in smoky Bingo halls to make this moment possible. From the time I dipped my foot in the Atlantic Ocean and began the cross-country *Journey*, this is the most shining example of philanthropy I have witnessed along the road. In the days that follow, I think of Bradley as I head down a highway that has now become a symbol. It's the road to a better life.

Making my way across the top of Toronto with a police escort along Highway 7, the road crew works overtime as traffic backs up with people wanting to donate. It's late afternoon in rush hour traffic when our daily routine suddenly comes to a halt.

It's five o'clock, and traffic heading west is moving past me quickly. Police cruisers with flashing lights are blocking the right lane as they provide our escort. In the single lane beside me, traffic is speeding past, with just a car length between vehicles, and motorists staring into the glare of the late afternoon sun. When one driver slows down to see what's happening, there are five sudden loud bangs and everything behind me comes to a stop. The hoods of five cars are bent like inverted V's with steam rising and engine fluids spilling onto the road. Fortunately, no one is hurt. The police officer behind me gets out of her cruiser and says, "Hang on a minute, I just have to go and talk to these fools!" When I mention to the officer my concern about whether or not we are involved in the accident she says, "No, they're just being idiots. You can't go 90 km/h one car length apart and expect that everything will be OK." When she asks if I want her to radio for another cruiser so we can continue, I tell her we have completed 32 of 33 km and it's probably best if we just add the one km to tomorrow's workload. Nobody says anything, but for the sake of the road crew and volunteers, this is one time I am glad to get off the road.

Still surrounded by police cruisers, it's a hot and sunny morning as I walk on toward Brampton. I'm surprised to see a middle-aged man in a shirt and tie, and not-very-practical leather shoes, ask for a bucket and a handful of brochures. It doesn't take long before Sarkis Assadourian, the area Member of Parliament, has loosened his tie and is soaked in sweat as he joins the rest of the volunteers dashing from vehicle to vehicle collecting donations. I've stood in front of cameras shaking hands with a lot of politicians over the past few months, but this is the first time I have seen a politician literally roll up his sleeves and go to work for us. Back at his constituency office, Sarkis has lots of bottled water and juices waiting for us, along with a good supply of butter tarts and a floral arrangement that includes all the provincial flowers from across Canada.

On the road I always try to stop and say hello to people in wheelchairs. The only time I slow down today is to go back along the sidewalk to greet a little blonde-haired boy in a wheelchair who is smiling as he struggles to catch up with me. He tells me he's in grade two and he wants to be a wrestler! He's a really neat kid, and despite the chest brace that holds him straight, he has the heart and courage of a lion. He gives graciously the donation he has saved. I bend down and kiss the top of his head and take his tiny arm into my hand as we shake hands and I say goodbye.

The summer days are now with us, and I'm walking familiar roads where the crowds begin to steadily build. We are now close enough

260

to home that people can reach us by car and that means the makeup of the road crew changes almost daily. Suddenly it seems like everyone wants to help.

The air horns from tractor-trailers are now a steady sound of encouragement. Truck drivers are pulling their rigs to the side of the road to make a donation. The Ontario Provincial Police have made *Jesse's Journey* a priority, and police cruisers and motorcycles are with us throughout the day. Leaving Toronto, one of the motorcycle policemen chases a driver who ignored instructions and passed me on the right. On the motor home at lunch, the officer tells us the driver was a young kid and he let him go with a seatbelt warning and a suggestion that it might be a good idea to, "Find some folding stuff and make a donation." The young driver thought that was a pretty good deal.

On the first day of August, I walk through Georgetown and Acton. It's my 115th day on the road. There is a steady stream of people along the roadside who applaud as they shake my hand and make a donation. I think it's a little funny when people call me 'Sir,' or sometimes 'Jesse.' It really doesn't matter. What is important is that they are taking part in *Jesse's Journey*. One man pulls his car to the side of the road and walks back to meet me and make a donation. As he shakes my hand he says, "You're making us all proud to be Canadian."

My home province is responding, and the days on the road are becoming chaotic. There are people with cameras waiting to include me in a family picture, people who want me to sign something, and still others who want to press a 'guardian angel' pin into my hand and tell me about a lost loved one. I do my best to try to accommodate everyone, but I'm concerned about losing time and falling behind in distance. I think Ed is the first to realize I'm arriving at the motor home for my breaks later and more tired. He takes it upon himself to begin screening my time.

261

Through Guelph and Kitchener, sponsors and media join people at the roadside waiting to greet us. In Guelph I pose for a newspaper picture with Vic Barrett, who greets me from his wheelchair. A victim of Duchenne, there is something different about Vic. At 33, he is the oldest person I have met with Duchenne. That gives me a great reason for hope, as I move on down the road to where a young couple from Cambridge, who I'd met earlier in Newfoundland, are waiting to say hello again. I never find out their names, but they remind me that we met while they were on their way to St. John's to attend the funeral of the woman's father. I do remember them, and recall telling the young lady that there would be "better days ahead." Standing here in the sunshine, with the woman holding their baby, it's clear that these are better days. Shaking hands, they thank me for what I am doing. Once again I feel like I've been on the road for a long time.

A chance meeting along the road on a Sunday afternoon leads to an unforgettable evening in Guelph. An Italian father and son, Joe and Domenic Ciaravella, applaud as I pass the end of the road that leads to their family business. The older man, a proud father, watches as his handsome young son, a man in his mid-twenties, comes forward and makes a donation on behalf of their family. At the same time, Joe Ciaravella hands his business card to our road manager, Trish Federkow, and offers to feed us at the family's banquet hall. I've just returned to the road after having lunch, so Trish thanks the man for his offer and we move along.

When Trish catches up to me and tells me about the offer to feed us, I say, "Trish, run back and see if they'd like to provide us with supper." When Trish looks at me quizzically and says "Really?" I say, "Yes, because people like this don't make that kind of offer unless they really mean it."

It turned out that the Ciaravellas were delighted at the thought we'd join them for supper. I didn't know what to expect, but at the end of a dry and dusty day on the road, Joe, his wife Olga, and their son

Domenic welcomed a hot and tired road crew of twelve people. The stage was set for another magical moment to unfold for *Jesse's Journey*.

Between the time Joe and Domenic first laid eyes on our troupe of volunteers coming down the road, and the time we arrived for supper, the Ciaravella's had set up a banquet table. Silverware and china with red candles on a white tablecloth weren't what we were used to at night. After the introductions were made, we sat down to steaming bowls of pasta and spaghetti sauce, and bread was brought from the kitchen. I remember looking down the table at Bevin and wondering if he was familiar with Italian custom. If Bevin's eyes lit up at the sight of homemade spaghetti, I had to laugh when I saw how his eyes looked like saucers when the second course of chicken arrived from the kitchen. Everyone laughed when Bevin said, "There's more?" We were very relaxed and everyone was enjoying the food that kept coming from the kitchen.

After dessert I stood up and thanked Joe, Olga and Domenic on behalf of our entire group. I told them all about *Jesse's Journey – A Father's Tribute* and explained how the gift of a meal was so welcome. It was then that Joe asked Domenic to get fresh glasses for everyone and to bring a bottle of champagne. When all the glasses had been filled Joe toasted *Jesse's Journey*, and he spoke of us as new friends as he wished us well. It was one of just two occasions on the road when I drank something with alcohol in it. When you meet good people like the Ciaravella family of Guelph, Ontario, that's what you do.

In Kitchener, hospital workers in light blue uniforms join me on the road. Making our way past the Kitchener-Waterloo Hospital, I see a young teenage girl sitting in a wheelchair, with her parents at her side, waiting to see *Jesse's Journey* pass by. Although it's a warm day, she has a blanket over her pyjamas. There are tubes from her wrist to a plastic bag of clear fluid hanging from the metal pole beside her. A 'halo' of steel rods holds her head firmly in place.

For a moment *Jesse's Journey* comes to a halt as I jog across the road to gently shake her hand and to thank the young girl and her parents for coming out to see us. I don't know if I brightened her day, but I knew her smile certainly brightened mine.

Under sunny skies the road routine continues along the highway to New Hamburg and Stratford. There are police escort cruisers and fire engines. Sometimes they're antiques spewing out smoke as I walk on shaking as many hands as possible. Listening to people applaud and hearing them say things like 'good work,' I know that those words belong to Jesse, the young man who is the spark plug for all that we have been able to accomplish – the young man I will be reunited with tomorrow.

Walking through the rural communities, we reach the small farm community of Embro, northwest of Woodstock, where Al and Anne Matheson were just kids when they bought the grocery store in the village. They were both 21 and they had just married. They had their whole lives ahead of them.

Thirty years later, on a hot summer afternoon, they are waiting to greet me, standing in the tall grass at the side of the road, not far from the grocery store they still own. No one has to explain to the Mathesons what *Jesse's Journey* is all about. They've already been there.

Dale Matheson was born in 1974. It was just two months before Christmas of 1978 when the Mathesons learned that their 4 year old son had been diagnosed with Duchenne. "I knew about Duchenne," says Anne, "My brother, who died in 1972 at the age of 20, was three years younger than me. We were a family of seven, and we never knew where it came from. The doctors always told my mother that it was a mutation at birth, but actually she must have, unknowingly, been the carrier." When Dale was diagnosed, the couple was finally referred to a genetics counsellor.

Dennis, the couple's second child, was born the year that Dale was diagnosed. The Mathesons waited until Dennis was six months old before having him tested, hoping against hope that he would be spared. Again, it was just before Christmas when they received the news that Dennis also had Duchenne. Anne says, "I know things have changed a lot since that time, but back then we didn't have a clue that I was a carrier. My sister never married or had any children, she was so afraid, even though tests showed she was not a carrier."

Al remembers driving back home to Embro after Dennis had been diagnosed and saying to Anne, "Well, I guess we won't have to worry about any more children because we won't have time. I'll be pushing one wheelchair, and you'll have the other." It was a bitter statement born out of the shock of the moment, and one that would eventually become the reality in the lives of Anne and Al. But at that moment, the knowledge that they now had two sons with Duchenne was almost too much to bear. Lost in their own thoughts, wondering what had hit them, the couple drove home in silence.

It was about this time that Anne and Al made the decision to take things one day at a time. Anne recalls, "We decided that we wouldn't worry about what might happen 10 years down the road, because the future will look after itself; we can't control it, so why let it run our lives right now?"

The Mathesons began focusing on each new day as it came, and concentrating on their sons. Anne says "We realized that whatever happened in the future, we still had each other, and we held tight to that."

While both Dale and Dennis, despite the disease, made it through school, only Dale would pursue a post-secondary education. When Dennis was in grade eleven, his health started to deteriorate. So he left school to help out at the family store whenever he felt well enough to handle the computer, as that was something he enjoyed.

Then in 1995 the unthinkable happened, and the family learned that Dennis had congestive heart failure. "We just couldn't believe it," Al recalls of the visit to the doctors and the trip home after the new diagnosis. "Dennis was pretty glum. He knew the consequences; he was an adult at 17 and the doctor laid it all out for the three of us. Basically they gave him just a few months. It was pretty difficult to cope with that."

But cope they did, and the Mathesons did everything they could to help their son. But in 1997 Dennis had to be hospitalized on two occasions.

Anne remembers the night her youngest child lost his battle with the disease that had been with him for a lifetime. "I had already settled Dale for the night and was getting Dennis into bed when he began to have trouble breathing, and telling me that he needed to go to Emergency right away. He knew what was happening, I'm sure of it."

And so they raced toward the hospital in Woodstock, taking Dennis on what would be his final journey down a familiar road. "I knew there was something seriously wrong," Anne recalls with a sad smile as she thinks back on that night, "because Dennis didn't caution me, as he always did, to slow down on the loose gravel, but instead he kept telling me to speed up."

At the hospital, Dennis was placed on life support. "We knew his wishes," says Al. "He never wanted to be on a ventilator."

Dennis Matheson, with his parents at his side as they had been for a lifetime, lost his valiant fight for life that night in 1997. He was 19 years old.

In August of 1999 Dale turned 25. Al thanks his son for getting the family through a most difficult time. "When we lost Dennis, Dale was our support," says his father Al. "He held us together."

Far from giving in to the disease that has been with him all of his life, Dale went on to the University of Western Ontario as a part-time student, studying genetics as a science and working toward his B.Sc. "He loves it," smiles his proud dad. "He just showed us a mark he received on his last project, an 80 percent."

"Sometimes," says Anne sadly, "he asks 'Mom, why should I continue going to school?' and there are days when he just doesn't feel much like going. You can tell it's wearing on him, but he always bounces back, and is determined to get his degree."

Sadly, the Mathesons lost their second son Dale on May 31st, 2001. He was 26 years old.

When I pushed Jesse through the crowds of people that lined the streets of London to welcome us home in 1995, Al was one of the many dads who walked along with me. Al remembered the generosity of the crowds and how much he wished his own two boys could have been there to share the moment. In the days that followed, Anne, together with her mother-in-law Betty, became a part of *Jesse's Journey*. Anne says that from the moment they heard of the wheelchair marathon across Ontario, "We would have done anything in the world to help, but having two boys in wheelchairs kept us tied pretty close to home." Al interjects, "But I can tell you, we were there with them in spirit, every step of the way across Ontario, and later across Canada."

Each summer for the past five years, the Mathesons have hosted a 'Sample Fest,' an evening where customers can taste the various products from the Food Town grocery store in Embro, with the proceeds going to *Jesse's Journey*. As Anne says, "We too have our inspiration right here at home." And, you can still stop in at the grocery store, where there's always a hot coffee ready and waiting. Al keeps the coffee brewing for the customers, and when the donation jar fills up, *Jesse's Journey* is ready to help genetic research take another step forward toward the answer parents pray for.

It's been a hard road for the Mathesons with the diagnosis and eventual loss of both of their sons after so much of their lives was given over to caring for the boys. But there is no sense of self-pity in the Mathesons. Instead what comes across is two people who have kept their relationship alive in the worst of times. On the summer day in 1998 when we met along the road while Dale was still alive, Al and Anne Matheson stood out as symbols of courage.

The green cornfields of southwestern Ontario are now standing tall in the summer sun. Under a bright sky there are families cheering us on at virtually every farm gate as *Jesse's Journey* moves south along Highway 19 toward Woodstock. From babies and little kids to grandparents sitting in lawn chairs waiting for our arrival, there are hundreds of hands to shake. While I greet as many people as I can, I'm anxious to keep moving because I know that after more than four months of walking the highway, a little further up the road, Jesse will be waiting for me.

Part of my early morning routine includes the daily radio interviews back home. The rotation means that I talk with each station's morning show hosts once a week. It's one thing to tell people in a radio interview about the expressions on the faces of people along the road, and the story those people have to tell. It's quite different watching the reaction of the morning show hosts who join us on the road, as they see firsthand the kind of excitement that we are generating.

The summer day I meet up with Jesse, 50 year old Rich Grevin and his co-host Elaine Sawyer from Q97.5-FM in London are walking the road with me and seeing *Jesse's Journey* in action. As we walk along shaking hands with people and receiving donations, I tell Rich and Elaine that Jesse has given me instructions on the telephone for when we meet later in the day.

All parents seem to come with the same flaw. We never really want to let go of our children, to recognize that they are no longer just kids. We seem blinded to the reality that when they're 18 years old, they don't want you hugging them in public. Knowing there was a good chance the media would be there, Jesse had asked me not to make a big fuss when I met him. We had made a deal: one hug, one pat on the head and a handshake. It was the best bargain I could negotiate.

Jesse had always sounded very strong whenever we spoke on the telephone. Despite that, I couldn't help but wonder if I would see a change in him. Would the disease he has lived with all his life have made a further advance? Coming over the crest of the hill leading into Woodstock, there is a crowd of people, cameras and microphones and in the middle of the gathering, sitting in his wheelchair, there is Jesse. Breaking into a jog toward him, I'm relieved to see that he doesn't appear to have changed at all since I left home in April. Remembering our deal, I give him one hug, one pat on the head and shake his hand. Then, with bagpipes and police cruisers, and Jesse by my side, I have a feeling of being almost home. It's the second time Jesse and I have been welcomed by thousands of people on the streets of Woodstock.

Slowly we make our way through the crowd and I'm ushered onto a stage that has been set up in front of the Old Town Hall in downtown Woodstock. Amidst a huge crowd of parents, and kids and balloons surrounding the fountain in front of the Old Town Hall, there are speeches and donations. I'm in such a good mood when I speak to the crowd that I actually confess that when I was in high school, I once put soap in the fountain in the square. The result was huge clumps of bubbles floating into the air in downtown Woodstock. It was just a high school prank and I figure this was a pretty safe moment to make a confession.

It's raining by the time we leave Woodstock, but Rich Grevin and Elaine Sawyer stay with me for the remainder of the day. Despite the wet weather, there are still people along the roadway as we walk west, ending our day in Beachville, where a letter in the village's museum makes reference to the first recorded baseball game in North America. The game was played in the village in June of 1838. That was a year before the Abner Doubleday game in Cooperstown, New York.

When they finally have a chance to sit down on board the motor home at the end of the day, I think both Rich and Elaine have sore muscles. If they have, they're well-earned. Unlacing my shoes, I look up to see Elaine's father, Alec Patterson, as he looks proudly at his daughter who is wet from the rain, tired from the walk and smiling at her accomplishment. It was much later that Rich Grevin recalled what he remembered most from the day he walked the road as part of *Jesse's Journey*. Somewhere along the way there was a young boy who made a donation, and as I did so often, I shared a 'high five' with him and said, "You're the best!" For Rich, I think that young boy may have represented every father's son.

It must have had quite an impact on Rich because months later he still had a lump in his throat as he recalled that little boy. The meeting with the youngster had been a memorable occasion. It had been a brief moment along the highway – a moment like so many others that had slipped my memory and faded into the wake of *Jesse's Journey* as we moved along. Still, I was glad both Rich and Elaine had taken the time to come out to the road to share in the experience of it. From that point on, as I moved further across the country, our weekly interviews seemed to have even more meaning. I know that both Rich and Elaine can visualize exactly what is happening along the road. They've been there; they've experienced the generosity of the thousands of people who want to help make life better for kids like Jesse. And for Rich Grevin, another father in a chain of so many fathers across the country, there will always be that little boy and that one special moment along the road.

Back in Beachville next morning, it's raining heavily when the motor home stops where we had finished the day before. Road conditions

270

are not good and Trish is double-checking with the police escort to make sure it's safe to start our day. When we are given the green light to go, I step onto the road to begin the walk that will take me home to London. It's going to be a wet homecoming.

All along the road through Ingersoll and Thamesford, there are people waiting in the rain. Sometimes, when it's pouring heavily, they wait in their cars. As I get closer they step out into the rain to make a donation and offer words of encouragement. Although I'm being slowed by the huge turnout of people, I still try my best to reach through car windows to shake hands with seniors and grandparents who are there because they are thankful they have healthy grandchildren.

The rain is still falling when I reach Thamesford, on the outskirts of London, where service clubs' donations amount to $4 per person for everyone living in the village. From the open back of a transport truck I speak to a smiling group of people, some of whom have been standing in the rain for most of the morning. Some of them have umbrellas. Many of them don't. Thamesford is the home of my friend Ron Calhoun, and it's hard to tell which one of us is prouder of the people of Thamesford. When it's time to move on to London, I'm cautioned about the crowds ahead and the need to keep moving as quickly as possible, but nothing could prepare me for the onslaught waiting on the streets of London.

The motor home has been our 'home away from home' for more than four months. Besides providing transportation and shelter, the motor home has played many roles, from office to medical headquarters, but today it is definitely a command post. We are behind schedule as we leave Thamesford just past midday. Despite the fact that there are people waiting in the rain, Trish insists I stop for a quick lunch before we head into London. Ed Coxworthy, the Newfie jack-of-all-trades, who is driving the motor home, does his best to keep the chaos to a minimum. We usually welcome people on board but today access has been limited to media people, the road crew and volunteers who are emptying donation buckets of the money they contain. Even then the motor home seems to be full of people. There is no rest after lunch. Looking at Ed, I say, "I don't want to keep these people waiting." And with that I step off the motor home, plunge into the crowd and get back to work.

If there is one thing Jesse and I accomplished in our adventures on the road, it was bringing people a greater understanding of the word genetics. As I begin reaching out to the hands – young and old and big and small that are reaching out to me – I know the effort Jesse made when we were together in 1995 has struck a resounding chord with the people of London and southwestern Ontario.

The road ahead of me, which is lined with people, is both physically and emotionally draining. It's difficult to imagine the effect it has when people are clapping as you pass by and their eyes are welling up as they say things like, "We love you, John. Good work. Congratulations. Keep it going. God bless you, John." And all along the way people want to shake hands.

While women are more emotional, the men in the crowd, who maybe don't even say anything, seem to send me a message in the way they squeeze my hand. It's as if their support for what I am doing is to be measured by the strength of their grip. In a matter of minutes, my hand is aching. It's a relief when I can stop and talk to little kids in brightly-coloured rain capes, who look at me and say, "Are you really Jesse's dad?" That, more than anything else, helps keep me on an even keel as I move along the street.

Steve Casey, who had been with me in Nova Scotia, is at my side. In the crush of people, I'm relying on Steve to guide me to where I'm supposed to go. Steve has been part of the group planning our arrival in London, helping to coordinate police involvement, and looking after getting the necessary permits for us to be on the road. "It was totally unreal," Steve recalls. "There were thousands of people in the streets, people in the parks, people everywhere."

Looking back later, Steve recalls, "It was one of the best things I've ever been involved in. It might sound trite, but it really did give me a whole new perspective on life. I found I was able to look at situations with a keener eye and I was able to find within myself the truly important things in my life – my family being at the top of that list, and then the things that could wait for another day."

Steve reflected upon what *Jesse's Journey* had done for a lot of people. "It wasn't just that John Davidson was walking across Canada. It was about the lives that he and Jesse touched along the way because – make no mistake about it, Jesse was there with him every minute of every day – in John's mind, and in the hearts of all who saw the sacrifice that needed to be made for the cause of those afflicted with a genetic disease. As a father, I don't know if I would have the same courage if one of my boys were to have been diagnosed as Jesse was, but I like to think that John would have done the same for me if I were in his shoes."

Entering London, Steve guides me through the crowd at a Wal-Mart store where the employees and management donate $8,000 to *Jesse's Journey*. That donation marks the beginning of a continuing relationship with Wal-Mart in London.

By the time we reach downtown London, I'm really getting tired. Then when I look up, Sherene and Jesse are coming toward me, and once again I kiss my wife in the middle of the street in front of a crowd of people.

Escorted by the London Police Pipe and Drum Band and their colour guard, Jesse and Sherene join the road crew volunteers who are working harder than ever as they scramble along both sides of the road collecting donations. As we make our way to City Hall, I continue shaking hands along the street and waving to people high above me on the balconies of apartment buildings.

In the heart of the city, the wet pavement reflects the colours of the umbrellas held by people in the crowd. It's almost funny how, with so many people cheering, the sound of the pipes and drums and the flash of cameras every now and then, I sometimes see things as if they are in slow motion. I remember looking across the street at one point and seeing a girl standing at the side of the road with a metal halo holding her head in place. I jogged over to meet 21 year old Tory Bowman, who had broken her neck in a car accident earlier in the summer while working as a tree planter in Prince George, British Columbia. I thanked her for coming out on a rainy August afternoon to see us arriving home.

I had written my name in a lot of city guest books since the *Journey* began back in Newfoundland, but penning my signature in London is just a little different. Watching Sherene and Jesse sign their names in the city's guest book, I think about how we are really signing on behalf of all the volunteers who have helped along the way.

The signing of the guest book is followed by the unveiling of a plaque at the base of the sugar maple tree that Jesse and I had planted with Queen Elizabeth in 1997. Then it's on to the bandshell in Victoria Park, where hundreds of people standing in the rain welcome us home. After speeches from the politicians, London Mayor, Dianne Haskett, announces the city will be making a $25,000 donation to *Jesse's Journey.*

Media interviews are next, and then, after more than four months on the road, and with five more months ahead of me, we're going home. The little white dog that looks like a floor mop with a wagging tail jumps onto my lap. In a matter of minutes both Charlie and I are sound asleep. It's the end of the first day in London.

The weekend schedule brings another series of events and appearances. While the road team is highly visible everywhere they go, the home team operates away from the spotlight, making sure that all the pieces fit together every day. Two women, whose only communication link is the telephone, keep the *Journey* moving ahead.

Maureen Golovchenko, our *Journey* director, had seen the 'road team' in action for a couple of days in eastern Ontario. The road team on the other hand, has never seen the home team in operation. Maybe it's just as well. Wherever we are, Trish has made it clear to everyone on the road that I'm not to be bothered with any of the dozens of problems that have to be ironed out by the home team every day. "John's job," Trish tells them, "is to walk 33 km a day."

Maureen views the whole project as a wheel, with all the spokes representing the various facets that have to be dealt with every day. Transportation, accommodation, volunteers, sponsors and media are some of the main spokes, and the home team makes up the hub of the wheel. Maureen describes the project as being like a big quilt. Everyone involved is contributing their little patch and it's her job to sew all the patches together.

One of the highlights of the hot and muggy weekend in London is a rally at the University of Western Ontario. There's plenty of live music and seeing the long lineup of supporters from various groups who have come out to make a donation to *Jesse's Journey* is a very humbling experience. CFPL-TV news director George Clark and news anchor Kate Young, both of whom joined Jesse and me on the road in 1995, are the show's hosts.

George and I have been friends for more than thirty years, starting when he was a cub reporter at CFPL-TV in the mid 1960's. George knew that I probably wouldn't be coming back to work at the television station when I left to push Jesse across Ontario in 1995. He also had no doubt that we would make it. When it came to the cross-Canada walk, George wasn't quite as sure. He knew my age, and that 8000 km is a long way to walk. But on a sweltering afternoon in London, George also knew that this is where I was meant to be.

The weekend appearances give me a chance to meet and personally thank some of the hundreds of people who have put their creative juices to work for *Jesse's Journey*. At a mall in London we pose for a picture with the staff and management of a gift shop called *The Brandy Tree*. This is a group of people I've never met and they are presenting *Jesse's Journey* with a cheque for $18,000 raised from the sale of 'Beanie Babies.'

One of our appearances in London, before heading back to the highway, is at a 'cruise night' car show, where nostalgia is the name of the game. Chrome that is polished to a fine lustre and fins from the '50s and '60s make up a large part of this regular Sunday night gathering. For people walking through the rows and rows of classic cars and listening to the softer side of rock music from that era, it's a trip down memory lane. This is where radio talk show host Jim Chapman, himself a classic car buff, presents *Jesse's Journey* with a cheque for $13,000 donated by his listeners.

On the 10th of August in bright sunshine, I step back onto the road. By the end of the day London has disappeared behind me. Ahead are five more months on the edge of the highway. As I smile and shake hands with the people I pass, my mind is racing ahead. While it's been a gorgeous summer day in southwestern Ontario, I know that fall is just around the corner. According to the schedule, I won't reach Manitoba until the 9th of October. That means we'll be crossing the Prairies in November and the Rocky Mountains in December. I'll just have to take it one day at a time, starting with today.

Although Jesse isn't with me on this *Journey*, people still donate, as they had done on hot summer days three years before. Sometimes they come from a distance to be at the side of the road. Passing through the village of Arva, there is no fanfare as the people of Armo Tool, a machine shop company that services the auto industry, donate more than $4,000 to *Jesse's Journey*. As I walk the road, the employees of that company are hard at work miles from the route we are following.

The 30 km stretch of highway from London to Lucan is a familiar piece of road. I walked it several times in the seven months of training before beginning the cross Canada walk. On those days I had always been alone. Now, provincial police are clearing the way, and ahead a tremendous show of support is waiting for us.

In Lucan, *Jesse's Journey* turns into a festival. By the time I reach the firehall on the main street, the crowd has spilled out onto Highway 4, which runs right through the centre of the village. For the next hour, the road through Lucan is closed. It's a blistering hot afternoon, and with a microphone in my hand, I stand on the hood of a car to speak to the crowd. My feet are baking with the heat from the hot metal surface I'm standing on, but I want to make sure I acknowledge all the service clubs in Lucan who have come out to take part in *Jesse's Journey.* Looking at the crowd, I see the proud faces of the men and women of the Royal Canadian Legion, most of them no longer young. Despite the temperature and humidity, they are dressed in navy blue blazers, and some of them are wearing ribbons and medals from campaigns fought long ago. In the crowd there are the gently wrinkled faces of grey-haired seniors. There are strong-looking fathers who work with their hands, some of them with a rural tan from hours of farm work. There are teenagers hiding behind sunglasses and little children in baseball hats, T-shirts, shorts and running shoes, darting in and out of the crowd. But most of all, there is a strong sense of community and a caring about one another. This is small-town Canada at its best. This is Lucan, Ontario, the village that on a steamy hot day in August donates $20,000 to help further research into genetic illnesses.

After walking through Grand Bend at the end of the day, Sherene and I spend a few minutes together watching the sun set over Lake Huron. It will be more than a year before we will again have a chance to watch a sunset at the lake.

It's now the season for corn on the cob and tomatoes, and both are available from vegetable stands popping up along Highway 23 as we pass through Woodham and Kirkton, moving north to Mitchell. Families waiting along the highway to make a donation to *Jesse's Journey* make sure that the motor home is well stocked with fresh fruit and vegetables. While the sun is warm, the harvest is another sign that fall is not that far off. My mind wanders again to the days ahead on the Prairies. I wonder what I will face.

Mitchell is the home of hockey legend Howie Morenz of the Montreal Canadiens. When he played in Stratford, Ontario, he was nicknamed 'The Stratford Streak.' Morenz was just 35 years old when he died of an embolism in 1937 after breaking his leg in a freak accident during a game in Montreal. Twelve thousand people attended his funeral at the Montreal Forum. With the medical knowledge that's available now, Howie Morenz would likely have survived the on-ice collision that eventually took his life. Walking into Mitchell, I think about how the advances in medicine that we enjoy today came about as the result of research. The thought gives me one more reason to keep moving ahead.

From Mitchell and thoughts of hockey, *Jesse's Journey* shifts sports as we move on to St. Marys, the home of the Canadian Baseball Hall of Fame. The town's quarries are the source of the limestone used to build the Town Hall, opera house, museum, and library as well as several churches. Called "The Stone Town," picturesque St. Marys, with a population of 6,000 people, is nestled in a beautifully treed valley where the Thames River flows over the dam located in the heart of the town.

The Canadian Baseball Hall of Fame had been housed in a somewhat temporary location at Exhibition Stadium in Toronto before finding a permanent home in St. Marys in the mid-90s. The baseball diamond at the site of the Hall of Fame is every fan's dream of what a diamond should look like, with rich green grass, a well-manicured infield and crisp white chalk lines. There are thousands of people here on an unforgettable summer night when I'm asked to walk the bases with hundreds of school children.

The stop in St. Marys is one of the best night time opportunities I've had to speak to a huge audience about the need for research – to ensure that all children are able to play baseball and to have a chance to chase their dreams. At the end of the day, as my legs are being stretched and massaged, I'm aware that the rest I had hoped for in London didn't materialize and I'm close to pushing my endurance to its physical limit. I write my journal and fall asleep.

In the morning, I sleep in the motor home as we drive to our start point outside of Mitchell. The road to Listowel takes us through Bornholm, Monkton, Newry, and Atwood. There are donations from each of the villages, and from service clubs and people we meet along the road. It's nice to fit in again to the routine of the road, with breaks and meals that fall at the right time, and a comfortable groove of 125 paces to the minute.

The sound of pipes and drums breaks the quiet of a hot August afternoon on the main street of Listowel as police cruisers guide us to the town's clock tower for a civic reception. Earlier at the mall on the outskirts of town, there were donations from the Zehr's and Zeller's stores. It's a good afternoon as I'm joined on the road by employees of the K-Mart in Goderich, who have driven almost 100 km to take part in the walk. They too are people I haven't met before and they bring with them a cheque for $1,000.

There are few opportunities to relax and enjoy a home-cooked meal on the road. We've become so used to ordering from menus that most nights we make a game of it. Before anyone opens their menu, somebody on the road crew describes in their best "The Price is Right" voice, a hot beef sandwich with all the trimmings. It's then up to everyone at the table to 'bid' on the sandwich so we can see who comes closest to the actual retail value without going over the price! There's no prize, but we all become experts on the pricing of hot beef sandwiches. The servers sometimes look at us as if we have been on the road for just a little too long. We don't care. It's our way of unwinding at the end of a long day. But in Listowel we're treated to a real home-cooked meal.

Don and Pat Meadows, the parents of my good friend Dave Meadows from Halifax, are very familiar with *Jesse's Journey*. They were on the road with us during the original crossing of Ontario. It was Pat who was beside Jesse and me as I pushed Jesse's wheelchair up one of the toughest of climbs, Jackfish Hill in northern Ontario.

It's been a long time since we sat down to a family dinner with a tablecloth, china and silverware. Pat and Don's daughter, Mary Lou, who has returned to Canada after living in Israel for a number of years, serves us a meal of chicken and rice, with peach pie for dessert. There's no hot beef sandwich game tonight. It's at moments like this, as everyone talks during dinner, that I keep sneaking a peek at my watch. The deadline for sleep never seems to go away. Before we leave for our motel, Don pours everyone a glass of wine and we toast the *Journey*. It's the second time I taste something with alcohol during our time on the road. It will also be the last. The routine is that demanding.

Back at our motel for the night, Ed takes the motor home to be fuelled. In my room there is a brown paper package containing *Jesse's Journey* shirts that have been shipped from London to replace those that are looking a little tattered and worn. Somehow they've been mislabelled. What is supposed to be a large-sized shirt turns out to be an extra, extra large. When I hear Ed arriving back with the motor home, I stand in the doorway of my motel room facing the parking lot, wearing one of the new shirts, which hangs past my knees! As the headlights of the motor home swing around and capture me standing in the motel room doorway, Ed starts laughing. It's the perfect moment for another of Ed's Newfoundland expressions. "Johnny," he says, "you look like a sack of spuds, without the spuds!"

Through the rural areas of Palmerston and Harriston there are farm families along the roadside. Although stopping to shake hands and to take pictures isn't a problem, I still haven't found the walking

Sherene and I smiled as we met in downtown London after being apart for four months.

Keeping the vans neat and organized was an endless task. Here Trish Federkow loads some giant "presentation" cheques and buckets used for collecting money, back on board one of the two vans.

In the rain, Jesse, Sherene and I were escorted by the London Police colour guard and pipe and drum band to a reception at Victoria Park.

Some days there were huge crowds. Some days there was no one at all. As fall approached I was making my way through midwestern Ontario.

Students across the country, who related to Jesse as "another school kid" turned out at rallies like this group at East Elgin Secondary in Aylmer, Ontario to raise money for Jesse's Journey.

If Jesse was the inspiration for the road team in 1998, he also inspired the home team. Heading the home team was Journey Director Maureen Golovchenko, who guided the day to day activities at the office in London.

groove that I'm most comfortable with. I'm sure I'll rediscover it, but it's been missing on most days since we left London.

During lunch at a roadside picnic table, I find myself looking at some tabletop graffiti. Someone has carved deep into the table the words: 'What would Jesus Do?' Right beside those words someone else had very neatly responded in ink, "Well, for one thing He wouldn't have defaced this picnic table!"

In the afternoon, I'm spending time on the road with a man whose baby daughter was diagnosed with cancer when she was one month old. He and his wife lost their little girl eleven months later, when she was just one year old. Now he organizes the annual Terry Fox Run in the area.

Later that day, I'm surrounded by an excited group of Beavers, Cubs and Brownies – little children who have come out to the road with their leaders to make a donation and to march along the highway in front of a real police car. They want to be able to say they took part in *Jesse's Journey.* There is no way of knowing at the time how much it means, but walking along with little kids I always hope that, somewhere down life's road when they get involved in helping their communities, maybe they'll think back to this as one of their first experiences with giving.

After the Beavers, Cubs and Brownies leave, a woman with two canes is standing at the end of a country road, waiting to make a donation. When I stop to shake her hand she says, "You're good stuff." I thank her and walk on, thinking the exact same thing about her. She is one of so many people we meet each day, and seldom do I ever learn their names. By night time their faces begin to fade from memory as I write in my journal.

It's Friday, August the 14th, 1998, and my 128th day on the road. The highlight of the day is at the afternoon break when I answer the motor home cell phone and Sherene's voice is on the other end of

281

the line. She has a brief message for me. *Jesse's Journey – A Father's Tribute* has just passed the $1,000,000 mark! That's great news. I'm very happy and extremely proud of everyone involved, both on the road and back home in London, because we have all worked so hard to reach that mark. Despite the joy I feel, I'm more tired than usual. That's happened a lot lately, and Ron Calhoun wants me to see a doctor when we reach the halfway mark at Collingwood.

I can never imagine what volunteers are thinking when they come to join us for a week. Bonnie Kolkman, Elly McMillan and Judy Young are like most of the volunteers on their first day. They're very quiet, watching, listening and learning as Trish walks them through the routine of how things work in a 24-hour period on the road. Bonnie, Elly and Judy work for a company called Marketing Communication Inc. (MCI), which donated its design services to create the graphic effects on the motor home and vans. The company has also coordinated and produced all of our promotional literature, including the colour brochure the volunteers hand out. By the end of the week, these three quiet women won't be 'rookies' any more. They will have been through what all the volunteers before them have experienced. They will have sweated as they work the road handing out brochures. They will have done laundry, helped prepare and clean up after meals, and sometimes driven the motor home. They will have laughed and maybe sometimes cried. And when it's over, they won't want to go home.

The entire road crew was together in Harriston, almost 100 km north of London, on Ed's 59th birthday. At dinner with the Lions Club we gave Ed some fitting gifts, including a fly swatter and an apron. In order to take a picture around the birthday cake, we had to squeeze together so tightly that one of the Lions in the back row was being pushed against a set of double doors behind him. Before we could get the picture taken, the double doors flew open and the man who was nicknamed the 'Lion King,' disappeared out of sight and tumbled into the next room. That's when Bonnie turned to me with wide eyes and said, "Holy Flyin' Lions!"

One of the things Bonnie, Elly and Judy probably didn't expect was to experience a slice of country and western life. On a Saturday morning, at our first break, George Hewitt, whose television show *Open Roads* aired in about 300 different markets, invites us to stop by his ranch for lunch. George's daughter Robyn, sitting in the saddle atop her horse 'Tuffy,' greets us at the farm gate. It isn't long before George and his wife Gail have hamburgers and hot dogs sizzling on the barbecue.

From the back of George's home, which sits on a hilltop west of Flesherton, there's a panoramic view overlooking the treed valley below and the Saugeen River that winds its way through it. Inside the house, there's a western theme saluting the cowboy heroes of yesteryear with memorabilia from the westerns that marked the early days of black and white television. Amidst the wagon wheels and pictures from rodeos are life-size cardboard figures of John Wayne, Roy Rogers and 'The Lone Ranger', Clayton Moore. The walls are covered with autographed pictures of country and western stars who George has crossed paths with in the years he worked on *Open Roads*. George, his wife Gail, and daughter Robin not only provided lunch, but also made a generous donation before we headed off down the road. *Jesse's Journey* had made three new friends.

Out on the road emotions are often raw – not because of our problems, but because we sometimes encounter stories that are difficult to handle. Across the road on the way to Flesherton, there's a pretty little girl wearing a bright green dress, sitting in a stroller. Even from a distance I can see it's a stroller designed for special needs. Her mother and grandmother wave to me, perhaps just happy to say they had been there the day when *Jesse's Journey* passed by. It's a hot afternoon and I know we're running late, but I stop and jog across the road to meet the little girl who has suffered severe brain damage. *Jesse's Journey* will be on the road for almost 300 days, but for this little girl, her mother and grandmother, this is the only day they'll get to see us. At the end of the day, we stay on the road just a little longer.

There are lots of donations on the road through Mt. Forest and Durham, and on the Saturday afternoon we reach Flesherton, I'm caught in a traffic jam of women and tears. It's time to say goodbye to Bonnie, Elly and Judy, who are no longer rookies, and naturally, they want to stay with us. It's the end of the day and we are in a restaurant in Flesherton, and three dinners are getting cold as Bonnie, Elly and Judy have all left the table and gone to the ladies' room to have a good cry. When two of our new volunteers, Jo Ann Reid and Mary Kraul go to cheer them up, I'm left sitting with five dinners that are getting cold. I don't want to guess what our newest volunteers must be thinking about the week ahead. The good news is Jo Ann has been here before, travelling with Jesse and me in 1995, and she knows exactly what Bonnie, Elly and Judy are going through. *Jesse's Journey* is often a life-changing experience and volunteers never want to go home.

For a little while in Collingwood, it feels like old times, as Jesse joins me for part of the day. The heat and humidity are almost unbearable when I break through the banner that unofficially marks the halfway point across Canada. Physically and emotionally, I'm feeling completely spent. I haven't been sleeping well, and I struggle to laugh as I say goodbye to Jesse. It's almost more than I can handle, knowing that it will be five months before we'll see each other again.

Sitting on the edge of the bed in the motor home, I'm fighting my worst fears about the future. With my elbows resting on my knees and my head hanging down, I'm pretty close to tears.

Luckily, Ed and I were the only two people on the motor home, and Ed could tell I was feeling pretty low. He reached out, put his hand on my shoulder and said, "Don't you worry, Johnny. We'll make it." I tied my shoelaces, poured some water over my head and stepped back onto the road. It was time to move on.

Red maple leaves, another sign that fall is coming, are blowing along the sidewalk in Elmvale enroute to Midland. The crowds have thinned and, alone on the road, there's more time to think about life. It becomes clearer each day that life isn't about the cars we drive, the houses we live in, our bank accounts, the jobs we have or the toys we own. Life is about character and what we're willing to do and what we want our legacy to be. I've already answered that question in my mind. I know what I'm willing to do.

When it comes to the word legacy, Thursday, August 18th, 1998 is the beginning of a bitter lesson in politics. That's the day I begin to realize that whatever the legacy of *Jesse's Journey* is to be, we are going to have to create it ourselves. In the middle of the afternoon, there's a buzz amongst the road crew as CBC Radio airs a story about the Government of Ontario and a $1,000,000 donation. There's probably a good reason for the crew to be excited. The provincial minister of Energy, Science and Technology, Jim Wilson, had been in Collingwood when I broke through the banner marking the halfway point in my cross-Canada walk. The minister said at the time, "The request for $1,000,000 is before cabinet now. I'd hate to miss a chance to help." And from my home town of London, the province's Intergovernmental Affairs Minister, London MPP Dianne Cunningham, said, "I'm very optimistic discussions will go favourably."

When it comes to politics and money, the gap between good intentions and financial reality can be very wide. Until a commitment of dollars to any project becomes a reality, it's little more than good intent that's left an impression with the public. An impression can carry political value if the public perception is that a commitment has been fulfilled. Still, it's action, or the lack of it, which tells the true story.

I had walked with and posed for the cameras with enough politicians to know that what gets said, the impression the public is left with, and what actually happens aren't always the same thing. The end

285

result was that when the headlines had been forgotten and the radio and television stories had faded away, the Government of Ontario never did make a donation to *Jesse's Journey*. I thought back to the controversy and embarrassment created by the $10 donation, in Moncton, New Brunswick. That city may have been ridiculed over its donation but it was $10 more than the government of my home province donated. I know a lot of politicians and I like a lot of politicians. I just don't understand them. Politics is a strange business.

In Midland, Ontario, my reserve tank of energy finally hits empty. Even though I've been tired, I still haven't been able to sleep, so last night I took a sleeping pill. But as soon as I'm on the motor home for breakfast, Ed can tell I'm struggling. Six kilometres into the day, Trish decides she has seen enough. I'm sluggish, and for the first time in 134 days, I have to get some rest. The crew is concerned, and they whisk me back to our motel. The room is quickly blacked out and the phone disconnected. Putting in a set of earplugs, I fall asleep almost instantly. Waking up six hours later, I can't believe that I've slept that long. My body has been working overtime since leaving London and the wear and tear has finally caught up with me. But in the morning, after a good afternoon and night's sleep, I'm up early, rested, and ready to go.

Our start point for the day is across the highway from the twin towers of the Martyrs Shrine just outside of Midland. The morning air is noticeably colder as we wait for the Provincial Police escort to arrive. As a youngster, my family had vacationed in Midland, so I had been to the Martyrs Shrine, but doing the math, I calculate that it's been more than 35 years since I was last here. While we are waiting for the police Ed and I climb the stairs of the shrine, which contains the relics of Jean de Brébeuf, and four other Jesuits who were martyred by the Iroquois. All five were canonized in 1930.

The building I remembered as a kid seems so much smaller. There are a few people silently worshipping at the front of the church as Ed and I quietly enter to have a look at the stained glass windows, gold coloured statues and candles inside their red glass canisters. As a kid I remembered seeing people making an offering before lighting a candle. But times seem to have changed.

Ed decides to light a candle for his daughter Kari. After placing $10 in the box, he discovers there are no matches. That's because there are no candles. The yellow flames surrounded by red glass that I remember have been replaced by small electric lights, probably for safety reasons. Instead of lighting a candle, you now just push a button to turn on your 'candle.' The problem is that when Ed pushes the button his 'light' doesn't come on. He spends the rest of the day making me laugh by telling me about how he's going to send a letter to Rome to tell the Pope that he owes him $10!

We have been spoiled over the past month by the visits of friends from home who come out to help collect donations along the road. Not only do they work the highway, they usually bring homemade meals for the road crew. But by the time we reach Parry Sound, there are fewer and fewer visits. Each time we say *goodbye* to people, we know there's little chance we will see them again until we fly home early next year – and that's if we are able to make it to Victoria.

It's late summer as *Jesse's Journey* makes its way up Highway 69 leading to Sudbury along one of the most dangerous stretches of road I've been on so far. There's just a single lane in each direction, and very little shoulder to work with, on a highway that's jammed with holiday traffic. The cars, trucks, vans and campers, nearly all hauling boats on trailers, make the highway seem like everybody in Ontario owns a motor boat. In a funny way, it also looks like most of the boats in the province are being driven around on land. But in reality, this stretch of road is no laughing matter.

287

Our provincial police escort is worried about the speed and the volume of traffic. There has been a fatal accident just the night before. A woman died when her car collided with a transport truck, and the road was closed for several hours. In the afternoon the highway is closed again following another accident. The bumper-to-bumper traffic is stalled on the pavement and for the first time that I can remember, I'm walking past traffic that's usually zipping past me. The road crew takes advantage of the captive audience and they hand our buckets through the windows of just about every car and truck we pass as we move along. It's a case of 'when God gives you lemons, make lemonade.'

The 165 km from Parry Sound to Sudbury is one of the most desolate pieces of highway in Ontario. Along Highway 69, in this sparsely populated area of the province, there are only four villages – Nobel, Pointe au Baril Station, Bigwood and Estaire. Along this quiet stretch of road I start to recapture the pace I've been looking for since leaving London. Approaching Labour Day weekend, the air temperature cools as we leave behind the hot, sticky days of summer and pick up the pace, heading toward fall.

Highway 69 isn't the easiest road for people to stop and make a donation, but quite often people stop where the motor home is parked. One day at lunchtime, a father and his young son knock on the door of the motor home. When they come aboard, it's a proud man who watches his son shake hands with me and donate two weeks' worth of allowance to *Jesse's Journey*.

Every day there are words of encouragement along the highway. A young man in a T-shirt, riding in the passenger seat of a pick-up trucks says, "Good job man," as he holds his hands out the window of the truck and applauds. The truck with its huge 'Chevy' logo on the back is loaded down with lumber. It looks a bit like a scene from a television commercial.

A man driving a Mercedes Benz calls out, "Go for it man!" He is among the many people who give us the 'thumbs up' sign when they meet us. A couple from Ingersoll who stop to make a donation say, "It's a very courageous thing you're doing." And a man and his wife from St. Thomas say, "Good luck, John. You make fathers proud." Messages like these drive me on, even when dollars are scarce. I never let go of the thought that I am doing what I feel fathers are supposed to do – and that's to do everything in your power to provide your kids with the best possible quality of life.

South of Sudbury on my 139th road day, I reach the 4,000 km mark. Walking north, I settle back into our regular daily routine as we get ready to rejoin the Trans-Canada and to turn west toward Sault Ste. Marie and the portion of the *Journey* that will take us across the top of Lake Superior.

Day after day, and night after night across the country, I do my best to explain to individuals and groups making a donation to *Jesse's Journey* that "this is not our money. It's your money and we are merely the stewards of those dollars." I remind people that in the years ahead as our endowment fund continues to grow, "No government is going to cancel the program and no company is going to downsize the program." And I remind them that the dollars they have donated are going to be hard at work year after year, seeking the answer to genetic illnesses.

Leading the way in corporate support, our friends from Manulife Financial continue to exceed their commitment to donate $1,000 each time I pass one of their branch offices. The Manulife family in Sudbury welcomes us to the Nickel Capital and Canada's biggest producer of copper, with a donation of more than $2,500. And at a midday barbecue, employees of the Royal Bank donate another $1,600. Piece by piece, the endowment fund is being built.

There is an interesting incident on the road to Sudbury. After I jog past a construction zone, one of the workers jumps on a front-end loader and drives down the highway to catch up with us and make a donation. There probably aren't too many people that can say they've been chased down the Trans-Canada Highway by a front-end loader.

At night in Sudbury, the red-hot slag from the smelters creates a fiery glow against a backdrop of blackness. Before darkness falls we are welcomed again at the home of Bernie and Helen Quesnel, a couple who hosted us when we crossed Ontario in 1995. The Quesnels, who are retired, share a special kind of creativity. Bernie uses the scroll saw in his workshop to create dozens of wooden pieces, many of them seasonal figures like Santa Claus. Helen's delicate touch with the paintbrush brings the figures to life. Like many grandparents, they wish it were as easy to fashion a healthy life for their grandson Ryan, another youngster with Duchenne.

The swimming pool in the Quesnels' backyard brings back memories of a summer night three years earlier when we lifted Jesse from his wheelchair into the pool to help him cool off after a hot day on the highway. Jesse's attendant, Sean Bagshaw, showed his youthfulness and sense of humour as he propped Jesse up on a combination air mattress and floating chair. With a pair of sunglasses to give Jesse a Jack Nicholson look, we snapped pictures of him smiling and hamming it up as the 'Big Cheese.'

Along the Trans-Canada Highway to Lively, just west of Sudbury, donations continue to come from a variety of sources. There are members of a car club with their vehicles parked on a hilltop by the side of the road. There are people who stop at the motor home or meet us at dinner who want to contribute. There are people playing golf who leave their clubs behind and come up to the roadside to make a donation. There's a man with two stainless steel knees who joins me on the road for a while. And there are those who want to walk along for a bit, perhaps just to know in their hearts that they were part of the *Journey*.

The days on the road are often long. But as I walk west on the highway Jesse and I shared three summers before, there's also a touch of nostalgia. Sometimes I can remember the road with some of its twists and turns before they appear. Nearing Espanola, another pulp town, we pass through Nairn Centre, where the sawmill produces enough sawn timber annually to build 18,000 houses. At the end of another day on the road, a familiar laneway takes me back to one of the prettiest places Jesse and I had seen, the Anishinabe Spiritual Retreat on Lake Anderson, just south of Espanola.

In a way it seems as if time has stood still. The nuns, Sister Dorothy and Sister Pat, welcome us again with open arms. And right beside the nuns, the slightly older golden retrievers, 'Frisky' and 'Mooch' are happily wagging their tails. It's another of the few moments along the way that feels a lot like 'going home.'

There is no one I talk with more along the road than Trish. Among Trish's many responsibilities, she looks after stretching my legs and doing the muscle work that has become more and more necessary now that I've been on the road for almost 150 days. Trish has been getting pressured to make sure I undergo another medical, and soon. We both know that at some point I'm going to have to take a day away from the road. It's at Espanola, on the final weekend in August, after 144 days on the road, that I finally decide to take the day off. Trish makes the phone calls that have to be made to juggle events further down the road.

The colour change in the leaves is more noticeable as Ed and I climb a hill and sit on a tree stump overlooking Lake Anderson. The sky is clear blue and the sun is warm on our faces as I enjoy a morning where I don't have to keep looking at my watch to see if we are on time.

With a big chunk of Ontario still to be crossed, and four more provinces after that, Ed and I avoid talking about the road ahead. We both know what we face. Instead, we talk about our families and the workload they are facing while *Jesse's Journey* makes its way across Canada. We talk about the gardens we didn't get to plant, the lawns that someone else is cutting, and all the things that are going to have to be trimmed, fertilized, fixed, oiled, cleaned or painted when we go home. But that list is just a bunch of things. In time they all will get fixed or replaced. It's our families we miss. We miss the wives who share each day of our lives. It isn't just because they're there to share in the moments of joy, or the tough times, but because they bring the music of laughter and a sense of balance to each day. We miss that when we are apart. We miss seeing our kids and we miss making our way through the parental minefield. We even miss the noise they make. As for Ed, the one he misses most is his pride and joy – his grandson, Scotty.

The decision to take a one-day break at Espanola gives everyone a chance to escape from the daily routine. It's a watershed in a way, because sometimes we get so busy with what we are doing that we forget why we are doing it. The rest gives all of us a chance to remind ourselves why we're here.

Ontario is province number six. The part of Canada I have already walked tells the story of the struggles among the British, the French, the Americans, and Canada's Native People. Northern Ontario's history is rooted in the story of survival in the rough-and-tumble world of the fur trade, fir trees and mining. Beyond Espanola and the E. B. Eddy forest reserve, (three times the size of Prince Edward Island), the countryside becomes more rugged as farmland disappears and the pulp and paper mills begin to dominate.

On the last day of August, on the Trans-Canada between Massey and Spanish, Bevin is waiting with his video camera. He has spray-painted a bright red line across the road, and added arrows pointing east and west, to St. John's and Victoria. Both distances are also there in red – 4,151 km. I'm now officially halfway across Canada.

Chapter Eighteen

THE SECOND HALF

"A good plan today is better than a perfect plan tomorrow" –
General George Patton

It's very quiet along the road as I walk past Serpent River, where the road north from the Trans-Canada takes you to Elliott Lake. Beyond Spragge, Pronto and Algoma Mills lies Blind River, named by the voyageurs who couldn't find the river's outlet to Lake Huron. The name stuck. Among the few people along the road, there is a conservation officer who stops. He wants to shake hands and say, "I'm a dad too." I spend my time getting used to the increase in the number of logging trucks and tractor-trailers with heavy-duty equipment.

The officer driving the provincial police escort cruiser, and whoever is driving the van that follows behind me, both start watching their rear view mirrors for trucks with oversized loads coming up behind us. When the escort people honk, I move to my right, further away from the road. That too will become just a part of the routine for the next four months.

September 2nd, west of Blind River on the Trans-Canada Highway between Iron Bridge and Thessalon, Ontario, is the first day since the Maritimes that I can see my breath in the air. I spend another day walking 33 km. We raise $60. The days ahead are looking lean.

It's raining when I pass through Thessalon and Bruce Mines. I work the road in 5 km blocks in what turns out to be an 'on again off again' day for rain gear. There's a reception in Thessalon where the town, as well as the town and township fire departments, make donations. There's a cheque presentation from employees of the Royal Bank at Bruce Mines, and donations from representatives of both the town and township councils.

293

My first reminder we are really in the North Country comes when a black bear crosses the highway in front of me just before I reach Bruce Mines. My second reminder is in Bruce Mines as I read the sign on the side of the store, advising that it sells "ice, lottery tickets and fishing licenses." From my travels with Jesse I know that beyond Sault Ste. Marie, these signs become even more detailed. One sign boasts "ice cream, bait, and firewood along with movies, hunting licenses and fireworks," dependent, I suppose, on the time of the year.

I don't know if it's the thought of 'ice cream and bait' that does it, but somewhere along the road I lose my appetite. Even though the meals are good, for a few days I don't feel much like eating. At the same time, every ten or eleven days my body clock seems to cycle around to where I just can't eat another restaurant meal and I have a light supper either in my room or on the motor home. Trish has wanted me to change my diet for some time, and when these two situations collide, she decides this is the time to make the change. Trish wants me to increase the amount of fruit I'm eating. And, as the weather gets colder, my mornings will be starting with Ed's legendary Newfoundland porridge.

On Day 150, laughter rejoins the *Journey* as we reach Sault Ste. Marie. It's been decided that here is where I am to have a full medical and a blood test. The appointment is arranged for Saturday night of the Labour Day weekend.

After the usual poking and prodding, I'm asked to make a fist while a needle is injected into a vein in my arm and three small vials are filled with blood. Passing the time, I talk with the doctor and ask him, "Do you ever take a look at somebody before you get started and think to yourself, 'Boy, I wouldn't be surprised if we find something wrong here.'" He's a good guy and says in a very matter-of-fact way, "Not very often. Besides, people who walk here from St. John's, Newfoundland aren't usually very sick!" We both have a good laugh as he wishes me luck and thirty minutes after the blood test he gives me the green light to keep going.

294

On the morning we leave Sault Ste. Marie, Bevin and his fiancée Renata Van Loon have to say goodbyes again. I feel bad for Bevin who has had his share of tearful farewells. Bevin's sister was in tears when she said goodbye back in Flesherton, knowing she wouldn't see her brother again until her wedding day in the fall. I remembered hugging his sister, Serena. Knowing I wouldn't see her for several months, I'd said, "Let me be the first to kiss the bride." Now it's Bevin's fiancée Renata who is fighting tears as she leaves for home. On the road with *Jesse's Journey,* both of these young women have been tireless workers.

I can remember all those days I'd looked back and seen Serena and Renata, tanned from the sun and soaked with sweat as they collected donations on the highways of southern Ontario. Sometimes they surprised us, especially Bevin, when they arrived to help out. And every time they arrived, they brought food – homemade meals that meant we didn't have to eat in a restaurant. But now it's time for another goodbye. These are always stressful moments and I don't know how many more times Bevin and his fiancée can stand to do this.

After Labour Day, the early morning sun creates an illusion of warmth over Lake Superior, the coldest of the Great Lakes. Standing at the top of 'One Mile Hill' north of Sault Ste. Marie, the road takes a dramatic plunge before stretching off to the horizon. Cars and trucks at the bottom of the hill look tiny as I start my descent, and I wonder for a moment how, three years earlier, I managed to push Jesse up this hill.

Somewhere, beyond that point on the horizon where the earth meets the sky, is Victoria and the end of the *Journey.* Regardless of what happens in the way of financial success and our ability to fund research, I'll have done my best. Thousands of good people will have joined the walk at one time or another, and supported our project. Thousands of ordinary Canadians will have shown us their generosity. Whenever I feel my spirits lag a little, I have to remind myself why I'm out here and I tell myself again that doing nothing

295

was never an option. Someone needed to come out here to send a message. I just had a better reason than most people for being that someone.

Walking north along the Trans-Canada Highway toward Batchawana Bay, with Lake Superior gleaming in the sun on my left, the leaves of the trees on the right hand side of the road are beginning to change colour. It's the first week of September and people who stop at the side of the road are parents driving their sons and daughters north to Lakehead University at Thunder Bay to begin another year of school. Some of the kids look to be in their early twenties – not much younger than our road manager, Trish. She was about the same age when she graduated from the University of Western Ontario in 1995, the year she first met Jesse and me. The day we reach Batchawana Bay, Trish turns 27. We mark the event with cabbage rolls and a little birthday celebration.

One of the toughest individual challenges in walking across Canada is the steep climb at Montreal River Harbour. Arriving at the foot of the hill at the end of our day on the road, I know my legs are going to get a serious test first thing in the morning.

On the 11th of September it takes me almost an hour to get to the top of the hill at Montreal River Harbour. When I reach the peak, I'm greeted by a couple from Kingston who applaud my arrival. I'm a little rubber-kneed, but after pouring some cold water over my head and resting a moment while I catch my breath, I can see we've been rewarded with a spectacular view looking out over Lake Superior. I don't often think about Terry Fox, but on this particular morning I do. I say to the road crew, "I don't know how somebody with just one leg ever managed to climb up that hill."

North of Batchawana Bay, the Trans-Canada is scenic but at the same time starts to become very difficult. Visibility is often limited by the jagged rock cuts where the road has been blasted out of the Canadian Shield. The resulting road has sharp twists and turns and very little shoulder, and at times the tight turns make life extremely dangerous. While the escort van stays tucked in close behind me, the provincial police cruiser is sometimes out of my sight about a kilometre back with its lights flashing, letting truckers know there is something to look out for on the road ahead.

The drivers of logging trucks and tractor-trailers are very good about giving us a wide berth when they pass. Lots of them let go with a blast of the air horn as a sign of encouragement. I think they probably use their CB radios to keep each other posted as to our location on the highway. Where the Trans-Canada passes through Lake Superior Provincial Park, a couple of truckers stop right on the highway and yell a message to me, warning about bears up ahead. It's been a hot summer and there have been few berries, so the bears are on the move, looking for food.

At the end of the day, we mark the road and head back to Montreal River Harbour and the Trail's End Lodge where Sherene is waiting for me. This will be the last time we see each other for almost five months.

The lodge has a rocky beach where the Montreal River spills into Lake Superior. When Sherene and I walk down toward the shore, the owner of the lodge cautions us not to stray too far, because of the number of sightings of bears. We sit by the water and talk for a few minutes before heading back to our cabin. It's a toss-up as to which of us is the most tired. Sherene's flight had been delayed and when it finally arrived in Sault Ste. Marie, there was the long drive to Montreal River Harbour. For me, the hills of northern Ontario have left me drained at the end of the day. On board the motor home, we both try hard not to fall asleep as we share a candlelight soup-and-sandwich supper before calling it a day.

Phil Spencer, who retired in 1989 with the military rank of Brigadier General, joins us on the road as we head north to Wawa. Joining Phil on the volunteer patrol is Gord Wainman, a former reporter with the

London Free Press. Ed, the commander of the motor home, also looks after the Department of Nicknames. Ed takes one look at Gord's white hair, and for the rest of his time on the road Gord is known as 'Snowman.' It's another in a long list of nicknames that go all the way back to Newfoundland. They were all terms of endearment whether you were called Starvin, Cueball, Stretch, Pappy, Ducky or Honey.

Phil Spencer spent 35 years serving his country in Canada's Armed Forces and he has two very personal reasons for taking part in *Jesse's Journey.* Phil comes from a family of eight children, the eldest of whom had been diagnosed with Hodgkins Disease when he was 28 years old and who had died when he was 50.

Phil's 24 year old son, Chris, had gone through the diagnosis and removal of a tumour which turned out to be non-malignant, but the thought of what might have been remains with his father as he prepares to take his turn on the road in northern Ontario.

From the Montreal River to Wawa, the Trans-Canada Highway typifies the old line about 'good news/bad news.' The hills become steeper and the task of walking becomes more grueling as we make our way north of Superior. On the other hand, the good news is the spectacularly rugged beautiful scenery along this stretch. Wawa is the home of one of the most noted landmarks in Canada, 'The Big Goose.' The nine-metre-high steel Canada goose stands at the entrance to Wawa, which is an Ojibwa word that means "wild goose."

Holding Sherene's hand I arrive in Wawa on a sunny Saturday afternoon. This is Sherene's final day on the road with us before heading home. The *Journey* convoy of vans and the motor home is escorted by fire trucks and police cars to a reception at the town's Community Centre. There are lots of people at the reception and among them is my friend Pirkko, the woman who – three years earlier – invited Jesse to her farm at Hawk Junction. The summer night that Jesse named a ten-day old pony "Snowy" is still one of my fondest memories from our trip across Ontario. Pirkko has remarried, and is now Pirkko Houston. She introduces me to her new husband, Andrew, and their two-month-old baby, Andrew Junior. It's nice to see that life has taken a happy turn for the woman who gave us such a special moment in 1995.

Physically, the toughest part of the walk across Canada lies between Wawa and Nipigon, on the northern shore of Lake Superior. The steep and seemingly endless hills are in control and for days on end, they dictate the agenda. Along this piece of the Trans-Canada Highway it's important to 'listen' to your body and not push it beyond its physical limit, while at the same time mentally focusing on completing just one hill at a time, one day at a time.

North from Wawa to White River the Trans-Canada Highway is 100 km of nothing but hills, rocks and trees. I sleep at every opportunity. To battle muscle fatigue, the work that is already being done on my legs three times a day must become more intense. The massage work on my calves and thigh muscles becomes much deeper.

White River, besides laying claim to being the coldest place in Canada, is also the birthplace of Winnie-the-Pooh. In 1914 Captain Harry Colebourn was on board a World War One troop-train that had stopped in White River. From a trapper, Captain Colebourn bought a black bear cub that had wandered out of the woods. He named the bear Winnipeg after his hometown, and then Colebourn and the bear, along with the rest of the troops, crossed the Atlantic to London, England. Before leaving for the fighting in Europe, Captain Colebourn gave the bear cub to the London zoo. When the author, A. A. Milne, visited the zoo with his son Christopher Robin, he saw the bear and started writing stories about 'Winnie' and his friends. As we know, these stories, which were first published in 1926, are still in bookstores today.

In the park in White River there's a moment when the past and the present seem to meet. *Jesse's Journey*, a project geared toward making life better for people with genetic illnesses – especially children – receives a special donation. It is from the people of White River and we accept it at the site of the statue marking the birthplace of the storybook character who has delighted children for decades.

The Trans-Canada Highway from White River to Marathon is another lonely stretch of road, with no towns or villages. I try to sleep on the motor home during the drive out to our start point in the morning and on the drive back at the end of the day.

The grey, rainy days have made the sand and gravel at the side of the road very soft. There is a close call while I'm walking the highway. Further up the road, the motor home is forced off the road by a tractor-trailer. Luckily, no one is hurt. The motor home ends up leaning on an angle, up to its axles in soft sand. The truck driver stops to help, and he and Ed manage to rock the motor home free with no damage.

The days heading to Marathon are uneventful. It's funny the lengths we sometimes go to, to make the time go faster. There's an afternoon on the road when the kilometres click by as Gord Wainman and I search our memory banks to recall things from our childhood. We talk about cap guns, peashooters, Dinky Toys, marbles, chestnuts, baseball cards and jackknives. We recall the black and white pictures of Toronto Maple Leaf and Montreal Canadien hockey heroes you could send away for with the labels from Beehive Corn Syrup. And we talk about when we were ten or eleven year old hockey players, how accurate we were at consistently shooting pucks through a hole where a board was missing on the side of the garage.

It's fun talking about a time when every kid you knew – boys and girls, played hockey or figure skated, rode bicycles and went swimming. It seemed like we could run and play forever. Then a young American couple, a mother and father, pull their car to the side of the road. As they make a donation, I receive a cold reminder that not every child's youth is as easy as mine had been. They tell me about how their young daughter is about to undergo the same operation as baseball player Dave Dravecky.

It was in June of 1991 when cancer cut short the career of the 35 year old Dravecky, a pitcher with the San Francisco Giants. The former all-star had to have his left arm surgically removed after a cancerous lump was discovered. This couple's little girl was scheduled to lose her arm in a month.

There is never any warning and nothing can prepare you for these intensely personal moments when people want to share their stories about their families and their children. As they wish me luck and drive off, I can't help thinking about their little girl. My reason for being here has just been underscored once again. It's time to move on.

On the Trans-Canada, our visitors from France catch up with us on a soggy and wet morning, in the drizzle that's falling as I near Marathon. They've been shooting videotape of Jesse in London, and now they want to see Jesse's dad and the road crew at work. While northern Ontario can look breathtaking in the sunlight, it can be equally depressing when the sky is grey. Everywhere around us water is dripping from the sharp angles of wet rocks, but we'll have to make do.

As the camera crew begins shooting video to be aired in December when Jesse travels to France, I can tell right away that it's going to be a long day. Television production work isn't something that happens quickly, and in order for the cameraman to get just the right shot, I'm asked several times to repeat sections of the road I've already walked.

For months, Bevin has been climbing to the tops of hills, scrambling up the sides of mountains and looking for clearings in the trees to videotape the story of *Jesse's Journey*. The knowledge he's acquired about the terrain helps the visitors from France find great camera angles to get the shots they are looking for.

301

At one point, we need two-way radios to coordinate a shot as I walk across a long bridge spanning a wide valley of fir trees. The camera crew is more than a kilometre behind me, high on a lookout point that provides a panoramic view of Lake Superior, the valley below and the railroad tracks that wind through the valley.

Returning to the scenic lookout for lunch, the camera lens probes our every move, capturing the behind the scenes look at *Jesse's Journey*. After lunch as I lie down and have my legs stretched and massaged, Richard, the television producer from France, asks if he can do an interview. Although I've been asked a lot of questions in the months on the road, Richard penetrates my mind in a way that hasn't happened before, with questions that deal with both a father's dreams and reality.

At Marathon, during a break on the motor home, it starts pouring rain. I know that, to keep them dry, my feet will have to be wrapped in plastic bags inside my running shoes. To keep my feet tough and to prevent blisters, I'm still soaking them three times a day in sea salt and water. I guess it's working because when Ed is stretching my legs, he says, "Johnny, you've got feet like pig's ears."

The cast of characters changes again at Marathon. The television crew leaves for Winnipeg to begin a series of flights that will take them back home to France. Bevin returns from doing advance work with the media and police in Thunder Bay. Trish goes home for a break. When I arrive for breakfast, Ted Eadinger, who is replacing Trish as Road Manager, looks up from a bowl of Ed's porridge, smiles and says, "Hi, it's me again." Ted had been with us in Quebec, and although neither one of us knows it, for Ted, the most interesting part of the *Journey* is still to come.

The night before, we had walked across the Trans-Canada from our motel on one side of the highway to have supper at the restaurant on the opposite side. Looking both east and west as I crossed the highway, there was nothing in sight in either direction. It strikes me as funny that there are stretches of road on Canada's national highway, where every once in a while, you could almost set up nets and play road hockey.

Built by Marathon Paper of Wisconsin, the pulp and paper town of Marathon, Ontario was established in 1944. Marathon really boomed when gold was discovered at nearby Hemlo, which today is the site of Canada's three largest gold mines. It's at Marathon that Gary Alan Price, who had been with me in Newfoundland, joins me for just a single day after driving all the way from London with his father, Al. In eastern Ontario, Al Price - at 71 years of age had become the oldest person to become a member of the '33' club. Before this day is over Gary will match his dad's accomplishment for distance as he too logs a full day with me along Canada's national highway.

There are few people along the road as we wind our way across the top of Lake Superior to Terrace Bay, arriving on the first day of fall. Jesse and I had recorded one of our most memorable moments from 1995 at this same roadside motel where we are staying in Terrace Bay – another pulp and paper town, this one built by Kimberly-Clark in the 1940s.

It had been very hot in the summer of 1995, and after lunch I had been lying down for a rest in my motel room. When I looked up, Jesse was at the door in his wheelchair. "Dad," he said, "there's twelve guys out here on motorcycles." When I asked what they were like, Jesse said, "They're big! You know, they have big beards, big leather outfits and big tattoos. They're just big Dad, trust me." When I asked what they wanted, Jesse said, "They want to have their picture taken with me." So, Jesse had his picture taken with twelve 'bikers.'

Lying back on the bed at that time, I had thought to myself, "I'm a fairly intelligent guy, so let me just think about this for a moment. Twelve big tough guys on motorcycles are probably drug dealers of some kind. They're likely involved with a strip club and generally speaking, they're probably bad news."

303

Jesse told me later that after having their picture taken, these twelve big tough guys handed him $500 in cash. Still thinking the worst, I didn't bother to ask where that money had come from. It didn't matter, because I would have been wrong.

It turned out that our twelve 'bikers' were on their way to Thunder Bay to take part in a 'Ride for Sight' program. It wasn't what I thought they were all about, but ever since that time, whenever I'm in a car at a red light and I look over and see a big tough-looking guy sitting on a motorcycle beside me, I don't see the same person any more. Jesse's experience with the motorcyclists had reminded me that we should never judge a book by its cover.

I add a lapel pin from Terrace Bay to the bulging collection that began in Newfoundland, and I walk on to the neighbouring town of Schreiber, where half of the population is of Italian descent. Most residents can trace their roots to the southern Italian town of Siderno Marina. Starting in 1883, their ancestors began arriving in Canada and settling in Schreiber, where they went to work on the Canadian Pacific Railway.

From Schreiber west to Rossport, the trade-off continues. The hills are steep and demanding, but the view from the top of each one is its own reward. At this point the Trans-Canada Highway hugs the north shore of Lake Superior. The dramatic rise and fall of the Canadian Shield gave engineers a huge challenge in carving a roadway through the rock. The result is a road that plunges, climbs and twists, offering spectacular scenery at almost every turn. Villages that aren't right on the highway are sometimes missed in the rush to get to the bigger cities. Rossport is one of the north shore's little secrets. Before doubling back to the Rossport Inn, the day ends with a long, steep climb. I never like ending my day at the bottom of a hill. I always want to start the next day at the top. Ted Eadinger is with me as we make the final climb of the day. We are halfway up the hill when we hear the honk from the escort van, letting us know we have reached our distance for the day. We keep on going and I'm glad we do. At the top of the hill we meet a couple from Aylmer, Ontario who donate $200. It makes it all worthwhile, especially on a day when only three cars have stopped.

The Rossport Inn, which opened in 1884, is owned by Ned Basher and is the oldest operating hotel on Lake Superior's north shore. An American who flew fighter missions in Vietnam, Ned recalls that he knew the Inn very well from when he used to come to Rossport as a youngster. As an adult, flying from a base in the United States, training missions took him out over Lake Superior where he could look down at the Inn he would one day own.

The Inn sits on a hill, with a view of the water and the islands that protect the bay. Just below the Inn, the railroad tracks run along the shoreline. The motor home is parked across from the Inn, just beyond the point where the tracks bend with the shoreline. Sitting in the dark, you could swear the high-powered headlights on the engines of the freight trains that pass are coming right through the motor home before they veer off at the last second. The noise and vibration kept things a little too exciting for Ed, who slept on the motor home at Rossport. In the morning he looked both groggy and slightly shell-shocked as he laughed at breakfast, telling us he'd had a dream that a freight train "tore the arse-end right off the motor home!"

There's a beautiful dawn the morning we leave Rossport. As the sun climbs into the sky, I start climbing the hills that lead to Nipigon. Nipigon is the western end of the toughest section of the Ontario highway. There are still lots of hills to climb, but I know that the road ahead will soon become more manageable.

Late in the day, when the shadows are getting long, I jog what seems like an endless expanse of bridge, high above the Nipigon River, Lake Superior's largest tributary. The police sometimes refer to the bridge as the 'Nipigon Net' because everything on rubber that moves across Canada has to cross the bridge at Nipigon. That's where the police set themselves up when they're looking for people who they believe are trying to make a dash to the West Coast.

On the far side of the bridge, I climb the hill leading into Nipigon with Ted Eadinger at my side. I keep thinking to myself, 'Poor Ted, he keeps getting the short end of the stick. Every time I have a big hill to climb, it seems to be his turn to be out on the road with me.' I'm always amazed at Ted's ability to hang in there on the tough climbs. He huffs and puffs a bit as we make our way up the hills, but in the spirit of what this journey is all about, he never gives up. Besides, Ted knows that quitting is not an option. Nipigon also marks the beginning of the 100 km of the Trans-Canada from Nipigon to Thunder Bay known as "The Terry Fox Courage Highway."

Sunday, September 27th, I reach the edge of Thunder Bay. A couple of former *London Free Press* reporters, Mac Haig and Bob Weber, are our newest 'rookies.' One of the strangest things that happens the morning of their first day on the road is seeing a motorist waving to us from where he has pulled his car to the side of the road almost a kilometre ahead of us. Oddly, he then drives off long before we reach the spot where he'd parked. But on the ground, pinned under a rock, we find a $5 bill and a day-old copy of *The London Free Press*.

After lunch, I get a big mental boost as I pass the five-thousand kilometre mark. Late in the afternoon we reach the Terry Fox Monument. I ask Ted to join me as we walk up the hill to the monument. It seems fitting. After all, Ted has been on the road for a lot of the steep hills, and I think he deserves to make this little climb.

The Terry Fox Monument looks out over Lake Superior, and is close to the point on the Trans-Canada Highway where the one-legged runner was forced to suspend his 'Marathon of Hope' in September of 1980. The sun is shining and even though it's now fall, there are still a few tour buses in the parking lot. This stop is like none other.

It's quiet, and people seem lost in their own thoughts as they gaze up at the larger-than-life bronze statue of Terry Fox, the courageous young Canadian whose contribution to cancer research has outlived him. Their faces look solemn as they remember the curly-haired runner with the hippity-hop stride and the huge smile, making his way across the country. At the monument, some people with cameras take pictures. Others just stare and wipe their eyes. There's a feeling of respect tinged with awe. The words carved in the stone base of the monument recount the story of Terry's 5,432 km run for cancer research. When I look at the word 'research', I get a sense of kinship. Perhaps just a little more than others, I understand what drove Terry on, day after day. Again, it's time to move on.

It is Thursday, October 1st, and it's snowing. We are at Shebaqua Corners, northwest of Thunder Bay. It's the first snow I've seen since leaving Newfoundland.

The 180 km from Shebaqua Corners to Ignace is another lonely stretch of highway, which means a long drive in the morning to reach our start point, and another long drive back at night. In Thunder Bay, there's a lot of media attention, and there are major donations at receptions hosted by both Manulife and the Royal Bank. Back on the highway on the way to Ignace, we pass through just three widely-separated villages, Raith, Upsala and English River. The snow disappears quickly but it's a reminder about what lays ahead. In the mornings now, it's still dark when I head out to the motor home. With the engine running, the lights on, and the windows steamed up, the motor home always looks warm.

On board, Ed's infamous porridge with raisins and cinnamon is simmering on the stove. In a matter of minutes the orange juice, porridge, toast, jam, coffee and tea are finished. The dishes are cleaned up, fresh water is loaded on board and everything is secured. The morning radio interviews are done and the Ontario Provincial Police are contacted. Before the sun is up, we are on our way again. The frosty mornings are another sign that the clock marking the change of the seasons is ticking even louder. The landscape is changing from a carpet of green to a carpet of green and yellow. There are only a few maple trees to provide the brilliant splashes of red we're used to in southern Ontario. The road is starting to flatten out which gives my back a chance to recover from the pounding it has taken on the hills between Sault Ste. Marie and Thunder Bay.

On most days, the sun still warms us in the afternoon. On the road Mac Haig, a fan of Maurice Richard and the Montreal Canadiens, shares stories with me about growing up in Belleville, Ontario in the glory days when the National Hockey League had just six teams. Almost as if we're kids trading hockey cards, I share with Mac some of the highway trivia I've learned. I tell Mac about things like the little silver and green diamond-shaped signs located at the beginning and end of sections of guardrail. At the front end of the guardrail, the top half of the diamond is green; and at the end of the guardrail, the bottom half of the diamond is green. The signs tell the snow-plough driver when to pick the blade up and when to put it down to prevent shearing off the guardrails in deep snow. It isn't a great mystery, but it helps pass the time as the kilometre count continues.

Before we reach Upsala we pass the official time marker and reset our watches back an hour to Central Time. If we're thinking that we are pretty smart with all our highway trivia and a free hour to catch an extra nap because of the time change, that goes out the window when we reach the town. Everything in Upsala operates on Eastern Standard Time!

Summer is now over and there is little traffic on the Trans-Canada Highway. Along the CPR tracks that run parallel to the road, the engineers of freight trains sound their horns and wave. From the industrial heartland of Canada, flatcars carrying containers stacked one on top of the other roll west. In the opposite direction, there seems to be an endless stream of brown and yellow grain cars heading east, each with the words Canadian Wheat Board and a yellow sheaf of wheat painted on the side. The wheat from the

Prairies is bound for ships waiting in Thunder Bay. Those ships, carrying part of Canada's annual harvest of 50 million metric tonnes of wheat, will be racing to reach the Atlantic Ocean before the winter freeze-up locks the Great Lakes in ice.

At the lunch break on my 180th day on the road, Ed has parked the motor home in a wide-open area beside the highway, just south of English River. The ground, which looks like it has been smoothed with some kind of grader, is full of what look like fresh wood chips. Back a distance from the highway, not far from where the motor home is parked, there are two white wooden crosses that tell the story. The crosses, each about three feet high, are side by side. Flowers have been left at the base of both of the crosses.

The police officer escorting us says there was a double fatality at this spot a couple of weeks earlier. The drivers of two tractor-trailers hauling wood chips died when their vehicles collided. The officer seems a little surprised when Ed tells him exactly what time the accident happened. Ed is holding up a wristwatch he found while waiting for us to arrive for lunch. The crystal is shattered, and the hands of the watch are stopped at 8:45, the exact time of the crash. Before moving on in the afternoon, Ed takes some heavy-duty clear tape and attaches the watch to one of the crosses. It just seems to belong there.

South of Ignace, a green Ministry of Natural Resources truck stops on the opposite side of the road. The tall uniformed officer, who walks across the highway, smiles at me and says, "So what time do you want the pizza to be ready?"

This is my friend Bruce Tomlinson, an enforcement officer with the Ministry of Natural Resources. He and his wife Kathy and their kids welcomed Jesse and me and our road crew into their home in 1995. Bruce just wants us to know the door is still open and they'll be expecting us for dinner. I have been looking forward to this stop because I have a couple of little presents to deliver. The home team in London has shipped us a framed print of Jesse and me on the road in 1995. The other gift is long overdue. I have with me a box full of unopened hockey cards that I promised to give to Bruce's son, Luke.

Dressed in his uniform and wearing a holstered gun on his belt, Bruce is a very imposing figure. Dressed casually and making homemade pizza in his kitchen, Bruce takes on a different persona. Bruce's wife Kathy is a Justice of the Peace who has family roots in Newfoundland. On our second night in Ignace, we are at the Tomlinsons again - this time for a Newfoundland 'Jiggs' dinner' of salt beef, cabbage, turnip, potatoes and roast beef. For Ed Coxworthy, it's a bit of a homecoming in the middle of northern Ontario.

At night, before going to bed, I usually turn on the television to check the weather for the next day. Flipping through the channels, I stop when I see a picture of Gene Autry. The 'Singing Cowboy' has died at his home in California at the age of 91. It's been a bad year for cowboy heroes from the days of black and white television. Earlier in the summer 'The King of the Cowboys', Roy Rogers, died at 86. The pages of my journal tell me that 'Buffalo Bob' Smith from the Howdy Doody Show of the 1950's died earlier in the year, as did singer Frank Sinatra, who was 82.

We've been in a dead zone for cell phones for the past few days and when I finally get to talk to Sherene, she tells me that Jesse is feeling a bit down. I can't think of a time I wanted to be home more than at this moment. It's one of the few times I think about just how long I've been away.

There is often a counterpoint to some of the down times. When I walk out to the motor home in the morning my day starts with a smile when I walk past a pick-up truck with a bumper sticker that says, "If you're opposed to logging, try using plastic toilet paper!" And so it goes.

The morning we set off for Dryden, the jet trails in the sky are very short. We use that as a barometer to tell us there isn't much moisture in the air and that it will likely be a dry day. We don't know yet how right we are. Here it is October 9th and I'm wearing a T-shirt and shorts, after a couple of wet days I'd spent putting on and taking off the fluorescent-orange rain suit. Although the sun is shining, I'm still wondering how much longer our luck will last with these bonus days of fall.

Arriving in Dryden, a group of Wal-Mart employees meet us at the mall on the edge of town. Among the group who joins us on the road is a young couple, both doctors in Dryden, whose 4 year old son has Duchenne. After the police escort us to the Royal Bank branch in Dryden, the little boy sits on my knee, and we pose for pictures as we cut a big chocolate cake together. This little guy looks a lot like Jesse did at that age.

Dryden is another northern Ontario pulp and paper town. Sometimes I forget how rugged the surrounding area is until we see a moose or, as happened when I looked out the window of our motel in the morning, a coyote standing on top of a pile of railroad ties.

On the road to Kenora, the last town before the Manitoba border, people continue to stop. At Vermillion Bay, a couple of days away from Kenora, I have to go back and repeat a 4 km section of road to make up for a construction zone. After completing that section of road for the second time, a female worker who is directing traffic with a flag at the beginning of the construction zone, makes a donation and wishes me luck.

There are people heading east and people heading west who stop. Among them is an older couple travelling together with their collie dog, seeing Canada and the United States from the cab of a transport truck. The lady uses a cane and has difficulty walking. Her husband says he doesn't want to be worrying about her while he's out on the road, so they travel along together. I have never really looked inside

311

the cab of a transport truck before, and I'm surprised to see there is a stove, a microwave oven, bathroom facilities, a bed, and even a television. These folks are on their way to Vancouver with a load of furniture. From Vancouver, they'll be carrying something else to Kansas City, and then a different load again back home to London.

A young man from Kitchener, on his way to medical school in Calgary, is thrilled when he stops to meet me. His name is Tony Bella and he is so excited he gets out his video camera and I end up doing an impromptu speech at the side of the road. He wants to be able to share with his class in Calgary this story of a father and son and their family's efforts to help fund science and research. Standing on the side of the Trans-Canada Highway, talking to a video camera, I find myself doing whatever it takes to help spread the word about the need for research dollars.

Later I meet a man from Poplar Hill, in southern Ontario. He's doing some pipeline work between Ignace and Dryden. For him it's an emotional moment as he shakes my hand and apologizes about not having much money. He gives us $100.

On Thanksgiving Sunday it's raining steadily at the end of our day, west of Vermillion Bay. Only two people have stopped all day.

After lunch Ed takes the motor home back to Vermillion Bay to start preparing our Thanksgiving dinner. Later, in the gathering dusk, the light that spills from the steamed-up windows give a warm glow to the larger-than-life picture of Jesse's smiling face on the side of the motor home. On board, I can hear the voices of people who have gone from being road crew to being road family. I have a lot to be thankful for.

Opening the door of the motor home, I'm met by the wonderful smell of a turkey cooking in the oven. Everyone is in a really good mood, and they all seem to be busy getting ready for dinner. I climb

In June of 1995, Jesse and I are seen climbing Jackfish Hill, north of Wawa in a painting by Canadian artist Ken Jackson.

I paused to survey the view from the top of Jackfish Hill in 1998. This is the location used for the painting above.

At the foot of Jackfish Hill in Northern Ontario, the late summer sunlight created a carpet of green and blue as the days grew shorter and the weather turned colder.

Halfway across Canada Bevin Palmateer's handiwork indicates St. John's, Newfoundland, and Victoria, British Columbia, are both 4,151 km away.

The permanent road team pose for a roadside shot. From left: Bevin Palmateer, Trish Federkow, myself and Ed Coxworthy.

In 1998 Jesse was always on my mind as I walked alone through Northern Ontario. In 1995, it was in places like Terrace Bay that Jesse really experienced nature. This picture was taken at the foot of Aguosaban Falls, which spills into Lake Superior at Terrace Bay. It was here that Jesse caught a salmon in 1995.

Around the north shore of Lake Superior, nature played a large part in dictating where the Trans Canada Highway would be built. Rock cuts and blind corners made us very conscious of safety as I walked a brief "flat" portion at the crest of another hill.

Physically, the hills from Wawa to Nipigon were the most punishing. Although the climbs seemed endless, looking out over Lake Superior, the scenery was spectacular.

Crossing Canada and feeling like the hills of Northern Ontario were punishing me physically, I thought back to how hard Jesse had worked in 1995. At that time I couldn't always see Jesse's face from my position behind the wheelchair. It wasn't until later when I saw pictures like this one that I realized how, at times, the journey was very tiring for Jesse.

aboard to the usual chorus of friendly insults suggesting that I hurry up and shut the door, along with the standard inquiry about whether or not I was born in a barn.

With the turkey and Newfoundland dressing with summer savory, we have ham, potatoes, turnip, carrots, cabbage, yellow peas-pudding and gravy. We even have some of those little packages of cranberry sauce that somebody managed to 'borrow' from a restaurant somewhere along the way. And we have an apple crisp that Trish made for dessert. Life on board the motor home seems pretty good. Twenty-four hours later it will be a different story.

Thanksgiving Monday, Mother Nature decides to throw everything she has at us. It's raining at the start of the day and it just keeps getting worse. By midday the wind is blowing hard. Before lunch, I complete 22 km in a combination of rain, sleet, ice pellets and snow. To make matters worse, there is no shoulder on the road, and trying to get through the wet sand and gravel at the edge of the pavement is like walking in porridge. Finally, the snow stops, but it's still windy and raining. The good news is we have a police escort and lots of flashing lights.

Even though the truckers slow down as they pass me, I'm still blown off the road twice by a combination of high wind and tire spray from the transports. I finish my 33 km just after five o'clock. Then things get worse.

Ed has waited for me with the motor home while everyone else has gone on ahead to a pre-arranged dinner in Kenora. As Ed and I drive on toward town, a gauge on the instrument panel shows the engine is overheating. That diagnosis is confirmed within seconds when we notice steam coming from the engine compartment. With the emergency lights flashing, Ed slows the motor home to a crawl, and as soon as he hears the engine lifters starting to make a noise, he immediately pulls to the side of the road and stops.

313

We are out of cell range and can't reach either Bevin or Trish. So we do the only thing we can do. We wait. After the engine cools, we start it up again, and move forward about a kilometre before we have to stop again. Now we are within cell range, but Murphy's Law is still playing with us. It's the end of the day and Trish and Bevin have turned their phones off.

After talking over our options, we decide to call the police. When the operator asks if we want to declare an emergency, we say "yes," but not because we're in any personal danger. There is very little shoulder to park on and although we have our emergency lights flashing, the back end of the motor home is sticking out on the road surface.

When we don't show up for supper, Trish and Bevin eventually call to find out what's happened. We tell them to stay where they are and within half an hour we limp into Kenora, in the dark, attached to a tow truck. To add insult to injury, we haven't collected a penny all day.

I was never so happy to see that motor home as I was the next morning when Ed rejoined us on the highway. Once again, he looked a little the worse for wear, having spent the night parked beside a refrigeration transport with its motor running. Our problem was that the motor home's ten-cylinder engine had blown a frost plug. All of the frost plugs have now been replaced and we are back in business. It's something that could have happened to anybody, but I still wonder why it happened to us. Maybe that's what you get when you forget to say grace at dinner on Thanksgiving Day!

In Kenora, the largest town on the Lake of the Woods, the pulp mill has been on strike since June. When the CPR arrived at Kenora in 1879, so did the lumber industry. And now, more than a hundred years later, there are signs that Kenora is still reliant on the wealth of the forests. Some of the people on the streets appear to be hanging around with nothing to do. That's what happens when people are without work. There will be few donations in a town that's waiting for the end of a strike that has crippled the town's major industry.

At the Town Hall in Kenora, the mayor presents everyone with town pins. And, despite tough economic times, there are cheque presentations from men's and women's groups, showing that generosity knows no bounds and that people facing hard times still want to share what they have.

From Kenora, the Manitoba border is just over 50 km away. The sun is shining as I walk past McLeod Park and one of the most famous pieces of 'highway art' in North America. "Huskie the Muskie" champions Kenora as a sport fishing paradise. "Huskie the Muskie" joins a long list of highway art that includes The Big Goose at Wawa, The Big Apple, The Big Nickel, the World's Biggest Axe and The World's Biggest Chair. There was the 80-tonne lobster at Shediac, New Brunswick, and Jumbo the Elephant in St. Thomas, Ontario.

Among the last people to stop in Ontario are two young men from Newfoundland who are heading west to seek their fortune in the 'oil patch' of Alberta. They seem to have everything they own strapped to the roof of their car. The scene reminds me of Bruce Tomlinson in Ignace saying that over the years he has seen hundreds of cars just like the one parked in front of me, and with every one of them there's a story. Some are heading east to the Promised Land and just as many are heading west to the Promised Land. The two young men make a $10 donation to *Jesse's Journey* and wish me well. I have a funny feeling they don't have $10 to give. But then again, these people are Newfoundlanders, and they're typical of the people from the island that leads Canada when it comes to giving.

Chapter Nineteen

ON TO MANITOBA

"I don't even know what street Canada is on" –
Al Capone

Late in the day on Thursday, October 15th, I take my final steps in
Ontario and cross the border into Manitoba. I have been on the road
for 191 days since dipping my shoes in the Atlantic Ocean at Quidi
Vidi, Newfoundland. It has taken me 98 days to walk the entire
length of my home province. It's the second time in my life I have
walked across Ontario. With six provinces now behind me, ahead are
the Prairies, the Rockies and the Canadian winter. But at last, the end
is in sight.

The first day in a new province always seems like a bit of a loss. The
distance that's completed on the road stands by itself: it isn't being
added to anything. There's no feeling of building on something that's
already been completed. It's been the same in every other province
and that's the way it is when we arrive in Falcon Lake to spend our
first night in Manitoba.

I can't get over how fast things become flat. After crossing
the Ontario-Manitoba border, there are a couple of little hills
followed by a big valley and then suddenly we're on the Prairies.
It's that quick.

My daily routine requires some adjustments now that we are in the
Central time zone. The radio interviews in Ontario have to be done
an hour earlier. This is only going to become more difficult
as we move further west. The two nights at Falcon Lake, I stay in
my room at night and try to catch up on sleep. Coming out of
Ontario my back has been bothering me, so I welcome the flat
terrain of Manitoba.

One of the first problems we have to face in Manitoba is
fighting the flu bug, which has tagged along for the ride as

we switched provinces. The two former reporters, Mac Haig and Bob Weber, have both been knocked out of commission as we move on toward Hadashville. They may have been easy prey for the flu bug, as they were probably exhausted. They've been on the road as volunteers for twenty-one days since joining us before we reached Thunder Bay. To complicate matters, Trish is also fighting the flu.

Trish is a *Journey* veteran who knows the realities of life on the road, and life on the motor home. After coaching the wrestling team at university, working with a crew of guys doesn't seem to bother her – or if it does, she never lets on. I'm probably a little old-fashioned and even though Trish seems to 'tune out' when someone lets slips with the odd swear word, I still see myself as a sort of father figure looking out for a daughter.

Once again with just the guys on the road after Trish heads home for a break, I put an empty plastic cup in the cup holder on the kitchen table of the motor home. I tell the guys it's going to cost a person 25 cents every time they swear. Little do I know that this plastic cup will become the source of a lot of laughs and do more to build team spirit than I can ever imagine. It's also a minor source of revenue. Some of the guys deposit a couple of dollars in the cup and use it as a kind of bank account that they withdraw from until their slip-ups have eaten up their deposit. As quarters are being dropped into the cup, we are about to welcome aboard our next volunteers, two retired schoolteachers from London – Carolyn Brennan and Marilyn Richmond. The week ahead is going to be a language test of a different kind.

Having Carolyn and Marilyn on board is great. For me, it's a little bit like having your mom there to look after you. As volunteers they're quick self-starters who plunge right into the work, doing the laundry, buying the groceries and getting a card and birthday cake for Mac Haig, who will celebrate his 60th birthday with us on his last day on the road with *Jesse's Journey*.

318

I call home from where we're staying in Hadashville, another little Manitoba community, sandwiched between Winnipeg and the Ontario border. We're staying at a motel with a bar that features country and western music. It's been a long time since I talked to Sherene, Jesse and Tim back in London and Tyler, who's working for the summer in Banff. When I call home, Jesse seems very up as he tells me a couple of his marks from school. I tell Tim that I was interviewed in Kenora by a reporter whose name was Tim Davidson! I tell Sherene that I miss her.

The next day at lunch when I report that Jesse has earned an 89 in English and a 97 in Marketing, Carolyn and Marilyn smile and seem pleased. I guess once you're a teacher, you're always a teacher. And these two are special. They never bat an eye when another quarter or two lands in the plastic cup on the table.

On the road I try to shift gears mentally as the Trans-Canada Highway now runs straight all the way to Winnipeg. I see very quickly how boredom can become a problem.

People who are on the move across Canada are among those who stop. There's a young couple making the long haul from Peterborough to Victoria, four young guys from Falcon Lake helping a friend move to Winnipeg and a mother and daughter from London relocating to Jasper. They all make donations before driving off into the distance, their vehicles still visible for a long time on the flat land.

In the past few days, there has been a dramatic increase in the amount of wildlife along the highway. Late one afternoon, just before we left Ontario, Bevin was walking with me when two deer crossed the road. There was no traffic at the time, and in the quiet their hooves clicked and clacked on the hard surface of the highway, making a strange sound as if the deer were tap dancing. And then, as quickly as they had appeared, they had vanished into the woods on the opposite side of the road.

The wildlife doesn't seem to be nearly as shy in Manitoba. Leaving Hadashville, a white-tailed deer stands for the longest time, just watching us walk down the road. While Ed is up ahead of us preparing lunch there are seven deer – two bucks, two does and three fawns who come boldly up to the motor home, just to see what's happening. It's a pastoral moment that is short-lived.

East of Winnipeg, the unrestrained anger of the weather seems to be asking me again just how much I'm willing to take. The rain that's mixed with ice pellets once again stings my face, and the high wind that sweeps across the open fields sometimes stops me from moving forward at all.

I'm back to wearing the fluorescent-orange rubber rain gear. Leaning into the wind that's rocking the motor home, I have to fight just to get the door open. Safely on board for my first break, the wind slams the door behind me.

My fingers feel numb and my eyes are red. As I slump into my seat at the kitchen table, cold water is dripping from my chin. Ed sets a cup of steaming hot chocolate in front of me before fetching another pair of clean, dry socks he has been warming on the heat vent. It isn't until I'm shedding the rain suit that I realize we have visitors.

I shake hands with 45 year old John Fehr and his wife Matilda who have driven out from Steinbach, Manitoba to make a donation. They know why I'm here.

The Fehrs had three children, two girls and a boy. Their son Randy died of DMD two and one-half years earlier when he was 21 years old. Cold and wet, I listen in silence as John Fehr, another father I have never met before, tells me the story of the final hours of his son's life.

It was almost springtime when Randy was taken to hospital in Steinbach on a Monday night in April of 1995. Near the end, Randy could barely speak. His father said he woke from a broken sleep at his son's bedside when he heard Randy say, "Cool." John said he thought Randy was cold and wanted a blanket. As John tucked a blanket around his only son, he heard Randy say in a whisper, "Neat."

John said, "Randy, what are you talking about?"

His son was very weak and perhaps mistook his father's voice for that of his mother. Randy responded, "Mom, you have to see this. Come with me." It was shortly after that, in the early morning hours of Friday, April 19th, 1995 that Randy Fehr died.

After pausing a moment at the end of the story, John took a deep breath. Then with a bit of a smile he broke the silence that had settled over the motor home and said he's sure that Randy is now in a much happier place.

Before they left, John Fehr, a dad from the little town of Steinbach, Manitoba, and his wife Matilda made a generous donation to *Jesse's Journey*. Before stepping down the stairs of the motor home, John smiled again and said that Randy was the kind of kid who was always happy and never complained. Thanking the Fehrs for their kindness, I felt emotionally drained as we shook hands again and said goodbye. Watching them drive away in the rain, the weather didn't really seem so bad anymore.

I know I met some other people along the road that day, but I barely remember any of them. Driving into Winnipeg at the end of the day, a long thin line of red sky ran along the horizon. It gave a strong hint that there would be better weather ahead.

For the next four nights we are based in Winnipeg, shuttling back and forth from the Trans-Canada Highway at the beginning and end of each day. Fortunately, Winnipeg has what is probably the country's most efficient ring road. Getting back and forth to the

321

highway is fairly easy, which is good because of the extra workload in these bigger centres, where there are always more radio, television and newspaper interviews to do. These provide us with more opportunities to talk about our project and the need for research dollars. Winnipeg is no exception.

During one of the early morning radio interviews, our friend Dr. Ron Worton joins me on the air by telephone from the Ottawa General Hospital Research Institute. It's comforting for me to know that while I've been on the road, Dr. Worton and his team, along with researchers around the world, have been working non-stop to unravel the genetic puzzle, the key to helping kids like Jesse.

Winnipeg also means another opportunity to meet some of the employees of sponsors of *Jesse's Journey*. After a breakfast speech to employees at the main branch of the Royal Bank in Winnipeg, four police cruisers provide an escort as employees of Manulife join me in walking through the heart of the city to the Manitoba Legislature. There they present me with a cheque for $2,000 as the company continues to meet and exceed its pledge to donate $1,000 every time I pass one of their branches. Manulife will end up donating more than $75,000.

As the road team slowly makes its way across the country, the home team back in London continues to oil the machinery from a distance, making sure everything runs as smoothly as possible. In Winnipeg the home team has made arrangements for us to acquire heavy-duty winter clothing and the proper footwear to withstand the sub-zero temperatures we will face in the weeks ahead. And as a bit of a bonus, I spend an hour having my muscles looked after by the massage therapist for the Winnipeg Blue Bombers.

Lynn Jarvis is used to working on the muscles of 250-pound linemen. When she looks down at me on her massage table, she must think she is working on the proverbial 98-pound weakling! My thigh

322

and calf muscles are being worked so deeply that I think I'm being tortured – until Lynn tells me that the football players usually roll a towel up like a piece of rope and bite on it while she works on them.

While she works on my muscles, Lynn has lots of questions about the *Journey*. When I mention that Jesse is going to France in December to help with the telethon, Lynn says she has been to France and visited the Louvre in Paris, perhaps the world's most famous art gallery. She tells me that the Mona Lisa is actually very small in relation to all the other paintings which are on display.

Through Winnipeg and beyond, the mornings start out being very foggy. After the sun burns off the fog, I'm walking the Trans-Canada Highway toward Portage la Prairie under a big blue Manitoba sky. For a couple of days the afternoon temperatures reach 22°C. It's now the 23rd of October, and in T-shirt and short pants I'm again wondering how much longer our luck can last with this kind of weather.

I mark my 200th day on the road in Portage la Prairie. That's the day the schoolteachers, Marilyn and Carolyn, go home. They've done a great job all week long, and never said a word when they heard the 'plink' of a quarter being tossed into the plastic cup on the kitchen table. It wasn't till it was time to say goodbye that Carolyn shocked us as she broke the week's silence she and Marilyn had kept when it came to swearing. In that regard they really were the "golden girls." Reaching into the pocket of her blue jeans, Carolyn pulled out a five-dollar bill, which she smacked down onto the table with a thud. And, as she stifled a laugh, she summarized the week she and Marilyn had spent with us by announcing loud and clear, "I just want all of you to know that we had a @#&%ing good time!"

The motor home rocked with laughter as Carolyn Brennan – the last person on the planet you'd expect to hear swear – and her friend Marilyn Richmond hugged us as they said goodbye.

It's a raw, cold Saturday morning when we meet the mayor of Portage la Prairie and members of the Lions Club at City Hall. The mayor presents us with pins and, like so many Lions Clubs before them, the Lions of Portage la Prairie present us with a cheque.

On the main street there's another of those moments you remember for a long time. Our RCMP escort brings along his young son who is about three and a half years old. The little boy, whose name is Justice, is dressed in his own miniature red serge RCMP uniform, complete in every detail, right down to the brown boy scout type hat.

This little boy has come to walk through town with me, so we set off together with his dad right behind us, driving the RCMP cruiser with its lights flashing. Part way through town the little guy gets tired, so I pick him up and carry him for a while before he decides he'd like to have a ride in the police car with his dad – undoubtedly the proudest father in Portage la Prairie that particular Saturday morning.

There's little traffic on the road as I walk through the Manitoba communities of Holland, Glenboro and Wawanesa on the way to Brandon. In Glenboro, I feel like the Pied Piper again as the kids from the local public school listen to our story and then join me as I walk back out to the highway.

Through Manitoba I learn a lot about wheat, canola and flax. A retired farmer from Holland, Manitoba, who tags along for the day, tells me that farmers in this part of the province get about $4 a bushel for wheat. The system involves an initial payment of perhaps $3.25 per bushel with a subsequent payment of $.75 per bushel, depending on the final price the government is able to negotiate with its customers. Farmers get about double that price for canola, which is used for margarine. Flax is another crop that's grown in Manitoba and it's used for making linseed oil and linoleum products. The other thing I learn is that wheat farmers in Manitoba get a larger yield per acre than farmers in Saskatchewan because Manitoba gets a more even rainfall.

Just after hearing about the crops that are grown in Manitoba, we received a donation that arrived in the most unusual manner. Coming toward us was a tractor-trailer hauling grain and the driver was flashing his lights on and off as he approached. At first I thought to myself that maybe he was in some kind of trouble and we should be prepared to jump out of the way. But as he drove by he threw something from the window of the cab and yelled "good luck" and just kept driving down the road. It turned out to be a five-dollar bill attached to a neatly-wrapped muffin, and held in place by a rubber band. It was the first time that we could say some research dollars had really arrived by 'air' mail.

It's now late fall. Through Brandon, Manitoba's second largest city, and heading toward the Saskatchewan border, traffic has thinned to a trickle. The holidayers are gone and now it seems the only people travelling the Trans-Canada Highway are those who have to be there.

Two-thirds of the farmland in Manitoba lies within 130 km of Brandon, another Canadian city that owes its birth in 1881 to the arrival of the railroad. The mayor of Brandon is in a celebratory mood when we arrive. Reg Atkinson has been re-elected Mayor only the night before. At a reception for the road crew, the mayor tells me how much he personally appreciated our efforts to raise money for research as his grandson had benefited from research after being diagnosed with leukemia.

For several days I have been expecting a rude awakening and to find that winter has suddenly arrived. But in the last days of October, the daytime temperature is still hovering around 15 or 16 degrees C. Even though the wind makes it feel colder, our luck with the weather is holding.

It may seem a contradiction in terms, but as the days grow shorter, they also seem to grow longer. Not only is there less daylight, but boredom is starting to set in. I still face another six weeks of being able to look in every direction across flat land to the horizon.

If necessity is the mother of invention, I need to invent something quickly to keep me from sinking into chronic boredom. So that's when we invent 'truck hockey', on the road to Virdon, Manitoba.

On the Trans-Canada, tractor-trailers now make up the majority of the traffic. What we call truck hockey operates a little bit like the NHL player draft. We put the names of the most popular trucking companies we've seen on the road on slips of paper, and in the morning at breakfast we hold a draw. Each player is given a point for every one of his or her trucks that passes us on the highway. It may sound pretty juvenile, but it helps fill in the hours as we move toward the Saskatchewan border.

On the first day of November, we adjust our start time to begin a half-hour earlier, at eight in the morning, to take full advantage of the available daylight. People continue making donations as I walk through Virdon, one of the last towns on the Trans-Canada Highway before leaving Manitoba. Virdon is the home of two people whose interests couldn't have been more opposite, and yet their creations have become household names. Bob Rockola made his mark in history as the inventor of the modern day jukebox, and the other notable from Virdon is Dr. Ballard of pet food fame.

Walking through Hargrave, Elkhorn, Kirkella and finally Fleming – the last town in Manitoba on the Trans-Canada Highway – there are a lot of little pieces of information noted on the pages of my journal. There's the day that someone left a donation of $40 pinned under a windshield wiper on one of the vans. There was no note, just two twenty-dollar bills flapping in the wind, left by a person – or persons – who would always know that they had taken part in *Jesse's Journey*. Maybe it's a Canadian thing, but no one had taken the money, which was very visible and had been there for quite a while.

Sherene's dad, Mowbray Sifton, left us at Virdon, after spending a week on the road doing the things that all the volunteers before him had done. Ed Coxworthy had nicknamed Mowbray 'Skipper.' Ed told me that in Newfoundland the title 'Skipper' goes to the oldest person on board, regardless of whether he is the captain. Mowbray, who had joined us the week before in Portage la Prairie, had the distinction of being the oldest walker on the road crew. He said that when it came to his score in golf he'd be happy to shoot his age. When it came to walking the highway, he did better than that. During his week on the road, Mowbray the 'Skipper' Sifton at 74 years old, logged 81 km as we moved on to province number eight.

Chapter Twenty

WINDY SASKATCHEWAN

*"Sow an act and you reap a habit. Sow a habit and you
reap a character. Sow a character and you reap a destiny"* –
Charles Reade

Pushing Jesse across Ontario in his wheelchair in 1995 and walking
across Canada in 1998, young school kids all across the country keep
amazing me with their straightforward 'let's help' attitude. They
seem to relate to the boy whose picture they see on the sides of the
motor home and vans. To them, perhaps Jesse is just another kid, but
he is a kid who represents a lot of kids who don't get to play hockey
or baseball and who aren't able to ride a bike or go swimming. Kids
understand that, and they take action.

During one of the morning radio interviews I hear how the kids and
teachers at one public school in London are working together to sell
paper 'footprints.' That project has raised $1,100. It has also helped
teach kids a priceless lesson about the true value of giving by
helping others.

Back on the Trans-Canada Highway a little later that morning,
I end up being surrounded by kids when we stop at the public
school at Wapella, Saskatchewan. The 100 kids at this little rural
school are kids who have never met Jesse, and yet they have raised
$40 with a penny drive and their no-nonsense 'let's help' attitude.
The kids get a good laugh when a reporter asks me to pick one of
the kids up for a picture. Standing in the middle of the entire school
population I ask "How about this little boy right here?" They all
laugh because they know the 'little boy' is actually a little girl! These
lighter moments always served as a pressure valve that released the
stress that had built up from long days on the road.

The *Jesse's Journey* road crew is once again an 'all guy' affair after
another changing of the guard. It's almost like a homecoming as
morning show radio host Peter Garland, who was there on Day 1 in
St. John's, Newfoundland, comes back to join us again. So does

Ted Eadinger, taking over as road manager after we say goodbye to Trish who heads home to Ontario to go back to school. For Ted a life-changing experience is not that far away.

Early in the morning in Broadview, Saskatchewan, I find myself in the Sweet Dreams Motel, pulling on long underwear for the first time since the previous winter. We've managed to dodge the snow bullet once again, but the temperature has now dropped to -9°C. At breakfast I realize how far west we are when I watch the morning news. There's a reporter doing a live report from Ottawa where it is broad daylight. Outside the Sweet Dreams Motel, it's still dark.

Radio has played a large part in *Jesse's Journey,* and the power of the airwaves is demonstrated again as I walk on toward Regina. I am still on the telephone doing a live interview with CBC Radio in Regina when people begin stopping along the highway. In the cold weather they don't stop for long. A couple of transport truck drivers pull over to make a donation and so does a man driving east from Regina. Dressed in a shirt and tie and without a coat, he doesn't seem bothered by the cold as he walks across the wide expanse of median and highway to shake hands and make a donation. A woman who stops asks me, "Are you the father?" She wants to shake my hand. As she mentions a niece who has been taken to Toronto for surgery, she tells me to keep going and says, "Don't give up." But I already know that quitting isn't among the options.

As we reach Wolesley, Saskatchewan, there are snow flurries in the air. Peter Garland begins his day at four o'clock in the morning to accommodate the time difference. Through the ether he conducts an auction from inside a motor home in Saskatchewan for his listeners in Ontario. That morning, the magic of radio gives *Jesse's Journey* a $5,000 boost.

Among the people we meet at Indian Head, in the heart of Saskatchewan's wheat-growing district, is a family of native people – a mom and dad and two young girls. Each of the girls makes a $20 donation, and I can see their father is deeply moved as he hugs me and wishes us well.

The Prairies can be bitterly cold in the fall. By nightfall on November 9th, we are in Regina, Saskatchewan, and into a deep freeze. The temperature in the morning is -28°C. Bevin and I make the rounds to a series of pre-arranged early morning radio interviews. From there it's back to the road. It's a day that involves a lot of shuffling back and forth. At noon, I'm back in Regina to speak to a combined meeting of five Rotary Clubs. Before returning to the road, we meet the employees of Manulife in Regina who present *Jesse's Journey* with a cheque for $1,500.

It's been a long cold day, and even though the sun has been shining, I finish my day in the dark. The real warmth comes when I hear the faraway voices of my family at the end of the day. Sometimes we think conversation is only meaningful if we have big news to share. On this night I am missing what might be called family music – the sound we mistakenly call noise. I wanted to hear voices asking, "Did somebody get the mail? Hey Jesse, look at this! Are the Leafs playing tonight? Just a minute I'll be right there. Did you take Charlie for a walk? Is there any more, Mom? I can't, I've got homework. Pass the milk, will ya?" In the silence of motel rooms night after night, I want to hear all the noise a family generates, the noise that's gone too soon when they move away.

After talking with Sherene and the younger boys at home, I dial our oldest son Tyler's phone number at the Centre for the Arts in Banff. It's Tyler's birthday! I can still picture all the kids with balloons, smiling at the camera in the years of chocolate cake and candles – the cake that always ended up everywhere. I think of how cake eventually became pizza with the gang, and then grew into going out to dinner to mark the occasion. We never really know where the time goes, but I realize we have now been parents for 21 years.

Ed has not missed a Remembrance Day service in 39 years, and on November 11th he goes to the Cenotaph in Regina. The weather in Regina can be extremely cold in November and, to accommodate veterans and seniors, two services are held – one at the Cenotaph and

331

the other indoors at the Agridome. Out on the highway in the early morning I have to put on a balaclava for the first time since April in Newfoundland. The temperature is -20°C and the wind chill leaves me feeling numb. On the motor home at my break, we tune in the Remembrance Day service from Ottawa and join the rest of the country in marking two minutes of silence at the eleventh hour of the eleventh day of the eleventh month.

Before we get back on the road, a young boy of about 11 or 12 comes across the Trans-Canada Highway to make a donation. Back on the road a man who stops to make a donation says, "This is a story that fits into Remembrance Day." Another man who shakes my hand tells me, "Keep it going."

West of Regina the railway tracks run parallel to the highway. Toward sunset, as the sky puts on a real prairie show, the tracks seem to light up like two bands of silver running to the horizon. In the morning when you look east toward the horizon, those same tracks are often a brilliant orange as they reflect the early morning sunrise. There are plenty of visual jewels in illusive Saskatchewan, but you have to know where to look. The province is falsely labeled flat and boring by people who haven't taken the time to look beyond the wheat fields.

The frigid weather, with the temperature hovering around -28°C for almost a week, finally warms as we approach Moose Jaw. You'd think in the months I've been on the road I would have found some interesting treasures along the side of the highway. But the truth is I haven't really found anything of value lying on the shoulder of the road.

Once we found about $5 in quarters, which we guessed had been in an ashtray that had been dumped out, since the coins were scattered on the ground along with a bunch of stubbed-out cigarettes. And one day I found a small miner's hammer, but by far the most common item on the shoulder of the road had to be bungee cords – the heavy stretchy pieces of rubber with hooks on each end for holding things in place. Hubcaps were a close second.

The day I reach Moose Jaw, I find one of those pouches that people tie around their waist. Inside there's a wallet with a driver's license and other pieces of identification. There are a few coins inside the wallet, but if there was any folding money, it is long gone. There's a news crew from Moose Jaw with us at the time, and the cameraman says he knows the person whose name is on the driver's license. We found out later that the person's car had been stolen the night before. After the money had been taken out of the wallet, the pouch had probably been thrown out the window. It isn't any big mystery we've solved, but it is more exciting than finding another bungee cord.

CFB Moose Jaw is the home base for Canada's most famous aerobatics team, the Snowbirds. And it's in Moose Jaw where one day on the motor home, I managed to fall asleep before lunch was ready. I was sound asleep and not aware that the motor home was moving. When I woke up, we were inside a truck wash, and it must have looked pretty funny as five of us sat eating lasagna while high-powered hoses blasted away the layer of dirt that had been splashed onto the side of the motor home by passing trucks. As I used the cell phone to return a call to the *London Free Press,* I said to the guys I was willing to bet that, at that very moment, there probably weren't too many Canadians doing telephone interviews with newspapers from motor homes inside truck washes.

That night, *Jesse's Journey* is in the spotlight at the arena in Moose Jaw. I'm introduced at centre ice and presented with a hockey sweater before dropping the ceremonial puck as the Moose Jaw Warriors host the Prince Albert Raiders. A week before, I had done the same thing in Regina as the Western Hockey League's Regina Pats played host to the Spokane Chiefs. The only difference tonight is, in Regina they ask you to take your hat off before they play the national anthem!

From Moose Jaw, the next major location I have my sights set on is Swift Current. While we have to struggle in the severe cold on the Prairies, the snow I dread facing has yet to cause a serious problem. I'm beginning to wonder if we might make it to Alberta before the heavy snow begins.

It's a Saturday morning in mid-November, and for the first time in a long time, Bevin Palmateer is with me on the road. He's been busy working ahead of us, scouting interviews and speaking engagements. It seems like weeks since we've had a chance to talk. Of all the people on the permanent road crew, Bevin has been the most fun to watch as he matures. He wasn't exactly short of confidence when we set out to cross Canada, but now that original confidence has multiplied several times.

The Saskatchewan sky puts on another amazing light show as the sun begins to fade late in the afternoon. The fields of yellow wheat stubble, that run for as far as the eye can see, seem to be lit from beneath as rural Saskatchewan takes on an amber glow. Marking the highway at the end of the day, we make the long drive back into Moose Jaw. In the lobby of our motel, the newspaper box confirms that Bevin has been hard at work. *Jesse's Journey – A Father's Tribute* is a front-page story.

In the morning, the winter we've been trying to beat in a race across the Prairies finally strikes. At seven o'clock on a Sunday morning in Moose Jaw, there isn't a lot of activity. The engine of the motor home is purring, and Ed has the porridge heating on the stove as I stow my red duffel bag on board. The sliding blinds at the breakfast table window are pulled down to keep out the cold. There are very few signs of life outside. In the yellowish glow from the streetlights, I can make out a taxicab idling in front of the donut shop next door. Further down the street, a few Christmas tree lights are blinking in the dark. The rest of the bags are loaded onto the motor home and into the vans with the knowledge that by the end of the day we will be in Chaplin, Saskatchewan – halfway between Moose Jaw and Swift Current.

We make the long drive in the dark out to our start point. There's an accumulation of snow at the side of the highway and walking is difficult. When daylight comes, I think I'm hallucinating when I look across the highway and see nothing but water. The mystery is solved a little later when I meet the mayor of Chaplin, Saskatchewan. What looks to me like a lake is actually one of six sodium sulfate pools. Each of the pools covers about 17 acres and is about 15 centimetres deep. The Mayor, Brent Sylvester, works at the plant where the sodium sulfate from the pools is spun in a centrifuge and separated from the dirt that's also been scooped up in the harvesting process. The majority of the end product is shipped to Lever Brothers and Procter and Gamble to be made into laundry soap. The area also produces seed potatoes, which are trucked to Idaho where they're planted and grown to become 'Idaho potatoes.'

The teachers and the 107 kids at the public school in Chaplin decided they would each bring in a roll of pennies to donate to *Jesse's Journey*. What would have been a donation of just over $50 turns out to be three times that amount. With an additional gift from the Student Council, these kids reach out to kids like Jesse with the familiar 'let's help' attitude.

When our convoy of motor home and vans rolls back into town at night, there isn't anyone on the streets of Chaplin. It's getting dark and snow is piling up in drifts in front of the combination hotel, restaurant and bar where we will be spending the night.

It's warm inside where about a dozen people, some of them with their kids, make us feel welcome. We give *Jesse's Journey* hats to the kids and there's plenty of western hospitality as we are asked lots of questions about our travels across the country. I have the feeling that *Jesse's Journey* is probably pretty big news in a town the size of Chaplin, Saskatchewan.

335

At daybreak, Ed drives the motor home ahead to Swift Current to have the oil changed. On the highway, it's bitterly cold and somewhat lonely. I sip tea from a flask at noon hour, after completing 15 km in the snow. I'm desperately missing our home away from home. And no one has stopped along the road all morning.

By nightfall the motor home is back, and in one of the most desolate areas of Saskatchewan, we settle down for the night in a motel right on the Trans-Canada in the little town of Morse. On nights like this one, after completing 33 km in the snow, research is a distant thought as we shovel snow away from the doors of our motel rooms to gain entry. The rooms are freezing cold as we wait for the little oil stoves in the corner of each room to generate some warmth. There will be no showers tonight, but at least the phone is working.

When I talk to Sherene, she tells me that she and Jesse have received their invitations to go to Paris, to take part in the telethon to raise money for research. I also talk to Mario Chioini, the high school teacher from London, who will accompany Jesse and Sherene to France and serve as interpreter and Jesse's assistant. Mario, who I first met on the streets of Edmunston, New Brunswick, sees the trip as a dream come true, even though he knows it won't be easy.

It's snowing heavily the morning I walk into Swift Current. Firefighters help collect money along the roads in town. During a reception at the Royal Bank, both the firefighters and our friends from the Lions Club make donations to *Jesse's Journey*. The day is full of radio, television and newspaper interviews with media in Swift Current and also Medicine Hat, Alberta. On the road, I do some of those interviews by cell phone as I keep walking to make up lost time. In the afternoon, I work until after dark to finish the final 14 km for the day. I'm physically and mentally tired. On the Trans-Canada again, no one has stopped. But I don't really care because my mind isn't on Swift Current, Saskatchewan. I'm just anxious to get to a telephone, because back home Jesse is fighting a cold.

Sometimes colds are seen as just another inconvenience in life. You might miss a few days of work. You have to listen to everybody's advice about getting rest, drinking plenty of orange juice and ginger ale and eating lots of chicken soup. A cold can feel like it's more of a nuisance than an illness. But for kids like Jesse, a cold can quickly become a very serious problem.

I know Sherene will be keeping a close watch on Jesse, but still, so far away from home, I feel helpless. After Ed works on my legs, he gives me a pat on the back as he leaves. He always knows when something is wrong.

The morning of Day 225, I do something I've never done before. I call home to find out how Jesse is doing as soon as I know it's breakfast time in Ontario. Sherene tells me Jesse is sleeping after a reasonably comfortable night. Sherene never complains, but I can tell by her voice that it's been a sleepless night for her. For a moment the long-range goals of the *Journey* seem far less important than the state of Jesse's health. Even though she says, "Don't worry, honey. We'll be fine," when I hang up the phone and step back onto the highway, for the first time since the beginning I think hard about going home.

We reach Gull Lake, Saskatchewan the next day, and at suppertime there's good news from home. Jesse is feeling better! Sherene says he's slept for a large part of the day. And Charlie has spent the day sleeping at the foot of his bed.

We have now made it to Gull Lake where we're roughing it again. My motel room is ice cold and this time there's no little oil stove to warm things up. I'm at one end of a line of rooms and the thermostat that controls the heat for the whole row turns out to be in a room at the other end of the row. I have two single beds so I take all the blankets off one, pile them on top of the other bed, and then crawl inside. The good news from home about Jesse makes all the difference in the world. I'm sound asleep in minutes.

We've shivered through a blast of winter on the Prairies and Saskatchewan isn't going to let us pass without feeling the powerful winds of November. From Gull Lake to Maple Creek, the last town in Saskatchewan before we reach the Alberta border, I put my head down and lean into the wind that is blowing hard with no sign that it's about to let up. Parked well off the side of the highway, the motor home is swaying back and forth in a ragged fashion as it is buffeted by the wind. At one point I feel close to collapsing from exhaustion when I climb onto the motor home at one of my breaks. In all the time we have been on the road, I have never encountered anything like the wind in Saskatchewan. The days that follow prove to be just as tough. It's 120 km to the Alberta border with a 70 km/h dry wind sometimes pushing me backwards. For days, the wind keeps blowing.

They say that, "When the going gets tough, the tough get going." They forgot to add that a sense of humour can help keep you going too. Near Maple Creek, Bevin puts on an impromptu sketch that looks like the Wild West meets the National Hockey League, and gives us the laugh we need as we fight the wind on our final days in Saskatchewan.

It's lunchtime and outside the motor home Bevin is standing in the wind, shooting some video for one of his weekly television reports back east. Beyond where Bevin is standing is a five-foot-high wire fence running parallel to the highway for as far as the eye can see. The fence is covered from top to bottom with tumbleweeds driven by the wind. The tumbleweeds make the fence look like a shaggy woollen wall.

The tumbleweeds, most of them bigger than a beach ball, are blowing past Bevin as he finishes his camera work. Giving us a nod that says, 'Hey, watch this,' Bevin puts on his best goalkeeper moves as he tries to stop the tumbleweeds that are flying by him. His antics look like a cross between a hockey goalie and rodeo rider wrestling cattle to the ground. Maybe you had to be there, but it was pretty funny.

Leaving Maple Creek, we log our final kilometres in Saskatchewan on Sunday, November 22nd. It's the 35th anniversary of the assassination of U.S. President, John F. Kennedy. Everyone in my generation knows exactly where they were and what they were doing when they heard the news that Kennedy had been shot. Bevin was ten months old at the time. My legs are suddenly telling me that maybe you should walk across Canada when you're 22, not 52.

In Saskatchewan, the motor home has almost always been visible as it has made one of the slowest motor vehicle crossings of the Prairies. Day after day, Ed has repeated the same pattern, driving seven or eight kilometres and then waiting for me to catch up. Now, as I walk toward Alberta, the landscape begins to change. Slowly the brown and yellow fields of wheat stubble are being replaced by grazing cattle.

At lunch one day we watch a couple of farmworkers rounding up some cattle that have strayed onto the railway tracks after slipping through an open gate. These cowboys were working hard to get their cattle under control. But the most remarkable herding job I saw on the Prairies wasn't done by cowboys on horses, but rather by a dog.

The motor home was parked right-angled to the highway and backed into a bit of a laneway. The laneway became an open field where about a hundred sheep were grazing. The landscape was flat, and the Trans-Canada Highway offered an exercise in perspective in both directions. To the east and the west the road – and the accompanying line of telephone poles that ran along side it – receded to the horizon where they disappeared. The sheep seemed free to wander wherever they wanted, except for the dog that was watching them.

Space is one thing they seem to have plenty of in western Canada. The median of the Trans-Canada Highway is sometimes more than 100 metres wide and this particular farm property sat well back from the road. At lunch I watched the sheepdog, which looked over at us once in a while. The dog seemed to have little more than a casual interest in our being there. It was obvious the dog was well trained and she was at work. Lying in the grass and looking back and forth, the dog watched the sheep with an imaginary line in her mind that they were not to cross. It was like a game, watching the sheep wander closer to the highway until they reached the imaginary line. That's when the sheepdog would stand up, and the sheep would turn and retreat back toward the field.

The monotony of flat land, straight road and an endless line of telephone poles is broken by the freight trains. They may joke in Saskatchewan that it's so flat that you can watch your dog run away from home for three days, but in reality when you look to the horizon you can sometimes see as many as three trains approaching. They crawl toward you, parallel to the highway, like long black snakes slithering in straight lines across the Prairies.

You see a train's powerful headlights long before you hear any sound. You might watch a train for several minutes, and hear nothing. Then, about thirty seconds before the train reaches you, you begin to hear it rumble along the tracks. The engineers send a greeting, as they lay on the air horn. The high-pitched authoritative sound rolls out across the open expanse of flat land.

On November 23rd, we say goodbye to Saskatchewan as I reach the Alberta border at midday. I'm now in province number nine.

Chapter Twenty-one

PROSPEROUS ALBERTA

"Perseverance is the hard work you do after you get
tired of doing the hard work you already did" –
                                        Newt Gingrich

On the road to Medicine Hat, Alberta, a steady stream of people comes into our lives. A mother who has a son with Cerebral Palsy stops and gives me a big hug. At break time, another mother climbs aboard the motor home. She is accompanied by her young son – a boy she'd been told would not likely be able to walk or talk. Happily, the doctors were wrong; he does both very well. Passing through Irvine, the Lions Club makes a donation of $500. And after lunch a man who stops to make a donation says, "That's in memory of my son." He drives off without saying anything else.

At City Hall in Medicine Hat, we are welcomed by employees of the Royal Bank, who donate $7,500. At night time in Redcliff, we are welcomed by the members of Lions and Lioness Clubs from the area, proudly wearing their bright red vests that identify Lions in Alberta. Up to this point all the Lions vests we had seen had been yellow. After dinner, I speak about the *Journey* across Canada and our quest to build an endowment geared toward funding research. The audience listens intently. Looking at their vests covered with club pins, I think about our earliest days on the road back in Newfoundland. The *Journey* started when the yellow-vested Lions and Lioness Clubs of Whitbourne, Newfoundland welcomed us with a fish n' brewis dinner. Now, almost nine months later, these clubs are still reaching out to help a father they've never met, in a cause many of them have never heard of before.

By the end of the night the Lions and Lioness of Redcliff have raised several thousand dollars and the dream is another step closer to becoming a reality.

It's late when we get back to our motel in Medicine Hat, and although it's even later in Ontario, I call home. Sherene tells me that

341

she and the boys are fine, and that Jesse is feeling positive and looking forward to the trip to France. I write my journal and head to bed. It's been a very good day.

It's now late November, and the foothills of the Rocky Mountains will soon replace the brown sod of the Prairies. But that is still a few days away. After more than six weeks of looking at a bald, treeless landscape, there is still more to come. From Medicine Hat to Brooks, it's sunny, but very cold, as the Trans-Canada Highway shifts from being a mostly east-west corridor, and turns northwest to Calgary. The road consists of 120 km of highway, telephone poles, 80 kilometre-an-hour winds and little else. At least the mornings are brighter, as we're now at the front end of a new time zone after making the switch from Central Time to Mountain Time. However that also means getting up even earlier to do the morning radio interviews to places in Ontario and as far back east as the Maritimes and Newfoundland.

A familiar and friendly face rejoins us in Brooks. Bob Seaton, who had been part of the convoy eight months earlier, was one of the people who had driven the motor home and vans east to the start position in St. John's. On the road we also meet up with Dr. Mark Poznansky, President and Principal Researcher at the John P. Robarts Research Institute in London, Ontario. He's in Calgary on business, and has driven more than 200 km to spend a couple of days taking part in *Jesse's Journey*.

We talk about bio-medical research and having a passion for getting things done. In the two days he spends with us, Dr. Poznansky walks 39 km.

In Brooks, I speak to a group of Rotarians and firefighters. After the formal presentation of donations, a young physiotherapist reaches into her purse for her chequebook and donates $1,000. She too believes in medical research and has a passion for getting things done.

It's bitterly cold and there's very little traffic on the road. We are working from the 'Mickey' van, as the motor home has gone on to Calgary to be serviced. At our first break, we receive a call from Kay Coxworthy. She is phoning from a Sunday afternoon concert being held on Bell Island in Newfoundland. Shivering at the side of the road on my way to Bassano, Alberta, I listen to the voices of Newfoundlanders, thousands of kilometres away. They are singing "Jingle Bells" to a father standing in the middle of Alberta with a telephone to his ear. It's yet another moment for the memory bank.

We don't have any milk for the tea this morning, but at least we have some cookies. Two truck drivers stop to make a donation and maybe this is our lucky day, as one of them gives us a box of shortbread cookies along with my first Christmas card. It isn't the first time – and it won't be the last – that just when we need something, there it is.

Bassano, bills itself as "The best in the West by a damsite." It is the site of the Bow River dams, which provide irrigation to more than 800 sq. km of land. Farmers here raise cattle, or grow wheat, oats and canola, as Bassano enjoys Alberta's longest growing season.

On the morning of the last day of November, I call home to London to say goodbye to Sherene, Jesse, and Mario Chioini, their travelling companion, as they leave for France. I tell them I'm confident they will all do a good job. The media is at our house in London as I talk to Jesse and wish him a safe trip. Sherene tells me that Air France has scheduled a news conference at the airport. Jesse – no longer a little boy but now a young man – is setting out to help others in a country he has never visited before. Hanging up the cell phone in the van and getting ready for the afternoon on the road, I feel a long way from home. At the same time, I feel proud of Jesse, who always measures life not by the things he can't do but rather by the things he does.

Between the two communities of Bassano and Strathmore, the Trans-Canada Highway runs north before making a ninety-degree turn to head west to Calgary. When you're on foot, there are things that happen along the highway that you can easily miss if you're travelling by car. Just before making that big sweeping curve, there's a long slow grade to climb and the highway gives you a feeling that it's rising. As you continue up the incline, the farm fields to the west drop off like a curtain falling away, and for the first time, far off in the distance beyond the foothills you can see the snow-capped beginnings of the Rocky Mountains. The blue sky and morning sun make this a dramatic moment. It also means the Prairies will soon be behind us. We are now well into "Wild Rose Country."

The thrill of finally seeing the Rocky Mountains has the edge dulled a little when I have to admit I'm not nearly as mentally sharp as I had been earlier in the *Journey*. There are times I'm not alert. My timing has slowed, and I'm struggling a bit more to make my distance each day. More and more, as I flip through the pages of my journal at night, I can see the entries that reflect how tired I am at the end of each day. To complicate matters, my back has been very sore for several days. Ed takes the lead role as the road crew turns its attention to working on my back and legs at every opportunity. There isn't any panic, but if I'm to finish at all, it will be the road crew that deserves the credit for keeping me going.

People stop at the motor home parked beside the highway, not to make a donation but to escape the snow and cold for a few minutes. At noon one day, a little girl comes on board with her dad to make a donation and to have a look at 'my house.' On another occasion Ed, who is himself a long way from home, ends up pouring coffee for a fellow Newfoundlander, a transport truck driver who stops to make a donation while hauling Christmas trees from Wisconsin to Calgary and Edmonton.

344

Saskatchewan isn't completely flat - but almost! I had to fight a mental battle against long periods of solitude for almost eight weeks.

Terry Fox said that the way to get across Canada was "one telephone pole at a time."
In Saskatchewan Terry's comment become a reality for me.

While a mountain can be fleeting when you drive past it in five minutes, it takes on a greater permanence when you spend five hours looking at it.

By the time I reached Banff, I was tired but confident about finishing the journey. I still faced another month on the road.

East of Calgary, in Strathmore, they know what hard work is all about. This town of six thousand people is where history was made on July 28, 1883. That's the day Canadian Pacific Railway workers set a record, laying more than 10 miles of track across the prairie in a single day, ending in what would become Strathmore. At that time, the CPR was in charge of naming the hamlets that sprang up at its sidings as the steel rails were laid across the country. There's no record as to who named the original site "Strathmore," but a Scot named James Ross was in charge of the project and he had a tendency to give the sidings Scottish names.

If Strathmore represents endurance and determination, then it's probably fitting that's where I should meet three men from the heartland of Ontario with those same characteristics.

Harry Norris, 53, Blythe Lannin, 56, and John Scott, 52 – all from the Mitchell area – were having coffee in a restaurant in Exeter, Ontario when they decided to fly to Calgary and take part in *Jesse's Journey*. By the time Harry, a retired high school principal, joins me on the road, he has a long list of people lined up to sponsor him for the distance he walks. On one of the days the threesome from Ontario is with us, Harry walks 33 km with me. What makes this a story of endurance and determination is that two years earlier Harris Norris had undergone double-bypass surgery.

Born when the rails arrived, Strathmore still exhibits a solid work ethic more than a hundred years later. Along the Trans-Canada Highway, which passes right through Strathmore, the thriving and energetic little community gives us a tremendous welcome. It's a humbling experience to have firefighters say it's an honour to meet me as they escort us into town with sirens blaring. At the side of the road, the 400 kids from the public school in Strathmore are chanting, "Go, John, go." As I shake hands with each of them, a young teenage girl says she is proud of me and that she thinks what I'm doing is really important. A group of women from the Royal Bank hug me and mention how happy they are to meet me. At night time

345

I speak to the Lions Club of Strathmore at their last meeting before Christmas. The turkey dinner, with all the trimmings, reminds me that we aren't going to be home for Christmas. It's clear and freezing cold when we drive back to our motel, and looking up at the stars in the black sky, I wonder how Jesse is making out in France.

Calgary and western hospitality go hand in hand. In earlier times, the home of the world-famous stampede conjured up images of cowboys and cattle ranching. The riches that lie beneath Alberta's soil - oil and natural gas – moved the city that hosted the 1988 Winter Olympics onto the world stage. In true western fashion, I'm presented with a white Stetson hat when I reach Calgary. The official welcome to 'Cowtown' takes place in the sunshine and frosty air at the Calgary city limits sign on the Trans-Canada Highway. Just before being swamped by television cameras, a lone figure breaks away from the crowd and jogs down the highway to greet me. Sean Bagshaw, Jesse's helper when we crossed Ontario three years earlier, wraps his arms around me in a bear hug. With a big smile, Sean says he wanted to make sure he was the first person to welcome me to Calgary.

My arrival is actually the second time in the same morning that I've entered Calgary. It was foggy and dark at five in the morning when Bevin Palmateer drove me into Calgary for an early morning television interview. Now back on the Trans-Canada, just as the sun is coming up, it's freezing cold and Ted Eadinger cautions me to keep checking my face for frostbite, as the temperature has plunged.

Wearing my white Stetson hat and feeling very much like a 'westerner', I am sworn in at the roadside as an official Calgarian. Employees of Royal Bank and Manulife, carrying sponsor banners, huddle together and stamp their feet to keep warm as they wait their turn to make a donation and to welcome us to Calgary. Sometimes there are familiar faces in the crowd, and here at the edge of Calgary, 25 year old Mike Stubbs is another of those faces. Mike and his wife Kiersta had been married for a year and a half when the radio career of the London Knights play-by-play announcer had taken them west to work on Calgary Flames broadcasts. Mike was part of the media scrum that followed the official welcoming ceremonies. Reporters shivered as they asked questions, while white puffs of their breath disappeared in the cold.

Facing a battery of microphones, cameras and newspaper reporters with notepads, I am again asked a lot of questions about the walk across Canada – questions about what I am doing and why. I welcome every chance I get to talk about the need to expand our knowledge through research, and to stress how research is where we'll find the answers to making life better for kids like Jesse. At the end of the day, *Jesse's Journey – A Father's Tribute* is officially in the heart of Calgary.

It is getting close to Christmas when we reach the prosperous western city. People are shopping for presents, and for the road crew the festivities in Calgary include taking part in the Santa Claus parade. The people who line the streets applaud when they see the *Jesse's Journey* banner, and we really get into the spirit of things as we toss some early Christmas presents into the crowd. The presents are *Jesse's Journey* T-shirts, which are rolled up tightly and bound by rubber bands. As my eyes scan the crowd along the roadside, I make a point of saying hello and giving a T-shirt to every child or young person sitting in a wheelchair watching the parade. Too often, all that some children get to do is to watch life's parade pass by. As we make our way along the parade route through Calgary, the smiles I receive from children in wheelchairs are gifts in themselves.

There are lots of group pictures taken in the afternoon as a delegation representing Rotary Clubs in the Calgary area stops by our hotel. As the cameras flash, one of the Rotarians who is talking to me about the difficulty of crossing the Rockies pats me on the back and says, "Give 'em hell, John!"

At the Saddledome we are the guests of the NHL's Calgary Flames as they play host to Phoenix. During an interview as part of the television broadcast, I receive a Calgary Flames shirt with *Jesse's Journey* stitched on the back. And during the Flames post-game radio show, hosted by my friend Mike Stubbs, I meet the Flames coach, Brian Sutter. I don't expect him to be in a very good mood since his team has lost 3-2 but Brian knows it's just a hockey game. He tells me he thinks I'm a "good dad" and says he's amazed at what I have been able to accomplish. As I introduce the members of the road team who are with me, I tell the coach it's really what our 'team' has been able to accomplish. I am just lucky enough to be leading the parade.

Calgary gives me a brief chance to rest both my lower back and my legs before setting out for Banff, Lake Louise and the British Columbia border. Focusing my mind on the Rockies, it suddenly dawns on me that Jesse and his mom, along with Mario, are on their way home from France. Not only am I hoping things went well, I'm hoping we haven't asked Jesse to take on too much. I decide to give Sherene, Jesse and Mario a day to adjust to the time change before calling home.

At lunchtime, west of Calgary, Ed picks out one of the most unusual places to park the motor home. At the crest of a hill, the motor home sits in the middle of the enormous median that divides the four lanes of the Trans-Canada Highway. The motor home is facing west, and from the front windshield the four lanes of the highway converge as they disappear in the distance. Under a clear blue sky, with just a few wisps of cloud to add to the picture, is a spectacular panoramic view of the Rocky Mountains.

On the highway leading to Canmore, Alberta, two transport truck drivers – a man and a woman – stop to make a contribution. The man says he has passed me several times as he's driven back and forth across the western provinces. He says, "Week after week I've watched you making your way across the Prairies, and now here you are."

Three teenagers, two boys and a girl, come running up the highway to make a donation. One of the young boys has on a Toronto Maple Leafs jersey, and all three have pierced ears and lots of earrings. They want to shake my hand and the young girl says, "This is a good thing that you're doing."

Just as it is getting dark and I am ending my day, a woman from a farmhouse in the distance walks down the road to make a donation. On board the motor home, as we head back to town for our final night in Calgary, I hear that Jesse, Sherene and Mario are all safely back home. I'm tired, but it's a good kind of tired, and I know I'll sleep well tonight.

We have packed up the red duffel bags for another move forward and there is only one piece of business left to attend to before driving out to our start point which is now well west of Calgary. I have one last medical checkup scheduled before we set out to cross the Rocky Mountains en route to Vancouver.

I know my body has taken quite a physical pounding since leaving Newfoundland in April, so I'm a little concerned about this final check-up. The doctor takes a long time checking me over before finally giving me the green light to keep going. Back on the road, just as I'm ready to head toward Canmore, I receive a call from home. With their body clocks back to working on Canadian time, Sherene and Jesse want me to know the telethon in France was a tremendous success. It raised $116,000,000 for research! And yes, Jesse did get to go up the Eiffel Tower.

That was just the kind of news I needed to hear on the day the Prairies disappeared and in a vicious wind, the challenge of crossing the Rocky Mountains began.

The Prairies, which started as soon as we crossed the border from Ontario to Manitoba, end just as quickly about 60 km west of Calgary. Heading into the mountains, there's a definite gap where you can look back and take a final look at the flat expanse of prairie leading back to Calgary. The wind rushing through the gap feels like it's ripping right through me. In the bitter cold, it's another of those days when I have to lean into the wind to keep moving forward. To make matters worse, the sand that's been spread on the road during earlier snowfalls feels like buckshot as it stings my face in the gusts of wind created by passing trucks. I spend most of the day on the road by myself, because I don't see any point in our volunteers fighting the wind. They are our most valuable assets and while we have managed to avoid colds and the flu, this isn't the time to push our luck. We are going to need these people to help get us across the Rockies.

Further into the gap in the mountains, there's a bend in the road; looking back, the Prairies have vanished. When Bevin hops out of the escort van to check on me and bring me some water I tell him, "Bevin, take a look around. We're going to be surrounded by mountains on all sides for the next month." Although it's windy and cold, we both know that after eight weeks on the Prairies we're glad to be here, even if we have no idea of the challenge these mountains pose.

A young couple on a ski trip to Banff stops to make a donation. They can't believe how long I have been on the road. An older woman who makes a donation says, "God bless you and thank you for what you're doing." And a tall, bearded tractor-trailer driver wants me to know that he has three kids at home and how thankful he is that they're all healthy. He looks like he has tears in his eyes, or maybe it's just the wind making his eyes water. I don't really know, I'm just glad he stopped.

Canmore started out in the 1880's as a railway and coal mining town. But now, more than a hundred years later, it has cashed in on its proximity to the mountains and become a paradise for yuppies. The stylish condominiums, trendy shops and motels are decked out in clear white Christmas lights. For the ski crowd, Canmore is a fashion statement. But just like all the other towns across Canada, it's the people who make the real difference.

At the edge of town a smiling group of Royal Bank employees join us for the walk into Canmore. We share stories about our travels across Canada, and hear about the choices in their lives that have brought these people here to their home in the shadow of the Rocky Mountains. Each of them has a different story to tell, but all of them have asked themselves what was important to them and where did they really want to be in life. Like most of the people I've met, they are an interesting group. When we reach town, the mayor and representatives of both the Lions Club and the Rotary Club make financial contributions to *Jesse's Journey*.

Reaching Banff National Park, there's no charge for the motor home or the vans as park employees wave us through and welcome us to one of the most beautiful places in Alberta. At one of our breaks, after I catch up to the motor home, Ed tells us about seeing a bear, which was actually going into a cave up on one of the mountains. Sitting down to a hot cup of tea, I'm sorry I've missed seeing that, but I too had a special moment for the memory bank. On the road, a cute little girl of about seven or eight came running back from her mom's pick-up truck to meet me. She wanted to make a donation, and as she shook my hand she said, "I hope your son is going to be okay." Guiding her back to her mom's truck, it strikes me again about how kids don't have an agenda, they just want to help.

I'm not sure whether I'm looking for some magic elixir or just a chance to rest my tired muscles in hot water, but when I reach Banff, we all go for a soothing soak in the hot springs. In Newfoundland, I had been too early for the icebergs, and in Ontario too early to see the leaves changing colour. Then on the Prairies, I had been too late to see the yellow fields of wheat blowing in the wind. Arriving after the harvest, I was left with only the stubble to look at. But in scenic Banff, a town of eight thousand people that plays host to as many as five million tourists a year, the hot springs are always waiting, no matter when you arrive.

351

Having had my hair cut in Fredericton, New Brunswick at Canada's only licensed barbershop, I suppose I shouldn't have been surprised by what I saw in a bookstore in Banff. But then again, it was still a bit of a surprise at the end of another day on the road to see a dog signing books! In a small bookshop on the main street of Banff, a little girl was getting her book 'pawtographed' by a dog. The story was that the owner of the shop had written a book about the dog and if you bought a copy of the book, you could get it 'signed' by the dog. The owner would touch the dog's paw on an inkpad and then press the paw on one of the inside pages of the book and presto – a 'pawtograph'. Only in Canada.

Leaving for Lake Louise in the early morning, it's almost pitch black along the shoulder of the Trans-Canada Highway, which is cradled between the mountains. From the escort van, Ted Eadinger honks the horn to get my attention so he can point out the sunrise in the eastern sky. The black of the Alberta sky is being pushed aside by a rich red and lavender colour. It's one of those scenes that, despite its grandeur, looks almost tacky. It's a bit like the paintings you see on one of those Sunday morning television commercials promoting a 'starving artists' show and sale.

The wind has died down, and in the sunshine the kilometres between Banff and Lake Louise are sheer magic, as light and shadow play like a giant kaleidoscope on the green of the fir trees and the snow-capped mountains. But like a kaleidoscope, the picture soon changes.

Lake Louise, Canada's most famous lake, known for its turquoise waters, is named for Princess Louise Caroline Alberta, a daughter of Queen Victoria. Photographed by millions of tourists, the lake is emblazoned on postcards mailed all over the world. We are a day away from Lake Louise when the weather changes drastically. The Trans-Canada Highway, and everything that can be seen from the road leading to Lake Louise, is covered in a sheet of ice. A steady rain, falling from low clouds, keeps polishing the already slippery ice. Getting a foothold is as difficult as wearing new socks on a wooden floor that's been waxed and polished.

Up and down the icy two-lane road, trucks move forward a few feet at a time, their wheels turning so slowly that you can read the manufacturer's names on the dripping wet tires. One by one the tractor-trailers creep slowly past us, each with all its hazard lights flashing. Walking past trucks that have slid off the road, the day quickly turns into a nail-biting affair for the volunteers in the escort van behind me. At this point we aren't worried about donations, as safety is our number one concern. The next day it starts to snow.

From the Chateau Lake Louise, which was built in 1928 to replace the original CPR hotel built in 1890, the lake probably looks very pretty under a fresh blanket of snow. While our rooms are on the lakeside of the Chateau, it doesn't matter. By the time our little snow-covered convoy arrives in the dark, there is nothing to see from the windows except a black night. A dozen floors below us, there's a yellow glow from the light standards in the empty parking lot where the motor home and vans look like children's toys. The snow clouds hide the moon, and there's no way to visually confirm that Lake Louise is actually there. In the morning, the same blackness is all we see from our windows, as we slip away in the dark to reach our start point.

There's really no way of explaining luck or the lack of it, but one of the strangest stories that involved both good and bad luck came our way on the snow-filled Trans-Canada on our last day in Alberta. Our jack-of-all-trades, Ed Coxworthy, along with Bevin Palmateer, had moved the motor home ahead and they were waiting for us to catch up. Ed had taken with him a rotating yellow light that was mounted on top of one of the escort vans.

The flashing light was broken, and Ed was going to try to repair it. The trouble turned out to be the plug on the end of the wire. It was a piece of black plastic that plugged into what used to be called the cigarette lighter. These are now called utility outlets because they run everything from CD players to air pumps. The bottom line was that the black plastic piece was broken beyond repair and we were going

353

to have to make do without the light until we reached someplace where the broken piece could be replaced.

Well, the bad luck in this story is that the motor home got stuck in the snow at the side of the road – not badly, but still it was stuck. When we were still in Ontario, Ed had the foresight to buy two things before the bad weather came. First, he bought an all-weather snowsuit at a place called 'The Trading Post' in northern Ontario. I kidded Ed about how original that name was as it was one of about 50 places we passed which were all called 'The Trading Post.' The second thing Ed bought was a shovel for each vehicle.

After shovelling the snow out from under the motor home tires, Ed and Bevin managed to rock the motor home back and forth, and finally free it from the snow. That's when the good luck took over. When they finished the job, Ed spotted a piece of wire sticking out of the fresh snow, right where the door and steps opened out from the motor home. Ed decided to pull the wire to see what was on the other end of it. After a couple of tugs the wire came free, and on the other end of it was the exact type of plug Ed was looking for to fix the rotating light!

He and Bevin were still laughing about their good luck when we arrived for our first break of the day. We didn't know whether to believe them or not, but they both swore it was a true story. If it was, what were the odds of that happening? Either way, Ed fixed the flashing light, and we were back in business.

It's snowing heavily in the afternoon and it takes me a long time to finish the final 11 km for the day. The fresh snow makes it a bit like walking in porridge, and I get hit a couple of times by stones kicked up by passing transport trucks. It's like standing next to a welder and feeling the sting of tiny bits of hot metal hitting your skin.

The shortest day of the year is just over a week away, and it's dark and snowing heavily when I finish my day on the road. The headlights of the escort van are shining on Bevin, who is standing at the roadside, the lens of his video camera up to his eye. If it hadn't been for him, I wouldn't have seen the huge stone marker that sits back from the side of the road. It's just past five o'clock in the afternoon on Sunday December 13th, and I have reached British Columbia. We are now in province number ten. The end is almost in sight.

Chapter Twenty-two

BEAUTIFUL BRITISH COLUMBIA

*"Never give in! Never give in! Never, never, never – in
nothing great or small, large or petty. Never give in
except to convictions of honor and good sense" –*

Winston Churchill

I had always thought that if we made it to Winnipeg then we might
have a chance at completing the *Journey*. I had also made up my
mind that if I stepped into British Columbia, I would definitely make
it to Victoria. It was pretty simple, really. I would just keep telling
myself, "I didn't come to the tenth province not to finish."

The Canadian Pacific Railway's spiral tunnels at Kicking Horse
Pass, between Lake Louise, Alberta, and Field, British Columbia, are
an engineering marvel. Seven hundred thousand people a year stop
in British Columbia's Yoho National Park to watch trains wind
through the tunnels, which are even more of an engineering marvel
when you realize they were completed in 1909. Over a distance of
7.4 km, the tunnels permit trains travelling east or west to iron out
the 130 m difference in height between the top and the bottom of
Kicking Horse Pass.

The pattern for the spiral tunnels came from a railway design in
Switzerland where switchbacks and looping tunnels cut through the
mountains to eliminate steep grades. At Kicking Horse Pass, the
lower spiral tunnel circles through Mount Ogden before switching
back to where the upper spiral tunnel curves through Cathedral
Crags. As many as 30 trains a day make the 47-minute journey
through the spiral tunnels. Walking the Trans-Canada, I arrive just in
time to see the engine of a freight train emerge from one end of the
lower tunnel while the last of the cars it is pulling has yet to
disappear into the same tunnel.

From Field, British Columbia, the highway rises and falls as it winds
through the mountains to Golden. The government of British
Columbia has advised us that I will not be allowed to walk the 16

km of road leading into Golden. Looking at that piece of road as we drive into Golden at the end of the day, I'm not surprised by the ban.

The narrow road, which is under construction, is full of sharp hairpin turns. On the passenger side of the motor home, the broken rock face, which at times rises about 75 metres above the road, is draped with netting to prevent falling rock from hitting vehicles below. On the opposite side of the two-lane road, beyond the concrete guardrail, the lights of Golden, B.C. blink in the darkness far below. Tractor-trailers and logging trucks in low gear are making the slow climb up the hill out of Golden. The following morning, making the hair-raising drive back to the start point east of Golden, the road reminds me of every story I have ever read about buses tumbling down the sides of mountains in South America. From our start point I walk until I reach the beginning of the 16 dangerous kilometres that lead into Golden. Heading back to our day's start point once again, I repeat the 16 km I just finished so we can account for the section I'm not allowed to walk. It's been that way all across Canada.

In Golden, where the Columbia and Kicking Horse Rivers converge, we are greeted by a group of firefighters, the mayor and representatives from the Rotary Club, the Kinette Club and the Shriners. We have supper on the motor home where Ed Coxworthy has made a Newfoundland 'Jiggs Dinner.' Ann Hutchison, who has now been with us in six provinces, has decorated a cake for dessert. It has the 'less than' symbol and the number 1000 km. The countdown is on. In the morning, the distance still to be completed in the walk across Canada, will drop to three figures!

From the very beginning, when I first sketched in my mind the plans for *Jesse's Journey – A Father's Tribute*, there was something that couldn't be avoided. I knew I would have to make the trek through Rogers Pass in December. At the organizational meetings in London, long before setting out on the road, no one had talked about what everyone silently thought of as the toughest part of the journey along the Trans-Canada Highway.

The highway through Rogers Pass was completed in 1962, and runs parallel to the railway tracks. The incredible story of the railway began long before anyone even thought about building a highway. It has now been 120 years since the CPR commissioned Maj. A. B. Rogers to find a route through the Selkirk Mountains. Major Rogers, who had never been to the mountains before, was 52 years old when he discovered the pass that would bear his name. Historians have noted that he was a foul-mouthed man who chewed tobacco and that he didn't care about the $5,000 he would earn for finding a passage through the mountains. More than anything else, he wanted his name attached to the route that would lead to the Pacific. The Rogers Pass was the linchpin in completing the tracks that would unite Canada. But laying those tracks would be no easy job. The ravines on the east side of the pass would have to be bridged, and on the west side of the pass there were steep grades that meant a long series of loops were going to have to be built. Thirteen bridges would have to be built crossing the Illecillewait River between Rogers Pass and Revelstoke. In 1885, during its first winter, snow closed the railway line and the following year, thirty-one snowsheds had to be constructed to keep the trains moving through the Rogers Pass.

I don't know whether our volunteers are simply in a hurry to get through the Pass, or maybe I'm just feeling the effects of more than eight months on the road, but for the first time I can remember, I have to ask everybody on the crew if they can slow down when they are out with me. My left ankle is bothering me, and I'm having trouble keeping up with them on the road. Muscle fatigue is again a problem and I've been very slow making the climb toward the summit of Rogers Pass.

Our fear about battling heavy snows here seems unfounded. Until today, the biggest problem in the Pass has been the sand that gets in your eyes and your teeth and chokes you to the point where it's difficult to breathe when trucks pass by, sending yet another cloud of gritty dust swirling into the air.

359

There has been no real reason for us to make the switch to Pacific Time. To make radio interviews in eastern Canada that much easier, we have all decided to stay on Alberta time until we reach Revelstoke in a couple of days.

We are now just one week away from Christmas, and I have almost reached the summit of the Rogers Pass in Glacier National Park. It's been a difficult climb, in bone-chilling temperatures. The Pass is taking a long time to complete as I have to go back and repeat some sections three times to make up the distance that's lost because it's not safe to walk through the snowsheds where it's dark and there's only a single lane in each direction.

In making the climb to the top of Rogers Pass, Ed leaves the motor home and for the first time in our travels together, he joins me on the road. Ed, who is a smoker, has only one lung. No one has been allowed to smoke on board the motor home or in any of the vehicles – and although I might be wrong, I'd be willing to bet that it won't be long before Ed gives up cigarettes. If you have the stamina to walk through Rogers Pass in the winter, you probably have what it takes to quit smoking.

On the 18th of December in Glacier National Park, Ed Coxworthy, who had toasted dozens of loaves of bread and poured hundreds of gallons of orange juice and milk as we made our way across Canada, for once didn't have to cook supper. That's because Peter Garland was celebrating his 58th birthday and his wife Ann Hutchison created a gourmet dinner in the kitchen on the motor home. Peter will always remember spending his 58th birthday shivering as we walked through Rogers Pass.

When I called home on December 18th, Sherene told me that Jesse was feeling a little down. He's a handsome young man, but he's a handsome young man in a wheelchair. Sherene says she thinks he's feeling a little low because he doesn't have a girlfriend. Sometimes life can seem pretty unfair, but at the same time, life doesn't make any promises. I know Jesse will bounce back tomorrow because he's that kind of kid. But still, tonight, I'm wishing I could be home.

360

This morning it's -20°C, and we have decided to leave the motor home at a motel at the summit of the Rogers Pass as we head east back through the snowsheds to our start point. We'll catch up with the motor home at lunchtime at one of the snowplough turnarounds.

In the cold, I have to keep checking the skin on my face for frostbite. By midday we are in the sunshine and finally reach the marker at the summit of Rogers Pass. We stop to take some pictures and by early afternoon we have caught up with the motor home, where Ed has hot soup and toasted bacon sandwiches waiting for us. As my back and legs are being worked on, I fall asleep knowing that in the afternoon we'll be heading downhill from the summit.

Heading down into a valley, we lose daylight sooner than we thought. I finish my distance for the day in the dark. Then we head back to the summit of Rogers Pass for a final night in Glacier National Park before moving on to Revelstoke. Getting through Rogers Pass and the park, where there are more than 400 glaciers, we've been lucky. Other than the extreme cold, we have escaped unscathed from an area where the annual snowfall has been known to reach as much as 23 metres. But, in one of the most active areas for avalanches, our luck is about to run out.

In the sub-zero morning temperature, the motor home and both vans are covered in a thick layer of frost. Ed has the motor home running and warming up, but the vans have yet to be started. After scraping the frost from the vans, they finally turn over and we leave them to warm up as we retreat to the motor home for breakfast. Suddenly, we all look at each other when we hear a strange grinding sound. We don't know where it's coming from, but we know that whatever it is, it isn't good.

It only takes a second for Ed to realize the sound is coming from the 'Mickey' van, before he springs into action. Without stopping to put on his coat, Ed is out the door of the motor home and shuts off the engine of the van. When he lifts the hood, he finds the source of the grinding sound. It isn't serious damage, but the bad news is, we've lost a fanbelt. The worse news is, we're a long way from help and we need both vans. Ed, the jack-of-all-trades, is in for another test.

Ed decides there might be a way to fix the problem and keep both vans on the road. He removes the fan belt from the second van and with a fish-filleting knife he carefully slices along the centre of the rubber to make two belts out of one. Ed loops these half-belts back onto their pulleys, and we cross our fingers as he starts the engines. Both belts hold and, for the moment at least, both van engines are running smoothly. The other problem is that the windshield-washer hose on the 'Mickey' van was severed by the shredded fan belt as it whipped around inside the engine compartment.

Luckily, the windshield-washer hose from the motor home is long enough that Ed is able to cut a piece off to repair the damaged hose on the 'Mickey' van. After heating each end of this very thin hose, Ed uses a ballpoint pen to enlarge the hose because it isn't a perfect match for the van. When he's finished we have a makeshift windshield washer hose for the van. It isn't perfect but we decide that if we are careful, we can probably make it through the day until we reach Revelstoke where we can get everything repaired. The whole episode reminds me of Kay Coxworthy telling me back in Newfoundland, "You take my Ed with you. He can fix anything. He can even weld the rear end back into a cat from the inside!" Kay would be meeting us in Revelstoke the next morning and I'd be able to tell her how close to the truth she was with her description of Ed's handyman talents.

On the days leading up to our Christmas in the Rocky Mountains, everyone tries to stay busy, mostly to keep from thinking about family and friends back home. The holidays can be a very stressful time and it's funny how we remember the little things. We manage to have our own sugar-and-spice moments on board the motor home. In Revelstoke five days before Christmas, Ann Hutchison switches our usual healthy dessert of fruit to ice cream topped with melted caramel, bananas and peanuts. Over tea and coffee, we decorate a tiny 15 centimetre Christmas tree, a gift from Peter Garland. Peter has also brought along a tiny wreath, complete with flashing Christmas lights. The wreath, which fits easily into the palm of my hand, is just the right size for the motor home. Peter and Ann have been tremendous volunteers, each of them walking with me in six provinces. They'll be leaving us in the morning to fly home for Christmas.

The merchants of Revelstoke present us with a huge Christmas basket of 'goodies' at a reception to welcome us to the town that was first known as 'The Capital of Canada's Alps.' After listening to our story, the mayor of Revelstoke writes out a cheque and he makes a generous donation. He joins representatives of the Lions Club, the Rotary Club and the firefighters in making presentations to *Jesse's Journey.*

On the morning of December 22nd, it's -16°C as we hug and say goodbye to the volunteers who are heading home for Christmas. The 'core' members of the road crew will be staying in British Columbia. This is also the morning a new recruit arrives who will spend Christmas in the Rockies with us. More than one life is about to be changed.

Dianne Steward, who was born in the South of England, is a former medical secretary. With strawberry-blonde hair, sparkling blue eyes, and a lovely English accent, there isn't anything to indicate that her self-esteem is at rock bottom. Dianne, who has been on her own since the break-up of her marriage, had been working as a volunteer with the home team in London. Feeling the need for a different Christmas, she called the office one day to say, "If somebody on the road team wants to come home for Christmas, I could go to British Columbia." After a snow-delayed flight to Kelowna, and a late night drive through the mountains with an RCMP officer, Dianne arrived in Revelstoke at 2:30 in the morning. And five hours later she was ready to go to work.

Kay Coxworthy arrives from Newfoundland to round out our skeleton crew of six who will celebrate Christmas in the little town of Sicamous, British Columbia. With Ed and Kay Coxworthy, Dianne Steward, Ted Eadinger, Bevin Palmateer and me, *Jesse's Journey* will keep moving south toward the Okanagan Valley.

The road to Sicamous winds through some of the most majestic scenery in Canada. Just west of Revelstoke, surrounded by mountains, lies Craigellachie, one of the most famous landmarks in Canadian history. It was at Craigellachie on November 7th, 1885 that the last spike was driven, completing the Canadian Pacific Railway. At lunchtime, two days before Christmas, I take a picture of Dianne and Ted standing together in front of the stone cairn that marks the exact spot at Craigellachie where the last spike was hammered home.

Few people stop along the road and by nightfall, we're in Sicamous, 'The Houseboat Capital of Canada.' A light snow is falling when we reach the Monashee Motel where we will spend Christmas Eve and Christmas Day. Jesse's older brother, Tyler, is due to arrive by bus from Vancouver and if the snow in the mountains isn't too heavy, he should be in Sicamous in time for Christmas.

The Lions and Rotarians of Sicamous have worked together to decorate the rooms our little group will call 'home' this Christmas. As the motor home and vans roll across the fresh snow that covers the parking lot, above us there's a string of snow-covered Christmas lights hanging from the railing outside of our rooms. It's a little difficult to realize that we're 'home' for the holidays.

The Lions and Rotarians here are a great bunch of people, and they have really gone out of their way to make sure we have a Merry Christmas. To make things easier for us, we learn people's names in relation to where they work. Soon we're talking with our new friends, 'hardware store John' and 'grocery store Bob.' Our first night in Sicamous we are taken for a drive to look at the Christmas lights.

I didn't think a town as small as this would have very many lights, but they sure do, and with the snow falling, and the company of new-found friends, suddenly Sicamous does feel like home.

The tour of the lights is followed by a tour of a houseboat. The hundreds of houseboats manufactured in Sicamous are shipped all over the world. There are two levels to the houseboat we board. There is a hot tub in the master bedroom on the second level, and on the main level the flames from a gas fireplace give the family room a toasty glow as snowflakes fall outside. The kitchen has a huge island workstation – and with a fridge and freezer, convection oven and microwave oven, there doesn't seem to be anything missing. That houseboat could be rented for about $4,000 a week. The purchase price is $286,000.

Following the houseboat tour, we all go to Moose Mulligan's Pub, where we are formally welcomed to Sicamous. With a glass of ginger ale I make a toast and thank the group for all they have done to make our little troop of 'Easterners' feel at home for Christmas. By this time it is getting late, everyone is tired and wanting to get some sleep. We have one more day to go before we will take Christmas Day off.

The morning of Christmas Eve is quiet in Sicamous. Outside our motel huge snowflakes fall softly to the ground. The day that starts out so peacefully will eventually prove to be tiring, dangerous, and beautiful all at the same time. After we reach our start point east of town, we begin our walk as the snow continues to fall. The firefighters join us on the road to help collect donations. Heading toward town they sound the siren every now and then, which on the day before Christmas in Sicamous, attracts a lot of attention.
The snow is still falling as we head back to the motor home where Ed has lunch waiting for us. The motor home is almost completely covered with snow when we arrive. Ed says Tyler will probably be late arriving. He's heard on the radio that buses from Vancouver to the interior of B.C. are running late because of the snow. What he

doesn't tell me is that there has been a crash involving a Greyhound bus and a tractor-trailer. Fortunately no one was killed. We find out later that Tyler was on the bus in front of the one involved in the accident.

By now, it's snowing very heavily and we debate whether or not it's safe to continue in the afternoon. After the snowplough clears the road, I decide to give it a try. Ed takes the motor home back into Sicamous where it will stay until after Christmas. With Ted driving the escort van, I stay on the road to complete two more sections of 7 km each.

A young boy of 11 or 12 has to fight his way through the snow in the median to cross the road and make a donation. Seeing him safely on his way, the snow keeps getting deeper, and even though it's beautiful, it's starting to get dangerous. I have completed 26 km in heavy snow. By late afternoon, visibility is so poor that transport trucks are using their flashing lights as they creep past me. In the fading light we head back into Sicamous. It's time to stop for Christmas.

Everything was silent on Christmas morning, when we walked across the road to the Husky truck stop for a breakfast of orange juice, bacon and eggs, and pancakes. Tyler has joined us after arriving safely on Christmas Eve while I was still out on the road. There isn't a car in sight as we walk across the Trans-Canada Highway and we joke about getting some sticks for a game of road hockey.

On the motor home, the days leading up to Christmas had been a bit of a charade as everybody looked for places to hide little gifts. Just when you thought you had the ideal spot, you'd discover something already hidden there. In the afternoon, when we gathered for dinner and to exchange gifts, it was amazing to see how many presents there were that had all been hidden somewhere on the motor home or in the vans.

The rooms that Tyler and I are using as our 'home base' in the motel have a small kitchen area with a stove. The Lions and Rotarians who decorated the rooms with Christmas lights have also provided us with a turkey. By the middle of the afternoon the smell of a turkey cooking in the oven lets everyone know it is definitely Christmas.

We have a couple of arborite tables with chrome legs. We push these together, and add a collection of mismatched chairs. With a tablecloth and a couple of candles, we sit down to enjoy a Christmas dinner that none of us will ever forget, particularly Ted and Dianne who perhaps didn't know it at the time but they were spending their first Christmas together.

After dinner there is a lot of laughter as we open gifts. Every now and then, 'Bruce the Spruce,' the foot-tall sound-activated singing Christmas tree springs into action with another round of 'Jingle Bells'! It brings gales of laughter every time the mechanical jaw of 'Bruce the Spruce' starts flapping. Throughout the day, the phone lines are kept humming as everyone calls families back in Ontario and Newfoundland.

On Boxing Day, we are back on the road, leaving the Trans-Canada as I begin walking Highway 97A which will take us south to Vernon and down through the Okanagan Valley. The road is more narrow than the Trans-Canada, and at break time, as Ed tries to pull the motor home as far as possible to the side of the road, it gets stuck in the snow. To keep to our schedule, Ted and I walk ahead to Enderby, while a farmer with a tractor helps Ed free the motor home.

In the little town of Enderby, members of the Lions Club demonstrate just what service clubs do, as they leave their families for part of the day, to meet us and make a donation of $250 to *Jesse's Journey*. One of the Lions who came out to walk with me tells me about his daughter, who is a paraplegic. She was injured in a skiing accident 15 years earlier and now she gives lectures on having a positive attitude. I didn't get to meet this man's daughter, but from the way he describes her, she reminds me of Jesse and his outlook on life.

Moving further down into the Okanagan Valley in the afternoon, it's noticeably warmer as the sun is shining and the temperature starts to climb. We finish the day in the dark, and then drive into Vernon, B.C. I now have just twenty-five days left before reaching the finish line in Victoria. But now I have a new problem to deal with.

There are few people who know the real condition of my legs and back. Although my feet are soaked in sea salt and water three times a day to keep them tough, they are now in bad shape. As far back as Calgary some nasty cracks developed in my feet, and in the past few days they have started to bleed. Now my toes are turning an ugly shade of grey and black. The question is, can I keep everything going for the remaining distance?

The first thing I do is to alter my expectations about the weather. The snow is still falling and it's discouraging, because mentally, I prepared myself for a slightly easier trip once I cleared the Rogers Pass and started down into the Okanagan Valley. That hasn't been the case, so it's back to the drawing board. I calculate that it probably won't snow on Vancouver Island on the last four days of the *Journey*. That means I have to prepare myself for a possible twenty-one days of snow and tough going. With that thought in mind, anything better than heavy snow will be a bonus.

In Armstrong we have breakfast with the Lions, who donate $500 to our project. On the road, milder temperatures are both good and bad news. It's difficult to walk through the snow, which has turned to slush on the side of the road. Slogging through the water and slush is tiring, and I'm really sweating. The good news is that it has turned warm enough to make the switch back to my spring jacket. While I'm having tea and oranges at my second break, I leaf through a grocery store tabloid that someone has left behind. My horoscope says my travelling is supposed to end soon.

368

As the snow keeps falling, I make my way south from Vernon to Kelowna. People still stop to make donations in the early part of the afternoon, but as the snow keeps falling, the Ministry of Transport people ask us to leave the road because of the deteriorating weather. We are happy to oblige, and back at the motel the Rotary Club of Vernon donates $500 to us. I call home early to talk to Sherene. We are both in a good mood, perhaps because we know that we will soon be together. Back home Sherene has made a lot of appearances on behalf of *Jesse's Journey*, and she is now comfortable speaking in front of an audience. Sherene has blossomed into being an outgoing person and I joke with her that when I come home, there's a good chance I'll want to be a homebody, at least for a while.

South from Vernon lies Kelowna and the start of the Okanagan Valley's wine industry. Along the highway are rows and rows of leafless grapevines waiting for spring to arrive. British Columbia's wine industry began in 1860 when a missionary named Father Pandosy planted the first grapevines in the Okanagan. The wine was primarily for religious purposes. It wasn't until 1932 that the first commercial winery opened in the valley. For the first time in days, the sun is shining and there's a hint of spring.

The snow is now showing its first signs of melting, and along the road the spray from trucks leaves us covered in a wet layer of mud. The wash of mud and water is certainly tolerable when I hear about the problems behind us. Snow has closed the Trans-Canada Highway from Revelstoke to Sicamous. It seems as if we've been travelling in some kind of protective bubble when we hear that they're now experiencing avalanches back in the Rogers Pass. I remember feeling a great sense of relief when we finally cleared the avalanche zone as we came through the Rockies.

I finish my 33 km for the day in record time at 4:20 in the afternoon. I'm glad to finish early, because time has become a very important commodity now that we are in the Pacific time zone. The three-hour difference means getting up at 4:00 a.m. to do interviews with radio stations in eastern Canada. I'm starting to feel like I'm running on adrenaline.

As the team moves toward its final weeks, there seems to be an event to go to and a speech to be made almost every night. I keep telling myself to hang on for a few more days.

As we pass through Kelowna, the first man I meet on the road shakes my hand and donates $100. Donations continue as I cross the bridge that takes you from the east to the west side of Lake Okanagan. Traffic is backed up a long way, but people don't seem to mind as they smile, wave, honk their horns and reach for their wallets.

Donations continue to come from both the young and the not-so-young. At the Royal Bank in Westbank, two little boys each give us $20. They have their picture taken with me in front of staff members who are all wearing *Jesse's Journey* T-shirts. At the motor home, Ed receives a $50 donation from a widow who stops to chat for a while. She tells Ed and Kay that every year on her late husband's birthday, she always buys herself something new to wear. And then she looks up, smiles and says to the sky, "Honey, your taste is getting better every year."

The weather in the Okanagan Valley changes in a big hurry. On the road that afternoon, fog sets in so thick that even with our powerful strobe lights it's difficult to see us. It's far too dangerous to stay on the road. We're forced to go back to Kelowna.

South of Kelowna on the morning of New Year's Eve, I'm thankful the prediction of more fog has proven false. As we get started I joke with everybody that tomorrow we will be able to say, "This is the year we are going to finish the walk!"

The sun is shining and the scenery is pretty as I walk south through Peachland and Summerland toward Penticton. The orchards, fruit fields and vineyards in this part of the Okanagan Valley are blessed with 2,000 hours of sunshine each year, making the whole area the fruit basket of British Columbia.

A young RCMP officer is among the people who stop as soon as I am on the road. Despite being shielded by sunglasses, he is visibly moved by the story of *Jesse's Journey*. And there's a young man who leaves his car running as he stops to make a donation, only to find he has locked himself out of his car. We give him a cell phone to call his roommate who has an extra key for the car. He feels embarrassed. We are just grateful he stopped.

It's a bit scary along the road as people stop right on the highway in the driving lane. They just want to shake hands and make a donation. A woman who stops says she doesn't have any money but she wants to give us a bottle of champagne so we can ring in the New Year at midnight. It's certainly a different kind of donation.

At the end of our day on the road in British Columbia, it's just three hours until midnight in Ontario and the beginning of 1999. Sherene sounds tired when I call home to wish everyone a Happy New Year. The sound of her voice reminds me that I'm not the only one who has had to pay a price to make this project work. The daily road routine may be taking its toll, yet for all the months I've been away, Sherene has been paying the same price back home, far from the attention we've been receiving. While a team of volunteers has surrounded me every day, Sherene has been alone – quietly doing her best to look after the workload that we normally share. Maybe I underestimated the challenges Sherene had to face while I would be away, but I knew the strength of her determination and resolve to see things through. Saying goodbye to each other and to 1998, there are just twenty days left on the road.

We spend New Year's Eve in Penticton, which is Salish for "a place to live forever." At dinner, Bevin borrows wristwatches from everyone and after resetting them, he lines them all up on his left arm so he can tell us when it's midnight in each time zone in Canada, starting in Newfoundland. In the heart of the Okanagan Valley, western Canada's premiere wine-making district, I toast the New Year with a non-alcoholic wine and go to bed.

On New Year's Day, the streets are deserted as Bevin and I drive to an early morning in-studio interview at a country radio station that has a signal which carries from the United States border well into the interior of B.C. A sign in the newsroom says, "All the technology in the world won't help if the people you're putting on the air aren't good communicators. At the end of the day, news is still storytelling and writing."

Leaving Penticton, people along the road are applauding and donating very generously. We have an RCMP escort as I climb the long slow grade heading south to Olalla and Keremeos. Looking out over Lake Okanagan, we are at the same height as the small planes on the glide path as they make their descent into Penticton.

The road to Keremeos is narrow, and at some points the cliffs rise straight up from the edge of the road. There are several hairpin turns and very little shoulder, making the road difficult to walk. Reaching the town that calls itself the "Fruitstand Capital of Canada," I'm joined on the road by an RCMP officer in his scarlet dress uniform as well as members of the Keremeos Lions Club. More than three dozen wooden fruit stands sit empty and abandoned on the side of the road, waiting for that time of year when they will be full of the valley's harvest of apricots, peaches and plums. Like so many Lions Clubs have done across Canada, the Lions of Keremeos present us with a donation and pins for the road team. The Keremeos pin shows a tall mountain, the snow-filled creases of which make up the letter "K." Looking up from the main street I can see the mountain and the snow, looking just as they are displayed on the pin.

Morning comes early. The night before, we drove back to Olalla, where I made a speech to the Lions Club. This morning the day started at 4:00 a.m. with a telephone interview with *Breakfast Television* in Halifax. After what has seemed like a very short night, the weatherman hasn't been all that kind. The road is covered with freezing rain, which is making footing difficult especially on the banked curves. Ed tries to warm us up at noon hour with a steaming-hot bowl of chili, but the rain and low-hanging clouds that obscure the tops of the mountains make it a dreary day. On the road, a man and his two young daughters stop to make a donation. He says that I am a great inspiration. Little does he know that he was my inspiration on a day when almost no one stopped along the road.

It's still raining at the end of the day, and in the dark we come to an accident scene that's lit up by the flashing yellow lights of a tow truck. A van has skidded off the icy road and plunged down the side of the mountain. The van is lying on its roof in jagged rocks next to the river at the bottom of the cliff. Cables have been attached to the van to haul it back up to the road. I ask the tow truck operator if anybody has been killed? He says nobody has been killed, but the driver of the van has been taken to hospital. When he takes a second look at me he says, "Are you the guy who's walking across Canada for his son?" When I say yes, he tells me to "Keep her going, pal. You're doing a good job." Inside, I'm hoping I can 'keep her going' for another fifteen days.

Through the Similkameen Valley, the road to Princeton passes through Hedley. The Nickel Plate Mine here, which operated for more than 50 years, generated more than $47,000,000 in gold, silver and copper before shutting down in 1955. The mine seems to reflect the 'boom-and-bust' history and the promise of riches attached to this part of the country in Canada's early years. It makes it clear to me that slow steady growth is probably a much safer course.

In the foothills of the Cascade Mountains, I struggle with the ice along the twists and turns in the narrow road leading to Princeton. There are few donations, and at the end of the day, after speaking to the Rotary Club at noon hour and the Lions Club at night, all I want to do is have my legs worked on and go to sleep.

We are now in Manning Provincial Park, south of Princeton, and the snowdrifts along the side of the road are between four and five metres high. I'm so tired I can't remember exactly where we started the day. All I can remember is that it has been an uphill climb most of the day. The only good news is that we are climbing up and out of the fog on a dangerous road that we have somehow misread. It's much narrower than we thought, and full of blind hairpin turns that have forced us to use the two-way radios to play what we call 'cat-and-mouse.'

Cat-and-mouse is a very tiresome and dangerous piece of work that involves walking the road without the escort van behind me as protection. On the blind curves, the van holds its position with the strobe lights flashing while I disappear around the next curve in the road and hurry ahead to find another safe spot for the van to stop – this on a road that has almost no shoulder. Then we use the two-way radio to call and tell the people in the van that it is safe to move up to the next spot, where they can tuck in at the side of the road, and we begin again. The van, in turn, will radio us to let us know when a logging truck has passed them and will soon reach us as it slowly climbs the hill. I keep my eyes looking frontward while the volunteer on the road with me keeps an eye out for the trucks coming up behind us. When the trucks show up, we step off the road to let them pass. The system works well and gives us a margin of safety, except when there's a tractor-trailer or logging truck coming down the mountain in the opposite direction and we all meet at the same spot. Throughout the day, I keep thinking that this section of road is much more dangerous than the Rogers Pass, the area we had spent so much time worrying about.

It's late in the day when two men in a pick-up truck stop to make a donation. Again they ask if I'm the man walking across Canada for his son. When I tell the older of the two men, "Yes, that's me," he wants to shake my hand. Extending my arm to shake hands with the younger man, he apologizes that his hands are so grimy. I tell him, "there's no need to apologize, that's honest dirt."

Back at Manning Park Lodge, which is buried under a thick blanket of snow, I ask Ed if he could work on my back, legs and feet as soon as we get checked in. There are no telephones in our rooms so I can't call home. The lodge does have one interesting feature. Along the lit pathways that cut through a courtyard leading to the restaurant portion of the complex, some trees that had to be taken down have been felled at about the 2.5 metre height. Carvers have then created, in great detail, bears that are standing on their hind legs. The effect is quite dramatic and a lot better than looking at tree stumps.

From Manning Park, heading toward Hope, there are very steep grades with signs warning truck drivers to check their brakes before beginning their descent. On some of these steep hills there are runaway lanes on the right hand side of the road. These are emergency escape lanes to bring a runaway truck to a safe stop. The lanes, which turn upward like a ski jump, are made from tonnes of sand. The idea is that a truck without brakes would run up one of these lanes and quickly come to a halt without being damaged.

The jagged peaks, thick forests, and plunging gorges in and around Hope, served as the backdrop for the Sylvester Stallone movie First Blood. But Hope is not about 'Rambo'like characters. It's a quiet community nestled in giant fir trees where hope for a better future is reflected in the town's Friendship Gardens. The gardens commemorate a dark period in Canada's history, the internment of 2,000 Japanese-Canadians at Tashme Camp near Hope, during the Second World War.

The road crew at the moment includes Doug Goodman, who is back for a third tour of duty after volunteering in Quebec and Saskatchewan. This week's rookie member of the road crew is London lawyer Jennifer Smout.

Almost six feet tall, Jennifer is a slender, athletic-looking redhead who was a rower at the University of Western Ontario where she graduated with a law degree in 1985. In Hope, Jennifer and Doug set out on their own personal mission that brought them face to face with the spirit of hope.

Jennifer and Doug went searching for a cake to celebrate our reaching the 8,000-kilometre mark, and late in the afternoon when they walked into a bake shop in Hope, the magic that seemed to follow *Jesse's Journey* began again.

The cakes had all been sold, and the shop was ready to close for the day. The owner of the shop, who had noticed our vans around town and had seen me on television, could sense that reaching the 8,000-km mark was a pretty big deal for all of us. So, while Jennifer was still talking, the owner picked up the phone and called her baker who had already finished his shift and gone home. As Jennifer listened, she asked her baker if he could come back and bake just one more cake. She said, "You know that guy who's walking across Canada… well, he's here in Hope. He's walked 8,000 km and they need a cake, so can you come in and make it?"

Jennifer, who had her fingers crossed, breathed a sigh of relief when the lady held the phone away from her ear and said, "What colour do you want?" Jennifer and Doug didn't really care about colour, they were just happy to have a cake. The next question was, "What do you want on it?" That's when Jennifer and Doug had a bright idea which the bake shop owner thought was pretty funny.

That night when we returned to our motel after speaking to a dinner meeting of Lions, Rotarians and members of the Hope Chamber of Commerce, I was called to a meeting on board the motor home. What I thought was going to be another routine briefing about departure times and distances turned out to be a surprise party. The smiles on the faces of the road team told me they had pulled one over on me! There in the middle of the dinner table was a huge white

I took this picture of Ted Eadinger and Dianne Steward on the day they met, December 22nd, 1998 in front of the stone cairn at Craigellachie. It was here that the "last spike" was driven to complete the CPR on November 7, 1885.

The majesty of the Rockies gave me a lot to think about as I crossed British Columbia.

Through Rogers Pass in early December, the temperature was bitterly cold.

On board the ferry from Mill Bay to Brentwood Bay two days before reaching Victoria, I took a moment to think about all that our team had been able to accomplish.

286 days after "wetting a shoe" at Quidi Vidi, Newfoundland, I got a real soaker in the waters of the Pacific Ocean at the foot of Beacon Hill Park in Victoria, British Columbia.

cake trimmed with blue, green and yellow icing spelling out the words, "8001 And Beyond Hope!"

Hope's Mayor Wilfried Viktor and his mother are both on the road with us early this morning as we leave Hope, heading to Chilliwack. Among the people along the road who make donations are a couple of ladies with a box full of goodies for us. They're holding a sign wishing us luck.

Saturday January 9th, Jennifer and Doug both stay on the road for the entire day and complete 33 km. It is the second time Doug Goodman has worked a full day on the road, the first being back in Quebec. At the end of the day we reach Chilliwack. The number of days left is now down to single digits. The schedule shows we have seven more moves to make and we are now just nine road days away from finishing. It's a good feeling.

I adjusted my thinking back in Revelstoke, telling myself to prepare for snow every day until we reach the end. Anything better than snow will be a bonus. Now that we are pretty well out of the mountains, I'm making another adjustment, telling myself to prepare for rain for the rest of the *Journey*.

The day we reach Mission, B.C. is one of the wettest days of the entire *Journey*. It rains steadily all day and by mid-afternoon, radio reports indicate that more than 40 millimetres of rain has fallen. For those of us who still relate some things to the old imperial system of measurement, that means we have had more than two inches of rain.

Doug recalls one of the earlier days in British Columbia when it rained all day. Until today, that had been the heaviest and steadiest rain he'd ever seen in his life. He remembered the rain being so heavy that it had soaked through his Gore-Tex rain suit. That's what had stuck in his mind as he watched me climbing one of the steepest grades in the province, soaking wet, and putting one foot ahead of the other making my way up a punishing grade. It's a hill I don't remember. It's just what we did day after day.

On Day 277, Bevin finally walks a full 33 km with me for the first time since leaving St. John's, Newfoundland. Bevin's schedule has never permitted him the time to spend a whole day on the road, although we've probably been together on the highway on more than 200 occasions. He kept saying he was going to spend a whole day with me, and that day finally arrives in the rain heading to Mission.

Through his video reports, *Jesse's Journey* has been a kind of 'serial adventure' for Bevin. Physically we've seen his hair colour change from blonde to red to dark brown and he's gone from having a beard to no beard and just about everything in between. But the biggest changes haven't been physical. Watching Bevin as the days have passed by, one by one, has reminded me that while growing old is mandatory, growing up is optional.

I tried to imagine what would have happened if someone had told Bevin in April of 1997 that one year later he would be walking away from Kilometre "0" with me in St. John's, Newfoundland, taking the first tentative steps of an 8300-km walk across Canada. It would probably have been something to laugh about with his buddies and then forget in a hurry.

Back then, Bevin was a young man in a hurry in a fast-paced world. But when it came to the *Journey* being a life-changing experience for those who took part, Bevin was no exception. In the months we've been together on the road, he has wrestled with a ton of emotions and the end result has been an overall maturing. His priorities in life have changed. Walking along in the rain, Bevin is telling me about going into big cities where busy people who were in a big hurry had a 'get out of my way' attitude. It was different in the smaller towns, where people seemed happier and showed a greater caring about each other. The *Journey* has made Bevin ask himself about what really matters in life.

From our earliest days in Newfoundland, Bevin has seen people from all walks of life pitch in to do whatever has to be done – from

378

carrying water for the motor home to doing the laundry, washing the dishes, driving the vans and collecting money. He's noticed that there were no egos on the road. It didn't matter if you were the CEO of a Fortune 500 company or a clerk in a grocery store. Out here everyone is equal, and through the good times and the bad, everyone has stayed focused on the reason we're here.

Passing Ruby Creek on the way to Mission, Bevin and I are walking alongside two sets of railway tracks leading to Vancouver. People who want to shake my hand have been stopping along the road. Some of them say it's a remarkable thing I'm doing. That's not right. What's remarkable is what Bevin is doing, along with everyone who has taken part in *Jesse's Journey*.

It's still raining at lunchtime when a group of Lions with a donation join us on the road. They give us a lot of information about some things we can see and some things we can't. Underneath the road we're walking on, there are telephone lines and two natural gas lines that service Vancouver. Along the Fraser River, they point out where the salmon run occurs as well as the log boom that keeps debris from floating downstream and becoming a hazard for shipping. The Lions tell us that the inmates at two prisons in the area cut the logs that are hauled from the river into firewood for use by campers.

It's still wet when we reach the top of another steep hill and stop at a natural spring where we use a couple of styrofoam cups to toast Bevin's day on the road. A man and a woman in a pick-up truck stop to fill some containers with the pure spring water. They leave a donation of $100. It seems funny to be enjoying the clear-tasting water when all day long water has been our major problem! I've been changing shoes constantly and on the motor home there are running shoes drying in front of every available vent.

Bevin has never been the kind of guy who can just sit around. Most days on the road, right after lunch when I'm lying down, I usually hear the click, click, and click of Bevin hitting rocks with a baseball bat. He's gone through four bats – three wooden bats and one aluminum bat. The funniest day for that game was near Sault Ste. Marie when Ed told Bevin he would pitch some stones for him to hit. Bevin didn't see it coming when Ed, who likes a good prank, tossed Bevin an egg instead of a rock. That moment became part of the *Journey's* folklore.

Leaving Mission in the dark, we head out to our start point. By the time we get underway, the weather is warm. After what seems like an eternity of grey wet days, the sun is finally shining. Passing through Maple Ridge, two members of the Lions Club present *Jesse's Journey* with a cheque for $1,000.

People continue to stop and make donations as I move along the road toward Port Coquitlam. Two ladies are choked with emotion when they stop to meet me. They have a friend whose son suffers from the same disease as Jesse. The little boy is just six years old and already in a wheelchair. These two women with tears in their eyes know why I've spent the past nine months on the road. Further along the road there's a father waiting to meet me and to donate $5. His son's name is also Jesse.

Jesse's Journey receives a tremendous welcome when we reach Port Coquitlam, the home of Marathon of Hope runner Terry Fox. The mayor welcomes us and presents me with a key to the city. There's an excellent high school orchestra, boys and girls in matching green sweaters, playing music as corporate sponsors, service clubs, individuals and students gather for the formal presentation of several financial donations. It has been a tremendous welcome, and after speaking to the crowd, I'm introduced privately to Fred Fox, Terry's brother. He's a really nice guy and it's a pleasure meeting him. At the end of the ceremony the orchestra plays "O Canada." It is a very proud moment.

While I'm meeting high school and grade school kids after the reception in Port Coquitlam, Jennifer Smout meets someone special.

Her name is Alicia, and her long blonde hair is done up neatly in pigtails. She's about 11 years old and after the first snowfall of the year, she rounded up her friends and went out to shovel driveways to raise money for *Jesse's Journey*. She was standing in the crowd with her mom and $42 in coins she and her friends raised by shoveling snow. When Jennifer asked the little girl if she would like to meet me, she was a little shy. But since her mom was coming along, she decided it would be okay. When we met, I asked Alicia how she managed to raise $42 for *Jesse's Journey*. When she explained, I was glad this story unfolded in Port Coquitlam, where they know what it means to give to research.

Port Moody is next, as *Jesse's Journey* edges closer to Vancouver. It's a little scary in the traffic, even with a police escort. There are grade school kids with balloons and banners along the way. Some of them are very small, and they're on the opposite side of the road, and I'm worried that they'll try to run across the road. The police hold up traffic while I jog across the road to meet the kids who are really yelling and cheering. I shake hands with each of them, and one young girl who might have been in grade six or seven says, "I'm really proud of you."

On board the motor home, Ed has a hot lunch of chili and toast waiting for me. We're running late after stopping at the City Hall in Port Moody. Heading toward the Second Narrows Bridge and North Vancouver, things are about to get hectic. And, this isn't an easy day for Ed Coxworthy either. His mind is somewhere else. In Toronto tomorrow, his daughter Kari is to undergo surgery for cancer. Kari wants her mom and dad to stay where they are with *Jesse's Journey*. There's nothing they can do in Toronto except worry. It's not an easy day on board the motor home, but through it all, Ed still manages to keep us laughing. People cope in many ways.

With a police escort through Burnaby, there are a lot of people applauding, yelling encouragement and making donations as we inch our way toward the Iron Worker's Memorial Bridge crossing over the Second Narrows to North Vancouver. The chaos of getting through another big city repeats itself, as there's a flurry of radio and television interviews to be done on the fly, and another round of newspaper interviews. It's dark and pouring rain when we reach our finish point at Centennial Theatre, where the mayors of both North and West Vancouver welcome us.

One of the hardest things to do in a big city is move the motor home through very heavy traffic, especially when you're not familiar with the road system. In the downpour we've been experiencing since late afternoon, and with the windshield wipers sweeping back and forth, the *Jesse's Journey* motor home slips into the stream of traffic making its way into downtown Vancouver. In the morning the whole procedure has to be repeated in the opposite direction as we cross the Lions Gate Bridge to reach our start point in North Vancouver.

Things seem like they are happening in slow motion as the distance to Horseshoe Bay and the ferry terminal becomes shorter. It's another of those times when everything seems to be unfolding like a series of still pictures. There are the flashing lights from the RCMP escort vehicle and cameramen running to get in front of me. In the sunshine along the Sea-to-Sky Highway, I stop at a waterfall and splash several scoops of water on my face. And then, almost before I know it, I'm walking across the grass that leads to water's edge at Horseshoe Bay. I have finished walking the length of mainland Canada. There is only Vancouver Island left to complete, and in just a few days *Jesse's Journey – A Father's Tribute*, which began on an island on Canada's Atlantic coast, will finish on an island on Canada's Pacific coast. The end of the *Journey* is near, even if it's hard to believe.

Before leaving Vancouver, I'm a guest on VTV's Vicky Gabereau Show along with Dr. Michael Hayden, the Senior Scientist at the Centre for Molecular Medicine and Therapeutics in Vancouver. Dr. Hayden explains how each of the three million genes in the human body is made up of a different series of the four letters of DNA.

He describes the riddle of the human genome as being a bit like taking three million letters in a foreign language and trying to come up with a dictionary.

After a day of shaking hands and posing for pictures and a series of corporate and promotional appearances, I'm anxious to get back to our motel for our final night in Vancouver. The day has turned cool and it's cloudy and grey as I walk across the parking lot, heading from the motor home to the Bayshore Inn on Vancouver's waterfront. Then I hear Jesse's voice as he calls out, "Hey, Dad!" from a balcony above me. In just a couple of minutes we are all together and I hug Sherene, Jesse and Tim – family members I haven't seen since August of last year.

On the morning of our last Saturday of the *Journey*, Sherene joins us for a bowl of hot porridge on board the motor home before our convoy leaves for Horseshoe Bay, where we will board the ferry for the crossing to Vancouver Island. Sherene will stay behind with Jesse and Tim and join us in Victoria in a couple of days.

The sky is grey, the water is grey, and it's raining as we dock in Nanaimo to start the final portion of the *Journey*. Members of the Lions Club had been in Horseshoe Bay to see us off, and as I walk off the ferry on Vancouver Island, the Lions of Nanaimo are among the service clubs, firefighters and a piper who are all ready to welcome us to the Island. Later in the day, there are lots of people who make donations along the road through Nanaimo. On the southern edge of the city known for the 'Nanaimo bar' candy confection, stands one of the most impressive 'welcome' signs in all of Canada. There are huge flagpoles with giant metal sheets that suggest sails under a full wind. The blue trim and flags atop the 'masts' create the effect of a tall ship. It leaves little doubt Nanaimo is an ocean playground with a rich seafaring heritage.

With just four days to go it keeps raining, but now there's very little chance of seeing snow again. In British Columbia, they like to refer to rain as 'liquid sunshine.' I still see it as rain. And although it's wet, the road to Victoria is mostly flat. One man who stops to make a donation brings along a walking stick he has carved with the words *"Jesse's Journey – Coast to Coast."* Each time I open the door to the motor home, there are familiar faces as people from home are starting to gather in Victoria for the completion of the walk.

At Ladysmith, which used to be known as Oyster Bay, members of the road crew are the guests of honour at a banquet hosted by the town's service clubs. There are about 200 people on hand, and by the end of the night almost $4,000 has been raised to help fund genetic research.

Walking on from Ladysmith to Duncan, the clock continues to tick toward the time I'll finish in Victoria. Through Lake Cowichan, it's still raining, but today I only have to complete 20 km. The schedule has been fine-tuned for the last days of the *Journey* so that I will have just 11 km to complete on the final day.

I don't know if it's the anticipation of reaching the finish line in just over 48 hours, but I haven't slept well, and the excitement that's been building along the road has left me tired again. The phone calls are coming fast and furious from radio stations stretching from Vancouver back to Newfoundland. The interviews begin at five o'clock in the morning, and every few minutes someone is sticking a cell phone into my hand to talk to another reporter or broadcaster.

On the road, a woman who throws her arms around me says, "I love a man with guts." Another woman, who obviously knows about Jesse, shakes my hand as she quietly asks me, "How's he doing?"

Despite the number of people who are now with us, Ed does his best to maintain our daily routine, and even prepares scalloped potatoes and ham for our lunch. After my midday rest, and a somewhat broken sleep, I step off the motor home into a group of 30 people who have flown in from London to be on hand for the final steps.

Among those who have come west is Peter Geene, a Lion who has been working with Lions Clubs across the country since the time I first set out from Newfoundland. The home team in London nicknamed Peter 'The Lion King' for his ability to get things organized.

Ruth McCallum, a young woman who flew to British Columbia for the conclusion of the road portion of *Jesse's Journey,* is one of the hundreds of volunteers across the country who worked long and hard, far from the limelight. Ruth is the spark plug who ignited Manulife, the company whose show of unity across Canada has been a shining example of what can be accomplished when corporations decide to roll up their sleeves to help.

When I finish my distance for the day, we return to Duncan, "The City of Totems." Passing through here a few hours earlier, I had admired the dozens of totem poles in the downtown area. I am sure we are in Duncan because I have the name of the town written on my hand as a reminder. This may sound strange, but in the past few days I have had to write the names of the places where I'm speaking on my hand. I'm having trouble remembering where I am. In the evenings, in order to keep our road distance true, there has been a lot of shuffling back and forth among different communities to attend banquets and make speeches. Between that and the heavy early morning phone traffic to eastern Canada, I now feel like the tank is empty and I'm just running on fumes. I'm really very tired, and it's difficult to stay focused.

In Duncan, a native artist presents me with a print of a very intriguing painting. The picture is a close-up of the eye of a bear cub, and in the reflection you can see the mother bear catching a fish in a stream as she shows her cub how to fish. The artist is here and he provides an excellent description of the picture and the story behind it – how it reflects the responsibility of one generation to help the next, not just by telling them what we have learned but by demonstrating all the 'how-to' techniques that we have acquired.

On the morning of my second-to-last day on the road, wisps of cloud hang in the tops of the fir trees as I walk through Mill Bay, chipping away at the few kilometres left before reaching Victoria and the Pacific Ocean. Waiting for the Brentwood ferry to take us across Saanich Inlet to Brentwood Bay, a group of young kids from a private school peppers me with questions about *Jesse's Journey* and the things I've seen as I've walked across Canada. They're very polite and seem a little surprised that someone as old as I am could walk all the way across the country.

As we cross Saanich Inlet to Brentwood Bay, the ferry captain lets me take the wheel for a minute. When I step off the ferry, Sherene is waiting for me with a group of family and friends. The group that will be with me for the next 24 hours continues to grow, as we move closer and closer to the finish.

At the end of the day in Victoria, the road crew's red duffel bags are unloaded from the vehicles in what will be our last 'move.' After nine-and-a-half months on the road, the stage is now set for the final day – with 11 km left to complete in my walk across the entire breadth of Canada.

It's January 20, 1999, the morning of the 286th day of my *Journey* across the country. It's also my birthday. By the end of the day, we will have raised $2,000,000 to launch the Jesse Davidson Endowment Fund, a fund that is eventually going to generate a million dollars a year toward genetic research.

Getting ready for the last day, there's a touch of melancholy – similar to that final morning in 1995 when Jesse and I reached Ottawa at the end of our *Journey* across Ontario. I'm aware that, at the end of this day, people will be shifting their focus away from the routine they have followed for almost ten months. The *Journey* road crew will disband as people will catch flights home to the families and lives that have been put on hold for nearly a year. In time, the road portion of *Jesse's Journey* will fade from people's minds, but until then, there's one more day to complete.

When I climb aboard the motor home for the final time, I can't help thinking about things as being a series of "last of's." I sit down to what will be my last bowl of Ed Coxworthy's Newfoundland porridge. Since I woke up, I've been making the last of the phone calls. The radio interviews are still ahead.

Along the road, radio has been the lifeline that has let us stay in touch with all the people who wanted to follow the story of *Jesse's Journey*. That powerful link has endured since last spring, when my friend Peter Garland broadcast his morning radio show from City Hall in St. John's Newfoundland. That was April 10th, 1998, the morning I had dipped my running shoes into the Atlantic Ocean. And now, in just a few minutes, Peter and CFPL Radio in London will be there again, this time in front of the legislature in Victoria, broadcasting live to an audience in Ontario. For Peter these will be two special broadcasts in a memorable career in radio.

For the final time, *Jesse's Journey – A Father's Tribute* checks in again with stations in London, Toronto and as far away as Newfoundland, connecting with people who are still cheering us on. Through a satellite hookup, I do an interview with CBC television's Colleen Jones in Halifax. It's taken until the final day for the meaning of the *Journey* to sink in at Canada's public television network. Standing in front of the legislature in Victoria, I listen in my earpiece as an interviewer on the other side of the country tells me she's going home to hug her kids.

During the final few kilometres, there are school kids along the side of the road, and lots of horns honking from the traffic that's streaming by as motorists give us the 'thumbs up' sign.

At lunch time the commotion continues, with people coming and going as everyone gets into position for the finale of the *Journey*. The onslaught of interviews continues. Amidst all the chaos, I sit down for the last lunch to be served on the motor home. I'm not seated for long before I spring up to hug a tiny lady with a big smile.

She's there among the crowd of well-wishers, with a card of congratulations for 'Jesse's dad'. I'd spoken to Miggsie Lawson ten times as I'd made my way across the country. The portable cell phone in the motor home would ring like clockwork on the day I'd step into a new province. On the other end of the line, I'd hear a lady bubbling with enthusiasm as she called to make a donation each time I reached another provincial border. On days when the going was slow, hearing Miggsie's voice was a tonic that would give me a lift to get back in the game and to give it my best.

Lying face down on the bed in the back of the motor home, my legs are being worked on for the last time. A lot of people have kept me in shape over the past nine and a half months. They are the ones who came to the rescue when the alarm bells went off as I reached British Columbia. That's when it had become apparent that muscle fatigue was definitely a problem, and we still had almost a month to go and another thousand kilometres to complete.

There are 3 km left to go when I get back on the road in the afternoon. Thinking back to the beginning, I remember the mental image I had in St. John's, when I had visualized the 286 days on one side of my mind as 286 little boxes of work to be done. At the end of that first day, I mentally moved one of those little boxes to the other side, to the 'completed' pile. And then in Ontario, a day finally came when I had more stacked up on the 'completed' side of my mind than there were on the 'still to go' side. At the end of this day, I can mentally move that last unit of work over to the 'completed' side.

Suddenly, the final kilometres have gone by in a blur of smiles, handshakes, pats on the back, words of congratulations, cheers and applause, and there is the sound of a band, sirens blaring, horns honking and people coming up to hug me. Then, almost before I know it, and almost as if St. John's were just yesterday, my mom and dad are standing in front of me holding the banner that marks the finish – 8,272 km from where I started. Breaking through that banner, I wrap my arms around Sherene. She looks happy, and at the same time relieved that we have all made it safely across the country. Hugging Jesse and Tyler and Tim, I too feel a sense of relief that the road portion of *Jesse's Journey* is over.

From the top of Beacon Hill, I take the jug of water from the Atlantic Ocean down to the shore, where the Pacific Ocean laps against the rocks and the hundreds of logs that have broken away from booms and washed ashore.

With his mom at his side, Jesse is at the top of the hill watching from his wheelchair as television cameras and newspaper photographers wait to capture these final moments. After dipping my running shoes in the warm Pacific, I pour the water we have carried from the East Coast of Newfoundland into the waters on the West Coast of British Columbia. When the bottle of Atlantic water is half empty, I fill it to the top again with water from the Pacific, sealing the top and shaking the bottle to mix the waters of two oceans. That bottle will go back onto the motor home to be taken back home to London.

From Beacon Hill Park we're escorted back into Victoria, to the steps of the British Columbia Legislature. At the Legislature there's a naval military band, RCMP officers in their red tunics, motorcycle police and best of all – friends and family.

A huge crowd has gathered and there's an atmosphere of celebration at the legislature, where we are welcomed by Victoria's town crier. There are speeches by municipal politicians from both Victoria and my home town of London. There are words of congratulations from the Province of British Columbia, from my own Member of Parliament who was there, and a letter of thanks for what we had done from the Prime Minister of Canada.

Standing on the steps of the legislature in Victoria and knowing in my heart that we have all done our best, I tell myself that *Jesse's Journey* is not over. If there is something we've learned, it's that we will never give up and each of us who has shared this *Journey* knows that one day we will reach our goal.

There was a farewell gathering that night at the naval base at Esquimalt. There were pictures taken, lots of *Journey* stories told, and I had a chance to publicly thank my family and all the volunteers who had worked with us, both on the home team and on the road team. We had raised $1,500,000 in 1995, which we had dedicated to research. And now in 1998-99, with the walk across Canada, we had raised another $2,000,000 to launch the Jesse Davidson Endowment Fund.

Battered and exhausted, we had raised awareness of the need for genetic research and the need to invest in science. We had told the story of the devastation that Duchenne Muscular Dystrophy causes families. It was a story thousands of Canadians had never heard before, just as they had never before heard of the genetic disease that strikes only boys. While we had done what we set out to do, there was more work ahead of us. In the morning we would head east to tackle that job.

After 286 days on the road, 8,272 km walked, $2,000,000 raised, and the satisfaction of knowing that we could always say we did our best – we were going home.

WHEN THEY WENT HOME

Jesse Davidson graduated from high school in 1999 and now attends Fanshawe College in London where he is enrolled in the Hotel Management program.

The Governor General of Canada, the Honourable Adrienne Clarkson, presented John and Jesse Davidson with the Meritorious Service Medal at a ceremony at the Citadel in Quebec City in November of 2000. While Jesse was unable to attend, his mother Sherene accepted the award on his behalf.

In June of 2000, The Guinness Book of World Records recognized John Davidson's 286-day *Journey* as a world record for the fastest crossing of Canada on foot.

Bevin Palmateer and Renata Van Loon were married on September 3rd, 1999. They are both working in television in London, Ontario.

Ed Coxworthy returned home to Bell Island, Newfoundland. He quit smoking in March of 2000.

Michael Woodward, a founding member of The Foundation for Gene and Cell Therapy, remains with *Jesse's Journey* as a member of the board and the Foundation secretary.

Mario Chioini, who escorted Sherene and Jesse Davidson to Paris, France, where they took part in the Association Francaise contre les Myopathies telethon, which raised $116M (Canadian) for the French Muscular Dystrophy Association, is now teaching school in Mexico.

Ted Eadinger and Dianne Steward were married on October 7, 2000. Ted is now the Managing Director at *Jesse's Journey*, where Dianne is a volunteer.

Maureen Golovchenko and Phil Spencer were married on August 26th, 2000. Maureen is now Executive Assistant to the mayor of London.

Trish "The Dish" Federkow returned to school. She is now working in Toronto in the field of human resources.

Sean "The Bagger" Bagshaw went on to medical school at the University of Calgary. He graduated and became Dr. Sean Bagshaw in the spring of 2000.

John Davidson returned home to his wife and family in London, Ontario. He continues to work on his dream of building an endowment fund that will one day generate at least a million dollars a year, every year forever, to find the answers to genetic illnesses.

Since it began its work, *Jesse's Journey-The Foundation for Gene and Cell Therapy* has raised more than $5,000,000 for research.

The *"Journey"* continues....

Graduating from W. Sherwood Fox Public School in London, Jesse never let a disability get in his way as he headed off to high school.

CANADA

PRIME MINISTER · PREMIER MINISTRE

January 20, 1999

Dear Mr. Davidson:

    It gives me great pleasure to extend my sincere congratulations to you as you complete your cross country walk to raise awareness and funds for genetic research.

    Jesse's Journey - A Father's Tribute *testifies to the depth of your commitment to your son and to others in the Canadian community who are afflicted with genetic diseases. As you complete your walk, you may take great pride in the knowledge that, together with Jesse and the members of the Road Team, you have greatly heightened Canadians' awareness of the urgent need for research into effective treatments and ultimately cures for such debilitating illnesses. For the past nine months, you made great personal sacrifices to maintain a pace of 33 kilometres a day, and you are to be commended for your perseverance and dedication. I am sure the support you received from your family, friends and numerous well-wishers from coast to coast made your arduous trek a rewarding experience.*

    I join with all Canadians in expressing great pride in your accomplishment. Please accept my best wishes as you arrive in Victoria.

    Yours sincerely,

Jean Chrétien

Mr. John Davidson

Team Roster

1998-99

Road Team
John Davidson
Trish Federko
Bevin Palmateer
Mike Woodward
Ed Coxworthy
Ted Eadinger

Drivers
Ron Calhoun
Bob Seaton
Don Black
Jane Black
Marvin Ralph
John Hodder
Urias Jones
Jerry Buchanan
Steve Casey
Patrick Casey
David Meadows
Susan Potts
Jane Morrison
Olive Bryanton
Rich Beharrell
Cindy Beharrell
Al Melanson
Hector Maillet
Evariste Cormier
Glen Sifton
Russell Press
Tobi Blue
Bob Gallagher
Donna Gallagher
Paul Page

Jane Morrison
Mario Chioini
Doug Goodman
Scott Shakir
Andre Trenqua
Marc Olivier Roy
Darren Walker
Dudley Briggs
Jeff Price
Al Price
Dorothy DeVille
Peter DeVille
Grace Roca
Lorraine Stirling
Willy Heidebrecht
Dwight Wesenger
Cathy Savage
Cindy Pierce
Rick Rumney
Elly McMillan
Bonnie Kolkman
Judy Young
Jo Ann Reed
Mary Krauel
Bill Wilson
Larry Rogers
Pat Carey
Joan Picken
Bob Picken
Phil Spencer
Gord Wainman
Mac Haig
Bob Weber
Carolyn Brennan

Marilyn Richmond
Bruce Fraser
Mowbray Sifton
Fred Nowitski
Nick Chrest
Peter Garland
Leon Brin
Diane Price
Melanie Weaver
Sheila Rowe
Bernie Range
Ann Hutchison
Dianne Steward
Sandi McCabe
Jim McCabe
Jennifer Smout
Ted Mills
Ken Slade

Home Team

Journey Director
Maureen Golovchenko

Team

Susan Arscott
Sue Bedell
Don Black
Jane Black
Ken Chaplin
Jim Chapman
George Clark
Gary Dallner
Jerry Daniel
Jack Davidson
Jesse Davidson
Sarah Davidson
Sherene Davidson
Clare Dear
Dorothy DeVille
Gary Ennett
Joanne Fordham
Irene Foster
Steve Garrison
Jenifer Georgas
Bryan Getchell
Mac Haig
Pam Higgin
Ron Hutton
Pete James
Colleen Jones
Jim Kernaghan
Bonnie Kolkman

Ted Kostecki
Elena Luryi
Brian Nuttall
Ruth McCallum
Maryann McDowell
Elly McMillan
Rena Morphy
King Perry
Wendy Perry
Gary Alan Price
Bonnie Quesnel
Dora Redman
Grace Roca
Bruce Rutledge
Darlene Sanderson
Donna Sifton
Doris Sifton
Jim Swan
Mary Jane Sinker
Phil Spencer
Dianne Steward
Gord Wainman
BobWeber
Jim Weir
Barry Wells
Mike Woodward
Judy Young
Kate Young

1995 Team Roster

Road Team

Jesse Davidson
John Davidson
Trish Federkow
Sean Bagshaw
Mike Woodward
John McHale

Drivers

Peter DeVille
Dorothy DeVille
Jack Davidson
Sarah Davidson
Jim Drinkwater
Liz Ayerst
Bill Wilson
Bill Teems
Ted Olexy
Don Meadows
Pat Meadows
Ron Kruger
Debbie Kruger
Bill Wilson
Maryann McDowell
Sylvia Burnke
Bernie Quesnelle
Peter Quesnelle
George Clark
John Lees
Aislinn Lees
Alene Lees
Nick Paparella
Doug Robertson
Mac Haig
Jim Easton

Phil Callander
Janet Ferguson
Jo Ann Reed
Don Mortenson
Don Mainstone
Perry Esler
Ed Busko
Glen Sifton
Ken Chaplin

Home Team

Ron Calhoun
Dean Chevalier
Sherene Davidson
Gary Alan Price
Donna Sifton
Doris Sifton
Glen Sifton
Richard Sifton
Mike Woodward

WHAT IT TAKES TO WALK ACROSS THE COUNTRY

635 loaves of bread
11 kilograms of brown sugar
572 litres of 2 percent milk
575 litres of orange juice
41 jars of jam
24 jars of peanut butter
3 bottles of cinnamon (popular on porridge)
Seven 2.25 kilogram bags of Quaker Oats
5,535 grams of raisins
227 kilograms of bananas
1200 apples
1200 oranges
11 kilograms of grapes
1500 tea bags
75 cans of chili
110 cans of Campbell's soup
48 cans of fruit cocktail
40 bags of nachos

6 pairs of running shoes

How to Reach Us

To make an online donation to *Jesse's Journey* and to help leave a lifetime legacy of research, and receive our semi-annual newsletter "The Road Ahead" please visit our website at:

www.jessesjourney.org or e-mail us at: fgct@jessesjourney.org

To order additional copies of *Jesse's Journey – A Canadian Story* contact us at:

Jesse's Journey-The Foundation for Gene and Cell Therapy
P. O. Box 5099
London, Ontario
N6A 4M8

Tel (519) 645-8855
Fax (519) 645-2242
e-mail: fgct@jessesjourney.org

Registered Charitable Organization 89509-7756-RR0001

If you haven't heard John Davidson speak about the magic of "Jesse's Journey" then you've been missing a great Canadian story!!

Award winning speaker John Davidson has spoken to hundreds of businesses, associations, educational audiences and community groups. He is available to speak to your company or organization to share the inspirational story of one Canadian father who is out to make a difference.

For more information about having John Davidson speak at your next meeting, convention or special event, please visit our website at www.johndavidson.ca

The telephone number is (519) 645-8855
The fax number is (519) 645-2242